Youth Employment
in Sub-Saharan Africa

Youth Employment in Sub-Saharan Africa

Deon Filmer and Louise Fox
with

Karen Brooks, Aparajita Goyal,
Taye Mengistae, Patrick Premand, Dena Ringold,
Siddharth Sharma, and Sergiy Zorya

A copublication of the Agence Française de Développement and the World Bank

Africa Development Forum Series

The **Africa Development Forum Series** was created in 2009 to focus on issues of significant relevance to Sub-Saharan Africa's social and economic development. Its aim is both to record the state of the art on a specific topic and to contribute to ongoing local, regional, and global policy debates. It is designed specifically to provide practitioners, scholars, and students with the most up-to-date research results while highlighting the promise, challenges, and opportunities that exist on the continent.

The series is sponsored by the Agence Française de Développement and the World Bank. The manuscripts chosen for publication represent the highest quality in each institution and have been selected for their relevance to the development agenda. Working together with a shared sense of mission and interdisciplinary purpose, the two institutions are committed to a common search for new insights and new ways of analyzing the development realities of the Sub-Saharan Africa region.

Advisory Committee Members

Agence Française de Développement
Jean-Yves Grosclaude, Director of Strategy
Alain Henry, Director of Research
Philippe Cabin, Head of Research Publishing Division

World Bank
Francisco H. G. Ferreira, Chief Economist, Africa Region
Richard Damania, Lead Economist, Africa Region
Stephen McGroarty, Executive Editor, Publishing and Knowledge Division

Sub-Saharan Africa

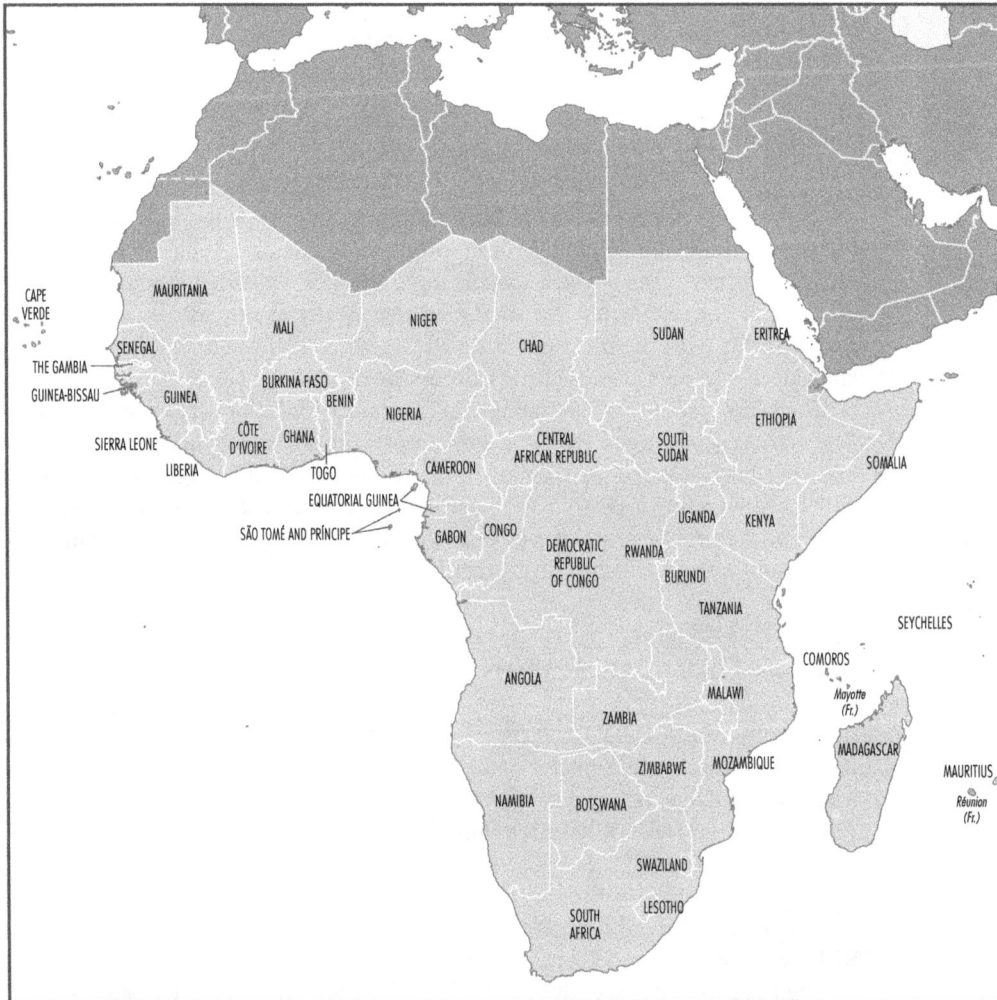

Throughout this report, "Africa" is shorthand for "Sub-Saharan Africa." In particular instances, "Sub-Saharan Africa" is retained to clarify comparisons across regions or to indicate a specific data set.

Titles in the African Development Forum Series

Africa's Infrastructure: A Time for Transformation (2010) edited by Vivien Foster and Cecilia Briceño-Garmendia

Gender Disparities in Africa's Labor Market (2010) edited by Jorge Saba Arbache, Alexandre Kolev, and Ewa Filipiak

Challenges for African Agriculture (2010) edited by Jean-Claude Deveze

Contemporary Migration to South Africa: A Regional Development Issue (2011) edited by Aurelia Segatti and Loren Landau

Light Manufacturing in Africa: Targeted Policies to Enhance Private Investment and Create Jobs (2012) by Hinh T. Dinh, Vincent Palmade, Vandana Chandra, and Frances Cossar

Informal Sector in Francophone Africa: Firm Size, Productivity, and Institutions (2012) by Nancy Benjamin and Ahmadou Aly Mbaye

Financing Africa's Cities: The Imperative of Local Investment (2012) by Thierry Paulais

Structural Transformation and Rural Change Revisited: Challenges for Late Developing Countries in a Globalizing World (2012) by Bruno Losch, Sandrine Fréguin-Gresh, and Eric Thomas White

The Political Economy of Decentralization in Sub-Saharan Africa: A New Implementation Model (2013) edited by Bernard Dafflon and Thierry Madiès

Empowering Women: Legal Rights and Economic Opportunities in Africa (2013) by Mary Hallward-Driemeier and Tazeen Hasan

Enterprising Women: Expanding Economic Opportunities in Africa (2013) by Mary Hallward-Driemeier

Urban Labor Markets in Sub-Saharan Africa (2013) edited by Philippe De Vreyer and François Roubaud

Securing Africa's Land for Shared Prosperity: A Program to Scale Up Reforms and Investments (2013) by Frank F. K. Byamugisha

All books in the Africa Development Forum series are available for free at https://openknowledge.worldbank.org/handle/10986/2150

Contents

Figures

Tables

Foreword

Africa is now the world's youngest continent.

While national populations in most parts of the world are aging, young people are now in the majority in many African countries. Whether they live in the cities and towns of a rapidly urbanizing Africa, or in rural villages and settlements; whether they come from middle-class backgrounds or from vulnerable families that are living in poverty, one thing is certain—these young people have high expectations, and African policy makers are increasingly concerned about how to meet them.

Today, jobs and opportunity for young people are consistently at the top of the development agenda in virtually every country on the continent.

Although data on employment is patchy and not generally comparable across African countries, we can nonetheless learn much from the available evidence. Contrary to popular perceptions, unemployment is but one of the main problems facing low-income countries in Africa. Beyond simple unemployment, Africa is challenged to address underemployment: in the absence of adequate social safety nets, young people are compelled to take low-productivity, low-wage jobs for their very survival.

While urban youth tend to be much more vocal about their challenges and aspirations, and highly visible in their job-seeking, millions of young men and women in rural and semi-urban areas struggle to find better-paying jobs and opportunities to escape poverty for themselves and their families.

With its comprehensive analysis of youth employment in Africa, this report updates how and where countries are creating jobs and looks to the future of promising new directions for the continent. It focuses on how policy makers can help young people walk through the front door of the labor market and into both fast-growing modern wage jobs as well as into other sustainable economic opportunities—improving income by raising productivity in the informal sector, where many young people will work for the foreseeable future.

Youth employment is not a one-dimensional challenge. Addressing it will require attention to the quality of basic education and training to improve young people's productivity, while also removing current obstacles that hinder progress in agriculture, household enterprises, and the modern wage sector.

If children do not know how to read or do basic mathematics at the end of their years in primary school, this basic skills gap has a profound impact on productivity in adulthood. If young people have weak access to land and to credit, their dreams of becoming entrepreneurs or working in high-paying, rewarding jobs will be dashed. If university graduates acquire degrees and knowledge that have little practical application in Africa's fast-changing labor force, then their investment of time and money will have been largely in vain, with few prospects for strong careers in the private sector.

I hope that this report will help African countries develop customized strategies to address youth employment and to invest in better information on how well these strategies are working.

Collectively we must redouble our efforts to meet the paramount challenge of youth employment so that young people can take advantage of the opportunities that are steadily growing across the continent whether in export-oriented manufacturing, high-productivity agriculture and agribusinesses, or profitable small enterprises.

Africa's future will be profoundly shaped by how well it manages this challenge.

Makhtar Diop

Vice President for Africa
The World Bank

Acknowledgments

This report was prepared by a core team led by Deon Filmer and Louise Fox and comprising Karen Brooks, Aparajita Goyal, Taye Mengistae, Patrick Premand, Dena Ringold, Siddharth Sharma, and Sergiy Zorya. Additional contributions were made by Shubha Chakravarty, Florence Kondylis, Obert Pimhidzai, Raju Singh, and Erik von Uexkull. The team was directed by Shantanayan Devarajan and Ritva Reinikka. Research assistance was provided by Jorge Munoz, Lena Nguyen, and Thokozani Kadzamira. The report was edited by Kelly Cassaday (overall) and Amy Gautam (who had primary editing responsibility for chapter 4). Several World Bank staff, as well as policy makers, academics, and other stakeholders provided comments at various stages of the development of this report. Richard Damania, Mary Hallward-Driemeier, Margaret Grosh, and Ravi Kanbur provided careful peer review comments. Any errors or omissions are the responsibility of the team.

About the Authors

Deon Filmer

Deon Filmer is a Lead Economist in the World Bank's research department and the HD Economics Unit of the Human Development department of the World Bank's Africa region. He works on issues of youth employment and skills, service delivery, and impact evaluation of policies and programs to improve human development outcomes. He has spent many years in the World Bank's research department where his research has covered the areas of education, health, social protection, and poverty analysis. He has published numerous articles in top-ranked economics journals. Recent work includes studies of the impact of demand-side programs on schooling outcomes; of the roles of poverty, orphanhood, and disability in explaining education inequalities; of the determinants of effective service delivery and the evaluation of interventions aimed at improving it; of the determinants of fertility behavior, and on trends in adult mortality around the world. He was a core team member of the *World Development Report 1995: Workers in an Integrating World* and *World Development Report 2004: Making Services Work for Poor People*, and a contributor to the *World Development Report 2007: Development and the Next Generation*. He holds PhD and MA degrees from Brown University.

Louise Fox

Louise Fox was, until her recent retirement from the World Bank, a Lead Economist in the Africa region of the World Bank. During her long career at the Bank, she worked on a wide range of topics; her specialties included the analysis of employment and labor markets, poverty and inequality, and the economics of social service delivery, with the overarching theme of the links among policies, outcomes, and poverty reduction. Prior to her position in the Africa region, Dr. Fox spent 13 years working on issues of labor market adjustment, poverty, and social protection in transition economies, including China and Mongolia, the Baltic States, and Eastern Europe. Before that she researched poverty, inequality, and macroeconomic adjustment in Latin America. Her most recent published work has been on the topics of poverty reduction and inclusive growth, the political economy of poverty reduction, and on employment, labor markets, and labor regulation, all with respect to Sub-Saharan Africa. She has also published in the areas of pension reform, reform of child welfare systems, social protection, public expenditures in the social sectors and poverty reduction, female-headed households and child welfare, stabilization policies and poverty reduction, the social costs of adjustment, and the economic history of poverty and inequality in Brazil. Dr. Fox received a PhD from Vanderbilt University.

Karen Brooks

Karen Brooks is Director of the CGIAR research program on Policies, Institutions and Markets. Brooks worked for the World Bank for 20 years. For the last 10 years of her tenure there, she managed analytical and operational programs in agriculture and rural development for the Africa region. Brooks also worked extensively in both the Europe and Central Asia and Africa regions; in the former on issues related to the transition from central planning, and in the latter on the investment and policy agenda associated with the renewed commitment to agricultural growth. Prior to joining the World Bank, she was Associate Professor in the Department of Applied Economics at the University of Minnesota. Brooks received both her PhD and MA degrees in Economics from the University of Chicago, where she was a National Science Foundation Graduate Fellow.

Aparajita Goyal

Aparajita Goyal is an Economist with the Agriculture team of the Africa region of the World Bank. Previously, she worked in the Bank's Agriculture and Environment Services department, as well as the Bank's Development Research Group. Her work has focused on microeconomic issues of development, with a particular emphasis on technological innovation in agriculture, access to markets, and intellectual property rights. Her work has been published in leading academic economics journals, and has also been featured in the popular press, including *Frontline, The Economist,* and the *Wall Street Journal.* She has previously worked with ActionAid in London and the Right to Food Campaign in India. She obtained a PhD in Economics from the University of Maryland and an MSc degree in Development Studies from the London School of Economics.

Taye Mengistae

Taye Mengistae is a Senior Economist with the Finance and Private Sector Development, Eastern and Southern Africa team of the World Bank's Africa region. Previously he was with the Bank's Development Research Group. He has published numerous articles in leading academic economic journals. His country work experience includes South Africa, Kenya, Ghana, Ethiopia, Zambia, India, China, and Pakistan. His main areas of research interest include globalization, export competitiveness, capital flows, innovation, and education. He holds a PhD from Oxford University and an MA degree from the University of Leeds.

Patrick Premand

Patrick Premand is a Senior Economist in the HD Economics Unit of the Human Development department of the World Bank's Africa region. He works on issues of youth employment and skills, early child nutrition and development, and the impact evaluation of policies and programs to improve human development outcomes. He has previously held positions in the Office of the Chief Economist for Human Development Department and in the Bank's Latin America and Caribbean region's Poverty team. He holds PhD and MSc degrees from Oxford University.

Dena Ringold

Dena Ringold is a Lead Economist in the Social Protection team of the World Bank's Africa region, with fifteen years experience working in Human Development at the World Bank. Her research interests include social inclusion of minorities, safety nets, and governance. Prior to joining the Africa region, she was a core team member of the *World Development Report 2013: Jobs,* and she previously worked in the Office of the Chief Economist for Human Development. Dena began her career at the Bank in the Europe and Central Asia (ECA) region, where she worked on operations and analytical programs with a focus on social protection and local service delivery in Central and Southeastern Europe. While in ECA she helped to initiate the Bank's first qualitative and quantitative analyses of the Roma minority and helped to set up the Roma Education Fund. She has also worked on social protection in the Latin American and Caribbean (LAC) region. In 2005, Dena was an Ian Axford Fellow in public policy based at the Ministry of Maori Development in Wellington, New Zealand. She holds an MSc in Economics and Government from the London School of Economics and a BA in History and Political Science from Swarthmore College.

Siddharth Sharma

Siddharth Sharma is an Economist in the Finance and Private Sector team of the World Bank's Europe and Central Asia Region. He previously worked in the Social Protection team of the Africa region and in the Poverty team of the Middle East and North Africa region. His research focus has been on labor markets, productivity, and firms. He has published academic papers in leading economics journals. He holds a PhD from Yale University, and an MA and BA from the University of Delhi

Sergiy Zorya

Segiy Zorya is a Senior Economist in the Sustainable Development team of the World Bank's East Asia and Pacific Region. He was previously with the Bank's Agriculture and Rural Development (ARD) Department. He works on issues pertaining rural policies and strategies, food prices, management of public expenditure, and global food security. Prior to ARD, he worked in three Bank regions: Europe and Central Asia, East Asia and Pacific, and Africa. His most recent work was in South Sudan, Tanzania, Uganda, and Zambia. Sergiy holds an MA degree in Agricultural Economics from the Agricultural University of Zhytomyr, Ukraine, and a PhD in Agricultural Economics from the Georg-August University of Goettingen, Germany.

Acronyms and Abbreviations

AfDB	African Development Bank
ALPs	accelerated learning programs
BARA	Bureau of Applied Research in Anthropology
CAADP	Comprehensive African Agriculture Development Programme
CECAM	Caisses d'Epargne et de Crédit Agricole Mutuelles (Madagascar)
CEMAC	Commission de la Communauté Economique et Monétaire de l'Afrique Centrale (Economic and Monetary Community of Central Africa)
CFA	Communauté Financière d'Afrique
COTVET	Council for TVET (Ghana)
CREATE	Consortium for Research on Educational Access, Transitions, and Equity
CREO	Comprehensive Review of Education Outcomes
CSAE	Centre for the Study of African Economies
DFID	Department for International Development (United Kingdom)
DHS	Demographic and Health Surveys
EPAG	Economic Empowerment of Adolescent Girls and Young Women (Liberia)
FAO	Food and Agriculture Organization (United Nations)
FET	further education and training
G2P	government to person
GDP	gross domestic product
GNI	gross national income
GRADE	Grupo de Análisis para el Desarrollo
HE	household enterprise
HIV/AIDS	human immunodeficiency virus/acquired immunodeficiency syndrome
ICT	information and communication technology
IDS	Institute of Development Studies
IFAD	International Fund for Agricultural Development
IFC	International Finance Corporation (World Bank Group)
IFPRI	International Food Policy Research Institute
IIEP	International Institute for Educational Planning
ILO	International Labour Organization
IMF	International Monetary Fund
IPA	Innovations for Poverty Action
IPAR	Institute of Policy Analysis and Research Rwanda
IPPG	Institutions and Pro-Poor Growth

KEPSA	Kenya Private Sector Alliance	SEZ	special economic zone
KYEP	Kenya Youth Empowerment Project	SfC	Saving for Change
		SfL	School for Life
LISGIS	Liberia Institute of Statistics and Geo-Information Services	SHG	self-help group
MFI	microfinance institution	SHIP	Survey-Based Harmonized Indicators Program
MICS	Multiple Indicator Cluster Survey	SIEF	Spanish Impact Evaluation Fund
MIJARC	Mouvement International de la Jeunesse Agricole et Rurale Catholique	SMEs	small and medium enterprises
		SPV	special-purpose vehicle
MIX	Microfinance Information Exchange	SSATP	Sub-Saharan Africa Transport Policy Program
MSME	micro, small, and medium enterprise	SUMATRA	Surface and Marine Transport Authority (Tanzania)
NBSSI	National Board for Small Scale Industries (Ghana)	TESDA	Technical Education and Skills Development Authority (the Philippines)
NGO	nongovernmental organization	TEVETA	Technical Education and Vocational Education and Training Association (Malawi)
OECD	Organisation for Economic Co-operation and Development		
OHADA	Organisation pour l'Harmonisation en Afrique du Droit des Affaires (Organization for the Harmonization of Business Law in Africa)	TFP	total factor productivity
		TICTS	Tanzania International Container Services
		TIMSS	Trends in Math and Science Study
		TPA	Tanzania Port Authority
OSBP	one-stop border post	TVET	technical vocational education and training
PMC	project management consultant		
PROMER	Promotion of Rural Entrepreneurship (Senegal)	TVVP	Technical and Vocational Vouchers Program (Kenya)
R&D	research and development	UEMOA	Union Economique et Monétaire Ouest Africaine (West African Economic and Monetary Union)
RCB	rural and community bank		
RCT	randomized controlled trial		
REP	Rural Enterprise Project (Ghana)	UNESCO	United Nations Educational, Scientific, and Cultural Organization
ROSCA	rotating savings and credit association		
		UNICEF	United Nations Children's Fund
SACCO	savings and credit cooperative	UNIDO	United Nations Industrial Development Organization
SACMEQ	Southern Africa Consortium for Measuring Educational Quality	USAID	United States Agency for International Development
SEWA	Self-Employed Women's Association (India)	VSLA	village savings and loan association

Overview

Youth Employment in Sub-Saharan Africa

Sub-Saharan Africa has just experienced one of the best decades of growth since the 1960s. Between 2000 and 2012, gross domestic product (GDP) grew more than 4.5 percent a year on average, compared to around 2 percent in the prior 20 years (World Bank various years). In 2012, the region's GDP growth was estimated at 4.7 percent—5.8 percent if South Africa is excluded (World Bank 2013). About one-quarter of countries in the region grew at 7 percent or better, and several African countries are among the fastest growing in the world. Medium-term growth prospects remain strong and should be supported by a rebounding global economy.

At the same time, many Africans are dissatisfied with this economic progress. According to the latest Afrobarometer data, 65 percent of the surveyed population consider economic conditions in their country to be the same or worse than the year prior, 53 percent rate their national economic condition as "very bad" or "fairly bad," and 48 percent say the same about their personal economic condition (Afrobarometer 2011–12. www.afrobarometer.org).

The incidence of poverty has fallen as Sub-Saharan economies have expanded, yet overall growth in Sub-Saharan Africa has not been as pro-poor as growth in other regions. Each 1 percent increase in average per capita consumption has been associated with a reduction in poverty of 0.69 percent; elsewhere in the world, that reduction has averaged just over 2 percent (World Bank 2013). In part, Africa's poverty reduction has been less marked because in many countries the source of growth is primarily oil, gas, and mineral extraction, not labor-intensive sectors such as agriculture or manufacturing. Young people, who have weaker links to the world of work than the general population, are therefore doubly disadvantaged.

Although the current generation of Africans entering the labor force is the most educated ever, many are finding that their prospects for employment and earnings differ very little from those of their parents. In a few countries, they are worse.

Youth in urban areas have been vocal about their dissatisfaction. Urban demonstrations consisting primarily of politically active and disaffected youth have become more common in African capitals. The causes of urban violence undoubtedly include factors much broader than employment status (such as inequality and exclusion), yet dissatisfaction with opportunities, especially in relation to expectations, can be a contributing factor. Understandably concerned, especially in light of the Arab Spring, policy makers in Sub-Saharan Africa are making youth employment a high priority. Focusing on urban youth, they are seeking policies and programs that can ameliorate the dissatisfaction of young people and ease their transition into adulthood by encouraging the creation of sustainable, productive employment.

But urban youth are only the most visible and audible part of the employment problem. The majority of young people still live in Africa's rural areas and small towns. Poorer and less educated than their urban counterparts, they too struggle to find pathways to adulthood, especially to stable, remunerative employment that allows them to support a family. For young women, the pathway can be especially treacherous. As they navigate the school-to-work transition, their control over their own destiny and their employment choices may be limited by social norms.

The challenge of youth employment in Africa may appear daunting, yet Africa's vibrant youth represent an enormous opportunity, particularly now, when populations in much of the world are aging rapidly. Youth not only need jobs, but also create them. Africa's growing labor force can be an asset in the global marketplace. Realizing this brighter vision for Africa's future, however, will require a clearer understanding of how to benefit from this asset. Meeting the youth employment challenge in all its dimensions—demographic, economic, and social—and understanding the forces that created the challenge, can open potential pathways toward a better life for young people and better prospects for the countries where they live.

This report begins by laying out the dynamics of the youth employment challenge in Sub-Saharan Africa today:

- The demographic transition, which created the youth bulge that is entering African labor

markets and can, in the longer term, stimulate economic growth and development

- The role of mineral exports—which have shaped the structure of recent economic growth but failed to sufficiently increase the number of wage jobs most desired by youth—and the prospects for reversing this trend in the future

- The largely untapped reservoir of opportunities in farming, at a time of high global prices for agricultural commodities and rising local and regional demand for food

- The massive expansion in access to education, which is adding many years of schooling, but much less learning, during childhood and youth

- The aspirations of youth and policy makers, which focus on the wage employment sector at the expense of more immediate opportunities in family farming and household enterprises.

Recognizing that it is the private sector that creates jobs, the report examines obstacles faced by households and firms in meeting the youth employment challenge. It focuses primarily on productivity—in agriculture, in nonfarm household enterprises (HEs), and in the modern wage sector—because productivity is the key to higher earnings as well as to more stable, less vulnerable, livelihoods. To respond to the policy makers' dilemma, the report identifies specific areas where government intervention can reduce those obstacles to productivity for households and firms, leading to brighter employment prospects for youth, their parents, and their own children.

Africa's Large Youth Population

Sub-Saharan Africa today faces an unprecedented opportunity. Half of the population is under 25 years of age. Each year between 2015 and 2035, there will be half a million more 15-year-olds than the year before. Meanwhile, the population in the rest of the world is, or will soon be, aging (figure O.1).

Africa's youth bulge offers a range of opportunities. First, the world's goods and services

Figure O.1 The structure of Sub-Saharan Africa's population is different than that in other regions

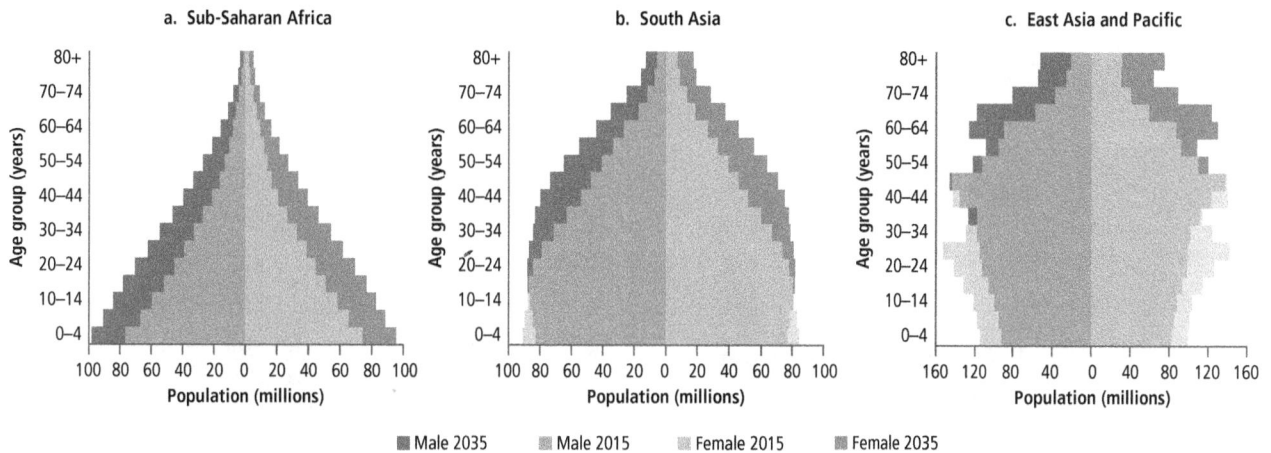

a. Sub-Saharan Africa   b. South Asia   c. East Asia and Pacific

■ Male 2035   ▓ Male 2015   ░ Female 2015   ▓ Female 2035

Source: Based on United Nations 2011.

cannot be produced without working-age labor. Sub-Saharan Africa, along with South Asia, can be the main supplier of the world's workforce, either by producing goods and services in the region or by sending workers to regions with a shortage of workers. Second, manufacturing wages in other regions are rising. Africa's labor force should compete for these jobs. Third, increasing concentrations of workers in urban areas can be a source of innovation and rapid economic growth (World Bank 2008). Young people will be at the forefront of these developments. Finally, if fertility continues to decline, rapid growth in Africa's workforce will mean that the number of working-age adults relative to "dependents" will rise from just around 1 in 1985 to close to 1.7 in 2050, providing the space for savings, investment, and sustained economic growth. Yet the demographic transition is not automatic. A critical concern is that the decline in fertility rates has stalled—or not even started—in many African countries. But it is also a critical concern that those of working age are able to be productive.

Growth, Jobs, and Africa's Labor Force—Now and in the Future

Despite 15 years of relatively rapid economic growth averaging more than 4.5 percent a year, almost all African countries still depend on primary commodities for their exports. The failure of this growth to reduce poverty is stark in several countries, including oil-rich Angola, Gabon, and Nigeria, and noticeable in others, such as Mozambique and Zambia. Labor-intensive manufactured exports—the force behind employment and economic transformation in East Asia—are far from taking off in Africa. In fact, manufacturing's share in GDP is lower in Sub-Saharan Africa today than it was in 1980; over the same period in Asia, it rose in both lower- and middle-income countries (figure O.2).

To understand the challenge of youth employment in this context, we start with where Africans work today (see box O.1 for an explanation of how this report defines employment). Contrary to popular perceptions, measured unemployment in low-income Africa is only 3 percent.[1] Even in lower-middle-income countries, unemployment is quite low (figure O.3).

These low unemployment rates may seem counterintuitive, given widespread concern about "unemployed youth," but most Africans simply cannot afford to be idle. Very few families can fully support a recent graduate while he or she seeks a job. That the unemployment rate is highest among university graduates—who mostly come from the top end of the income distribution—is no coincidence. Only in upper-income countries, with broader safety nets, does substantial unemployment persist,

Figure O.2 Over the past two decades, agriculture's share in GDP contracted in Africa, but manufacturing did not replace it

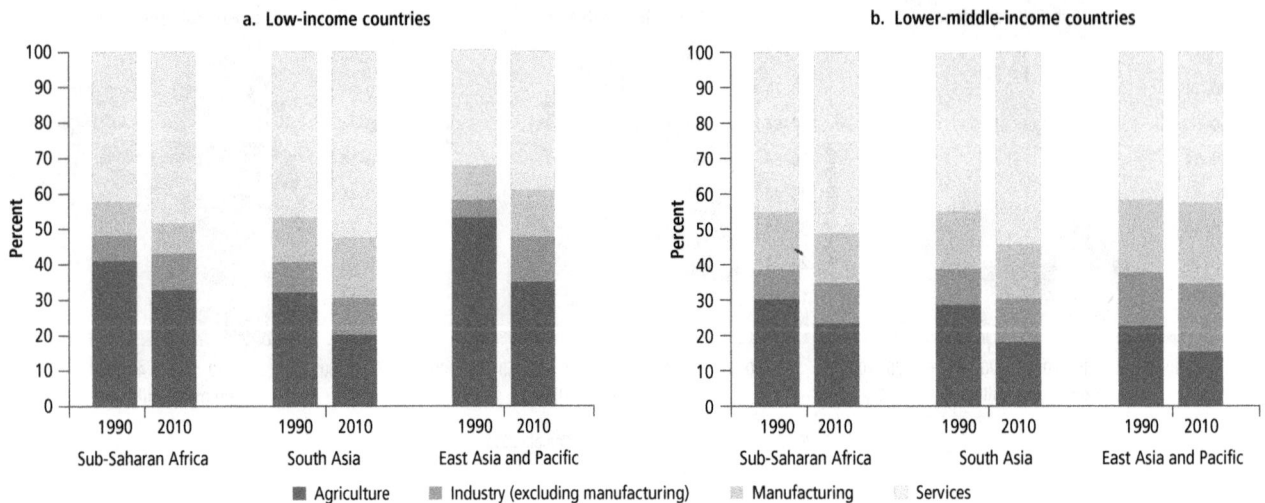

a. Low-income countries

b. Lower-middle-income countries

Agriculture   Industry (excluding manufacturing)   Manufacturing   Services

Source: World Bank various years.

Box O.1

What is a "job"?

In assessing the challenges of youth employment, it is important to take stock of what it means to have a job and to have employment. To some, having a job is synonymous with having a wage or salaried position with an employer. Most work in Africa is not structured that way, however. This study follows the approach adopted in the *World Development Report 2013: Jobs,* which defines jobs as "activities that generate actual or imputed income, monetary or in kind, formal or informal." That report also notes that not all forms or work can be considered jobs—for example, activities that are performed against the will of the worker or that violate basic human rights.

Across countries, including those in Sub-Saharan Africa, people report that jobs have a broader importance than the income they provide. Jobs can convey identity, status, and

self-confidence; they can contribute to an individual's overall life satisfaction. Not all jobs contribute to these dimensions of well-being. The type of job, working conditions, contract, benefits, and safety and security at work all matter. Beyond personal life satisfaction, jobs also contribute to social cohesion through various channels: jobs can shape identities and how individuals relate to one another, jobs can connect people to one another through networks, and the distribution of jobs within society and the perceptions about who has access to opportunities, and why, can shape people's expectations and aspirations for the future, their sense of having a stake in society, and their perceptions of fairness. All of these intrinsic aspects of jobs are particularly important for youth.

Source: World Bank 2012.

---

including among youth. Because the youth employment challenge is configured somewhat differently in Africa's resource-rich countries and some middle-income countries, they will need to approach the challenge in somewhat different ways (see box O.2).

Where do most Sub-Saharan Africans find employment? About 16 percent of those in the labor force have "wage jobs"—jobs that pay a

regular wage, sometimes with associated benefits. In low-income countries, these jobs are divided roughly equally between the public and private sectors, although the private share grows with per capita income. The industrial sector (mining, manufacturing, and construction) accounts for less than 20 percent of wage jobs (about 3 percent of total employment). The remaining jobs are either on family farms

(62 percent) or in household enterprises (22 percent), which may be collectively described as the informal sector (see box O.5 for a definition of household enterprises). These kinds of jobs—working a small plot of land, selling vegetables on the street, sewing clothes in one's home—often generate low earnings, partly because the "enterprises" tend to be tiny, typically involving only the family.

Will this pattern of employment persist? After all, countries that are not resource rich are creating private wage jobs at a rapid clip—often faster than GDP is growing. The kinds of jobs that are created will depend partly on the structure of growth that Africa attains. Growth and employment projections for this report assume that growth will remain strong (5–6 percent a year) and will be fueled by Africa's natural resources—minerals and agriculture. The mineral sector is not expected to create very many jobs. Increases in wage employment (as a share of total employment) will come from continued diversification of output and exports and from increased domestic demand for services as incomes grow. Since service employment is projected to grow faster than employment in industrial sectors, as it has in the past, most nonfarm employment will be created there. Based on these assumptions, the number of industrial sector wage and salary jobs is projected to increase 55 percent over the next 10 years. The problem is that this growth starts from such a small base that it does not even come close to absorbing the millions of young people entering the labor force each year. Because of the low base, the share of industrial wage jobs in total employment will rise only from 3 to 4.5 percent in Sub-Saharan Africa, still below the share in other developing regions. The share of wage jobs in the service sector is projected to rise from 13 to 22 percent.

In other words, over the next 10 years, at best only one in four of Sub-Saharan Africa's youth will find a wage job, and only a small fraction of those jobs will be "formal" jobs in modern enterprises. Most young people will end up working where their parents do—in family farms and household enterprises (figure O.4).

The employment challenge is therefore not just to create jobs in the formal sector, important as that may be, but to increase the produc-

Figure O.3 **Where are Africans working?**

Estimated structure of employment in Sub-Saharan Africa by country type, 2010

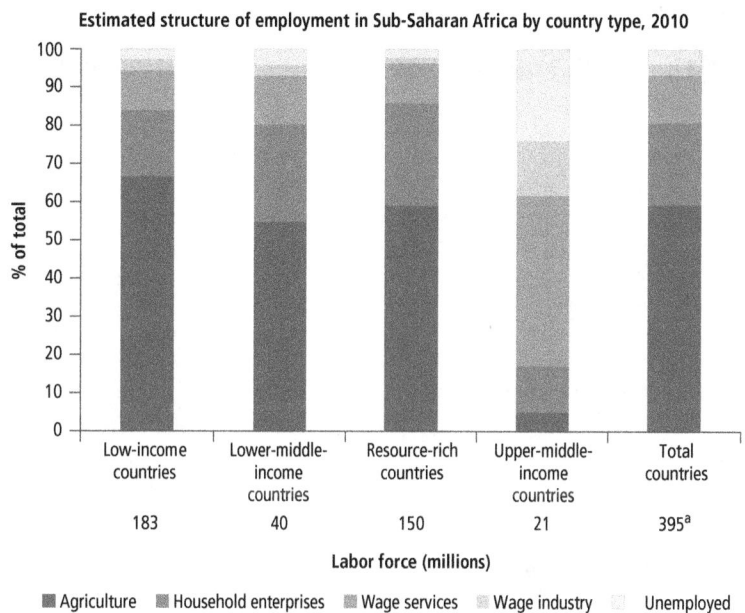

Source: Fox et al. 2013.
Note: On the horizontal axis, numbers show size of the labor force, ages 15–64, in each group. Resource-rich countries included are Angola, Chad, the Democratic Republic of Congo, Guinea, Nigeria, the Republic of Congo, Sudan and Republic of South Sudan, and Zambia.
a. Numbers do not add to total because of rounding.

tivity of the almost 80 percent of the workforce who will be in the informal sector—thereby addressing the underemployment associated with work in this sector. The size of the youth bulge in Africa and the current structure of the economy mean that the majority of this generation's workers will remain in the informal sector for the duration of their working lives. To be sure, in the long run these workers (or their children) will move to the formal sector, like their counterparts in East Asia and Latin America.

This focus on raising productivity in the informal sector may seem unusual, given the publicity around high unemployment among university graduates and the recent emphasis on creating jobs in the formal manufacturing sector (Dinh et al. 2012). But university graduates still represent only a tiny fraction (about 3–4 percent) of the labor force, come from the richest households, and have the best job prospects. Creating jobs in the formal sector is important and should be encouraged, but the reality is that even if African countries were able to attract an extraordinary infusion

The youth employment challenge in resource-rich and some middle-income countries in Africa

Resource-rich countries present particular challenges when it comes to employment. Natural resource rents, if poorly managed, lead to overvalued exchange rates and uncompetitive real wages. Such conditions severely hamper job creation in export-oriented sectors. At the same time, the few but highly paid employment opportunities in the natural resource sector encourage young people to "wait for a job"—behavior that can distort educational choices and aggravate skill mismatches in the labor market. Resource rents can also engender substantial governance problems that stifle growth in employment.

If countries manage their natural resource endowments well, however, they can amass the financial resources to support smart investments in human development, infrastructure, and the promotion of new sources of economic growth. Resource-rich countries noted for successfully growing their economies, such as Chile, Indonesia, and Malaysia, have diversified economically—to manufacturing (Indonesia

and Malaysia) or to non-resource-based primary commodities (Chile)—through sound macroeconomic policies, open trade and investment policies, strategies to build human capital, and a good business environment (Gelb and Grasmann 2010).

Youth employment problems in some middle-income countries, such as Mauritius and South Africa, resemble the crisis in youth unemployment occurring outside Sub-Saharan Africa. Especially in South Africa, unemployment is high (25–40 percent, depending on the definition used), youth unemployment is even higher, and the informal sector is very small. The challenge is to reduce unemployment, which involves understanding its determinants. While the symptoms and some of the causes may differ (for instance, labor regulations may play a significantly larger role in these more developed countries), some of the solutions proposed in this report for other countries are quite similar to those needed in South Africa—for example, steps to increase agricultural productivity or improve workers' foundational skills.

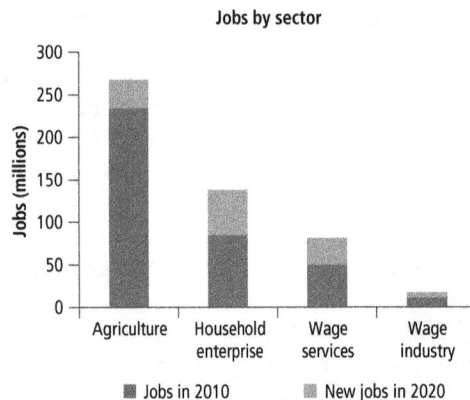

Figure O.4 **Informal will be normal in 2020**

Jobs by sector

Jobs (millions)

■ Jobs in 2010   ▨ New jobs in 2020

Source: Fox et al. 2013.
Note: The projected number of new jobs added by 2020 will be 125 million.

of private investment in very labor-intensive enterprises, the formal sector would draw only a small number of workers from the informal sector in the near future (see box O.3).

Even if it is realistic to emphasize the role of the informal sector, does this mean that we are

pessimistic about Africa's future? That we are denying African workers the hope of emerging from informal employment? On the contrary, raising the productivity of smallholder farms and household enterprises is precisely what will enable the formal sector to develop and thrive. It was the key to structural transformation in Asia and Latin America, and it is the key to Africa's future as well.

Youth's Transition to Productive Employment

Transition is the defining feature of youth (see World Bank 2006). The young leave school for work, eventually settling on a career. They grapple with the many decisions that influence when they start a family and how healthily they live (including decisions to engage in risky behaviors such as tobacco and alcohol use). Most young people also begin to engage in the rights and duties of citizens, such as voting in elections. The question, therefore, is

Box O.3

What will happen to employment if light manufacturing increases dramatically in Africa?

Some observers contend that the structure of employment could change more rapidly if Africa experienced a radical, "game-changing" departure from its current growth path (see Lin and Monga 2012; Dinh et al. 2012). What employment prospects would open to youth by 2020 if African countries picked up manufacturing industries and jobs from East Asia beginning in 2015, just as Asian countries such as Bangladesh, Cambodia, and Vietnam picked up industries and jobs from Japan and the Republic of Korea in the 1980s and 1990s?

To test the possibilities, we simulated this recent Asian experience in low-income and lower-middle-income countries of Africa.[a] For the simulation, the wage employment elasticity rises to 1.2 to match the historical wage employment elasticity estimated for Bangladesh, Cambodia, and Vietnam—meaning that employment in the industrial sector would grow 20 percent faster than value added, which implies very labor-intensive growth. The industrial growth projection for low- and lower-middle-income countries is also revised upward to 10 percent a year over 2015–20. This figure is slightly above the median and average industry growth rate experienced by Bangladesh, Cambodia, and Vietnam during the most recent decade (9.3 percent a year).

If this "game-changing" scenario could be realized, industrial wage employment would grow much faster across Afri-

ca's low- and lower-middle-income countries. The average annual growth of industrial wage employment would double over the decade to 12 percent a year, and total wage employment would grow 6 percent a year.

Ultimately, however, the structure of employment would change very little compared to today. Low-income countries could expect about 5 million more wage jobs a year, and lower-middle-income countries could expect about 2 million new wage jobs—a shift of 10 percent of total new jobs in these countries, representing a small change in the prospects for new entrants. These modest gains partly reflect the short period used for the projection (which covers 5 years, whereas the structural change in Vietnam unfolded over 20 years). They also reflect Africa's larger labor force and the lower base from which industrial development must start. Africa will need at least two decades to change the structure of employment sufficiently to offer dramatically different prospects to its youth, which underscores the importance of starting the change process now.

Source: Fox et al. 2013.
a. Africa's resource-rich countries are excluded from this simulation, because even resource-rich countries in East Asia did not achieve the transformation of employment simulated here.

how to help youth to make these transitions in a way that puts them on a pathway to productive employment. The particular challenges that young people—especially young women or poorer youth—encounter during these transitions increase the difficulty of finding a pathway to productive employment (although securing productive employment is important for all members of society, as box O.4 explains).

The transition from school to work as well as between sectors of employment (between farming and a wage job, for example) is particularly difficult for young Africans. Many lack the means, skills, knowledge, or connections to translate their education into productive employment. Nor is there a structured path to follow. Many young people combine school with work for many years (figure O.5). Some move straight into apprenticeships and

similar arrangements, but others do not. Evidence from urban Tanzania (Bridges et al. 2013) shows that some young people do odd jobs and are supported by their families for as long as five years before they settle into wage jobs or (mostly) self-employment. Moreover, first-generation school leavers aspiring to be wage workers lack a family history in formal employment. They may not have networks to help them to find jobs.

Young women may be particularly disadvantaged by other dimensions of the transition, such as family formation, compared with young men (figure O.6). Social norms tend to enforce job segregation by gender. For instance, young women in the household enterprise sector work mostly in narrowly defined fields such as dressmaking, even though a range of other occupations could be more lucrative.

Box O.4

Youth employment versus overall employment

A key part of improving employment opportunities for Africa's youth is to understand and address Africa's overall economic challenges. For that reason, much of the discussion in this report focuses on identifying policies that can increase the productivity of all employment—in agriculture, nonfarm household enterprises, and the modern wage sector. The report also identifies promising policies that focus specifically on helping youth to transition more successfully to higher-productivity work in each of those three sectors.

The focus on youth raises the question of whether it might be socially beneficial to support employment policies that favor youth over other members of society. Special efforts

to help young people to enter agriculture or start household enterprises do not generally reduce such opportunities for adults. But efforts to facilitate access of youth to the modern wage sector could potentially displace adults working in the sector. On the one hand, assistance for young people might have long-term benefits if it sets them on a productive path. On the other hand, older workers may have families and other economic dependents who rely on their income. There is no clear argument that social welfare will be improved by favoring younger workers over older ones. This report advocates seeking to increase the opportunities for all workers, while helping youth to overcome their particular constraints.

Figure O.5 The transition from school to work in Sub-Saharan Africa is slow

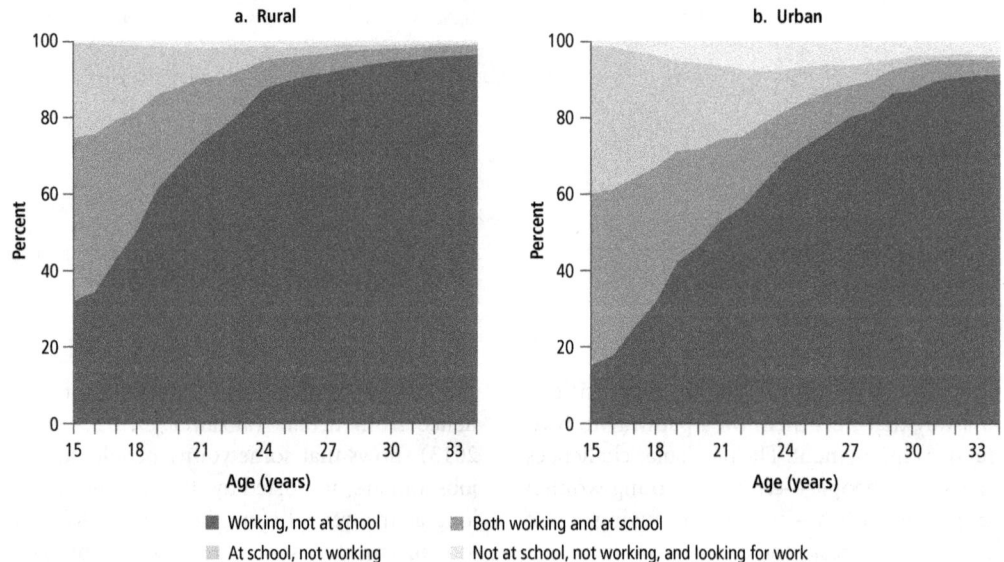

Source: Based on standardized and harmonized household and labor force surveys (see appendix).

Policy Priorities for Addressing Youth Employment

To understand the challenges constraining productivity and earnings for youth and to orient how policies should be targeted, this report considers the three main sectors where people work: agriculture, nonfarm household enterprises, and modern wage employment. It then distinguishes between two dimensions

that shape young people's potential to find a pathway to productive work in the three sectors: human capital and the business environment. Box O.5 describes this framework more fully.

On the human capital side, the role of basic education dominates interventions in all three sectors. As a complement, different approaches are needed to build post-school skills in agriculture, household enterprises, and the modern

Figure O.6 Family formation starts earlier for young women than for young men

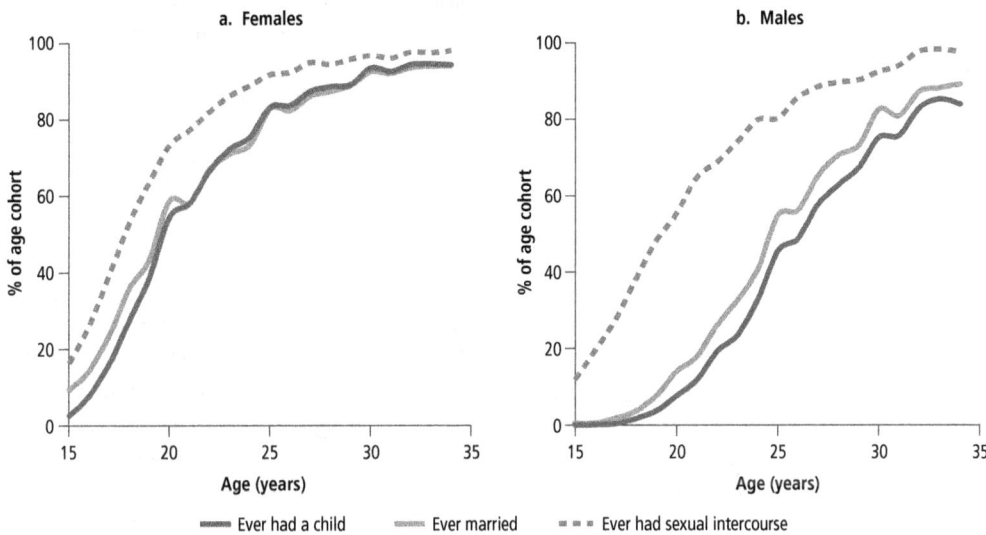

a. Females

b. Males

Legend: Ever had a child   Ever married   Ever had sexual intercourse

Source: Based on demographic and health survey data in 28 countries (see appendix).

Box O.5

Framework for analyzing youth employment

Three main sectors of employment:

Agriculture is where the vast majority of work takes place in Sub-Saharan Africa. Agriculture occupies more than 70 percent of the labor force in Africa's low-income countries and more than 50 percent in its lower-middle-income countries. African farmers are predominantly smallholders who consume a large share of what they produce. One recent collection of household surveys estimates that the share of own-consumption is around 50 percent (versus 20–30 percent outside of Sub-Saharan Africa).

Household enterprises are unincorporated, nonfarm businesses owned by households. They include self-employed people running businesses that may employ family members without pay, but may also employ less than five nonfamily workers on a continuous basis. The vast majority (70 percent) of nonfarm enterprises today are pure self-employment: just the owner operating the HE. About 20 percent of these enterprises include a family member in the operation, and only 10 percent have hired someone outside of the family.

The *modern wage sector* includes small, medium, and large firms that employ five or more workers on a continuous basis. It also includes the public sector, which in some countries is a large share of the modern wage sector. In the low- and lower-middle-income countries of Sub-Saharan Africa, roughly half of wage employment is in the public sector. In this report, we focus only on the private sector, where the potential for job growth is the greatest.

Two dimensions that shape the pathways to productive work:

- *Human capital*—the supply side, meaning the abilities, education, skills, family connections, networks, and other characteristics that are embedded in an individual and allow that person to find opportunities to be productive, increase earnings, and achieve income security
- *Business environment*—the factors outside the worker's immediate control that affect productivity (access to land, capital, and finance; infrastructure; technology; and markets), as well as the government policies, regulations, and programs that may affect the choice of economic activity and how the activity is conducted.

wage sector. On the business environment side, raising farm productivity requires enabling farmers to gain access to finance and secure land tenure; in the nonfarm HE sector, infrastructure services and access to finance as well as a space to operate will play critical roles; to boost modern sector wage jobs, business regulations and infrastructure will be important.

Human Capital: The Fundamental Role of Basic Education

Sub-Saharan Africa has seen a rapid increase in the number of children who complete primary school, from about 50 percent in 1991 to 70 percent in 2011. The average young Ghanaian or Zambian today has more schooling than the average French or Italian citizen had in 1960 (Pritchett 2013). The current cohort of youth in Sub-Saharan Africa will be the most schooled ever.

Educational attainment shapes employment opportunities, as reflected in the substantial variation in the educational profiles of young workers in each sector (figure O.7). Internationally benchmarked learning assessments suggest that many young people nevertheless lack the skills to compete in a global marketplace. Schooling is not learning. Deep deficiencies in the quality of education mean that the effect of schooling on productivity is far below its potential. The poor quality of education directly constrains productivity and hinders individuals from acquiring new skills.

Learning in primary school is often minimal: 80 percent of Malian third-graders and more than 70 percent of Ugandan third-graders cannot read a single word (Cloutier, Reinstadtler, and Beltran 2011). Even students who

complete primary school have low levels of basic skills: among sixth-graders 43 percent in Tanzania and 74 percent in Mozambique are at or below the "basic numeracy" level, while 44 percent in Mozambique cannot "read for meaning" (Hungi et al. 2010). A few years of low-quality basic education will not confer much of a gain in productivity if students never master even basic literacy and numeracy—although so-called "second-chance education" approaches offer some potential for catching up. For many, however, primary schooling is the highest level of schooling they will achieve. These results are especially troubling because they suggest that school leavers have a fragile foundation on which to build more specialized skills.

Even students who make it to the secondary level—those who will most likely head to the modern wage sector—are not globally competitive. In the most recent internationally benchmarked assessment of eighth- and ninth-grade students, 79 percent of Ghanaians and 76 percent of South Africans do not surpass the lowest measured level of math proficiency. For comparison, the international mean is 25 percent, and the corresponding scores are 67 percent for Indonesian students and 45 percent for Jordanian students.[2] Beyond these cognitive skills, many youth lack the behavioral and

Figure O.7 **Education shapes opportunities**

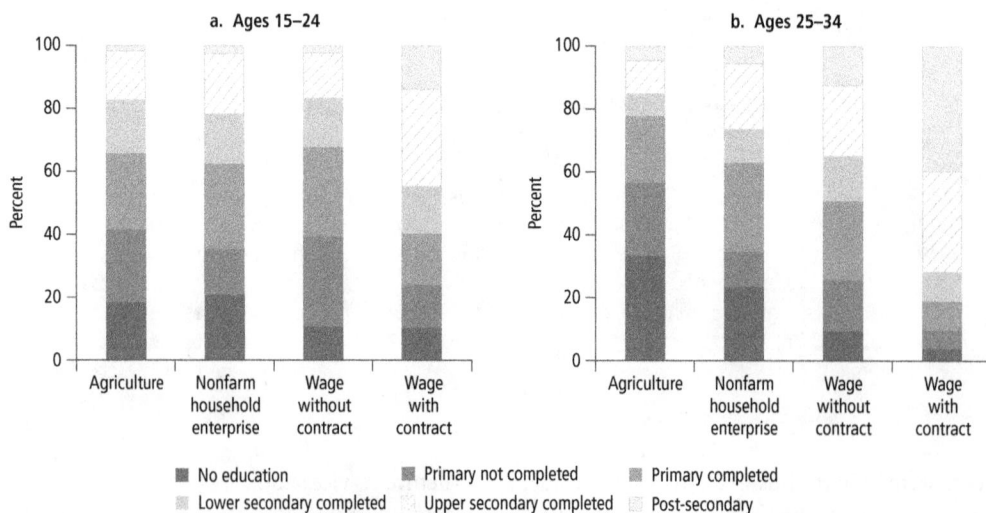

Source: Based on standardized and harmonized household and labor force surveys (see appendix).

socioemotional skills, sometimes called "soft skills," that are needed to get, keep, and be productive in a job.

Addressing this lack of learning is not easy. Surveys of schools reveal substantial failures in service delivery. For example, absenteeism among teachers is between 16 and 20 percent on a given day in Kenya, Senegal, and Tanzania, and primary school students in those countries experience only about two to three hours of learning a day.[3] Reforming the accountability framework that allows such poor performance to persist is key. Better information on performance must be complemented by targeted approaches that increase oversight by the people who are most affected: students and their parents. Steps to ensure that teachers are well prepared for teaching and supported in their tasks are critical for creating a cadre of high-performing professionals. The rise of private schools in Africa—schools that often deliver superior performance at lower cost—should not be stifled but should be encouraged and channeled to give larger numbers of students the opportunity to learn.

Improvements in basic education will lay the foundation for improvements in productivity. At the same time, to maximize young people's chances of transitioning successfully to remunerative employment, complementary actions are required to improve the business environment and develop human capital. Those actions will vary by sector of employment, as discussed next.

Raising the Productivity of Smallholder Farmers

Agriculture can and should be a sector of opportunity for Sub-Saharan Africa's youth. The growing demand for food means that there is scope for supply to take advantage of a growing market. And growth in demand is not limited to Africa's expanding domestic markets. Global food prices are at their highest point in several decades, and they are expected to remain high for at least the rest of the decade.

Africa is well positioned to produce for this large and potentially lucrative global market.

It has plentiful supplies of land and often of water, unlike other regions. If young people can gain access to these resources and use them in conjunction with strategies to make agriculture more productive, the results could be transformative for livelihoods and economic growth. More than two-thirds of the young people who work in rural areas already work in agriculture, and most will remain there, even if the nonfarm sector develops extremely rapidly.

Although agriculture is the most immediate means of generating income and employment for large numbers of young people, efforts to accelerate agricultural growth and improve food security in Africa have been conceptually separated from efforts to create jobs for young people. Yet these goals are highly complementary. Increasing young people's opportunities for productive work in rural areas is arguably the most important catalyst for Africa to reap its demographic dividend.

Low agricultural productivity is the primary impediment to overcome. Agricultural productivity remains lower in Africa than in any other region of the world, and agriculture is the least productive sector in African economies. This is true, despite the fact that total factor productivity, as well as land and labor productivity, have been increasing in African agriculture since the 1990s (Fuglie and Rada 2013; Nin-Pratt, Johnson, and Yu 2012). Productivity may increase further as food prices continue to rise, because the value of output for the same amount of inputs will increase, but these productivity indicators are far below levels achieved in other regions during their phases of rapid economic growth. Indeed, African countries are not following the trajectory of other regions in which productivity gains on farms, combined with higher productivity and more opportunities off the farm, shifted labor rapidly out of agriculture.

The effects of low agricultural productivity extend well beyond rural areas and farm households. An underappreciated result of low agricultural productivity in Africa is high domestic food prices. Local prices are poorly correlated with global prices, especially in the interior. When domestic prices are high, this increases the cost of food and pushes up wages, contributing to Africa's overall lack of competitiveness. High domestic prices undermine real earnings for everyone except those farmers who are net food sellers and whose production costs are relatively low. Greater agricultural productivity will reduce the domestic cost of food and create more and better-paying nonfarm jobs for everyone, especially youth.

Understanding why the least productive sector is also the largest may provide insight into how farmworkers can increase their productivity. Small-scale farmers may be caught in a trap that prevents them from generating sufficient earnings to invest in expanding production and productivity. The vast majority of African farmers work on tiny plots of land, often under uncertain tenure arrangements. They cannot take advantage of economies of scale (where they exist), modern agricultural inputs, and mechanization. Poor rural infrastructure (transport, electricity, and irrigation) frustrates farmers' efforts to obtain affordable inputs such as seed and fertilizer, market their output profitably, or harness new land for cultivation. The lack of irrigation makes agriculture more vulnerable to the vagaries of weather.

Low levels of education and pervasive health problems (two outcomes of the poor delivery of services) prevent farmers from increasing their own productivity, much less migrating to areas where agriculture or some other occupation might be more productive. Rural youth have significantly lower levels of education than their urban counterparts. Many endemic diseases are not difficult to manage or cure, but these areas of health policy often receive little attention despite their high cost to the rural economy. Illness, apart from reducing the labor available to farm households, can deplete savings through costly treatments and cause distress sales of assets.

For Africa to raise agricultural productivity sufficiently to support overall growth and provide a remunerative livelihood for those working in the sector, farming must shift rapidly from being an occupation of last resort and low productivity to one of technical dynamism and recognized opportunity (see box O.6 for a discussion of the link between productivity and jobs in agriculture). With much higher priority accorded to well-designed programs of public investment in agriculture, continued progress on regulatory and policy reform, and some attention to including young people, agriculture could absorb the large numbers of new job seekers and offer meaningful work with large public and private benefits.

Broadly speaking, three pathways are available for rural youth in agriculture: (1) full-time work on family farms, (2) part-time farm work, combined with running a household enterprise, which can include the sale of farm services or inputs, and (3) wage work. To increase the productivity of these pathways to agricultural employment, constraints need to be relaxed in at least four areas: credit and financial services, land policies, infrastructure, and skills.

Credit and Financial Services

Because they work in a risky environment and lack collateral, rural households face major constraints in obtaining capital and credit. Traditional financial institutions do not find it profitable to provide agricultural credit. Instead, various nongovernmental organizations (NGOs) and banks have been innovating with new instruments and institutions, some of which look promising. First started in Niger in 1991, village savings and loan associations (VSLAs)—where members save on a regular basis and lend money on terms determined by the group—have spread to 39, mostly African, countries. They hold great potential for assisting young people to save the funds to invest in a farm and to get access to credit, while also benefiting from the mentoring and access to information that come from being a member. VSLAs could help youth in rural areas to establish themselves in agriculture as well as in nonagriculture sectors.

Various institutional arrangements and incentive schemes can also widen access to credit. Examples include different forms of collateral (chattel mortgages and others), leasing (which requires no collateral, such as the DFCU Leasing Company in Uganda), linking credit to extension services (thereby addressing multiple constraints simultaneously, because young people also need information), and contract farming (in which the wholesaler provides credit for inputs).

None of these innovations in rural finance is exclusively for young people. Nor should

Box O.6

Does labor need to move out of agriculture as productivity grows?

If Africa's farms get bigger as productivity grows, will workers be pushed out of the sector and have nowhere to go? Some observers have raised this concern, and it is understandable. In other parts of the world, growth in productivity has been accompanied by an increase in farm size, a reduction in labor intensity, and the exit of labor from agriculture.

Africa's endowment of land and labor and its recent history offer perspectives to quell this concern. If land is available and crop area is still expanding, increased farm size need not displace labor, especially where the cost of capital to invest in mechanization is high. As shown in table BO.6.1, between 1960 and 2008, crop area in Africa expanded, the workforce in agriculture grew, and output per worker increased despite the larger number of workers per hectare. During the later years, from 1990 to 2008, the pace of growth in the labor force slowed relative to the expansion of land, and output per worker continued to increase.

Africa's farms can grow in number, size, and productivity without displacing labor. The subcontinent's experience with structural change in the twenty-first century is not likely to replicate the experience in other regions in earlier times. The current context is one of high global food prices, huge potential for growth in area and yield, few nontradable manufactured goods, and shifts in comparative advantage

in the developed world in favor of technology-intensive services and products. The cost of capital in Africa remains high, reflecting low saving rates, high costs of doing business, and rising demand for capital-intensive infrastructure investments. Agriculture's share in African GDP (and ability to employ labor) therefore could remain steady or even grow, rather than shrink, with development. Reserves of good

Table BO.6.1 **Increase in crop area harvested, agricultural labor force, and output per worker in Sub-Saharan Africa, 1960–2008 and 1990–2008**

% increase

Indicator	1960–2008	1990–2008
Crop area harvested	42	20
Agricultural labor force	125	21
Output per worker	21	9

Source: Fuglie and Rada 2013.

land, abundant water, and an energetic young labor force are tremendous assets at a time when the global economy urgently needs more food and fiber. Whether Africa can use these assets productively depends on finding ways to ease the constraints on access to land and address the barriers to agricultural growth highlighted in this report.

young people be segregated as a group and offered financial services designed specifically for them. The risks of working with this client base are high, and separating young people from a larger pool for sharing risks would make them even less attractive to financial institutions. A better approach is to support a range of innovations in finance that facilitate outreach to small farmers and rural entrepreneurs. When necessary, additional features should be added to enhance the ability of these programs to serve young people.

Land Policies

Insecure and unclear land rights, as well as constraints on renting or otherwise using land, pose problems for young people in agriculture. Some young people own land (albeit small plots), but ownership is strongly concentrated among older adults (figure O.8).

The problem of insecure and unclear land rights can be addressed by developing an inventory of registered land and improving land registration. Geographic information systems have made this process increasingly practical. Tenure security is also reinforced by improving land titling procedures. When farmers know that their land rights are secure, they are more likely to invest in improving their land. A recent impact evaluation of a land registration pilot in Rwanda shows that more secure land tenure increased investments in soil improvement by 9 percent among male farmers and 18 percent among female farmers (Ayalew Ali, Deininger, and Goldstein 2011).

Once land is registered and titled, land rental markets can develop. Land rental markets have been shown to promote commercial farming in Ghana and to encourage the transfer of land to smaller-scale farmers in Sudan. By contrast,

Figure O.8　Young people are unlikely to own land

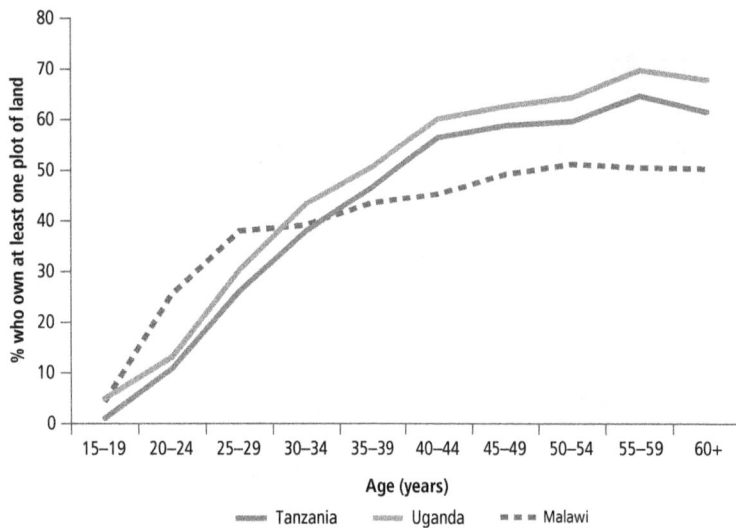

Source: Based on data from the World Bank's Living Standards Measurement Study, Integrated Surveys for Agriculture (2011 in Malawi, 2010 in Tanzania and Uganda).

restrictions on land rental markets have inhibited both the farm and nonfarm sectors, discouraging people with land from taking jobs in the nonfarm sector for fear of losing their land.

Agribusiness can increase productivity, and parts of Africa, especially the Guinea savannah, have huge potential for commercial agriculture on both large and small farms (Morris, Binswanger-Mkhize, and Byerlee 2009). Large commercial landholdings and agribusiness may prove politically contentious, however. How large farms are integrated into a diverse farm structure and how smallholders are compensated for land that they make available to large commercial operators are critical issues to resolve. Other ways of aggregating smallholders, such as producer associations or contract farming, could also be practical approaches for improving productivity when increasing the scale of production will contribute to lower costs.

Infrastructure

In some—but not all—cases, investments in rural infrastructure can have huge rates of return. Typically such investments occur in more densely populated areas (World Bank

2008), but even here, investments should be evaluated case by case and not accepted across the board. For example, paved rural roads are not always a good investment, especially in areas where motorized traffic is low. Paved roads are more expensive to maintain, so maintenance is often not funded; another issue is that roads are prone to becoming tools of political patronage (Raballand and Macchi 2009).

Skills

Given their low levels of formal education (figure O.7), youth in rural areas can increase their productivity with more and better schooling. In turn, higher productivity increases demand for schooling, triggering a virtuous cycle. The evidence used to identify externalities in education usually comes from agriculture: farmers learn from neighboring farmers, especially more educated ones, who are also more likely to adopt new technologies (Conley and Udry 2010; Rosenzweig 2012). All of these effects apply more strongly to young farmers.

In addition to basic education, high-productivity farming requires specific skills, such as skills in processing, marketing, machinery operation and repair, transport, logistics, and quality control. In some countries, agricultural vocational training institutes (some of which are associated with universities) traditionally have provided these skills. These institutes have a mixed track record, mostly owing to the disconnect between academic, lecture-style teaching and the need for on-the-ground, practical training.

Agricultural extension programs have a disappointing history in Africa, mainly because of poor incentives and accountability. Better results are coming from new programs that empower farmers by giving them a choice of providers and services from among a range of public, private, and nongovernmental agencies. Another approach, farmer field schools, involves participatory methods of learning, technology development, and dissemination and appears to be especially successful in building women's skills. Business incubators and rural alliances that bring together commercial buyers with producer organizations are further ways of boosting agricultural incomes. In all such efforts, the use of information and communication technology can benefit, and benefit from, the participation of young people.

Increasing the Productivity of Nonfarm Household Enterprises

The majority of people who work outside the farm sector are engaged in informal, household enterprises. Often such an enterprise is one pillar of a diversified livelihood strategy: Many households are engaged in the farm and nonfarm sectors at the same time (30–50 percent of rural households have a nonfarm HE). In urban areas, many households with an enterprise have a family member earning a wage income, a pattern that is likely to increase over time (Fox and Sohnesen 2012).

Although their productivity is relatively low, HEs provide earnings that are usually higher than anything their owners could obtain in the agriculture sector. Most HEs have no employees and are pure self-employment. Few include a family member as additional labor, and only 10 percent hire outside the family. Some are started in response to a local business opportunity (such as increased demand for a service), whereas others are started because the household lacks alternative means to earn a living.

What do HEs do? They mostly sell services (hairdressing, repairs) and internationally and locally produced consumer goods (used clothing, household supplies, vegetables, eggs). They also contribute to the industrial sector, transforming agricultural goods or natural resources into charcoal, bricks, iron work, or processed grain. Some pursue artisanal activities such as woodworking, dressmaking and tailoring, and construction.

HEs sell low-cost goods and services mainly for the local market, which lacks a modern service sector. In urban areas, the traders and hawkers substitute for convenience stores and shopping malls. The low-quality manufactured goods these enterprises produce, such as homemade bricks and furniture, eventually are replaced by higher-quality locally produced goods (made in brick and furniture factories) and imports. As a result, HEs that are involved in manufacturing do not persist as long as HEs that provide services.

Historically, HEs have tended to remain tiny or to disappear; very few grow into even small or medium enterprises. Data from West Africa show that, even after 10 years of operation, the capital stock of these businesses remains the same. Most enterprises never hire another worker. So the employment they provide, including the employment for young people, comes from seizing a business opportunity and starting a new enterprise.

Despite their small scale, HEs are an instrument for reducing poverty in Africa, with the potential for becoming an even more powerful one. They tend to be found in richer areas. Households with enterprises are less likely to be poor and are clustered in the middle quintiles of the income distribution. Rural households gain a higher hourly income from HEs than from agricultural work. In urban areas, some HE owners make more money than they would from a wage job. In fact, controlling for education and skills, the reported consumption of rural and urban households with an HE in Africa is no different from that of households in wage employment (Fox and Sohnesen 2012). Indeed, they also report being "happier" (Falco et al. 2013).

Most governments continue to ignore, neglect, or undermine the potential of this sector. Hawkers and sellers are regarded as an unattractive annoyance to be chased out of the business districts in capital cities. Advocates of formal employment criticize HEs for not offering the benefits and security of a wage job. Thinking that HEs can be transformed into small and medium enterprises—for which they have a strategy—governments try to formalize these informal enterprises. This transformation rarely takes place, however, because this is not the intention of the owners. Lacking support, HEs just try to survive. In Tanzania, the law prohibits businesses from operating without fixed premises, but it does not stop the government from collecting taxes and fees from those same enterprises. (This describes 80 percent of HEs.)

By contrast, Ghana, a country with a rich trading history dating to precolonial times, explicitly incorporates HEs in its strategy documents and the institutions that implement them. In 2006 the government established an objective to "enhance productivity and income/wages … in all sectors of the economy, including the informal economy" (Republic of Ghana 2006). The Trade Union Congress supports the development of HE organizations and their integration into the consultative mechanisms between government and the private sector.

To realize the potential of the HE sector for productive youth employment, national strategies that recognize the sector's potential and propose a supportive policy framework need to be developed. Such strategies should endorse the creation of independent HE associations to reduce the costs of reaching individual enterprises and to give this sector a voice in government decision making. Local interventions need to address three key areas: the local business climate in urban areas, access to credit and financial services, and skills.

Urban Policy

One of the most frequently cited constraints on the productivity of urban HEs is the lack of access to space and sometimes outright harassment, legal and extralegal, by local authorities. Insecurity of premises discourages entry (the main form of growth in this sector) as well as investment in the enterprise. Governments can help rather than hurt this sector by incorporating the growth of HEs in planning processes. Without planning, traders and vendors crowd sidewalks and roads, leading to massive congestion. Usually the situation escalates to a crisis, and authorities use police or security forces to "decongest" the city. Because the eviction policy is rarely permanent, the cycle usually resumes. If governments had planned for the growth of HEs and provided adequate space for them in the key areas of foot traffic in the city, employment growth and social stability would have followed.

Alongside planning, national policy makers can clarify land rights in urban jurisdictions, giving local governments scope to provide HEs with locations to operate. Overlapping land regulations and responsibilities make it diffi-cult to implement the law—if there is one. For example, in Dar es Salaam, Tanzania, local governments are not empowered to decide whether hawkers can use the land next to national roads. Just as land rental markets can facilitate access to agricultural land, they can facilitate access to space for HEs to do business.

In addition to secure space, HEs need services, such as security, sanitation, electricity, transport, and water supply. For the most part, they are willing to pay for these services (and do pay for them) through fees and taxes. In fact, HEs pay local business taxes at a higher rate than large businesses but often fail to receive any services. HEs have little leverage to improve this situation (Fox and Sohnesen 2012). Local authorities are not accountable to HEs, because ineffective political decentralization and weak legal status deprive HEs of a voice in local governance.

Credit and Financial Services

Lacking access to formal sources of finance, young people struggle to raise capital to start and operate a business. The problem is exacerbated by the fact that business and household finances are linked, so that lumpy household expenditures (school fees, repairs, and so on) and external shocks (family illness) spill over to the business. Virtually all HEs in Africa today report that their own funds or loans from friends and relatives enabled them to start their businesses, and the overwhelming majority of existing businesses report that they did not obtain any type of loan over the last 12 months. An expansion of credit cannot make up this gap and may even make it worse, as recent experiences in India have shown. To use credit effectively, a borrower has to be able to put aside money regularly to service the loan. For this purpose, the establishment of a savings mechanism is critical.

At the root of the credit problem for HEs is the lack of financial inclusion among households in Africa (World Bank 2014). Households not only lack sources of credit but also have difficulty finding reliable places to safeguard their savings. As a result, it is challenging for them to accumulate the funds to start or expand a business. This problem is especially acute for youth and for females. Research has shown that access to a secure place for savings is particularly important for women's ability to build up savings for a business (Dupas and Robinson 2013).

The challenge of providing access to financial services for poor people is a common one. Because of economies of scale, the spread of formal banking services (banks, postal savings, formal savings institutions other than banks) usually rises with income and urbanization—banks go where the money is. But this is not the whole story in Africa. FINDEX data show that even at the same level of income per capita, national policies can produce very different results (figure O.9). Low- and lower-middle-income countries such as Ghana, Kenya, and Rwanda have achieved greater financial access than other African and non-African countries at similar income levels. They have done so primarily by reducing the costs of serving small savers and those in remote areas.

In Kenya, banking access increased through the pioneering use of mobile banking technology. By increasing branchless banking, mobile banking allows accounts to be maintained at relatively little cost to savers and borrowers. Today, about half of the adult population of Kenya uses mobile banking. In Rwanda, government provided incentives for banks to develop low-cost products for small savers and for households to use banks by channeling payments to households through banks, including microfinance banks with a client base among lower-income households.[4] Ghana developed a system of rural banks to process payments to cocoa farmers; today these banks provide low-cost accounts in rural areas. Ghana and Rwanda are both encouraging the spread of mobile banking to further widen access to financial services. Countries in the Western and Central African monetary unions using the CFA currency (UEMOA and CEMAC) are also changing their regulations to foster more inclusion. Benin, which encouraged the establishment of microfinance institutions, was an early mover in this group.

Skills

Training can help to structure a pathway to youth employment in HEs. Training programs—both for entry and for improving incomes and sustainability—are the most commonly provided government and donor intervention to support HEs, whether or not they target youth. Programs provide (1) technical training in a specific sector (such as tailoring, metalworking, operating a bakery); (2) business

Figure O.9 At the same level of income per capita, national policies can produce very different levels of financial inclusion

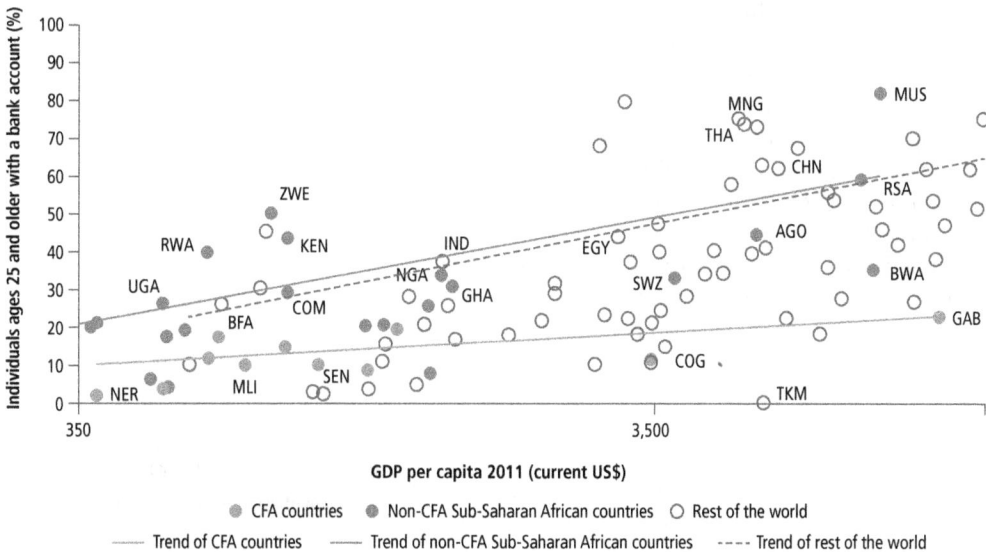

Source: Based on Global Financial Inclusion (Global Findex) Database, World Bank, Washington, DC, http://www.worldbank.org/globalfinder

Note: The x axis of this figure is on a log scale.

skills or financial literacy (such as basic accounting or money management); (3) behavioral and life skills; or (4) a mix of these skills. Programs specifically intended for youth focus primarily on providing the skills needed to enter the HE sector and have included all four types of training. Programs targeted at existing HEs tend to focus more on business skills to strengthen or expand HEs.

The good news for youth employment is that programs designed to facilitate entry (versus those focusing on productivity) appear to have had some success, so positive models are emerging. Apprenticeships and on-the-job training can help young people, provided that these programs are closely tied to market signals. For this reason, private providers, including existing businesses, are often the best source for this training. Youth often face multiple constraints in entering the HE sector, and the most promising pilots are delivering interventions that tackle multiple constraints (offering behavioral, business, or technical skills training together, or combining training with measures to tackle credit constraints through savings groups, grants, and other means). Many of these "bundled" interventions have been expensive, however, and they are yet to scale up in Africa.

Overall, despite the large number of training programs, evidence of their effectiveness in the HE sector in Africa remains thin. More systematic use of careful evaluations is clearly required, including impact evaluations that measure outcomes among program participants and compare them to a relevant group of nonparticipants. At the very minimum, governments should encourage all programs to track and report outcomes. At the same time, governments should not attempt to deliver training directly but rather focus their efforts on market-enhancing programs that disseminate information about training opportunities and enable disadvantaged youth to access training that is already available.

Improving Competitiveness to Boost Modern Sector Wage Jobs

Although small (16 percent of the labor force), the formal wage employment sector represents the engine for employment and growth in the medium to long term for Africa. No country has developed without this sector coming to dominate employment. This is the sector that can exploit economies of scale and produce for export. The multiplier effects to the household economy from the creation of wage jobs are strong. Most secondary-school graduates aspire to work in this sector. When these aspirations are not fulfilled and graduates must resort to working in the household enterprise sector, for example, the risks for social instability and political violence are high. While Africa's young people seem to have no special advantage or disadvantage when it comes to modern wage employment, they remain a consistent share of that employment when it grows (figure O.10).

The modern wage sector has been creating jobs at a fairly rapid pace in Sub-Saharan Africa—usually faster than GDP growth. The problem is that the sector has grown from such a small base that it still cannot absorb the millions of young people entering the labor force every year. To generate jobs at a rate that is commensurate with growth in the labor force, the export-oriented enterprises—with their potential to sell to global markets—will have

Figure O.10 **The share of youth in wage employment tracks the share in the general population**

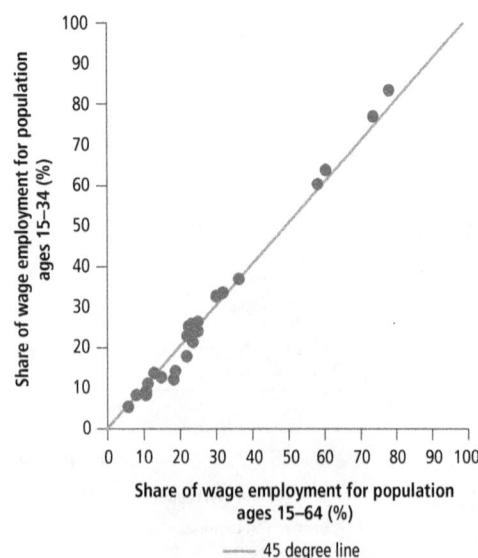

Source: Based on household and labor force surveys (most recent data available).

to be the engine for job creation in this sector. Since most African economies are small, access to external markets is the key to unleashing the modern wage sector's full potential. The scope for trade is wide. Even services are traded internationally, although these tend to call for relatively high-level skills still lacking in much of Sub-Saharan Africa. Moreover, the employment effects of trade go beyond exporting firms, as rising demand from the export sector—for inputs, consumer goods, and services—increases opportunities in other parts of the economy.

What factors are constraining export-oriented enterprises in Africa today? The main constraint on the growth of an export-oriented sector in Africa is low productivity.

The underlying causes are not identical across the continent, even if they have similar effects. In some countries, the cost of complementary inputs to labor (electricity, overland transport, and so on) is too high. Clearly, the cost of transporting goods across borders is prohibitively high in the region, and the need for better transport infrastructure, simpler customs procedures, and expedited inland border crossings is acute. In other countries, bureaucratic red tape delays investors' access to land or permits. The high costs of financial intermediation are starving firms and entrepreneurs of the capital needed to implement good ideas. In many countries, poor connectivity has fragmented local markets, suppressing competition and reducing the pressure to improve productivity. These business climate issues would be a problem for productivity (and hence, youth employment) even if firms only produced for domestic markets.

What can be done to increase Africa's low labor productivity? The entire business climate comes into play here, with some exceptions. For example, labor market regulations—considered an important determinant of productivity elsewhere—do not play a major role in Africa, except for South Africa. In many settings, regulations may exist on the books, but they are rarely enforced.

Infrastructure and the Business Climate

Infrastructure is a major problem, but building new infrastructure may not be the solution. Infrastructure policies and regulations block firms' access to infrastructure services, and building infrastructure without improving policies and institutions is unlikely to solve the problem. Conversely, improving policies such as electricity and water tariffs or trucking regulations can go a long way to improving services and attracting the private sector.

Expensive or limited financing prevents firms from investing to improve productivity and also keeps productive firms from growing. Banks in Africa set high collateral requirements and high risk premiums partly because they lack the credit information systems that help lenders to evaluate prospective customers. This problem can be addressed by policy and regulatory reform. Africa also needs better, well-enforced creditor rights, which will ease lending by providing protection for lenders when borrowers default. Improved creditor rights and contract enforcement will also allow borrowers to use a broader range of assets as collateral.

In developed economies, innovative new firms are constantly emerging and growing, while unproductive incumbents are leaving. This churning is a major source of aggregate productivity and employment growth in the modern wage sector. In Africa, this process is held back not only by financial constraints on entrepreneurs but also by difficult formal requirements for business entry or expansion. Governance issues, such as corruption in the granting of business licenses and other permits, hamper this process as well.

In short, the constraints to Africa's productivity are a combination of market and government failures. Government failures in particular either have been difficult to rectify—especially when they require economywide policies such as deregulation or tariff reform—or, when implemented, have not delivered results. Vested interests inside and outside government can prevent reforms or their implementation. Analysis of Ethiopia's light manufacturing sector shows that the leather goods industry could create 90,000 jobs (it currently employs 5,000). To unleash this potential, value-chain analysis shows that the government has to remove a series of policy-induced constraints, such as trade restrictions, anticompetitive practices, and financial regulations that affect the sector (Dinh et al. 2012). The scale of such a reform means that it could take some time.

A complementary approach is to create a localized environment—say, a special economic zone (SEZ), with the requisite infrastructure and deregulation—in which industries that could benefit from proximity can cluster and flourish. The government provides land and functioning infrastructure services for the SEZ. Although in China this approach attracted foreign investment and know-how and helped China to become an export manufacturing powerhouse, it has not yet been implemented successfully in Africa.

Besides giving careful thought to the design and implementation of these interventions, policy makers must evaluate each one in terms of its susceptibility to political capture, which plagued industrial policy when it was last attempted on a large scale in Africa. Any subsidy creates a rent. Politically powerful interests, if they capture those rents, will resist efforts to reduce them, even though that step is necessary for industries to compete in world markets.

Skills

Is demand for secondary-school graduates simply insufficient in Africa's modern wage sector, or is there a skills mismatch? In fact, both of these problems appear to be present. Secondary and post-secondary graduates say they have trouble finding a job because of lack of demand. There is a much larger supply of labor for unskilled (factory floor) jobs than for skilled jobs as mechanics and factory engineers or for office jobs as accountants and managers. Meanwhile, employers are requesting permits to import experienced skilled labor. Graduates at all levels without technical training and some work experience (where they can acquire and demonstrate the equally valuable "soft" skills) face an especially crowded job market, reflecting an "aspirational" mismatch as much as a skills mismatch.

As with the farm and HE sectors, perhaps the most important step toward resolving these problems in the modern wage sector is to get basic schooling right. Foundational skills are important for all types of wage workers, partly because they facilitate further training and on-the-job learning in firms.

To avoid creating more unemployable university graduates, higher education policies and curriculums also need to be geared toward private demand. Financing in public universities should include a private component (especially for those who can pay), so that signals from the private sector are received (Devarajan, Monga, and Zongo 2011). Such a shift would improve equity in access to higher education as tuition payments become means-tested rather than free across the board. Also, those who pay will demand value for money.

The Sub-Saharan African experience with technical vocational education and training (TVET) has been disappointing. Secondary and post-secondary vocational training costs at least three times more than basic secondary education, yet often provides no better foundation for private sector jobs. Training in government-run programs has not been geared to private sector needs.

Governments in Sub-Saharan Africa should focus on support for public goods in TVET such as quality assurance and information. To promote access to training for poor and disadvantaged youth, governments should provide financial support for training in either the public or the private sector. Information about the returns to alternative training options can help to align young people's training choices with the realities of the labor market. To the extent that governments support specific training options, those options should emphasize portable skills rather than the firm- or job-specific skills that employers should already have an incentive to provide. They should ensure that programs are closely linked to the private sector, potentially through public-private partnerships. Programs for disadvantaged youth that integrate training with internships show promise.

The visibly poor management practices in African firms suggest considerable scope for improving productivity by investing in business and management skills training and perhaps even in individualized management consulting. The evidence for such programs is mixed but promising, and governments should consider testing and refining them through careful piloting.

Building an Effective Youth Employment Policy

The challenge of youth employment in Africa is not amenable to simple solutions. It reflects the challenges and opportunities of countries themselves in a globalized world. The key employment issue is that productivity, and therefore earnings, are low, while aspirations, especially those of youth, are high—and perhaps higher than those of their parents. Despite progress in many countries, most youth in Africa today will not have an easy or structured path to a sustainable livelihood, one of the core aspects of adulthood. All stakeholders—governments, private firms, private and nongovernmental training providers, and young people themselves—have a role to play in supporting this transition.

Progress requires a comprehensive approach to relieve the constraints on human capital and the business environment that prevent the private sector from seizing opportunities and increasing productivity in agriculture, HEs, and the modern wage sector. Governments need to take a holistic view of how to address the situation—they need to "own" the whole problem.

A common tendency is to perceive government-provided technical and vocational skills training as the key. But such action, by itself, will not address the more fundamental problems. Government intervention should focus on public goods—those things that will support higher productivity in the economic activities of households and enterprises. Specific actions can relieve the most pressing constraints in the short term, such as increasing access to finance for HEs as well as modern firms; improving access to land and technology for young people to expand earnings in agriculture; building supportive infrastructure that enables all enterprises to be more productive; and opening access to regional markets so that firms can broaden the reach of their products. Table O.1 summarizes the priority actions.

It is equally urgent to undertake other actions to address constraints that will only yield payoffs in the medium term. For example, improvements in basic education, the foundation for developing all other skills, will take time to translate into higher productivity and better youth employment outcomes. Reforms to the business climate will require sustained effort, and it may take time for investors to respond. But policy makers must rise to these urgent challenges. Failure to act now means that future cohorts of young people may also lack clear pathways to productive work.

These priorities are, of course, only a general guide. Addressing the challenge in any given country will require a country-specific analysis. The framework put forward in this report, the general diagnostics that it provides, and the evidence that it marshals to illustrate successful or promising approaches provide a foundation for such an analysis and indicate policy directions to pursue. But a country-based analysis is required to address the specific local issues surrounding the following questions: What is constraining earnings growth in agriculture, HEs, and the modern wage sector? Why is it hard for youth to start HEs and work productively in them? Why isn't private investment in labor-intensive firms flowing in to increase the number of modern wage jobs on offer? What can and should government, NGOs, and other private sector actors do to ease the constraints that youth face in making the transition to productive employment?

The basis for a successful country-specific analysis will be more and better data on employment; such data are currently sparse and often of low quality (see the discussion in Fox and Pimhidzai 2013). The basis for building a much better evidence base of which approaches are potentially effective and cost-effective will be more experimentation with promising interventions—and careful evaluation of their impacts.

At its core, the youth employment challenge is closely aligned with the challenge of promoting inclusive growth, defined not only as growth in which the poorest segments of society share but also as growth in which young

Table O.1 Priority actions to take now to address the youth employment challenge

Area for intervention	"Do now for now": Actions to affect the current cohort of youth	"Do now for later": Actions to affect future cohorts of youth
Agriculture	1. Enable rental markets for land 2. Pilot intergenerational land transfer programs 3. Support high-quality, demand-driven extension services (covering information as well as skills) 4. Link agricultural credit to extension services	1. Establish effective land registration and transaction systems 2. Scale up intergenerational land transfer programs, based on lessons from pilot programs 3. Mainstream youth into smart interventions aimed at increasing productivity (producer organizations, livestock development, irrigation, and others) 4. Build skills through rapid improvements in education systems in rural areas
Agriculture and household enterprises	5. Promote rural village savings and loan associations and self-help groups 6. Enable financial inclusion for households 7. Use safety net programs as a platform to deliver interventions to disadvantaged youth	
Household enterprises	8. Develop a national strategy for household enterprises that reflects the voice of their owners and youth 9. Ensure access to workspace and infrastructure for household enterprises through improved urban policy 10. Leverage nongovernmental organizations to deliver interventions that support disadvantaged youth to enter the sector by addressing multiple constraints (building a range of skills together; building skills along with providing access to finance)	5. Build foundational skills through rapid improvements in education systems 6. Address infrastructure needs of household enterprises in urban development planning
Modern wage sector	11. Reduce the cost of infrastructure services by addressing quality and efficiency 12. Address logistics bottlenecks 13. Reduce corruption and the cost of business start-up 14. Reform technical and vocational education and training and pursue public-private partnerships for delivering demand-driven training	7. Increase the quantity of infrastructure services 8. Expand regional markets for products 9. Build foundational skills through rapid improvements in education systems 10. Improve access to credit through financial sector reform
Cross-cutting areas	15. Increase awareness of opportunities and pathways to self-employment, especially for young women 16. Consider second-chance education for basic skills	11. Promote early child development and nutrition to build a stronger foundation for skills development 12. Build behavioral skills (consider reforms within the school system) 13. Reduce fertility rates to lower the size of future youth cohorts (through more girls' education, improved maternal and child health, increased access to family planning) 14. Build better employment data and a stronger evidence base to identify country constraints, priorities, and opportunities

people's vitality is harnessed and rewarded. For African countries that meet this challenge, the benefits will build on each other. The demographic dividend will yield returns, and Africa's prosperity will grow and be shared.

Notes

1. Defined as having no work at all in the last seven days and actively looking for work (ILO 1982).
2. In Botswana form-two and in South Africa grade-nine students were tested, corresponding to nine years of schooling; in Ghana junior high school form-two students were tested, corresponding to eight years of schooling.
3. See www.sdindicators.org.
4. A similar approach was used in Mongolia.

References

Ayalew Ali, Daniel, Klaus Deininger, and Markus P. Goldstein. 2011. "Environmental and Gender Impacts of Land Tenure Regularization in Africa: Pilot Evidence from Rwanda." Policy Research Working Paper 5765, World Bank, Washington, DC, August.

Bridges, Sarah, Louise Fox, Alessio Gaggero, and Trudy Owens. 2013. "Labour Market Entry and Earnings: Evidence from Tanzanian Retrospective Data." Background paper presented at the CSAE Conference on Economic Development in Africa, Oxford University, March.

Cloutier, Marie-Hélène, C. Reinstadtler, and Isabel Beltran. 2011. "Making the Grade: Assessing Literacy and Numeracy in African Countries."

DIME Brief, Washington, DC, World Bank. http://go.worldbank.org/15Y7VXO7B0.

Conley, Timothy, and Christopher Udry. 2010. "Learning about a New Technology: Pineapple in Ghana." *American Economic Review* 100 (1): 35–69.

Devarajan, Shantayanan, Célestin Monga, and Tertius Zongo. 2011. "Making Higher Education Finance Work for Africa." *Journal of African Economies* 20 (supplement 3): iii133–54.

Dinh, Hinh T., Vincent Palmade, Vandana Chandra, and Frances Cossar. 2012. *Light Manufacturing in Africa: Targeted Policies to Enhance Private Investment and Create Jobs.* Washington, DC: World Bank.

Dupas, Pascaline, and Jonathan Robinson. 2013. "Savings Constraints and Microenterprise Development: Evidence from a Field Experiment in Kenya." *American Economic Journal: Applied Economics* 5 (1): 163–92.

Falco, Paolo, William F. Maloney, Bob Rijkers, and Mauricio Sarrias. 2013. "Heterogeneity in Subjective Well-Being: An Application to Occupational Allocation in Africa." Documento CEDE 2013–01, Universidad de los Andes, Department of Economics, Bogotá. http://dx.doi.org/10.2139/ssrn.2229328.

Fox, Louise, and Obert Pimhidzai. 2013. "Different Dreams, Same Bed: Collecting, Using, and Interpreting Employment Statistics in Sub-Saharan Africa: The Case of Uganda." Policy Research Working Paper 6436, World Bank, Washington, DC.

Fox, Louise, and Thomas Pave Sohnesen. 2012. "Household Enterprises in Sub-Saharan Africa: Why They Matter for Growth, Jobs, and Livelihoods." Policy Research Working Paper 6184, World Bank, Washington, DC.

Fox, Louise, Alun Thomas, Cleary Haines, and Jorge Huerta Munoz. 2013. "Africa's Got Work to Do: Employment Prospects in the New Century." IMF Working Paper 13–201, International Monetary Fund, Washington, DC.

Fuglie, Keith O., and Nicholas E. Rada. 2013. "Resources, Policies, and Agricultural Productivity in Sub-Saharan Africa." Economic Research Report 145368, U.S. Department of Agriculture, Economic Research Service, Washington, DC.

Gelb, Alan, and Sina Grasmann. 2010. "How Should Oil Exporters Spend Their Rents?" Working Paper 221, Center for Global Development, Washington, DC. http://dx.doi.org/10.2139/ssrn.1660570.

Ghana, Republic of. 2006. "Poverty Reduction Strategy Paper." National Development Planning Commission. IMF Country Report 06/225, IMF, Washington, DC, June.

Hungi, Njora, Demus Makuwa, Kenneth Ross, Mioko Saito, Stéphanie Dolata, Frank van Cappelle, Laura Paviot, and Jocelyne Vellien. 2010. "SACMEQ III Project Results: Pupil Achievement Levels in Reading and Mathematics." Working Document 1, Southern Africa Consortium for Measuring Educational Quality (SACMEQ), Harare. http://www.sacmeq.org/downloads/sacmeqIII/WD01_SACMEQ_III_Results_Pupil_Achievement.pdf.

ILO (International Labour Organization). 1982. "Resolution Concerning Statistics of the Economically Active Population, Employment, Unemployment, and Underemployment." Adopted by the Thirteenth International Conference of Labour Statisticians, Geneva.

Lin, Justin Yifu, and Célestin Monga. 2012. "Solving the Mystery of African Governance." *New Political Economy* 17 (5): 659–66.

Morris, Michael, Hans Binswanger-Mkhize, and Derek Byerlee. 2009. *Awakening Africa's Sleeping Giant: Prospects for Commercial Agriculture in the Guinea Savannah Zone and Beyond.* Washington, DC: World Bank.

Nin-Pratt, Alejandro, Michael Johnson, and Bingxin Yu. 2012. *Improved Performance of Agriculture in Africa South of the Sahara: Taking Off or Bouncing Back?* IFPRI Discussion Paper 01224. Washington, DC: International Food Policy Research Institute.

Pritchett, Lant. 2013. *The Rebirth of Education.* Washington, DC: Center for Global Development.

Raballand, Gaël, and Patricia Macchi. 2009. "Transport Prices and Costs: The Need to Revisit Donors' Policies in Transport in Africa." Working Paper 190, Bureau for Research and Economic Analysis of Development, Duke University. http://ipl.econ.duke.edu/bread/papers/working/190.pdf.

Rosenzweig, Mark R. 2012. "Microeconomic Approaches to Development: Schooling, Learning, and Growth." *Journal of Economic Perspectives* 24 (3): 81–96.

United Nations. 2011. *World Population Prospects: The 2010 Revision.* New York: Department of Economic and Social Affairs, Population Division. http://esa.un.org/wpp/Excel-Data/population.htm.

World Bank. 2006. *World Development Report 2007: Development and the Next Generation.* New York: Oxford University Press.

———. 2008. *World Development Report 2009: Reshaping Economic Geography.* New York: Oxford University Press.

———. 2012. *World Development Report 2013: Jobs.* New York: Oxford University Press.

———. 2013. *Africa's Pulse: An Analysis of Issues Shaping Africa's Economic Future* 7 (April).

———. 2014. *Global Financial Development Report 2014: Financial Inclusion.* Washington, DC: World Bank.

———. Various years. World Development Indicators. Washington, DC: World Bank. http://wdi.worldbank.org.

Chapter 1

Opportunities and Challenges for Youth Employment in Africa

Two trends are converging in Africa, with potentially profound effects on how Africa's economy will grow and where it will create jobs. First, Africa's economies, spurred by high prices for primary export commodities, are growing again after a hiatus of many decades. Output is shifting out of agriculture and largely into services, and employment is shifting slowly toward services. The second trend is that Africa's rapidly growing population will constitute the world's largest reservoir of working-age individuals for generations to come, and the majority of this population will be young. These trends mean that the structure of employment will continue to change in Africa, but the transformation will be slow.

Africa stands to gain economically, socially, and substantially from channeling the energy of its young labor force into more productive employment. The challenge is large and demands immediate attention, but it can be met. Industry—especially export manufacturing—has been a vibrant source of wage jobs in other regions, most notably East Asia. In Africa, industry is in the very early stages of development. It needs time and the right policy environment to grow. Governments must also focus on tapping the more immediate potential for productive employment in agriculture and household enterprises. This report assesses the specific challenges and opportunities related to youth employment on farms, in nonfarm household enterprises, and in modern wage jobs. It examines these issues and possible interventions in light of two types of binding constraints to higher productivity for young people in those sectors: constraints related to human capital and constraints related to the business environment.

Africa's Working-Age Population: Very Young and Growing Rapidly

The median person in Africa is 18 years old— 7 years younger than the median age in South

---

Throughout this report, "Africa" is shorthand for "Sub-Saharan Africa." In particular instances, "Sub-Saharan Africa" is retained to clarify comparisons across regions or to indicate a specific data set.

Asia, which is the next youngest region (figure 1.1). In other words, fully half of Africa's population is under 18 years old. Africa will remain the youngest region in the world in the decades to come, and the age gap with other regions will increase. According to projections by the United Nations, the median age in Africa will increase only to 21 in 2035 and to 24 in 2050. In other regions of the world, the median person in 2050 will be more than 35 years old—almost 45 in East Asia and the Pacific.

In Africa, the population structure resembles an Egyptian pyramid, with a narrow top and a wide base (figure 1.2). The wide base is Africa's "youth bulge"—Africa has twice as many 15-year-olds as 35-year-olds. In other regions of the world, the structure is elongated, reflecting a more even distribution across age groups. South Asia's demographic profile is closest to Africa's, whereas in East Asia and the Pacific, the pyramid is inverted, with a greater number of older than younger people. Projections suggest that the shape of the pyramid in Africa will remain as it is in the near future—just with more people at each age.

These population trends suggest that the number of young people entering Africa's working-age population will be rising for years to come. The United Nations estimates that in 2015 Sub-Saharan Africa will have 193 million people between the ages of 15 and 24; by 2035, it will have 295 million, and by 2050, 362 mil-

lion (figure 1.3). Each year between 2015 and 2035, there will be half a million more 15-year-olds than the year before. This rapid increase contrasts starkly with the Middle East and North Africa, where increases in the size of this cohort have steadied, and even with East Asia, where numbers are dominated by China and the size of this cohort is expected to fall from 350 million in 2010 to 225 million by 2050.[1] In South Asia, the size of the cohort is expected to increase, and then begin to decline after 2030.

Can Africa's Youth Bring an Economic Advantage?

Africa's young and growing working-age population compels attention for many reasons, not least because a rapidly expanding working-age population spearheaded the economic transformation that occurred in East Asia and the Pacific between 1965 and 1990. Over that period, the working-age population in East Asia and the Pacific rose by almost 500 million (from 541 million to 1.039 billion). More crucially, the number of "dependents" (ages 0–14 and 65 and over) increased by only 143 million (from 437 million to 580 million). The region had just over one working-age adult for each dependent in 1965, but by 1990 almost two working-age adults supported each dependent (figure 1.4). During those years, gross domestic product (GDP) per capita in East Asia and the Pacific increased from around US$1,300 to US$3,300. Based on cross-country analysis of the relationship between growth rates and the changing structure of the population, analysts have attributed one-third to half of East Asia's economic growth to changes in demography (Bloom and Williamson 1998; Bloom, Canning, and Malaney 2000).

East Asia's "demographic dividend" is argued to have transformed the economy through two main channels. The first was the increased availability of workers. More workers mean more output, and if there are more workers relative to the population, then output per capita will rise. The second channel was the continued expansion of the working-age population relative to the population as a

Figure 1.1 Africa's population is young and will remain so

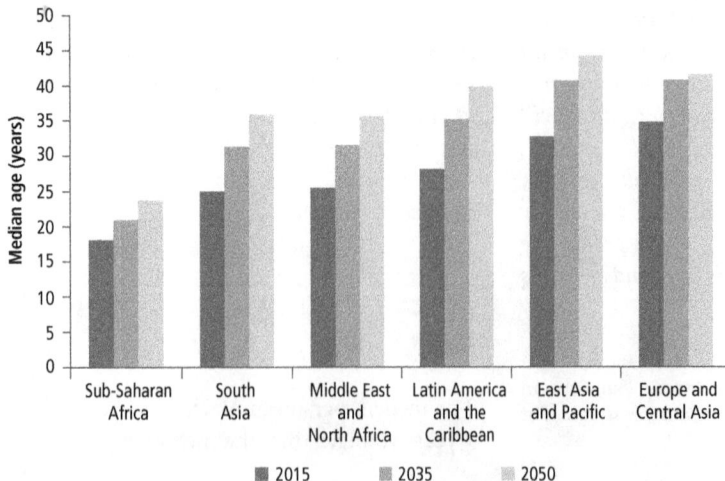

Source: Based on United Nations 2011.

Figure 1.2 The structure of Sub-Saharan Africa's population is different than that in other regions

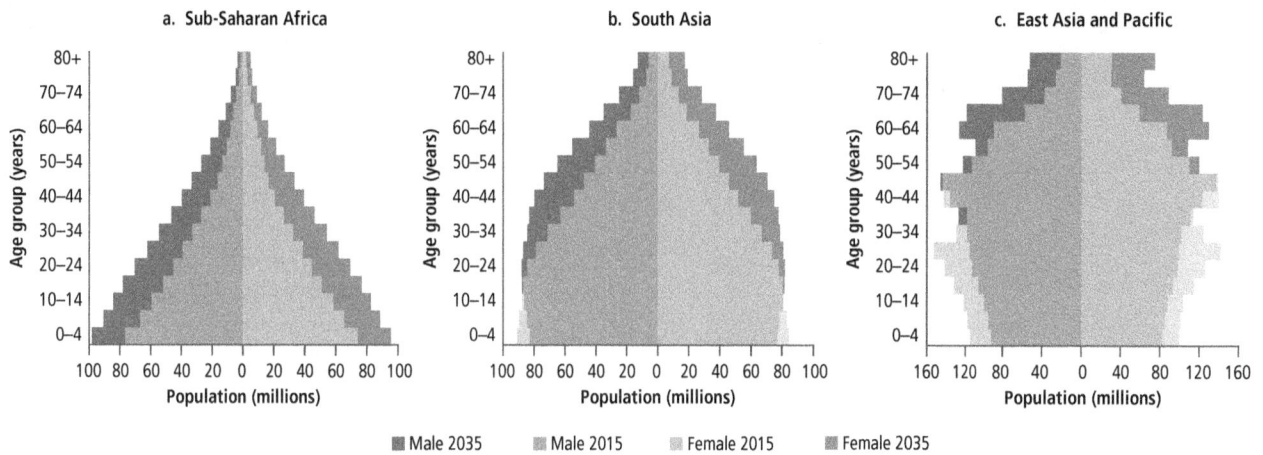

a. Sub-Saharan Africa   b. South Asia   c. East Asia and Pacific

■ Male 2035   ■ Male 2015   ■ Female 2015   ■ Female 2035

Source: Based on United Nations 2011.

Figure 1.3 Unlike in other regions, the number of young people in Sub-Saharan Africa will increase dramatically in the near future

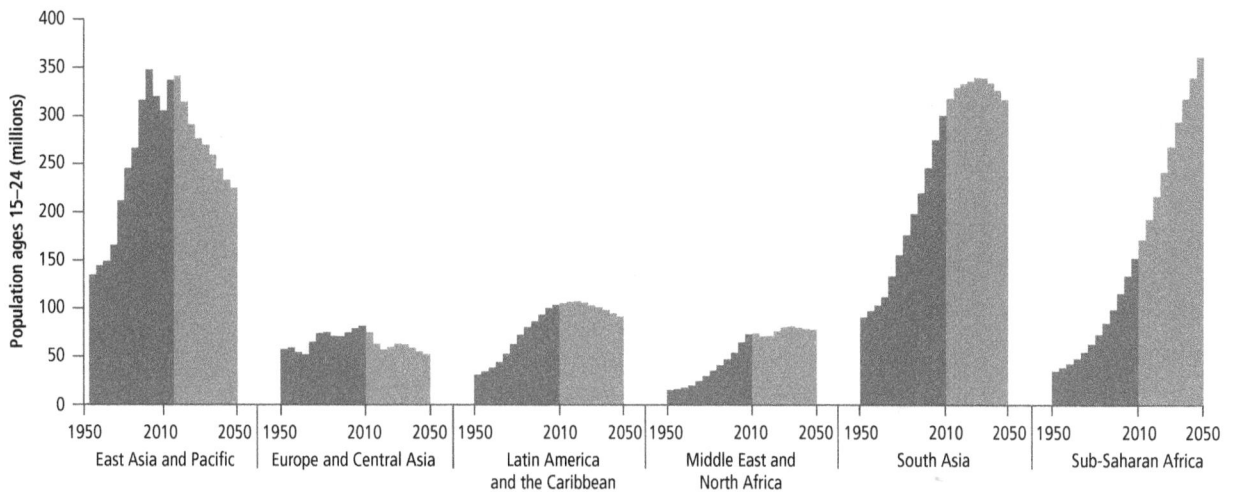

Source: Based on United Nations 2011.
Note: Each bar shows an estimate or a projection of the number of 15- to 24-year-olds for one year at five-year intervals.

whole, a result of the rapid decline in fertility. With fewer dependents, working-age adults can increase their savings—which can be converted into productive investments, which further stimulate economic growth.

For Africa to realize a demographic dividend of its own, it is not enough to have a large working-age population; fertility rates need to fall. Unless the number of dependents per working-age adult decreases rapidly, the potential benefits of a changing population structure

will not materialize. The rapid change in the ratio between the two groups (illustrated in figure 1.4) was critical for the boom in productivity in East Asia and the Pacific (Bloom and Williamson 1998).

Historically, declines in child mortality have preceded declines in fertility—a sequence that creates a true youth bulge (a bulge that is followed by a decline in the youth population once the number of children born falls). In Africa, child mortality has declined dramati-

Figure 1.4 In East Asia, the dependency ratio changed quickly; in Sub-Saharan Africa, it is changing, but slowly

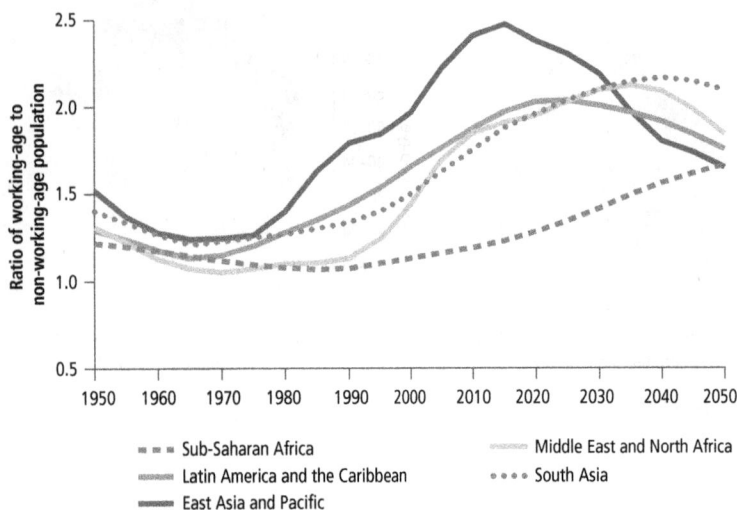

Source: Based on United Nations 2011.
Note: Working-age population is defined as individuals ages 15–64; non-working-age population is defined as individuals ages 0–14 and 65 and older.

cally in the past two decades, although some African countries still have the highest rates in the world. In the first decade or so of this century, the under-5 mortality rate fell from 160 to 70 in Benin, 219 to 129 in Burkina Faso, 166 to 88 in Ethiopia, 189 to 112 in Malawi, 274 to 127 in Niger, and 151 to 90 in Uganda.[2]

Africa's youth bulge will not taper off, however, unless fertility rates decline much more rapidly and systematically. In the 1970s the fertility rate in Asia and Latin America was identical to the rate in Africa today, but fertility is falling much more slowly in Africa today than in those regions at that time (Bongaarts and Casterline 2013). A more important consideration may be that fertility rates have declined inconsistently across Africa; in fact, the decline has stalled in several countries (figure 1.5).

Even with a rapidly changing population structure, the demographic dividend is not automatic. After all, as figure 1.4 shows, East Asia is not the only region where the population structure has changed. In Latin America, the ratio of working-age population to dependents rose from 1.1 in 1970 to 1.9 in 2010. In South Asia, it rose from 1.2 in 1975 to 1.8 in 2010.

"My father has never worked. He has spent his whole life here in this plantation which he inherited."
Tanzania

Two important differences help to explain why the changing population structure in South Asia and Latin America has not translated into a demographic dividend. First, the rate of increase has been much slower in those regions than in East Asia (where the ratio increased from 1.1 in 1970 to 1.8 by 1990). Second, as noted in the seminal analysis of the demographic dividend, East Asians had "the social, economic, and political institutions and policies that allowed them to realize the growth potential created by the transition" (Bloom and Williamson 1998).

Recent analysis has pointed to the economic threat posed in Africa by a growing population, low savings rate, and low productivity, which could mean a limited demographic dividend (Eastwood and Lipton 2011). An economic environment that is conducive to investment and growth—into which the population, with its large cohorts of young people, will arrive and find productive employment—is vital for Africa's growing labor force to have a positive effect on economic and social development. The next section discusses in some detail the types of jobs that exist and are likely to exist in Africa, because overall employment is a precondition of youth employment (see box 1.1). As chapter 2 discusses, young people have unclear and constrained pathways to productive work, and as the subsequent chapters in this report show, a range of policies will be necessary to enhance those pathways.

What Is a Job, and Where Do Most Africans Find One?

In assessing the challenges of youth employment in Africa, it is important to take stock of what it means to have a job and to have employment. To many, having a job is synonymous with having a wage or salaried position with an employer (see quote at left). The majority of work in Africa is not structured in such a way, however. This study follows the approach adopted in the *World Development Report 2013: Jobs,* which defines jobs as "activities that generate actual or imputed income, monetary or in kind, formal or informal" (World Bank 2012e). This includes part- or full-time in-household economic activities, such as subsistence farming, regardless of whether anything is ever sold. That report also notes that not all forms of work can be considered jobs. Examples include activities that are performed against the will of the worker and activities that violate basic human rights.

In many countries, including in Africa, people report that jobs have a broader importance beyond the income they provide (see focus note 1). Jobs can convey identity, status, and self-confidence; they can contribute to an individual's overall life satisfaction. Some jobs contribute to these dimensions of well-being more than others. The type of job, working conditions, contract, benefits, and safety and security at work all matter. Jobs also influence social cohesion by shaping individuals' identities and relations to one another and bringing them together in networks. The distribution of jobs within society and perceptions about who has access to opportunities, and why, can shape people's expectations and aspirations for the future, their sense of having a stake in society, and their perceptions of fairness. All of these intrinsic aspects of jobs are particularly important for youth.

In Africa, the vast majority of work takes place in agriculture. Agriculture occupies more than 70 percent of the labor force in Africa's low-income countries and more than 50 percent in its lower-middle-income countries. African farmers are predominantly smallholders who consume a large share of what they produce. Data from recently collected household surveys indicate that the share consumed is around 50 percent, compared with 20–30 percent outside of Africa (Losch, Freguin-Gresh, and White 2013).

Others find employment in household enterprises (HEs), which are unincorporated, nonfarm businesses owned by households. They include self-employed people who run a business that may employ family members without pay but also self-employed people who run a business that employs a small number of nonfamily workers on a casual basis.

Figure 1.5 The reduction in the total fertility rate has stalled in several African countries

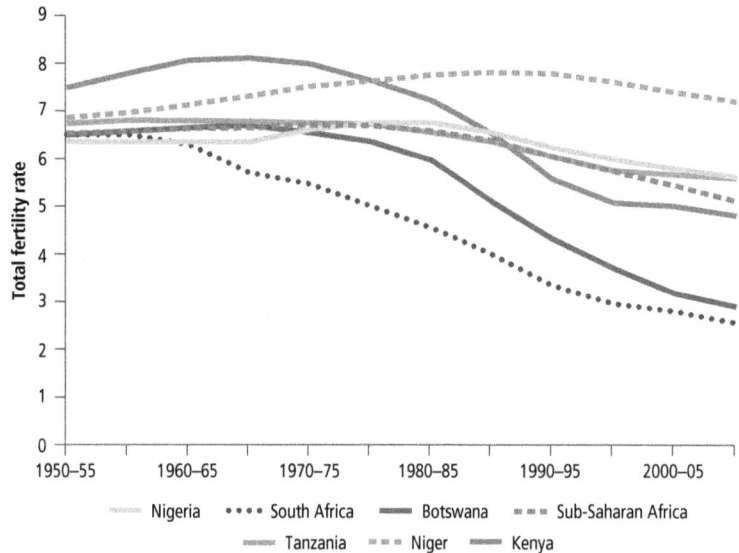

Source: United Nations 2011.

Box 1.1

Youth versus overall employment

A key part of improving employment opportunities for Africa's youth is to understand and address Africa's overall economic challenges. For that reason, much of the discussion in this report focuses on identifying policies that can increase the productivity of all employment—in agriculture, nonfarm household enterprises, and the modern wage sector. The report also identifies promising policies that focus specifically on helping young people to make a more successful transition to higher-productivity work in each of those three sectors.

The focus on youth raises the question of whether it might be socially beneficial to support employment policies that favor youth over other members of society. Special efforts to help young people to enter agriculture or start a household enterprise do not generally reduce such opportunities for adults, but targeted programs in the modern wage sector could have a detrimental effect on adult employment in the sector. On the one hand, assistance for young people might have long-term benefits if it sets them on a productive path. On the other hand, older workers may have families and other economic dependents who rely on their income. There is no clear argument that social welfare will be improved by displacing these older workers to the benefit of younger workers. Increasing the opportunities for all workers, while helping youth to overcome their particular constraints, is the strategy that this report advocates.

"We work mostly as subcontractors for the textile factories. . . . The entire village lives on the income from embroidery, smocking, and agriculture, which we do when we don't have work."
Madagascar

The vast majority (70 percent) of nonfarm HEs today are pure self-employment—just the owner operating the HE. About 20 percent of these enterprises include a family member in the operation, and only 10 percent have hired someone outside of the family.

The modern wage sector includes small, medium, and large firms that employ five or more workers on a continuous basis. It also includes the public sector, which in some countries is a large share of the modern wage sector. In the low- and lower-middle-income countries of Africa, roughly half of wage employment is in the public sector. This report focuses only on the private sector, where the potential for job growth is greatest.

Growth, Jobs, and Africa's Labor Force—Now and in the Future

Since 2000, Africa has seen more than a decade of economic growth, the longest continuous expansion in more than 50 years. Until the 2008–09 global economic crisis, Africa's GDP grew relatively rapidly, averaging 5 percent a year, and growth had resumed by 2010 (figure 1.6). Between 1998 and 2008, mineral-exporting countries experienced an exceptionally steep rise in GDP; 22 countries that are not oil producers averaged 4 percent growth or higher

(Chuhan-Pole and Angwafo 2011). The flow of private capital to Africa now exceeds the flow of foreign aid. As a result, the structure of output has changed: the share of GDP generated by agriculture is falling, and the share generated by industry and services is rising. By 2010, agriculture's share in GDP had fallen to 30 percent in low-income countries and 16 percent in lower-middle-income countries, while the share of the industrial and services sectors had increased.

The drivers of this growth were economic policy reforms, which were necessitated by misguided steps taken in the past, and higher commodity prices, which produced better terms of trade (Devarajan and Fengler 2013). These two factors allowed domestic demand, especially for private sector services and construction, to power growth. Africa's impressive growth trajectory has largely followed commodity prices, however, and African exports are still concentrated in primary commodities. In contrast, it was the rapid rise in export manufacturing that allowed East Asia to capture its demographic dividend. Over the past two decades, manufacturing's share of GDP actually fell in Africa, while rising in Asia's lower-income and middle-income countries (figure 1.7). Today, the share of manufactured goods in merchandise exports is 30 percent in Africa, compared with 50 percent in Latin America (another resource-rich region) and 60 percent in lower-middle-income countries on average. Manufactured exports have led growth in only one country in Africa: Mauritius. Indeed, Africa is so far behind East Asia that it will take some time to catch up.

The Structure of Employment in African Countries

Africa's dependence on commodity exports, aid, and domestic demand as sources of growth did not lead to a major transformation in employment (figure 1.9; see box 1.2 for an explanation of how employment estimates are derived and countries are classified). Although agriculture's share in GDP fell substantially, almost 60 percent of Africa's labor force in 2010 still reported that agriculture was their main economic activity.

Figure 1.6 Africa's growth miracle, 2005–12

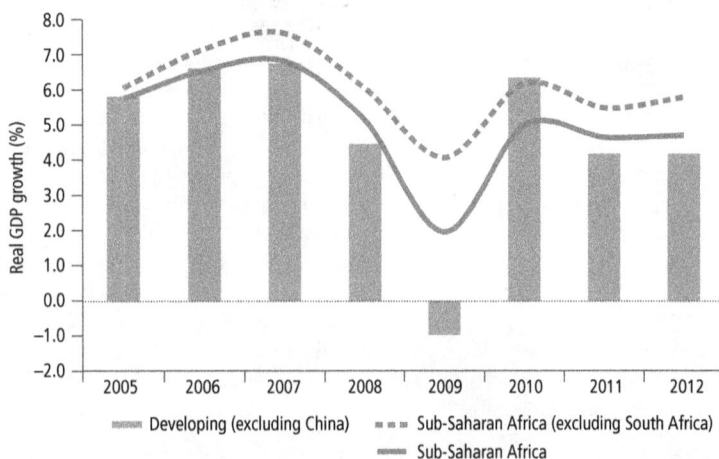

Source: World Bank 2012a.

Figure 1.7 Over the past two decades, agriculture's share in GDP contracted in Africa, but manufacturing did not replace it

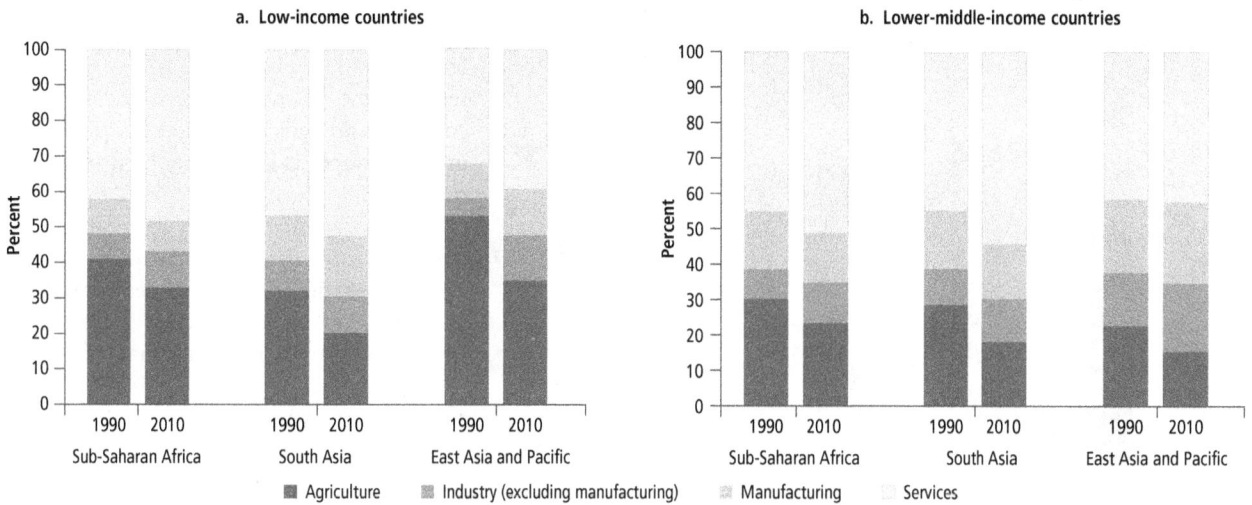

a. Low-income countries

b. Lower-middle-income countries

■ Agriculture   ▨ Industry (excluding manufacturing)   ▨ Manufacturing   ▨ Services

Source: World Bank various years.

Figure 1.8 Exports are a smaller share of GDP in Africa than in East Asia and a larger share than in South Asia, but African countries, even richer ones, export commodities, not manufactured goods

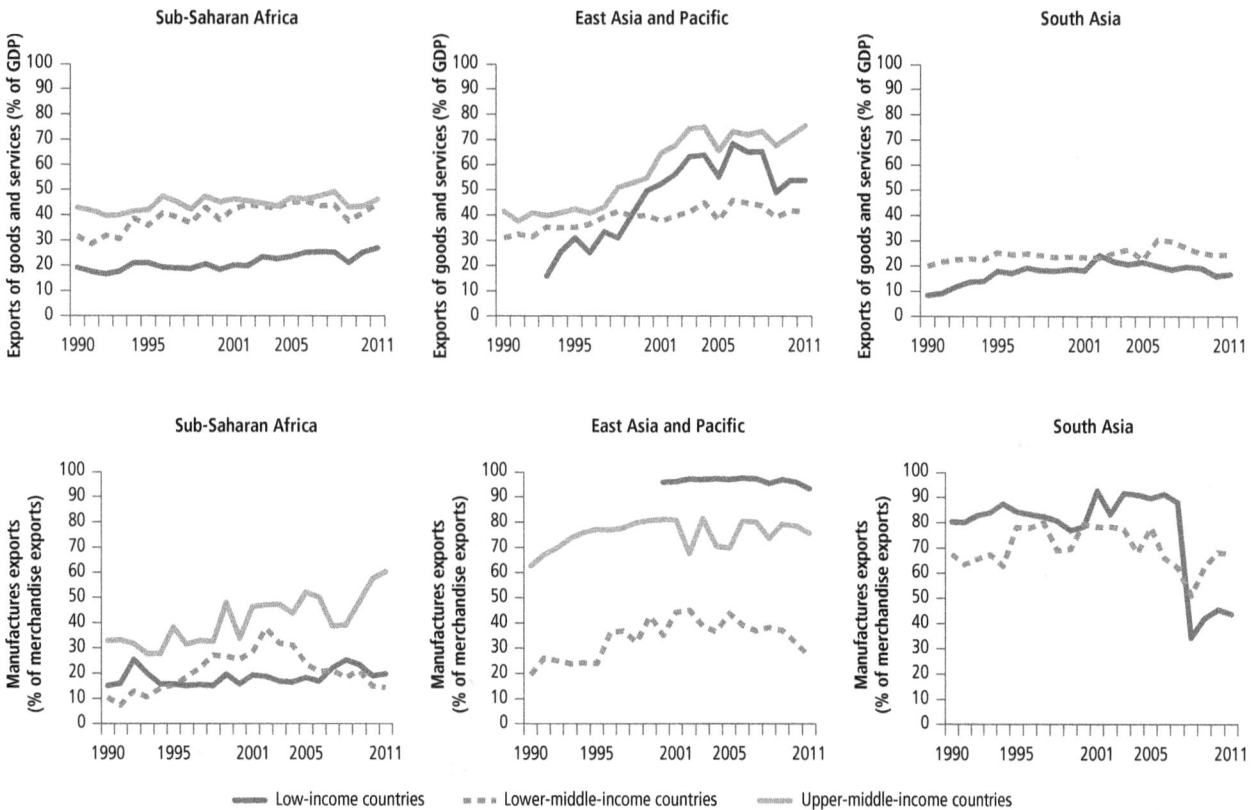

Sub-Saharan Africa   East Asia and Pacific   South Asia

——— Low-income countries   ▪ ▪ ▪ Lower-middle-income countries   ▨▨▨ Upper-middle-income countries

Source: World Bank various years.

Figure 1.9 **The majority of Sub-Saharan Africa's workers in low- and lower-middle-income countries work in agriculture and in nonfarm household enterprises**

Estimated structure of employment in Sub-Saharan Africa by country type, 2010

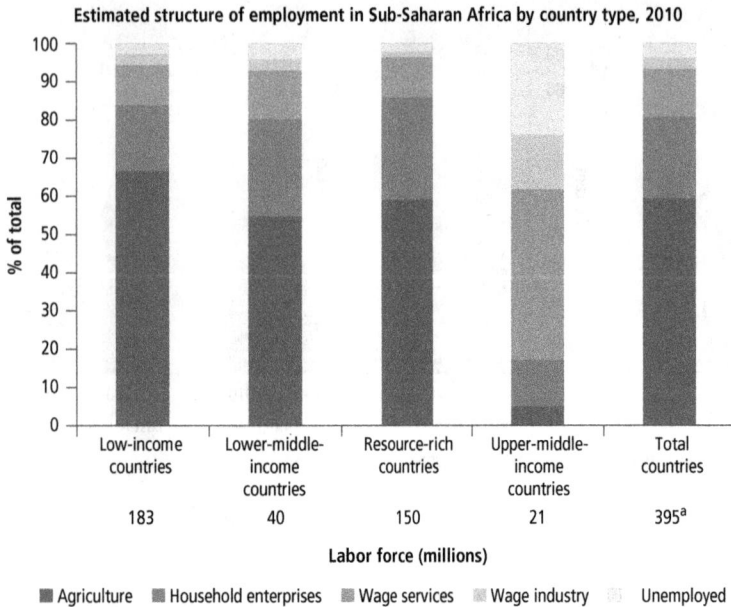

Agriculture   Household enterprises   Wage services   Wage industry   Unemployed

Source: Fox et al. 2013.
Note: On horizontal axis, numbers show size of labor force in each group. Country classification is based on per capita gross national income (GNI) in World Bank (various years). See box 1.2 for an explanation of how employment estimates are derived and countries are classified.
a. Numbers do not add to total because of rounding.

This result is not wholly unexpected: the transformation in labor always lags the transformation in output (more capital per worker is needed to employ people in more productive jobs). Yet the large share of the labor force

in agriculture combined with the persistently low growth in agricultural productivity help to explain the continued low incomes and poverty in Africa. The data confirm that unemployment remains low, except in upper-middle-income countries and especially in South Africa, where unemployment is stubbornly high (see focus note 4).

Africa's decade of growth was not "jobless," but patterns of employment growth differed across countries. Growth moved away from agriculture in some countries: for example, Ghana, Nigeria, Rwanda, Tanzania, and Uganda all experienced high growth in both wage and HE employment (figure 1.10). Mineral-exporting countries such as Cameroon and Mozambique experienced job growth but saw little or no transformation of the employment structure, although the creation of nonfarm employment in Nigeria over the last decade shows that diversification is possible in an African oil-exporting country.

In rapidly growing countries where growth did not depend significantly on mineral resources, employment followed output in shifting out of agriculture—the sector with the lowest productivity—and into higher-productivity industry and services. Those countries saw nonfarm wage and salary employment in the private sector advance at a rapid pace that often surpassed growth in GDP. Most of the increase in wage employment (public and pri-

---

Box 1.2

How are our employment estimates done?

Data on the structure of employment in Africa are difficult to obtain. Many countries do not collect these data frequently; often the data are not released until long after they have been collected; and in some cases, only published tabulations are released. Regardless of how they are released, the quality is often poor (Fox and Pimhidzai 2013). For these estimates, all possible data sources were consulted to get at least one observation on the structure of employment for each country over the period 2000–10 to form the baseline. We were able to do this for 28 of 47 countries in Africa, covering 73 percent of the labor force. For the other countries, we imputed a distribution of the labor force from the averages of similar countries. The size

of the labor force for each country was calculated by taking the United Nations projection for the working-age population in each country and applying a labor force participation rate. Countries were grouped according to income, with low income set at gross national income (GNI) per capita under US$1,000, lower-middle income at GNI per capita of US$1,000–US$4,000, and upper-middle income at GNI per capita above US$3,000. Resource-rich countries were estimated as a separate group. Figure 1.9 shows the baseline distribution estimated using this method by country group for 2010.

Source: Fox et al. 2013.

vate) occurred in the expanding services sector; growth in labor-intensive industry was slow, owing to the limited development of export manufacturing.

By 2010, the private sector was creating most of the wage jobs found in Africa (figure 1.11). Much of the increase in wage employment was in noncontract employment such as day labor or temporary jobs. These jobs, often called "informal wage employment," represent about half of all nonfarm wage jobs in Africa.

Despite the recent creation of private wage jobs, the share of wage employment remains low throughout Africa, partly because the public sector shed so many jobs in the 1980s and 1990s (Fox and Gaal 2008). Although most nonfarm wage employment was found in the public sector in the 1960s and 1970s, this pattern was reversed in non–resource-rich countries during their recent growth spurt. In contrast, economies that grew through increased mineral extraction maintained the pattern: the state distributed part of the resource rents in the form of public sector jobs. The public sector continues to provide most of the wage employment in resource-rich countries, because incentives for the private sector to create employment remain weak (box 1.3).

Private nonfarm employment grew the most rapidly in the HE sector, as rural and urban households used their extra income to start businesses (figure 1.10). The data presented here are likely to understate growth in the HE sector, because they show only primary employment, when in fact a sizable share of the labor force—up to 50 percent in some countries—undertakes two or more economic activities (jobs) over a 12-month period. Particularly in rural areas, where the majority of Africa's population still lives, a household is likely to report its HE as a secondary activity, after farming (Fox and Sohnesen 2012).

The Structure of Employment in Africa Compared with Other Regions

The share of the labor force in agriculture is not unusually high in Africa, especially in its lower-income countries. In Vietnam and the Lao People's Democratic Republic, where per capita income just exceeds US$1,000, 50 percent or more of the labor force still works in

Figure 1.10 Growth has moved the structure of employment away from agriculture in some countries, but not others

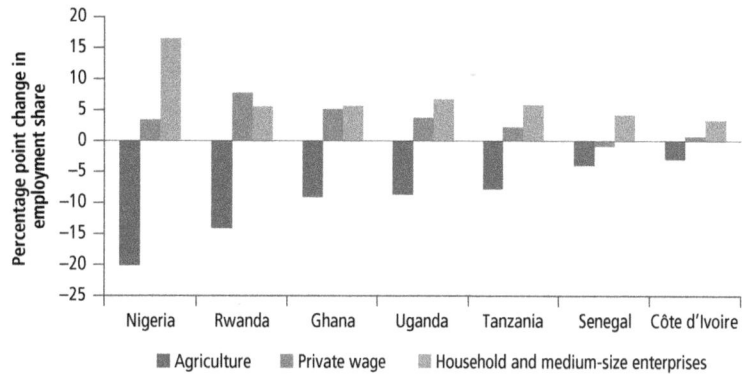

Source: Based on standardized and harmonized household and labor force surveys. See appendix A.

Figure 1.11 Most wage jobs are in the private sector (but not in resource-rich countries)

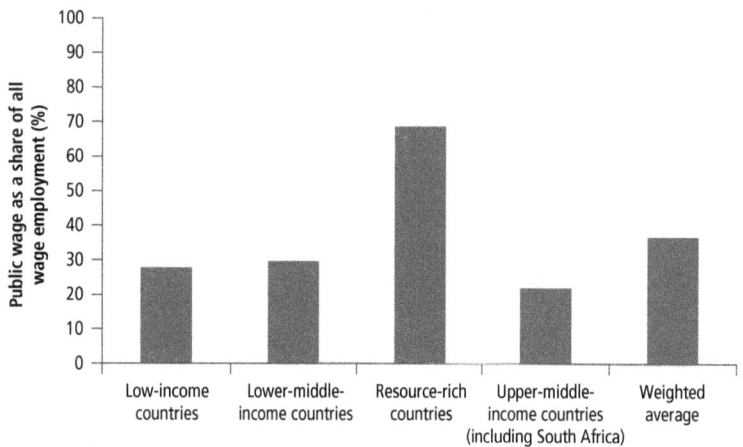

Source: Fox et al. 2013.

agriculture, which is about the average for Africa's lower-middle-income countries (table 1.1). The difference is that these East Asian countries have higher agricultural productivity, which has helped to reduce rural poverty to levels well below those in Africa. Africa and these East Asian countries may have the same share of the labor force in agriculture, but the persistently low growth in agricultural productivity in Africa prevents the African labor force from reducing poverty to the same extent as their Asian counterparts (IMF 2012). The HE sector is also large in all of the lower-income comparator countries, especially in Bangladesh, the poorest of the comparators.

Box 1.3

The challenge of diversifying output and employment in resource-rich countries: Examples from Central Africa

Debate remains lively on the existence and nature of the so-called "resource curse," but few doubt that youth employment faces special challenges in countries with large endowments of mineral resources. Resource rents, if not carefully managed, lead to overvalued exchange rates and contribute to noncompetitive wages. Both of these outcomes cripple the development of sectors that trade in goods other than mineral resources, particularly if a country's human capital or productive infrastructure has not improved as a result of its resource wealth. The traditional tradable sectors of the economy, including export-oriented agriculture, can shrink rapidly; at the same time, the industries based on extracting natural resources create few new wage-earning opportunities.

Most workers are left with few choices. They either revert to low-productivity subsistence farming or migrate to urban areas, where they often remain underemployed. The few opportunities for highly paid employment—in the natural resource sector and the public sector (where growth is fed by resource rents)—contribute to a pattern of youth unemployment in which young people simply opt to wait for a job in those sectors and develop a motivational bias against other forms of employment. The expectation of a public sector "desk job" distorts young people's educational choices and creates a large group of graduates whose skills are ill matched to the needs of the private sector.

Often natural resource wealth goes hand in hand with significant deficits in the institutional environment that hamper growth in private sector employment. When natural resource revenue is available, incentives for business climate reforms are reduced, and the public sector assumes an excessive role in economic activity.

The positive side of this story is that countries with extensive natural resources have substantial financial resources at their disposal to invest in human development, infrastructure, and the promotion of new sources of economic growth. A central concern is to ensure coherence across policies that promote human capital development, including specific programs for youth employment, and those that promote public investment in infrastructure and productive sectors. In Central Africa, for example, public expenditure reviews in Equatorial Guinea and Gabon found that public spending has overemphasized investments in physical infrastructure relative to human capital (World Bank 2010, 2012c). Despite high unemployment among well-educated youths, firms in newly emerging economic sectors have difficulty finding qualified personnel, indicating that the skills taught by the education system are not adequately aligned with efforts to promote new economic activities (World Bank 2012d, 2013). Arbitrary limits on the employment of foreigners can also be a significant business constraint, and even when expatriates are employed, all too little is done to transfer their expertise to locals. Often foreign contractors implement large-scale public investment projects that use very little domestic labor, even for low-skilled activities that could employ local youths in the short run. A review of youth employment programs in Cameroon found that they address a wide range of specific problems but lack coherence and are not clearly integrated with broader policies to remove binding constraints to growth and employment (World Bank 2012b).

Successful resource-rich countries outside Africa, such as Chile and Malaysia, have put skills and education at the center of their diversification strategies (Gelb 2010). Rather than "picking winners" and subsidizing specific sectors, such countries have used natural resource revenues strategically to identify and address constraints on skills in close cooperation with the private sector. This approach has effectively promoted economic diversification and youth employment.

The low share of the labor force in private industry is what makes the employment structure so different in low-income and lower-middle-income countries of Africa compared to the rapidly growing countries of Asia or Latin America (table 1.1). All the comparator countries except Lao PDR and Mongolia have a larger share of employment in industrial wage jobs, because they have a high number of manufacturing jobs. Clearly the importance of mineral rents in raising per capita incomes in Africa's lower-middle-income countries contributes to this discrepancy. Resource extraction does not generate many jobs, and high resource rents can create an economic structure unfriendly to private, labor-intensive industry (Gelb 2010). The economies of Lao PDR and Mongolia, both mineral exporters in East Asia,

Table 1.1 African countries have less wage employment than high-growth comparator countries
% of employment

Income level and region or country	Wage job			HE	Agriculture	Total
	All	Industry	Services			
Low income						
Sub-Saharan Africa	12.3	2.3	10.0	18.3	69.4	100.0
Bangladesh	25.7	10.8	14.9	27.7	46.6	100.0
Cambodia	23.3	11.1	12.2	21.0	55.7	100.0
Low-middle income						
Sub-Saharan Africa	13.9	2.0	11.9	31.1	55.1	100.0
Bolivia	43.0	12.6	30.4	28.1	28.9	100.0
Lao PDR	13.5	5.4	8.1	19.0	67.5	100.0
Mongolia	39.3	5.9	33.4	16.0	44.7	100.0
Nicaragua	43.9	13.3	30.6	22.9	33.2	100.0
Philippines	48.7	12.6	36.1	19.5	31.8	100.0
Vietnam	31.8	14.3	17.5	19.1	49.1	100.0

Source: Fox et al. 2013.

have structures similar to those in resource-rich African countries (figure 1.12). Even in this case, African countries with high levels of mineral exports stand out, because they have even less wage employment in industry than Lao PDR or Mongolia. Resources are not destiny, however, as Bolivia's successful performance in export-oriented manufacturing shows.

The lack of jobs in export-oriented manufacturing is not the only factor setting Africa apart. As discussed, the labor force is growing much faster in Africa than in Asia or Latin America, making it that much harder to transform the structure of employment. For example, because Vietnam's labor force grew at only two-thirds of the pace of Senegal's over the last decade (2.1 versus 3.1 percent a year), every dollar invested in creating labor-intensive manufacturing jobs will have a stronger effect on the structure of employment (measured as a share of the labor force) in Vietnam than in Senegal. In other words, Senegal needs 50 percent more investment in manufacturing than Vietnam needed, just to bring its share of employment in industry to the level in Vietnam in 2008.

In sum, after a decade of growth and job creation, the majority of Africa's labor force still works in its least productive sector—agriculture—which has yet to experience the sub-

stantial productivity growth seen in rapidly growing economies outside Africa. To create more productive employment, Africa still faces the dual challenge of increasing productivity in agriculture and diversifying employment out of agriculture.

Figure 1.12 Industrial wage employment has not risen with GDP in Africa the way it has in manufacturing exporters at similar income levels

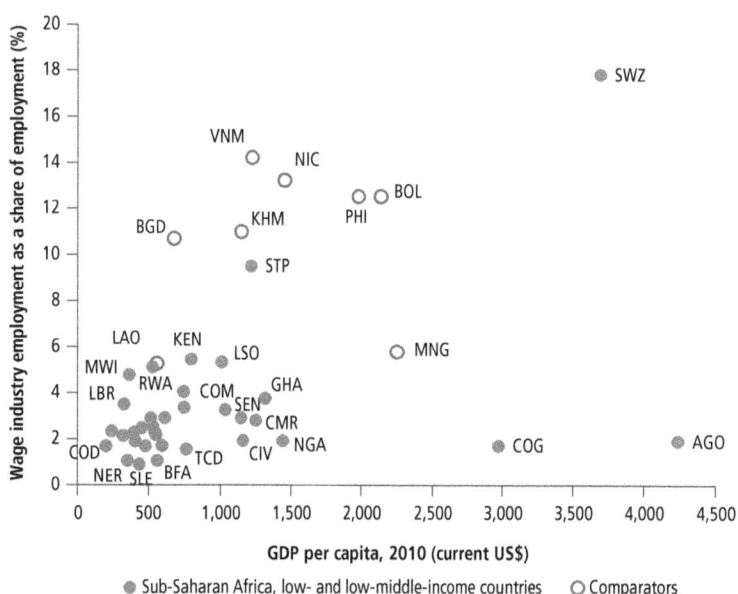

Source: World Bank various years for GDP; Fox et al. (2013) for employment structure in 2010.

"We both started this profession [silk production and weaving] when we were eight years old. There was no other option for us; this is our heritage, and we proudly continue this tradition."
Madagascar

What Can Africa Expect in the Future?

Africa's strong growth early in this decade has fueled expectations that by the end of the decade most of its population will live in countries with a per capita income (GNI) above US$1,000—what the World Bank defines as "middle income" (World Bank 2012a). Currently almost 60 percent of the labor force works in low-income countries, including those classified as resource rich, so this shift would be significant.

How might this continued strong growth influence the number and types of jobs available to Africans by 2020? And what would happen to employment if growth were even stronger? We developed two sets of employment projections to explore those questions. First, we project what might happen if the growth remains robust, following its present course. Next, we project what might happen to employment if Africa experiences a "game-changing" growth scenario, arising from a surge in export-oriented manufacturing. (For background on the data and methods used to develop the employment projections, see box 1.4.) The sections that follow outline the assumptions behind these scenarios and the resulting picture of employment.

Basic Scenario: Strong, Steady Growth Continues

In this scenario, the main sources of growth in Africa over the next decade are the same as those in the last decade, resulting in steady growth across country groups (table 1.2). *Agricultural growth* in lower-middle-income and low-income countries is projected to remain strong at about 5 percent a year, driven by increased factors of production (land and labor) and by increased labor productivity (from increased input use and improved access to markets). This growth will cause real incomes to rise for farmers, as demand for food crops from Africa is projected to remain high regionally and internationally, keeping prices at current real levels. Projected *industrial growth* in lower-middle-income and low-income countries reflects a combination of new mining projects and higher manufacturing output to serve the domestic market, but no major gains in manufacturing exports. Some countries with mining projects are projected to have very high industrial growth: Ghana at 19 percent a year, as oil production comes on stream; Liberia at 17 percent a year, from iron ore mining; and Sierra Leone, with an average industrial growth rate exceeding 50 percent, from iron ore min-

---

Box 1.4

How are our employment projections done?

For projecting the distribution of employment across sectors, the first step was to develop economic growth projections by sector for each country. These were made based on projections of area and yield for agricultural products and on projections of underlying sectoral benchmarks, such as electricity usage, cement usage, road and rail transport, telecommunications, and hotel stays, for the other sectors.

Then sectoral elasticities of employment with respect to growth were developed and applied. In developing the estimates for employment growth between 2010 and 2020, we consulted (1) computed sectoral elasticity estimates for some African countries for the previous decade, (2) computed estimates for selected Asian comparator countries from

the early 1990s through the late 2000s, and (3) computed estimates for African countries for which at least two high-quality employment and national accounts data points could be obtained. Using that data, we developed a set of median sector elasticities for each country grouping, sector, and type of nonagricultural job (see table B1.4.1). The industry and services elasticities for the middle-income countries are comparable to the other estimates. For low-income countries, the industry elasticities are considerably lower in Africa than in Asia (Bangladesh, Cambodia, and Vietnam), because industry growth has been much more labor intensive in the Asian countries. In contrast, the services employment elasticities are estimated to be slightly higher in Africa than in

Box 1.4

(continued)

Asia. The employment elasticity is much lower in industry for resource-rich countries than for low-income countries because of the importance of mining in the former group and the prevalence of labor-intensive production in the latter group. The agricultural sector elasticities are negative for South Africa and the middle-income countries because they have been losing agricultural employment over the past decade, in contrast to the earlier period (Kapsos 2005) and to middle-income countries in Asia.

Finally, the elasticities of employment were applied to the projected growth rates to project employment by sector for each country to 2020. Since elasticity estimates vary considerably across countries, the median estimate was adjusted in some countries based on the economic structure and projected future performance of the country. For example, the employment elasticity of industrial sector growth in Sierra Leone was adjusted downward from the median for low-

income countries, because the explosive growth anticipated in this sector will come from increased extraction of iron ore, which is not labor intensive. To close the model, the unemployment rate for low-income and lower-middle-income countries was held constant, and all projected employment not allocated to industry and services was assigned to agriculture. This feature of the model is consistent with agriculture's current function as the fallback economic activity for most households, but it means that employment estimates for agriculture in low-income and lower-middle-income countries are not based on growth elasticities. In middle-income countries, labor was allocated to each sector, with unemployment as the residual. The resulting baseline scenario shows only a modest decline in unemployment in these countries. The detailed country employment estimates were aggregated back into the country groupings. The final result is shown in figure 1.14.

Table B1.4.1 Growth elasticities of employment

a. Our elasticity parameters

Sector	Low income	Lower-middle income	Resource rich	Upper-middle income (except South Africa)	South Africa
Agriculture[a]				−0.8	−1.0
Wage industry	0.9	0.8	0.6	0.6	0.5
Nonwage industry	0.7	0.6	0.7	0.3	0.3
Wage services	0.8	0.8	0.8	0.7	0.5
Nonwage services	0.8	0.9	0.7	0.6	0.5

b. Comparators

Sector	Asia 1990–2010		ILO, SSA, 1990–2003[b]	
	Vietnam, Cambodia, Bangladesh	Indonesia, Philippines	Low- and lower-middle income	Upper-middle income
Agriculture	0.3	0.3	0.7	0.1
Wage industry	1.2	0.4	0.6	0.8
Nonwage industry	1.1	0.4	0.6	0.8
Wage services	0.7	0.7	0.8	0.7
Nonwage services	0.7	0.7	0.8	0.7

a. Agricultural employment closes the model for low-income, low-middle income, and resource-rich countries.
b. Data from Kapsos 2005.

Source: Fox et al. 2013.
Note: Resource-rich countries are defined here as Angola, Chad, the Democratic Republic of Congo, Guinea, Nigeria, the Republic of Congo, Sudan and Republic of South Sudan, and Zambia.

Table 1.2 Average annual growth, by sector and country income level, 2005–20
percent

Country group	Actual				Projected							
	2005–10				2010–15				2015–20			
	Real GDP	Agriculture	Industry	Services	Real GDP	Agriculture	Industry	Services	Real GDP	Agriculture	Industry	Services
Low income	6.5	4.8	6.6	7.7	6.2	5.0	7.9	6.2	6.4	5.8	7.3	6.2
Lower-middle income	4.4	4.1	4.9	4.5	5.5	4.1	9.9	4.0	5.9	4.7	6.9	5.8
Lower-middle income, except Ghana	3.3	3.9	3.4	3.2	4.9	4.3	6.6	4.4	5.8	4.9	7.1	5.4
Resource rich	6.8	7.5	3.1	11.9	6.8	6.5	4.6	9.5	6.4	6.4	3.7	8.5
South Africa	3.6	2.5	2.3	4.1	3.1	2.1	2.2	3.5	3.2	3.2	1.3	3.8
Other upper-middle income	3.0	1.5	1.5	4.8	4.6	3.2	4.7	5.1	4.5	4.7	4.1	4.9

Source: Fox et al. 2013.
Note: See box 1.4 for an explanation of how employment projections are derived and countries are classified.

ing. When those countries are excluded from their respective groups, a smoother pattern emerges for growth rates. Resource-rich countries, whose main export is expected to remain unprocessed minerals, will be distinguished by higher *growth in the services sector* (public sector growth funded by mineral rents). Upper-middle-income countries are projected to continue recovering from the slump that followed the financial crisis of 2007–08. They are expected to diversify their exports into services, giving a boost to that sector.

A key assumption behind this optimism is that Africa will not experience another major economic shock from external or internal sources, such as another major global recession that shatters demand for African exports, the outbreak of a regional conflict, or a prolonged climatic disaster in the region. Without such shocks, African countries could realize 10 years of growth averaging 4.5–6.0 percent a year, slightly above what was achieved during 2005–10, which included the shock to world financial markets.

Figures 1.13 and 1.14 present initial answers to the questions about the number and types of jobs that this kind of growth might create. Although industrial wage employment is projected to increase through continued modest diversification of output and exports, service employment is projected to keep growing faster than industrial employment because

the mining sector will not directly create very many jobs. By 2020, wage and salary jobs will account for 29 percent of the net new jobs but only 25 percent of the total jobs taken by new entrants (some new entrants will replace workers leaving the labor force). In other words, at best one in four African youth will find a wage job, and only a small fraction of such jobs will be "formal" jobs in modern enterprises. Unemployment is assumed to remain low in the low-income and lower-middle-income countries, and we project that it will fall slightly in the upper-middle-income countries if high growth rates are realized.

The HE sector is projected to create even more jobs than the wage sector, accounting for 45 percent of the net new jobs and employing 37 percent of new entrants through the start-up of new businesses. This sector feeds off demand for goods and services created by employment and earnings growth in the wage and agricultural sectors, so balanced growth is necessary to realize this part of the projection.

Because the majority of new jobs will need to be created in countries currently classified as low income (such as the Democratic Republic of Congo and Ethiopia), the agricultural sector will remain important for creating employment. In agriculture—unlike other sectors—the projection of new jobs (in low-income and lower-middle-income countries) is not based on demand for labor in the sector. Instead it repre-

Figure 1.13 Where will Africa's 125 million new jobs be created?

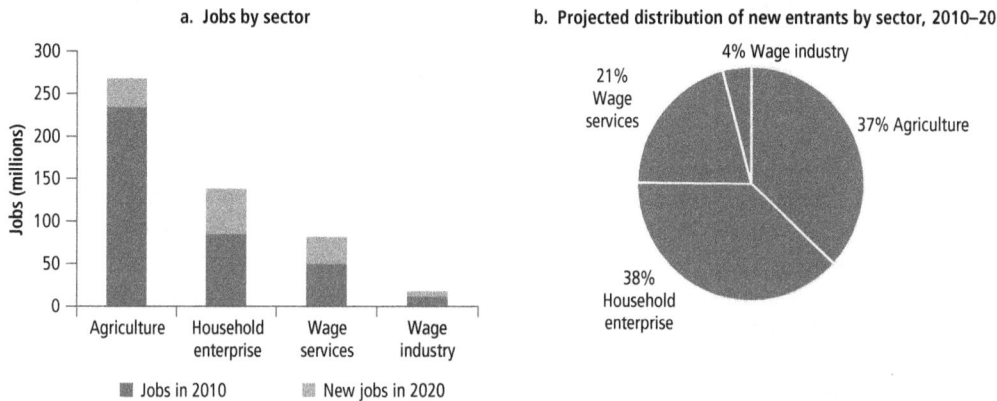

a. Jobs by sector

b. Projected distribution of new entrants by sector, 2010–20

■ Jobs in 2010   ▨ New jobs in 2020

Source: Fox et al. 2013.
Note: See box 1.4 for an explanation of how employment projections are derived and countries are classified.

sents the labor force that does not find a wage job or start a business (box 1.4). The absolute number of people working in agriculture is projected to rise by about 33 million. Since about 70 percent of those who will exit the labor force are now working in agriculture, the actual number of new entrants that agriculture needs to absorb is over 62 million, or about 38 percent of the new entrants. Stronger growth in other sectors could push this number down slightly, but it is unlikely that the labor force in agriculture will shrink over the next decade—young people seeking jobs will simply have no other place to go. If African agriculture realizes its potential, however, agricultural jobs will be more productive, higher-earning jobs than they are today.

Although the projection implies high growth in nonagricultural employment, the projected structure of employment shown in figure 1.14 is not much different from the current structure shown in figure 1.9. Agricultural employment will decline in all country groups, yet the share of industrial wage jobs in total employment will rise from 2.3 to only 3.2, below other developing regions, because those jobs are growing from such a small base.

How do these estimates compare with others in the literature? A recent McKinsey study contends that Africa will create about 122 million new jobs over the next 10 years and that almost half of them will be wage-paying jobs (Fine et al. 2012). Why is McKinsey's employment forecast considerably more optimistic than the one

Figure 1.14 Informal will remain normal in much of Sub-Saharan Africa

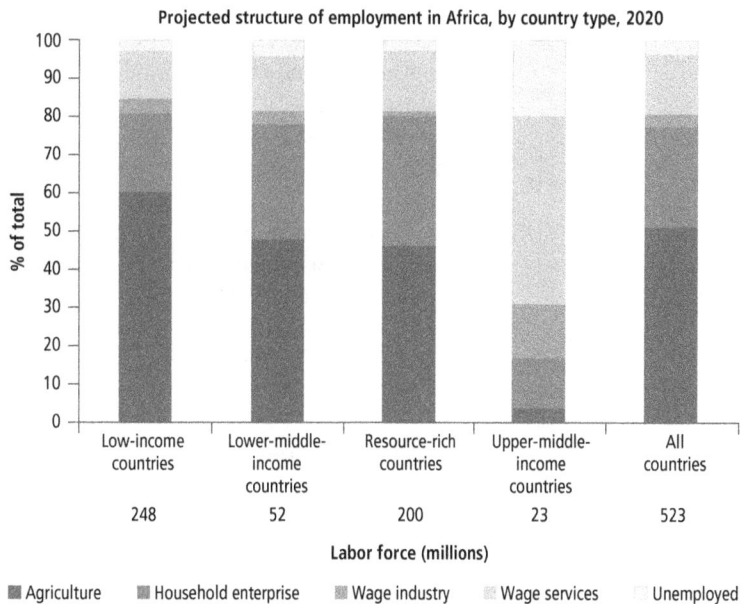

Projected structure of employment in Africa, by country type, 2020

Labor force (millions)

■ Agriculture   ■ Household enterprise   ▨ Wage industry   ▨ Wage services   ▨ Unemployed

Source: Fox et al. 2013.
Note: See box 1.4 for an explanation of how employment projections are derived and countries are classified.

provided here—30 million new wage jobs over the coming decade? The main difference is that we use Africa-specific data and projections to forecast the employment profile, whereas the McKinsey team uses data from fast-growing developing and emerging market countries on other continents.[3] That method clearly imparts an upward bias to McKinsey's results.

"Game-Changer" Scenario: A Surge in Labor-Intensive Export Manufacturing

Is there a better scenario for African jobs? The scenario just presented is already optimistic in the sense that it is based on sustained growth across Africa, but it is not based on a radical, "game-changing" departure from Africa's current growth path. Some observers contend that if Africa increases output in export-oriented, labor-intensive light manufacturing as dramatically as high-growth comparator countries in Asia managed to do, the structure of employment could change more rapidly (Lin and Monga 2012; Dinh et al. 2012). When growth in manufacturing employment was at its peak in Bangladesh, Cambodia, and Vietnam, those countries had annual growth rates of 10 percent or more in their industrial sectors and were creating industrial wage jobs at an even faster pace.

How would the structure of employment differ if low-income and lower-middle-income African countries changed their policies and investments to achieve a comparable performance? What employment prospects would be open to youth in those countries in 2015–20 if Africa picks up manufacturing industries and jobs from East Asia beginning in 2015, in much the same way that other East Asian countries picked up industries and jobs from Japan and the Republic of Korea in the 1980s and 1990s?

To test the possible implications of such a "game change" for employment in Africa, we simulated this recent Asian experience for low-income and lower-middle-income countries of Africa.[4] In this simulation, we raised the wage employment elasticity to 1.2 to match the historical wage employment elasticity estimated for Bangladesh, Cambodia, and Vietnam—meaning that employment in the industrial sector would grow 20 percent faster than value added, which implies very labor-intensive growth. The industrial growth projection for low-income and lower-middle-income countries was also revised upward to 10 percent a year over 2015–20. This figure is slightly above the median and average industry growth rate experienced by Bangladesh, Cambodia, and Vietnam over the most recent decade (9.3 percent a year). Figure 1.15 compares the structure of employment for the original and the alternative, "game-changing" scenario.

If the alternative scenario could be realized, industrial wage employment would grow much faster across Africa's low- and lower-middle-income countries, which would account for almost 60 percent of Africa's labor force in 2020. The average annual growth of industrial wage employment would double over the decade to 12 percent a year, and total wage employment would grow 6 percent a year. Yet even then the structure of employment would

Figure 1.15   Even game-changing growth will have limited effects on the distribution of employment in the near term

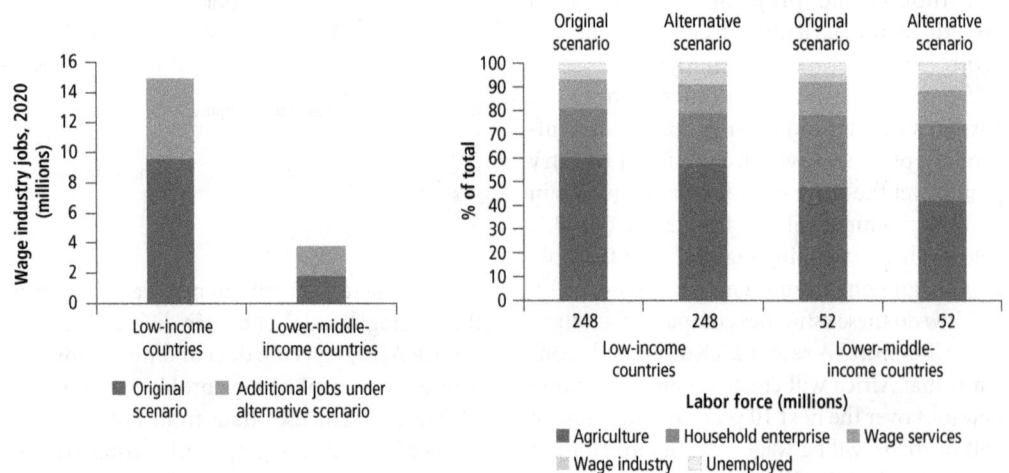

Source: Fox et al. forthcoming.
Note: See box 1.4 for an explanation of how employment projections are derived and countries are classified.

look about the same. Low-income countries could expect about 5 million more wage jobs a year, and lower-middle-income countries could expect about 2 million new wage jobs—a shift of 10 percent of total new jobs in these countries, representing a small change in the prospects for new entrants.

These modest gains partly reflect the short period used for the projection, which covers only five years, whereas the structural change in Vietnam took 20 years to unfold. They also reflect the larger labor force and the lower base from which industrial development would start. Africa will need at least two decades to change the structure of employment sufficiently to offer dramatically different prospects to its youth, which underscores the importance of starting the change process now.

Framework of This Report

Starting from the reality of youth in Africa—the size of the cohort and the events that shape their lives during the many transitions that youth entails—this report analyzes young people's employment prospects and experiences and examines how to create pathways leading to productive work. Using a simple analytical framework, the report develops a systematic and detailed understanding of the challenges involved in improving the productivity, earnings, and efficiency of the transitions of youth—as well as the various interventions that show promise in addressing those challenges (table 1.3). We focus on the three sectors in which productivity increases will be most critical: agriculture, nonfarm HEs, and the modern wage sector.

We distinguish two types of constraints that limit young people's potential for finding pathways to productive work in the three sectors:

1. *Human capital*. The supply side, or the abilities, education, skills, family connections, networks, beliefs, and other character traits that are embedded in an individual and allow that person to find opportunities to be productive, increase earnings, and achieve income security

2. *Business environment*. The factors outside a worker's immediate control that affect

Table 1.3 Framework of this report

Three sectors	Two dimensions
• Agriculture	• Human capital
• Nonfarm household enterprises	• Business environment
• Modern wage employment	

productivity (access to land, capital, and finance; infrastructure; technology; and markets), as well as the government policies, regulations, and programs that may affect the choice of economic activity and how the activity is conducted.

Chapters 4, 5, and 6 address each sector in turn (agriculture, HEs, and modern wage employment in the private sector). They delve into the particular ways that binding constraints related to the business environment and human capital influence young people's potential for productive employment, and they describe how those constraints might be relieved.

To provide the context for those chapters, chapter 2 discusses the transitions that characterize youth, particularly the overlapping transitions from school and to work. Chapter 3 looks at skills, an issue that cuts across all sectors of employment, focusing on the skills that are critical for productive employment and how they are acquired. The chapter assesses the role of schooling in producing education and learning and describes the wide landscape of apprenticeships and other forms of training that develop skills outside of school.

Notes

1. Excluding China, the estimates for East Asia and the Pacific are 115 million youth ages 15–24 in 2015 and 101 million in 2050. The decline in the cohort size begins in 2010 (as it does for China).

2. Figures are based on Demographic and Health Surveys (DHS) final reports (www.measuredhs.com).

3. McKinsey based its estimate on data for the Arab Republic of Egypt, Indonesia, Korea, Malaysia, Mexico, Pakistan, the Philippines, Thailand, and Turkey.

4. Africa's resource-rich countries were excluded from this simulation, because even the resource-rich countries in East Asia did not achieve the type of employment transformation simulated here.

References

Bloom, David E., David Canning, and Pia N. Malaney. 2000. "Population Dynamic and Economic Growth in Asia." *Population and Development Review* 26 (supplement): 257–90.

Bloom, David E., and Jeffrey Williamson. 1998. "Demographic Transitions and Economic Miracles in Emerging Asia." *World Bank Economic Review* 12 (3): 419–55.

Bongaarts, John, and John Casterline. 2013. "Fertility Transition: Is Sub-Saharan Africa Different?" *Population and Development Review* 38 (supplement 1): 153–68.

Chuhan-Pole, Punam, and Manka Angwafo, eds. 2011. *Yes Africa Can: Success Stories from a Dynamic Continent.* Washington, DC: World Bank.

Devarajan, Shantayanan, and Wolfgang Fengler. 2013. "Africa's Economic Boom: Why the Pessimists and the Optimists Are Both Right." *Foreign Affairs* (May–June): 68–81.

De Wolf, Stefan, Yves Rolland Rakotoarisoa, Laurence Vanpaeschen, and Honoré Rabekoto. 2008. *Madagascar: Le Grand Livre des Petits Métiers: Portraits of Daily Life Professions.* Belgium: Snoek Publishers.

Dinh, Hinh T., Vincent Palmade, Vandana Chandra, and Frances Cossar. 2012. "Light Manufacturing in Africa: Targeted Policies to Enhance Private Investment and Create Jobs." Agence Française de Développement and World Bank, Washington, DC.

Eastwood, Robert, and Michael Lipton. 2011. "Demographic Transition in Sub-Saharan Africa: How Big Will the Economic Dividend Be?" *Population Studies* 65 (1): 9–35.

Fine, David, Arend van Wamelen, Susan Lund, Armando Cabral, Mourad Taoufiki, Norbert Dörr, Acha Leke, Charles Roxburgh, Jörg Schubert, and Paul Cook. 2012. "Africa at Work: Job Creation and Inclusive Growth." McKinsey Global Institute, Washington, DC.

Fox, Louise, and Melissa S. Gaal. 2008. "Working out of Poverty: Job Creation and the Quality of Growth in Africa." World Bank, Washington, DC.

Fox, Louise, and Obert Pimhidzai. 2013. "Different Dreams, Same Bed: Collecting, Using, and Interpreting Employment Statistics in Sub-Saharan Africa: The Case of Uganda." Policy Research Working Paper 6436, World Bank, Washington, DC.

Fox, Louise, and Thomas Sohnesen. 2012. "Household Enterprises in Sub-Saharan Africa: Why They Matter for Growth, Jobs, and Livelihoods." Policy Research Working Paper 6184, World Bank, Washington, DC.

Fox, Louise, Alun Thomas, Cleary Haines, and Jorge Huerta Munoz. 2013. "Africa's Got Work to Do: Employment Prospects in the New Century." IMF Working Paper, International Monetary Fund, Washington, DC.

Gelb, A. 2010. "Economic Diversification in Resource-Rich Countries." Paper prepared for the conference on Natural Resources, Finance, and Development: Confronting Old and New Challenges, Central Bank of Algeria and the IMF Institute, Algiers, November 4–5.

IMF (International Monetary Fund). 2012. "Regional Economic Outlook: Sub-Saharan Africa Sustaining Growth amid Global Uncertainty." IMF, Washington, DC.

Kapsos, Stephen. 2005. "The Employment Intensity of Growth: Trends and Macroeconomic Determinants." Economic Strategy Paper 2005/12, International Labour Organization, Geneva.

Lin, Justin Yifu, and Célestin Monga. 2012. "Solving the Mystery of African Governance." *New Political Economy* 17 (5): 659–66.

Losch, Bruno, Sandrine Freguin-Gresh, and Eric Thomas White. 2013. *Structural Transformation and Rural Change Revisited.* Washington, DC: World Bank.

United Nations. 2011. *World Population Prospects: The 2010 Revision.* New York: United Nations, Department of Economic and Social Affairs, Population Division. http://esa.un.org/wpp/Excel-Data/population.htm.

World Bank. 2010. "Equatorial Guinea Public Expenditure Review." World Bank, Washington, DC.

———. 2012a. *Africa's Pulse* 6 (October). World Bank, Washington, DC.

———. 2012b. "Employment in Cameroon: Stock Take of Programs, Assessment of Existing Gaps and Opportunities, and Proposed Next Steps." World Bank, Washington, DC.

———. 2012c. "Gabon Public Expenditure Review: Better Management of Public Finance to Achieve Millennium Development Goals." World Bank, Washington, DC.

———. 2012d. "Gabon: Rapport sur la croissance et l'emploi." World Bank, Washington, DC.

———. 2012e. *World Development Report 2013: Jobs.* New York: Oxford University Press.

———. 2013. "Economic Growth in Equatorial Guinea: Paths to Inclusiveness and Sustainability." World Bank, Washington, DC.

———. Various years. World Development Indicators. Washington, DC: World Bank.

Jobs: More Than Just Income

A job—be it for a wage or not—is almost always more than just an income. A job affects a person's core sense of identity and at the same time establishes how a person is perceived by society. The kind of job that people do exerts a powerful influence on their social well-being and economic development. The *World Development Report 2013: Jobs* covers these themes in detail and serves as the basis for the brief discussion that follows.

The Value of Jobs

People throughout the world consider jobs to be more than a task or an income. Jobs say something about an individual's place and identity in society and contribute to an individual's satisfaction with life (World Bank 2012). In a 2012 survey in Sierra Leone, 90 percent of respondents judged their job to be somewhat or absolutely meaningful (Hatløy et al. 2012). Similarly, youths interviewed in a qualitative study in Ghana reported that they value jobs that allow them to acquire new knowledge and skills or to connect with other people through social networks (Anarfi, Anyidoho, and Verschoor 2008). The type of job, contract, benefits, and safety and security at work all influence such perceptions of well-being. This may explain why measures of job satisfaction are lower in Sub-Saharan Africa than in other regions across all types of jobs—agricultural, household enterprise, and modern wage (see figure F1.1).

In addition to their contribution to status, empowerment, identity, and well-being, jobs (including nonwage jobs) connect people through networks. Jobs connect people with others—of different backgrounds, ethnicities, and gender—with whom they would not otherwise interact and with information, including information about job opportunities. For example, a study of workers from different eth-

nic backgrounds in Rwanda's coffee industry found that workplace interactions are associated with better attitudes toward collaboration across ethnic boundaries and less distrust (Tobias and Boudreaux 2011).

Jobs in agriculture, too, can connect people through networks. Studies in Ghana and Uganda illustrate how farmers connected through networks can obtain information and increase productivity. In Ghana, pineapple farmers adjusted their use of fertilizer in response to the successful or unsuccessful experiences of their neighbors. Farmers just starting to cultivate pineapples are more likely to make changes based on information received from other farmers, showing the potential of on-the-job interactions and learning from others (Udry and Conley 2004). In rural Uganda, a recent randomized experiment studied the productivity effect of networks by pairing cotton farmers to stimulate the exchange of information. The pairs were encouraged to discuss farming activities, problems, and solutions and to set a target for increased cultivation. Farmers who participated in the project, especially women, significantly increased their productivity. Connecting farmers with other farmers outside their established social circles helped to spread information that otherwise would not have been shared (Vasilaky 2010).

While jobs can connect people through networks, they can also exclude. Across countries, most people find their jobs through connections with friends, relatives, and other acquaintances. In the 2012 jobs survey in Sierra Leone, 75 percent of respondents reported that their job is important for establishing contacts with others (Hatløy et al. 2012). Yet networks may have negative social consequences when they exclude people and groups who lack such connections. A case study of a weaving cluster in Ilorin, a city in the Yoruba Muslim part of western Nigeria, and a shoe and garment cluster in Aba, a city in the Igbo Christian area of

> *"[In my job] I meet a lot of people, learn how to express myself and how to go about personal communication."* Ghana

43

Figure F1.1 Jobs and life satisfaction across regions

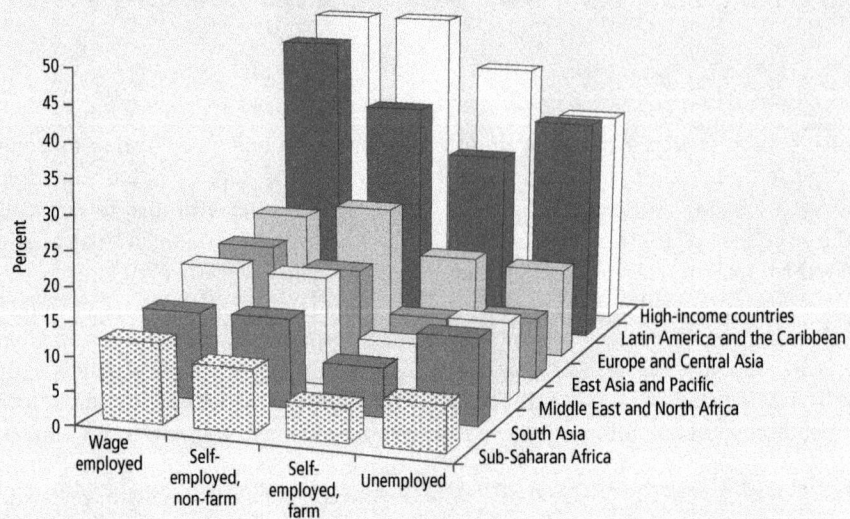

Source: World Bank 2012, based on Gallup 2009, 2010.
Note: Figure shows the share of respondents who rate their present life at 7 or higher and who anticipate that their life in five years will be at 8 or higher on a scale of 10.

eastern Nigeria, found that the greater inflow of producers increased the reliance on connections and social tensions. The poorest producers had no regular suppliers or credit networks, but depended mainly on customers from their own village (Meagher 2011).

Jobs and Aspirations

The distribution of jobs within a society can affect expectations and aspirations. As children and teenagers form goals for the future, their aspirations may be influenced by whether their parents have jobs and the types of jobs their parents have. Frustration and even social unrest may develop when education and effort are not rewarded or when people perceive the distribution of jobs to be unfair. In many countries in Africa, the conventional wisdom suggests that people, and youth in particular, prefer wage employment to other types of jobs, including jobs in farming and household enterprises, and that the lack of wage jobs can provoke social tensions. Wage employment, especially in urban areas, is perceived to be more lucrative and secure and to have a higher status. For example, young people interviewed for a qualitative study in Liberia explained that they

only consider "jobs" to be salaried employment, whereas other forms of livelihood and work activities do not qualify (World Bank 2013). In a similar study in Sierra Leone, youth considered "employment" to mean having a stable and salaried position. They held office jobs in particular esteem. Such jobs are often referred to as "Englishman" jobs. Positions in teaching and nursing are also often treated with respect. Young people refer to casual, informal jobs that provide low levels of daily income as "dishonorable jobs."

Wage jobs are not always the most coveted, however. The reality is more complex, based on the context, available opportunities, and characteristics of youth. In Ghana, wage work is not necessarily preferred among different types of employment (Falco et al. 2012). In fact, owners of informal firms that employ others are significantly happier than people working in the formal private sector. Young people explained that status, autonomy, and income cause them to prefer self-employment. A 22-year-old student explained, "Here in Ghana, you don't earn much by working for somebody. You are able to make more from your own business than from working for someone" (Anarfi, Anyidoho, and Verschoor 2008). An unemployed youth echoed that message: "There is nothing like doing [your own work], and it gives you the idea that, one day, I have to work hard and, if possible, establish my own company, employ people." Youth surveyed in Zambia expressed similar sentiments; those employed in wage jobs noted that they have to supplement their income with informal activities because of low pay as well as limited job security (PREM Poverty Reduction Group 2008).

Jobs and Development

Jobs have three transformational dimensions for individuals and society (World Bank 2012). The first one is *living standards*: poverty falls as people work their way out of hardship, especially in countries where the scope for redistribution is limited. The second is *productivity*: efficiency increases as workers get better at what they do and move from less productive jobs to more productive ones. The third is *social cohesion*: societies flourish as jobs create a sense of opportunity and get people from different ethnic and social backgrounds to work together.

When jobs are examined in light of their potential to contribute to those outcomes, it becomes clear that some jobs do more for development than others (figure F1.2). For policy makers, therefore, it is not only the number of jobs that matters, but their quality and contribution to a country's development. As discussed, individuals value jobs for the earnings and benefits they provide, along with their contributions to self-esteem and happiness. But some jobs have broader effects on society. Jobs for women can change the way households invest in the education and health of children. Jobs in cities support greater specialization and the exchange of ideas, making other jobs more productive. And in turbulent environments, jobs can contribute to peace and social cohesion (see box F1.1).

Often the individual and social perspectives on jobs coincide, but not always. Jobs with high pay and benefits may be coveted by individuals, but they may be less valuable to society if they are supported through government transfers or restrictive regulations, undermining the earnings or job opportunities of others. Because of gaps like these, jobs that look equivalent to an

Figure F1.2 Jobs drive development

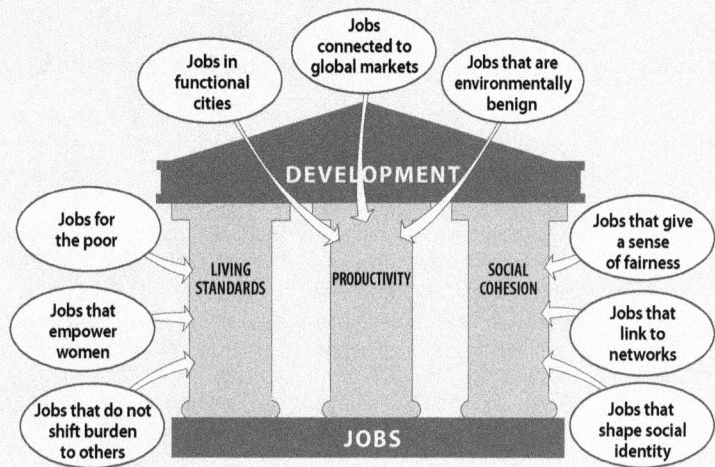

Source: World Bank 2012.

individual may have different effects on society. Good jobs for development are those with the highest value for society, taking into account not only the value they have to the people who hold them, but also the potential spillovers on others—positive or negative. Jobs that reduce poverty, connect the economy to global markets, or foster trust and civic engagement can do more for development than others.

The particular jobs that are good for development will vary with each country's level of development, demography, endowments, and institutions. For example,

- In *agrarian countries*, most people live in rural areas and their jobs are in agriculture. Making smallholder farming viable is critical because poverty rates are high. Higher agricultural productivity can help the development of off-farm employment. At the same time, urban jobs connected to world markets set the foundation for cities to become dynamic.

- In *conflict-affected countries*, the most immediate challenge is to support social cohesion. Employment for former combatants or youths vulnerable to participation in violence is particularly important. Construction can help, as it is labor intensive and can thrive even in a poor business environment.

Box F1.1

Employment, conflict, and violence: Is there a link?

Dissatisfaction with the quality and availability of jobs among youth in Africa has raised concerns in the media and in public debate about the risks of violence and social tensions. Across countries, however, the connections between jobs, conflict, and violence are not straightforward. Only limited and contradictory evidence on those connections is available from developing countries. Generally, the literature suggests that relationships between conflict, violence, and employment status are indirect and may operate through channels such as identity and social dynamics (Cramer 2010).

The literature linking crime to unemployment comes mostly from developed countries, and it finds no consistent link between unemployment and violent behavior. Studies from the United Kingdom and the United States have linked youth unemployment to property crime, including burglaries and vehicle break-ins (Bell and Blanchflower 2010). The evidence is weaker for violent crimes. The literature on unemployment and conflict presents more consistent results, and although causality is difficult to establish, there is evidence that poor economic performance, including youth unemployment, can be associated with conflict (Collier and Sambanis 2005; Urdal 2004). Other work fails to find empirical evidence for the relationship between youth unemployment and armed conflict, however, so the evidence remains mixed (Cramer 2010).

Overall, where unemployment is high or employment opportunities are poor, violence and tensions probably result from accumulated risk factors, such as exclusion, perceptions of opportunities, and family dynamics, rather than employment status alone. For example, young people may turn to gangs or other violent groups to compensate for the lack of ties they have in economic and social life. A longitudinal study of youth in Ecuador found that members of gangs involved with drugs and guns joined "because they were searching for the support, trust, and cohesion—social capital—that they maintained their families did not provide, as well as because of the lack of opportunities in the local context" (Moser 2009). Similarly, analysis in the United States found that gangs provide youth with the income, respect, and social ties that they are unable to find in jobs, particularly given the limited opportunities available in cities such as Chicago and New York that have lost stable manufacturing jobs (Padilla 1992).

- In *urbanizing countries*, productivity growth in agriculture frees people to work in cities. Jobs for women, typically in light manufacturing, can benefit households. Avoiding urban congestion and allowing the country to move up the value-added ladder are top priorities.
- In *resource-rich countries* foreign exchange earnings may be substantial, but the abundance may undermine the competitiveness of other activities and encourage the creation of jobs supported through transfers. Jobs that lead to a diversification of exports can have large development payoffs.

Ultimately the role of government is to ensure that the conditions are in place for strong private sector–led growth, to understand why there are not more good jobs for development in a particular country, and to remove or mitigate the constraints that prevent the creation of more of these jobs. The *World Development Report 2013: Jobs* outlines a three-layered policy approach:

- *Fundamentals.* Because jobs improve with development, it is necessary to create a policy framework that is conducive to growth. That task requires attending to macroeconomic stability, an enabling business environment, human capital accumulation, and the rule of law—including respect for rights.
- *Labor policies.* Labor policy should avoid the distortionary interventions that clog the creation of jobs in cities and in global value chains and that lack mechanisms for giving voice and protection to the most vulnerable workers, regardless of whether they are wage earners or not.
- *Priorities.* Because some jobs do more for development than others, it is necessary to understand where good jobs for development lie, given the country context. Policies should remove or offset the market imperfections and institutional failures that prevent the private sector from creating more good jobs for development.

References

Anarfi, John Kwasi, Nana Akua Anyidoho, and Arjan Verschoor. 2008. "The Economic Empowerment of Young People in Ghana." Report prepared for the World Bank, Washington, DC.

Bell, David, and David Blanchflower. 2010. "Youth Unemployment: Déjà Vu?" Discussion Paper Series 4705, Institute for the Study of Labor, Bonn.

Collier, Paul, and Nicholas Sambanis, eds. 2005. *Understanding Civil War.* Vol. 1: *Africa.* Washington, DC: World Bank.

Cramer, Christopher. 2010. "Unemployment and Participation in Violence." Background paper for *World Development Report 2011: Conflict, Security, and Development,* World Bank, Washington, DC.

Falco, Paolo, William F. Maloney, Bob Rijkers, and Mauricio Sarrias. 2012. "Heterogeneity in Subjective Well-Being: An Application to Occupational Allocation in Africa." Policy Research Working Paper 6244, World Bank, Washington, DC. doi: 10.1596/1813-9450-6244.

Hatløy, Anne, Tewodros Kebede, Huafeng Zhang, and Ingunn Bjørkhaug. 2012. "Perceptions of Good Jobs: Port Loko and Freetown, Sierra Leone." Background paper for the *World Development Report 2013,* World Bank, Washington, DC.

Meagher, Kate. 2011. "Informal Economies and Urban Governance in Nigeria: Popular Empowerment or Political Exclusion?" *African Studies Review* 54 (2): 47–72.

Moser, Caroline O. N. 2009. *Ordinary Families, Extraordinary Lives: Assets and Poverty Reduction in Guayaquil, 1978–2004.* Washington, DC: Brookings Institution Press.

Padilla, Felix M. 1992. *The Gang as an American Enterprise.* Piscataway: Rutgers University Press.

PREM Poverty Reduction Group. 2008. "The Economic Empowerment of Young People in Zambia." Report 51431, World Bank, Washington, DC.

Tobias, Jutta M., and Karol C. Boudreaux. 2011. "Entrepreneurship and Conflict Reduction in the Post-Genocide Rwandan Coffee Industry." *Journal of Small Business & Entrepreneurship* 24 (2).

Udry, Christopher, and Timothy G. Conley. 2004. "Social Networks in Ghana." Discussion Paper 888, Economic Growth Center, Yale University, New Haven, CT.

Urdal, Henrik. 2004. "The Devil in the Demographics: The Effect of Youth Bulges on Domestic Armed Conflict, 1950–2000." Social Development Paper 29740. World Bank, Washington, DC.

Vasilaky, Kathryn. 2010. "As Good as the Networks They Keep? Expanding Farmer's Social Networks Using Randomized Encouragement in Rural Uganda." Yale University, New Haven, CT. Processed.

World Bank. 2012. *World Development Report 2013: Jobs.* Washington, DC: World Bank.

———. 2013. *Understanding Youth Violence: Cases from Liberia and Sierra Leone.* Washington, DC: World Bank.

Chapter 2

Youth: A Time of Transitions

By definition, youth is a time of many transitions—from school, to work, through risky behaviors, to founding a family, and to exercising citizenship. These transitions, which are shaped by the opportunities available to each individual, as well as by social norms and aspirations developed during childhood and adolescence, have long-lasting consequences. For youths, the path from school to a livelihood in agriculture, household enterprise (HE), or wage employment can be particularly long. Young people in rural areas may work on their parents' farms for some time prior to establishing their own farm or HE. In urban areas, they may exit the labor force for a year or two and then spend several years seeking but not finding a wage job. They may also work in the family business to gain experience and save money to start their own HE or invest in a farm. Once young people start working in a sector—whether in agriculture, an HE, or a wage job—they tend to stay there, although mobility across sectors is slightly higher in urban than in rural areas. Migration can offer an opportunity to change these patterns and substantially increase earnings, but migration for employment is (perhaps surprisingly) low in Africa. For young women, the transition from school to high-productivity work entails additional challenges.

Often women's opportunities are circumscribed by social norms related to family responsibility, agency, and acceptable economic activities and by fears of harassment. Given these challenges, the pertinent policy question is how to make the paths to employment easier for young people to find and navigate.

Different countries and different institutions define youth differently. Broadly speaking, the United Nations defines youth as ranging from ages 15 to 24, the African Union defines youth as ranging between ages 15 and 35, and many Sub-Saharan countries apply their own definitions (such as ages 15–40 in Mali or ages 15–30 in Kenya). For this report, we do not define youth as a specific age range. Rather, we focus on the fact that youth is a period of transition—from school, to work, through risky behaviors, to founding a family, and to exercising citizenship (World Bank 2006). We present data for the various age ranges during which these transitions occur (most commonly ages 15–24 and 25–34). Generally we refer to the older group as "young adults" to distinguish them from the younger group.

The transitions of youth have long-lasting consequences. Clearly, the stage at which a young person leaves the education system and starts working is a key determinant of that person's skill level and career path, but an individual's stock of human capital is also formed through early work experience. A prolonged period of initial unemployment or an initial job that offers no opportunities for learning and growth can potentially hurt an individual's future productivity. Similarly, decisions regarding health and family made during adolescence and early adulthood can have long-term effects on an individual's health and career.

Because adolescence is a critical period of development, including for socioemotional skills, economic or health shocks occurring during that time can have long-lasting consequences.

Work experience is important not only because it is needed to master skills but because it affects adolescents' expectations, goals, and confidence. In some settings (primarily upper-income countries where a wage job is the norm for first employment), prolonged unemployment during youth can affect mental and physical health, and it has been linked to stress, depression, and illness later in life (Lundberg and Wuermli 2012).

Many types of market or government failures could potentially constrain these transitions. Examples include labor market rigidities that lengthen the school-to-work transition, inadequate information on the risks of certain choices, and lack of access to finance for pursuing higher education or starting a business. The remainder of this report examines such failures in depth. Enabling youth to manage these transitions better—in particular, to develop pathways to higher productivity and higher-earning jobs—is the central challenge for promoting youth employment in Sub-Saharan Africa.

Youth's Transition from School

More than 80 percent of 12-year-olds in the developing world are going to school. As expected, this number declines with age until, by the age of 24, few people remain in school. In Sub-Saharan Africa this transition is slow. About 50 percent of 18-year-olds in Africa

are still in school, but half of them are still in primary school (figure 2.1). Of the 16 percent of 24-year-olds who remain in school, nearly three-quarters are still in secondary or lower levels. Thus, in addition to their many peers who never attended school or left it at a premature age, many Africans leave school only in their late teens or 20s—without having acquired much education.

For far too many young Africans, this mismatch between age and academic level means that years of childhood and adolescence that should be spent learning in the classroom are being used inefficiently. A large part of early adulthood that should be invested in learning on the job and gaining experience is instead being used to finish school.

Aside from slow advancement through school, an unusually late start to school and interruptions to schooling combine to ensure much the same result. Young people graduate at a late age, even though they have not spent enough years in school. Understanding why these failures are endemic is essential to devising a supportive youth employment policy. Lengthy yet insufficient schooling may arise from the same factors that prevent many children from attending school in the first place or that force them to leave school at an early age,

Figure 2.1 Many 18-year-olds in Africa are still in school, but half of them are still in primary school

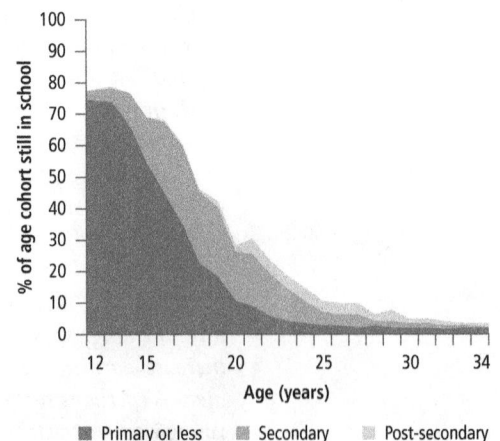

Source: Based on standardized and harmonized household and labor force surveys (see appendix).

such as the poor quality of schooling, difficulty of access, and lack of financial resources.

Another key question is the extent to which lengthy yet insufficient schooling is caused by children or youths starting to work at an age when they should be in school. Child labor is common in Africa (box 2.1), and strong evidence indicates that it is associated with lower school attendance and educational attainment. For some children, work marks a permanent end to schooling when they are still very young. For other children or young people, the effects

---

Box 2.1

Child labor in Sub-Saharan Africa

Many African children ages 5–14 engage in some type of work. Compared to other regions, Sub-Saharan Africa has the largest share of child labor (World Bank 2012b).

The worst types of child labor are unambiguously harmful to children and include all forms of slavery, bondage, military conscription, trafficking, and using, procuring, or offering children for prostitution, pornography, or other illicit activities. Extreme child labor leads to psychological and physical scarring, which in turn affects learning capacity and future earnings. For instance, in Uganda, child soldiering had a corrosive effect on human capital by keeping children away from school and creating high levels of psychological distress, especially among those who experienced the most violence (Blattman and Annan 2010).

Most children are involved in other forms of labor, such as working on the farm while going to school (particularly in agricultural households) as well as performing domestic work, selling, begging, and engaging in some type of manufacturing. The most recent round of the Multiple Indicator Cluster Survey (MICS) collected data on child work. It defines child labor among 5- to 11-year-olds as being engaged in economic activities (working, paid or unpaid, for someone who is not a member of the household, or working in a family business, on the farm, or selling goods in the street) for at least 1 hour in the 7 days prior to the survey or being engaged in domestic activities (also described as household chores) for at least 28 hours a week. Among 12- to 14-year-olds, only those who engage in economic activity for 14 hours or more or in domestic work for 28 hours or more in the 7 days prior to the survey were counted as engaged in child labor. According to these definitions, child labor among 5- to 11-year-olds is typically around 40–60 percent; child labor among 12- to 14-year-olds is typically closer to 20 percent (figure B2.1.1). In both age groups, the results from these surveys show that the majority of children work "for the family business" in either the farm or nonfarm sector.

Child labor tends to be more prevalent among poor households. Children in wealthier households may, in some settings, engage in labor if household assets and access to

finance, land, or other resources require more work from household members (World Bank 2012b).

Child labor is typically associated with delays in the accumulation of human capital, and it has been shown to reduce school attainment and school attendance (Beegle, Dehejia, and Gatti 2009). More limited evidence indicates that child labor leads to long-term "scarring" over and above its negative impact on schooling. Yet the long-term implications of child labor for young people's ability to engage in more productive activities or for their welfare in general remain unclear. In Tanzania, working in childhood increased the probability that boys would be involved in farming 10–13 years later, and it also pushed girls toward domestic work and early marriage (Beegle et al. 2008). However, child labor was also associated with an increased likelihood of wage work, which could be linked to higher living standards (Beegle, Dehejia, and Gatti 2009).

Figure B2.1.1 Percentage of children working

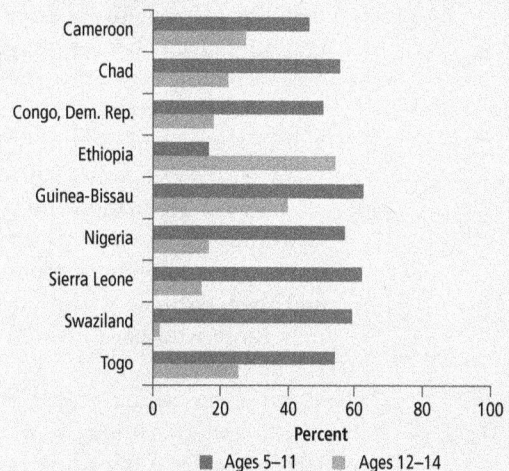

Sources: Multiple Indicator Cluster Survey Reports (MICS), various years (circa 2010). Available at www.childinfo.org.
Note: Child labor is defined as follows: (a) for ages 5–11, as economic activity for at least 1 hour a week or domestic work for at least 28 hours a week; (b) for ages 12–14, as economic activity for at least 14 hours a week or domestic work for at least 28 hours a week.

Figure 2.2 **School and work are often combined**

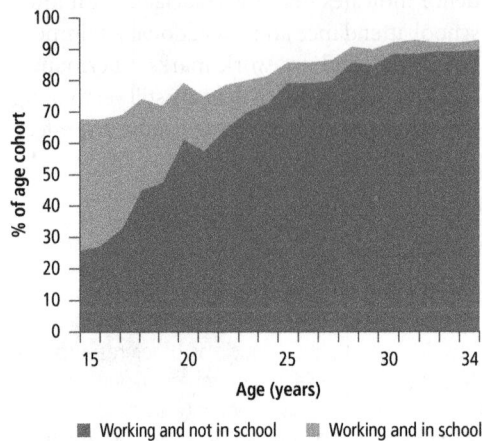

Source: Based on standardized and harmonized household and labor force surveys (see appendix).

of premature work may be less extreme but nonetheless limiting. Some children interrupt their schooling to perform intermittent work. Others engage in work that is "light" enough to allow them to attend school but that delays their progression through grades. Indeed, household surveys indicate that a sizable percentage of young people are both at work and in school; as many as 45 percent of 15-year-olds may fall in this category (figure 2.2). This work-school overlap becomes less common with age, declining to about 10 percent among 24-year-olds, presumably because they switch to full-time work.

As this discussion shows, for many individuals the transition from school to work is not a clearly demarcated progression from schooling to graduation and work. Often the transition is quite blurry—school and work overlap, or schooling is interrupted for work and then resumed—so policies that target only those who have just left school might not be enough.

For many young people in Sub-Saharan Africa, the transition from school begins relatively early. Although in most developing countries this transition can begin at any time between the ages of 12 and 24, it picks up after 18 years of age, crossing the 50 percent mark only among those in their early 20s. In contrast, more than 20 percent of 15-year-olds in Africa are already working exclusively (not counting those who are at work and in school). The incidence of exclusive work then rises rapidly. By age 20, it is well above 50 percent, and by age 25, it is at 75 percent.

Because a sizable number of those who reach working age have worked while attending school, as many as 70 percent of African youths complete the transition to work by the time they are 18. With age, the ranks of working youth increasingly comprise those who are exclusively at work.

The incidence of concurrent schooling and work is especially high in agriculture, where almost 90 percent of such work involves youth working on the family farm. In this context, young people may have fewer opportunities to leave the farm sector.

At the other end of the spectrum, the transition from school to work appears to be excessively long for some young people. About 17 percent of 26-year-olds and 10 percent of 34-year-olds are not working. This pattern does not vary by gender, so lower female labor force participation is an unlikely explanation. Some of these people may be in a temporary phase of unemployment between jobs. That, too, is unlikely to be the main explanation for their delayed transition to work, however, given the low share of wage employment among youth. Identifying the groups most likely to experience such difficulty in starting work should be a priority.

Traditional policies related to the school-to-work transition often use informational interventions and other strategies to link job seekers to employers, but their relevance in Africa is limited. As the next section discusses in greater detail, even though most young people are already working by the age of 20, most have not yet left the family enterprise or farm. At 18 years of age, nearly 70 percent of working youths are occupied in farming. At 24 years of age, nearly 60 percent of those working are still on the farm, and about 25 percent are in a nonfarm family enterprise or some form of self-employment. Only for cohorts in their mid-20s and onward does wage employment represent a notable share (more than 15 percent) of total employment.

Traditional school-to-work transition policies may, however, be more relevant to those in their mid-20s and early 30s who are yet to start working and are possibly looking for a wage job. Evidence from firm surveys shows that the majority of such jobs are found through social networks, leaving those with weak networks at a strong disadvantage (see the discussion of figure 2.9 later in this chapter).

Youth's Transition to Work

As young people begin to work less for their families and more for themselves (figure 2.3), they increasingly leave the family activity and strike out on their own. The vast majority become self-employed. By their early 30s,

more than 60 percent of men and 70 percent of women are working for themselves. Working for someone else increases modestly as people age, reaching about 30 percent for men and about 20 percent for women.

Given the slow transformation of the structure of employment, even after they become economically independent from their parents most people end up working in the same type of economic activity as their parents (box 2.2). In part because of the slow spread of education into rural areas and limited opportunities to enter nonfarm sectors, males born to households where the father was a farmer tended to become farmers themselves. Those born into households where the father had nonfarm work tended to end up in the nonfarm sector—usually because they grew up in an urban area and

Figure 2.3 Most Sub-Saharan African youths start out working for their families and then become self-employed

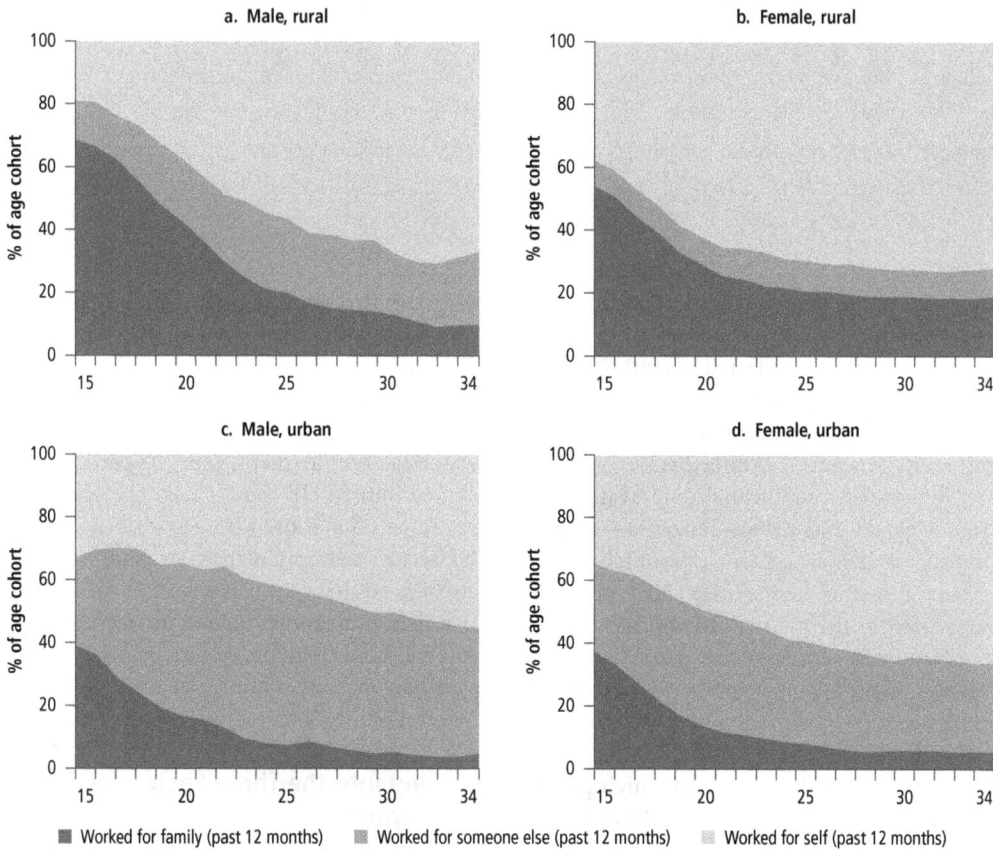

Source: Based on Demographic and Health Survey (DHS) data in 35 countries for females and 28 countries for males (see appendix).

Box 2.2

Intergenerational transmission of occupations in Africa

The trend for young people to end up in the same activity as their parents has deep roots. A study covering five African countries reveals strong patterns in the intergenerational transmission of occupations from fathers to sons. A farmer's son is much more likely to become a farmer than to exit agriculture (figure B2.2.1, panel a). In Madagascar, 87 percent of farmers' sons born in the 1960s are also farmers at the beginning of their working life, as are 72 percent in Uganda, 70 percent in Guinea, 69 percent in Ghana, and 64 percent in Côte d'Ivoire. In spite of the structural decline of agricultural employment, those numbers are not much lower than for previous generations. The intergenerational transmission of nonfarm employment is also substantial (figure B2.2.1, panel b). In Côte d'Ivoire, 93 percent of the sons born in the 1960s of nonfarmers end up being nonfarmers, compared to 89 percent in Guinea, 73 percent in Ghana, 69 percent in Madagascar, and 61 percent in Uganda. Overall, these patterns reveal limited intergenerational mobility.

Figure B2.2.1 Intergenerational transmission of employment sector in five African countries

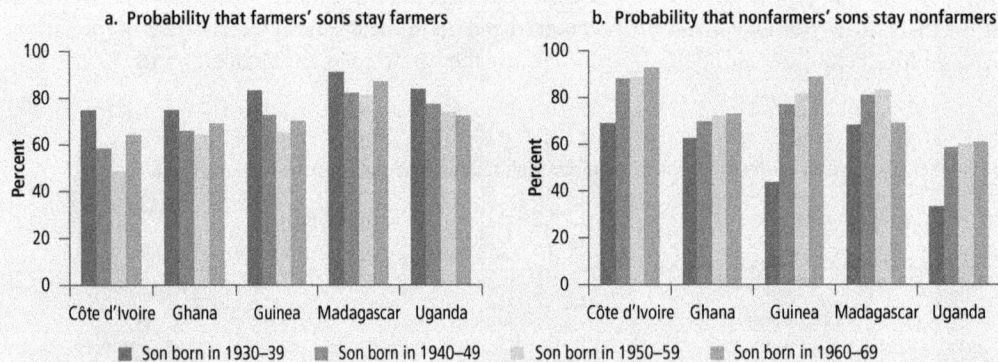

Source: Based on Bossuroy and Cogneau 2013.

encountered better opportunities for education and nonfarm employment. Data from urban areas in West Africa collected in 2001–02 show that more than 60 percent of those who were self-employed had fathers who were also self-employed (Pasquier-Doumer 2013).

The limited longitudinal data available—from Uganda and urban Tanzania—suggest that once individuals enter a type of job—agriculture, household enterprise (HE), nonfarm wage—few of them switch to another type of job. Nationally representative panel data from Uganda suggest that, overall, 61 percent of youth ages 20–29 in 2005 who were economically active had the same type of employment five years later, with an especially high persistence in agriculture (73 percent). Persistence is lower in HEs and wage work, but nevertheless high (at around 50 percent). Women were more likely to stay in the same type of employment over the two time periods—mainly because they were more likely to stay in agriculture.[1] In urban Tanzania, labor force histories collected from respondents who were 20–39 in 2005 showed that among those whose first job was wage employment, only 20 percent ever shifted into an HE (figure 2.4). The same survey reveals that those whose first job was in the HE sector (self-employment or family worker) also tended to stay in that sector. The transition that determines what type of job a young person will hold therefore occurs primarily when that person exits school, not through subsequent mobility across employment sectors.[2]

Moving into the Three Sectors of Employment

Given the relatively small amount of switching between sectors, the transition to the first type of work is key. But little is known about exactly how young people transition into the three main sectors of employment. The cross-sectional data used in this report do not record individual histories and thus hide variation between cohorts as well as within cohorts on the timing and efficiency of the transition. Longitudinal data from Tanzania and Uganda provide some insights, as they track individuals over time. Focus group data collected from African youths help to fill out the picture. As noted, however, the understanding of how young people make key choices leading to a transition to stable employment is unclear. What is clear is that the pathways and constraints are different depending on the type of activity concerned and an individual's location and gender.

As discussed, the transition into agriculture begins early. The vast majority of teenagers who work are working in agriculture (figure 2.5). At age 15, of the 60 percent of those who are working, almost 90 percent are working in agriculture. The share working outside agriculture increases steadily with age, largely because young people who leave school at higher grades enter other sectors. In rural areas, where limited educational opportunities prevent youths from staying in school for very long, agriculture employs more than 90 percent of 15- and 16-year-olds, and about 80 percent of young people ages 24 and older remain in agriculture (although some who report agriculture as their primary activity also have a nonfarm activity as well). Women who work are more likely to work in agriculture than men—and unlike men their probability of working in agriculture does not decrease much with age. One reason why so many women remain in agriculture is that they leave school sooner, so employment opportunities are set much earlier for females than for males.

Although agriculture is primarily a rural activity, young people and adults in secondary cities and periurban areas report working in agriculture as well. For example, almost 50 percent of youth ages 20–29 in urban Uganda in 2010 reported working in agriculture as their primary job, and at least 60 percent of those had entered the sector five years before. Young people in urban areas are less likely to stay in agriculture, however; it is often a stepping stone to starting a nonfarm business (figure 2.6).

Figure 2.4 Youths in urban Tanzania are unlikely to move between employment sectors during their working lives

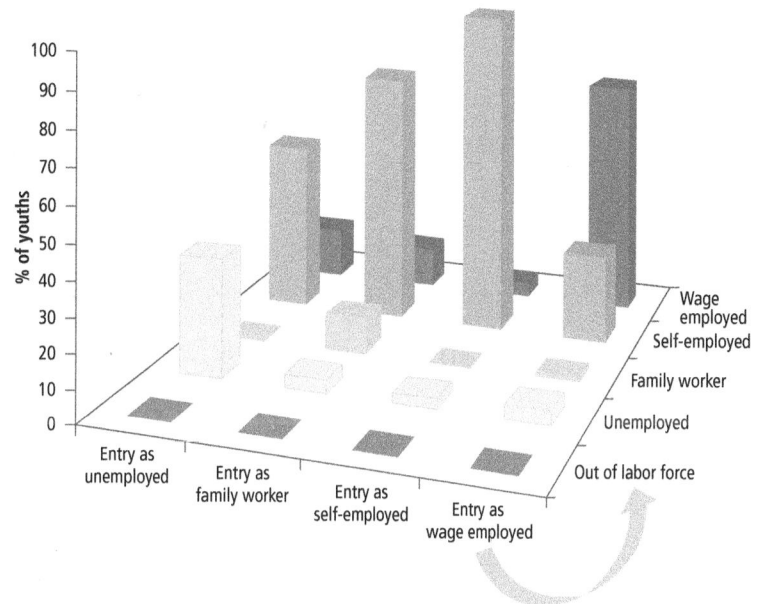

Source: Bridges et al. 2013.
Note: Sample includes youth ages 20–39 and in the labor force in 2005.

Like their adult counterparts, the young are more likely to work in an HE than in a wage job. At age 19, just over 5 percent work in an HE, while few work for a wage; by age 24, almost 20 percent work in an HE, and just over 10 percent are in a wage job; and by age 34, almost 30 percent work in an HE, and the share in wage work remains around 20 percent (figure 2.5). As they leave school, women, like men, who are not in agriculture are substantially more likely to work in an HE than to obtain wage employment. Longitudinal data from urban Tanzania suggest that many women enter this sector by helping out in a family business and then transitioning to their own HE. The same data also show that other women enter the HE sector only after a long period of searching for a wage job or failing to find one to their liking or with remuneration as high as they could earn in the HE sector (Falco et al. 2012).

Because it is based on primary occupation, which shows substantial persistence, this general picture conceals changes happening below the surface. Within the HE sector and agriculture alike, young people may start working with their parents and then acquire their own plot of

Figure 2.5 **Youth transitions to sector of employment vary across urban and rural areas and between male and female youths**

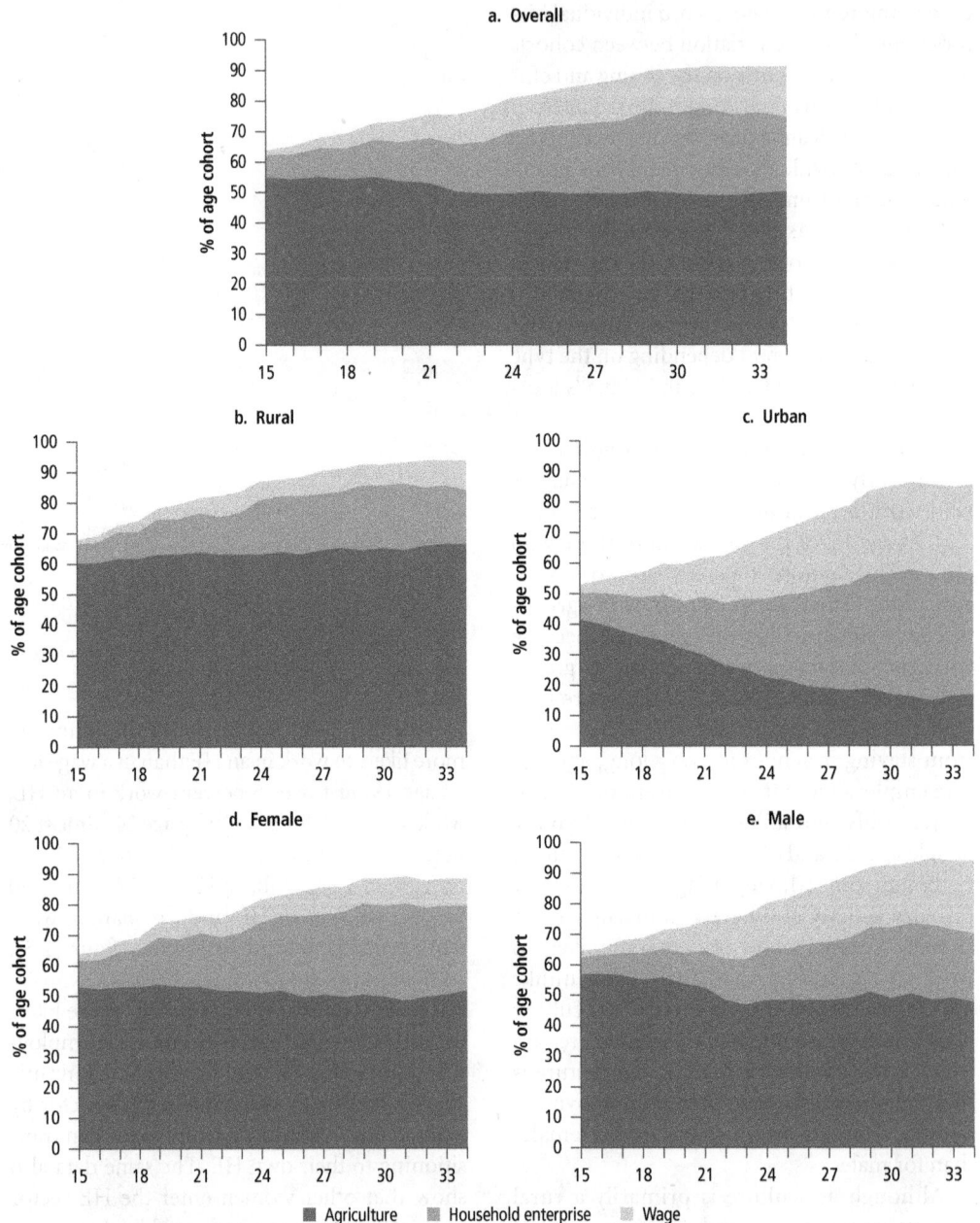

a. Overall

b. Rural   **c. Urban**

d. Female   **e. Male**

■ Agriculture   ▨ Household enterprise   ▨ Wage

Source: Based on standardized and harmonized household and labor force surveys (see appendix).

land or start their own business. In both rural and urban areas, multiple jobs are common. A young person may start out in agriculture but add nonfarm work as a second job. Even young people with a wage job may start out in casual labor but move to a more stable wage job or save enough money to start their own business. Labor force survey data from Tanzania indicate that by age 25 about half of those who had employment also pursued a secondary economic activity (figure 2.7). The probability of having multiple sources of employment is

Figure 2.6 Sectoral mobility among urban youth in Uganda

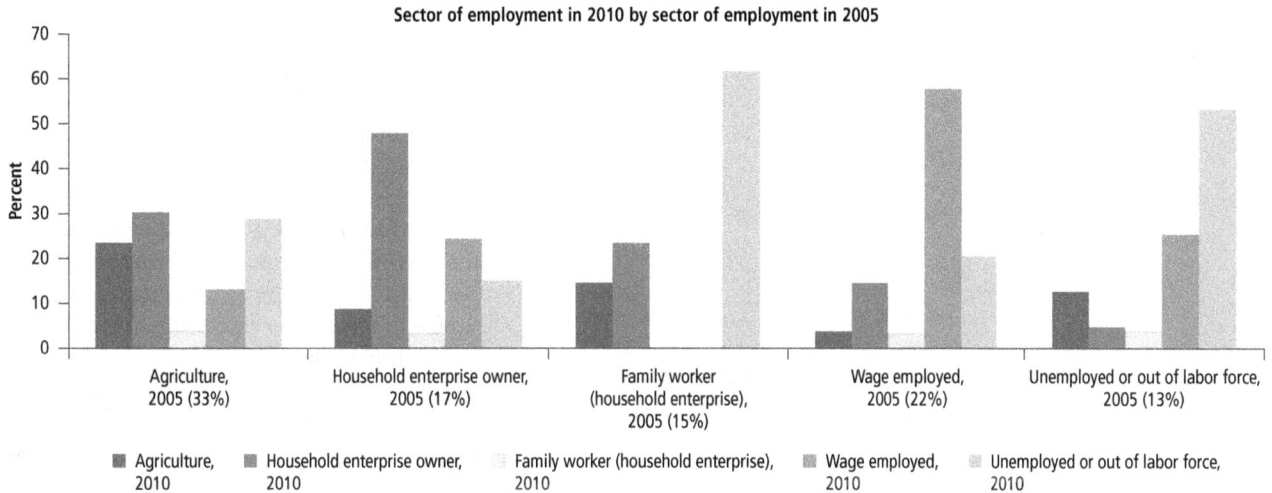

Sector of employment in 2010 by sector of employment in 2005

Legend: Agriculture, 2010 · Household enterprise owner, 2010 · Family worker (household enterprise), 2010 · Wage employed, 2010 · Unemployed or out of labor force, 2010

Source: Based on standardized and harmonized Uganda panel survey (see appendix).

much higher in rural areas. Having multiple jobs helps the worker to minimize the risks associated with operating a farm or HE and to cope with seasonal variation in employment opportunities and income. The higher probability of having multiple sources of employment in rural areas also suggests that mobility may be higher in rural areas than the data on primary economic activity indicate.

Young people find it particularly challenging to enter into modern wage employment. Employment histories of urban Tanzanian youths suggest that most did not enter directly into a wage job (20 percent; figure 2.4). However, 69 percent of those who entered a wage job remained in wage employment—26 percent became self-employed, and 4 percent became unemployed. Among the few young people who work for wages, less than half have a contract. Only around 20 percent of African teenagers with wage employment have a contract; this rate increases to around 50 percent for those in their mid-20s and around 60 percent for 30-year-olds (figure 2.8). Young people are most often engaged in casual wage employment, which can take the form of part-time or seasonal wage work. These arrangements are often verbal and of very short duration.

The desire for a wage job can lead urban youth to search a long time, without success. In urban Tanzania, young people reported hav-

Figure 2.7 In Tanzania, many work in two or more activities

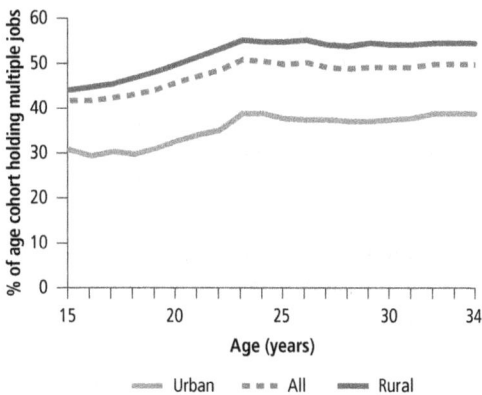

Source: Based on standardized and harmonized Tanzania labor force survey, 2005 (see appendix).

ing experienced long periods out of the labor force or in unemployment before entering into stable employment. In the longitudinal data, the average age of leaving school was two years less than the average age of entering the labor force, suggesting that even those who did not report entering the labor force as unemployed (for example, searching for a wage job) spent time idle or doing odd jobs of very short duration (Bridges et al. 2013). Most of those who reported a significant period of unemployment (not working and looking for a job) did

Figure 2.8 Younger people are most often engaged in casual wage employment

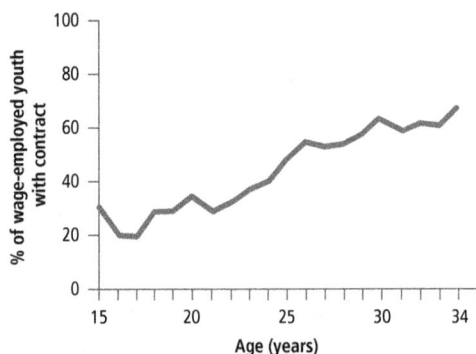

Source: Based on standardized and harmonized household and labor force surveys (see appendix).

not end up getting a wage job. Only 25 percent of those who were no longer unemployed at the time of the survey had found a wage job; the rest went into the HE sector (family or self-employment). The average duration of unemployment before becoming self-employed was close to 4.5 years.

If a young person is hoping for a wage job but ultimately settles for self-employment, 4.5 years is a long time to search for work before realizing that "informal is normal." The average duration of unemployment for those who entered the labor force as unemployed but managed to find a wage job in the end was 5.5 years. Youth entering as unemployed generally have higher education and come from wealthier families. Individuals who went through long spells of unemployment did not suffer an earnings penalty. If one makes it into wage employment, even a long job search can pay off, but the odds of finding a wage job are low (Bridges et al. 2013).

The importance of networks and contacts is one reason why the search for a wage job can be frustrating for youth. Across countries, most people get their jobs through contacts from family and friends, especially in the case of modern wage jobs. Almost 60 percent of enterprises surveyed in 14 countries report that their most recent position was filled through contacts with "family or friends" (figure 2.9). For a variety of reasons, including the difficulty of

getting information on the work-related characteristics of youth and the need to have a trustworthy workforce, employers prefer to rely on contacts to attract new entrants. Urban youths who participated in focus group discussions in Kenya complained that either a personal contact from the same ethnic group or a bribe or both were required simply to get anyone in a private firm to look at their résumé, even for those with postsecondary education (World Bank 2012a). As long as firms have an ample supply of entry-level candidates, this behavior is not likely to change.

Networks are important beyond the wage sector. In a survey in Ghana, most youths cited networks as important for getting any type of work. Young men mentioned that friends would tell them about work opportunities, especially in petty trading, street vending, farming and fishing, and construction. Young women tended to get referrals from family members for jobs in an HE, in many cases with other family members.

Moving into Employment through Migration

Urbanization is fundamentally altering Africa. Even though the share of the population living in urban areas remains well below the share in the rest of the world, in Africa urbanization has accelerated over the past couple of decades.

Figure 2.9 Personal networks are key to finding a job

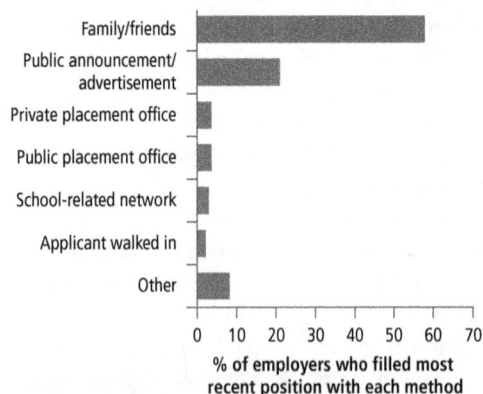

Source: Based on World Bank enterprise surveys (aggregated from surveys conducted in Angola, Botswana, Burundi, Cameroon, the Democratic Republic of Congo, The Gambia, Guinea, Mauritania, Namibia, Niger, Rwanda, Swaziland, Tanzania, and Uganda in 2006–07).

Census data from 42 Sub-Saharan African countries show that by 2010 two-fifths of Africa's urban population already lived in a big city (with a population of 1 million or more), while two-fifths lived in a small town (with less than 250,000 people; Dorosh and Thurlow 2013). The share of the population living in an urban area is expected to rise from 39 percent in 2010 to 57 percent in 2060 (Simkins 2013). Contrary to popular belief, fertility—not migration—still drives most urban population growth in Africa. After slowing from the 1960s to the 1990s, migration to urban areas has risen in recent years, but it is expected to constitute only about 30 percent of urban population growth between 2010 and 2060 (Simkins 2013).

Urbanization can be beneficial if it creates agglomeration effects that can be a source of long-term growth and structural transformation. Africa's urbanization has not yet delivered many of these beneficial effects. One reason is discussed in chapter 1: the lack of a manufacturing sector. The beneficial effects of agglomeration are more often seen in lower-income countries with the development of industy, not services, but the economy of African cities is dominated by services. Where agglomeration benefits occur in service clusters, the sectors, such as information technology, tend to require higher levels of education than most countries in Africa have. As a result, agglomeration forces are weak, and Africa remains a low-density continent (see World Bank 2008). At the same time, urban growth rates in some capital cities are very high and difficult to manage.

Africans tend to migrate within their country of origin (Sander and Maimbo 2003; McKenzie 2007; Simkins 2013). Few migrants come to Sub-Saharan Africa from outside the region, and international migration within the region is limited to a handful of "magnet" countries, such as Kenya, Nigeria, and South Africa (Simkins 2013). Most migration within countries occurs for purposes that are not directly related to employment, including education, marriage, or avoiding conflict or insecurity. Local moves in particular are often motivated by marriage. Longer moves, out of district boundaries, are more likely to be related to work. Much of the migration takes place between urban areas or between rural areas. Seasonal migration between rural areas is common in some countries, Niger for example, where it can involve up to one-third of the population (Simkins 2013).

A snapshot of migration patterns and their implications for employment mobility is provided by a recent study from Kegera, Tanzania. The study followed individuals from the predominantly rural region of Kagera in Tanzania who were 0–11 years old in 1991–94 (De Weerdt and Kutka 2013). Two decades later, in 2010, 56 percent of those individuals lived in the same or a neighboring village, 18 percent had moved to a village in the same region, 9 percent had moved to an urban area in the same region, and 8 percent had moved to another region. The main reason that young people had migrated was marriage (35 percent), followed by attending school (16 percent), looking for work (15 percent), and working (10 percent). Migration was associated with a substantial amount of employment mobility. Although 57 percent of youths ages 18–32 in 2010 who stayed in the village remained in agriculture, only 30 percent of those moving to a nearby town, and 3 percent of those moving to a city, were still working in agriculture (figure 2.10). Young people in cities were over three times more likely to be working for a wage and nearly twice as likely to be in nonfarm self-employment. These moves were associated with large increases in measured consumption. Young people who stayed in the village or moved to a local town saw incomes increase by 70 and 91 percent, respectively, between 1991 and 2010; those moving to a regional town had incomes 150 percent higher; and those who moved to a city had income gains of around 300 percent (De Weerdt and Kutka 2013). Most of these gains were associated with the move outside of agriculture.

Clearly, urban growth and migration from rural to urban areas can be a powerful engine for transforming the structure of employment. To ensure that the economic infrastructure can support both indigenous population growth and migrants, however, forward-looking urban planning and investments are required as part of an overall development strategy.

Figure 2.10 Migration increases mobility across sectors of employment

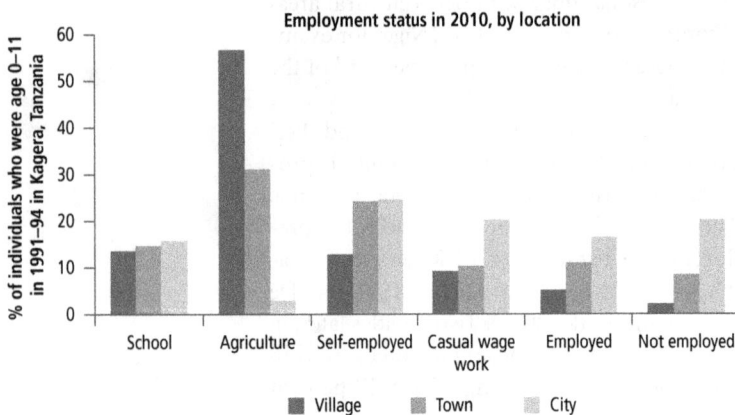

Employment status in 2010, by location

Source: De Weerdt and Kutka 2013.

The Parallel Transitions: Choices Influencing Health, Family Formation, and Civic Engagement

Certain decisions taken and habits formed during adolescence have lifelong consequences. Adolescence is when most individuals begin to have control over their own decisions and behaviors. It is also a period of experimentation, when youth start engaging in risky activities such as smoking and consuming alcohol. Youth is also the period in which sexual activity is initiated, family formation begins (figure 2.11) (see de Walque 2014). This is also the time when people begin to engage with society as citizens.

Taking Health Risks

Smoking is one of the leading preventable causes of death worldwide, and youth is when it is most likely to develop into a habit. Less than 10 percent of boys ages 13–15 smoke cigarettes in most of Africa, except the southern tip—Botswana, Namibia, and South Africa (Warren et al. 2009). This rate of tobacco use is one of the lowest in the developing world, but even so, the potential for damage should not be underestimated. As countries grow richer, they tend to pass through a cycle of tobacco prevalence (Eriksen, Mackay, and Ross 2012). The second stage of this cycle is when smoking prevalence tends to rise sharply.

Human immunodeficiency virus/acquired immune deficiency syndrome (HIV/AIDS) and teenage pregnancy are the two biggest dangers associated with teenage sexual activity, and both loom large in Africa. Sub-Saharan Africa is the region most severely affected by HIV. According to survey data collected between 2006 and 2011, the age-specific fertility rate for young women ages 15–19 (births per 1,000 women) was above 100 in all Sub-Saharan countries except Rwanda, and it surpassed 150 in Chad, Guinea, Lesotho, Madagascar, Malawi, Mali, Mozambique, and Zambia—rates that are at the higher end compared to rates in other developing regions (United Nations 2007).

In thinking about policies to prevent risky teenage behavior, it is important to consider how such behaviors are connected with the other youth transitions. For example, given the evidence that stress and mental health problems are associated with risky sexual activity and substance abuse among young people, the stress from idleness or job dissatisfaction could increase the chances of engaging in risky behavior. Another example is the rising evidence that school attendance lowers teenage sexual activity and pregnancy. A conditional cash transfer targeting young Malawian women (13–22 years of age) provided incentives to current students and dropouts to attend school and led to large increases in school enrollment as well as declines in early marriage, teenage pregnancy, sexual activity, and risky sexual behavior (Baird et al. 2010). Similarly, a study in Kenya finds that reducing the cost of schooling (by paying for uniforms) reduced dropout rates, teen marriage, and childbearing (Duflo et al. 2006). Schooling is not the only determinant, however. In the Malawi study, girls who received an *unconditional* cash transfer—a transfer not linked to school participation and performance—also had large reductions in sexual activity, teenage pregnancy, and marriage (Baird et al. 2011).

Starting a Family

Along with starting work, starting a family is one of the biggest decisions taken during youth. By the age of 25, nearly 80 percent of women in Africa have married and given birth (figure 2.11).[3] This transition happens later among men. While more than half of

Figure 2.11 Family formation starts earlier for young women than for young men

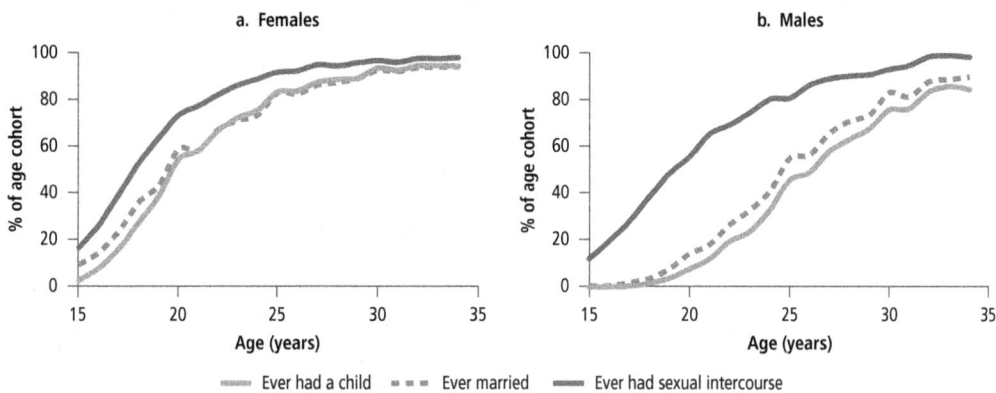

a. Females

b. Males

Ever had a child — — — Ever married —— Ever had sexual intercourse

Source: Analysis of DHS data for 28 countries (see appendix).

all women are married by the age of 20, the majority of men are likely to remain unmarried before the age of 25 and to marry only in their late 20s or early 30s.

Decisions about employment and family formation are linked. The decision to start a family is often taken after securing the means to support a family, which could be the reason why most men marry late. The linkages are particularly salient for women. Economically active women may decide to postpone marriage, schedule births later in life, and have fewer children on average than women who are not economically active. For example, in Asia and Latin America, women's employment in the garment sector has been linked to later age at marriage and lower fertility (Amin et al. 1998; McLeod et al. 2005). In the other direction, there is evidence—albeit mostly from developed countries—that childbearing lowers female labor force participation (Bloom et al. 2009). In Africa, where most employment is with the family farm or enterprise, the nature of the relationship between work and family formation may be different. Early marriage or childbearing may not prevent work so much as trap young women in low-productivity activities performed in the household.

While the main drivers of fertility are largely economic, public policy has a role in supporting healthier family formation, as financial or informational constraints may lead young parents in Africa to underinvest in family planning or maternal health services. Early pregnancy, which can have a large adverse impact on the health of both child and mother, should be of particular concern to policy makers. How young parents invest in their children will have a large impact on the well-being of future generations. Evidence is growing on the range of interventions that could prepare youth for this transition (summarized in World Bank 2003). For instance, micronutrient supplementation and food fortification for children and for young women before and during pregnancy are known to improve birth weight and subsequent child development, as are conditional cash transfers for the use of preventive health services. Other interventions, such as information campaigns on reproductive health, safe motherhood, and child health, look promising.

Exercising Citizenship

Along with participating in the civic discourse on important social, economic, and other issues, citizenship means having certain rights and obligations, such as the right to vote, which African youths exercise in large numbers (figure 2.12). Youth is also when individuals begin to express themselves as citizens in other ways, such as attending community meetings, joining with others to raise issues, or taking part in demonstrations. Survey data from 2008 indicate that in the past year between 60 and 70 percent of African youth ages 20–30 had engaged in at least one of those activities.[4]

Civic engagement is necessary for governments to take young people's ideas and aspirations into account effectively when formulating

Figure 2.12 As they get older, young people increasingly engage as citizens

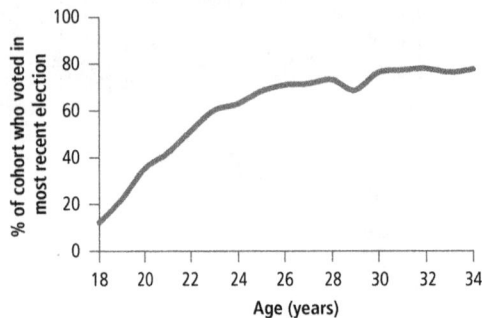

Source: Afrobarometer 2008.

policy. Such engagement is particularly relevant for policy to reflect an understanding of the types of work to which the young aspire and perhaps even to inform those aspirations. The common perception that the young are simply waiting for prized jobs in firms may have some truth, but it is unlikely to be relevant to most young people in Africa, who are predominantly rural and have little education. Some studies find that young people in low-income countries are concerned mainly about jobs that guarantee at least basic incomes and job security (Wietzke and McLeod 2012). But others suggest that the labor market aspirations of African youth are more heterogeneous. This complexity makes it all the more important to facilitate the civic channels through which the young can express themselves. If the young cannot engage as citizens, their frustrations about not being heard could foment economic and social instability. Civic organizations can also broaden access to economic opportunities for youth by providing better information and facilitating networks. This kind of action may be particularly important to previously excluded groups (such as women) and to youth from disadvantaged backgrounds.

Challenges for Females Transitioning to Work

Employment opportunities are more constrained for young women than for young men. Women are less likely to be able to leave agriculture, and they are also less likely to gain wage employment. Women's employment opportunities are constrained not only by the fact that they tend to exit school earlier, but also by gender-specific constraints associated with marriage and fertility choices. Women's employment opportunities are also more likely to be constrained by occupational segregation, social norms, or the fear of sexual harassment.

Many young women in Africa have to decide at the same time whether and how to enter the labor market and whether and when to have children. For some women, marrying and having children (or marrying early) can be a means to escape from poverty by relying on men for economic support. Although recent analysis suggests that young women in Africa are delaying having children in comparison with previous generations, fertility rates for young women remain much higher in Africa than in other regions (Sneeringer 2009). Across Africa, 25 percent of females ages 15–19 have already had their first child or are pregnant.[5] By the time they reach age 20, the average age at first job, they are already caring for young children.

Once faced with responsibility for child care, young women are constrained in their employment choices. They may choose not to work, they may work fewer hours than they otherwise would, or they may choose occupations that offer flexible schedules and home-based work. In Liberia, 41 percent of young women, compared to 31 percent of adult women and just 11 percent of young males, reported family responsibilities as a reason for "inactivity" (Ruiz Abril 2008). A time-use study in Guinea concluded that women, in particular, cannot increase the number of hours devoted to paid work because of their care duties (Bardasi and Wodon 2009). Where care options are limited, the need for flexible work arrangements pushes women from formal into informal work that can be combined with child care, such as HEs. The experience from developed countries suggests that while part-time work is often a good option for women seeking flexibility, it can often trap them in low-quality jobs even after that flexibility is no longer needed (World Bank 2011).

Gender segregation in jobs is evident throughout Sub-Saharan Africa, as in other developing regions. Men are concentrated in manufacturing, construction, mining, and transportation, while women are concentrated in retail trade, education, health, and social work. Gender segregation has potentially large effects on overall productivity and economic growth by allocating labor in a less than optimal way. Labor force surveys in Africa consistently find that women are concentrated in sectors with low wages and low productivity. For example, the 2010 Liberia labor force survey found that women are underrepresented in the growth sectors of mining, manufacturing, construction, and services (LISGIS 2011). Even though women have made strides in entering the services sector in the past 20 years, they continue to lag in industry (ILO 2012). When women strike out on their own as entrepreneurs, they still tend to work in less productive, female-dominated sectors. In agriculture, plots controlled by women are much more likely to be used for less profitable staple food crops, while male-controlled plots are used for cash crops (see World Bank 2011, ch. 5). These patterns are reinforced by the fact that training for women is often concentrated in less lucrative female-dominated trades, such as arts and crafts, tailoring, and hairdressing (discussed in chapter 3; Fox et al. 2011).

Social norms strongly shape women's employment opportunities. Expectations with respect to child care duties, mobility and transport, and occupational choice all play a role. When women do choose to work outside of the home, they often spend more time traveling on slower modes of transport; as a result, they are limited to employment options closer to home (Uteng 2011). Lack of agency also restricts their options. In a focus group in Bombouaka, Togo, young women said that a husband would likely veto a job that requires a woman to travel outside the village (Petesch and Rodríguez Caillava 2012).

Domestic and child care responsibilities and concerns about their reputations and safety make it much harder for women to travel: "If a woman is gone for a few days, people would start making up all sorts of bad stories about her. The norm is that a woman should stay at home and raise her children and look after the home," says a young woman from Ezinyathini, South Africa. In that village, another explains, "My parents would never allow me to go to other places. They think I will fall pregnant and bring shame upon the family name" (Petesch and Rodríguez Caillava 2012). A young woman who is well educated might be able to take a distant job—for instance, as a teacher.

Sexual harassment may also affect women's employment options. Nationally representative statistics on the prevalence of sexual harassment are hard to find, but smaller surveys have found that the perceived risk of harassment from bosses and other authority figures factors highly into a woman's choice of work. In qualitative assessments conducted in Liberia and Rwanda in advance of job training programs, young women reported a preference for self-employment or female-dominated industries because of the threat of sexual harassment.[6] Surveys have found similar sentiments among female entrepreneurs in Tanzania (Holla, Leonard, and Wilson 2010). Negative experiences with teachers in school (for example, teachers trading sex for grades) can reduce the willingness of prospective trainees to participate in training programs. Risks of harassment are particularly high for women who work in other people's homes, where the isolation of the work and the dependence on the employer for housing and food can make workers especially vulnerable to physical and sexual violence, nonpayment of wages, limitations on mobility, and (in extreme cases) forced labor.

Cross-border traders are particularly vulnerable. A recent survey of traders on the border between Rwanda and the Democratic Republic of Congo documented high rates of threats, harassment, and violence such as beatings, stripping, and even rape among the predominantly female traders (Brenton et al. 2011). A survey of Liberian female cross-border traders in 2007 revealed that, in addition to traditional challenges such as high duties, lack of market information, and lack of capital, women also reported high rates of sexual harassment and rape. The survey also found that women were more likely than men to join or to form groups to jointly transport goods to reduce costs, improve safety, and collectively resolve disputes with border authorities (UNWomen 2012).

"For women, distance becomes a barrier because of lack of bicycles and a bad eye on women who ride bicycles." Tanzania

"When I was looking for (secretarial) work here in Mombasa, I went to a certain company, and when I showed that boss my papers he said it was OK, but then I had to give him a date first." Kenya

Facilitating Transitions from School, to Work, and across Sectors of Employment

In all likelihood, most young people who enter into employment over the next 10 years in Sub-Saharan Africa will continue to work in the same sectors as the previous generation, with some expansion into the HE sector, especially in market towns and rural areas near population centers. The transition from school to work will continue to be unstructured and often slow for these youths. Agriculture is the gateway to work and, for many, will become the sector of lifetime employment. If productivity and earnings in agriculture do not improve, the wider economy in rural areas, where the majority of the population still lives, will be depressed, and the options for youth will shrink.

Once youth start working—whether in agriculture, HEs, or wage jobs—they tend to stay in the same sector, with mobility across sectors being slightly higher in urban than in rural areas. Migration offers an opportunity to change these patterns and substantially increase earnings. For young women, the transition from school to high-productivity work entails additional challenges. The remainder of this report identifies ways to support young people in making these transitions, by equipping them with the skills that will be needed wherever they work (chapter 3) and by ensuring that the business environment and their human capital are conducive to high productivity in agriculture (chapter 4), HEs (chapter 5), and the modern wage sector (chapter 6).

Notes

1. Based on analysis of Uganda national panel survey data.
2. The study is based on the Tanzania household urban panel survey, which collects retrospective information on previous jobs (Bridges et al. 2013).
3. The percentage of women who have given birth can include unmarried women.
4. Based on analysis of Afrobarometer round 4 surveys (Afrobarometer 2008) in 20 African countries: Benin, Botswana, Burkina Faso, Cape Verde, Ghana, Kenya, Lesotho, Liberia, Madagascar, Malawi, Mali, Mozambique, Namibia, Nigeria, Senegal, South Africa, Tanzania, Uganda, Zambia, and Zimbabwe.
5. Average across the most recent demographic and health surveys in Sub-Saharan Africa for which this indicator is available. Based on calculations using DHS StatCompiler.
6. In Liberia, 20 percent of those who reported a preference for self-employment mentioned avoiding sexual harassment as a reason for their preference (Ruiz Abril 2008).

References

Afrobarometer. 2008. Abrobarmeter Surveys Round 4. http://www.afrobarometer.org/.

Amin, Sajeda, Ian Diamond, Ruchira T. Naved, and Margaret Newby. 1998. "Transition to Adulthood of Female Garment-Factory Workers in Bangladesh." *Studies in Family Planning* 29 (2): 185–200.

Baird, Sarah, Ephraim Chirwa, Craig McIntosh, and Berk Özler. 2010. "The Short-Term Impacts of a Schooling Conditional Cash Transfer Program on the Sexual Behavior of Young Women." *Health Economics* 19 (1): 55–68. doi: 10.1002/hec.1569.

———. 2011. "Cash or Condition? Evidence from a Cash Transfer Experiment." *Quarterly Journal of Economics* 126 (4): 1709–53.

Bardasi, Elena, and Quentin Wodon. 2009. "Working Long Hours and Having No Choice: Time Poverty in Guinea." Policy Research Working Paper 4961, World Bank, Washington, DC.

Beegle, Kathleen, Rajeev H. Dehejia, and Roberta Gatti. 2009. "Why Should We Care about Child Labor? The Education, Labor Market, and Health Consequences of Child Labor." *Journal of Human Resources* 44 (4): 871–89.

Beegle, Kathleen, Rajeev H. Dehejia, Roberta Gatti, and Sofya Krutikova. 2008. "The Consequences of Child Labor: Evidence from Longitudinal Data in Rural Tanzania." Policy Research Working Paper 4677, World Bank, Washington, DC. doi: 10.1596/1813-9450-4677.

Blattman, Chistopher, and Jeannie Annan. 2010. "The Consequences of Child Soldiering." *Review of Economics and Statistics* 92 (4): 882–98.

Bloom, David E., David Canning, Günther Fink, and Jocelyn E. Finlay. 2009. "Fertility, Female Labor Force Participation, and the Demographic Dividend." *Journal of Economic Growth* 14 (2): 79–101.

Bossuroy, Thomas, and Denis Cogneau. 2013. "Social Mobility in Five African Countries." *Review of Income and Wealth* 59: s84–110. doi: 10.1111/roiw.12037

Brenton, Paul, Celestin Bashinge Bucekuderhwa, Caroline Hossein, Shiho Nagaki, and Jean Baptiste Ntagoma. 2011. "Risky Business: Poor Women Cross-Border Traders in the Great Lakes Region of Africa." Africa Trade Policy Notes 11, World Bank, Washington, DC.

Bridges, Sarah, Louise Fox, Alessio Gaggero, and Trudy Owens. 2013. "Labour Market Entry and Earnings: Evidence from Tanzanian Retrospective Data." Background paper presented at the CSAE Conference on Economic Development in Africa, Oxford University, March.

de Walque, Damien, ed. 2014. *Risking Your Health: Causes, Consequences, and Interventions to Prevent Risky Behaviors.* Washington, DC: World Bank.

De Weerdt, Joachim, and Andreas Kutka. 2013. "Urbanisation and Youth Employment in Tanzania: Preliminary Analysis." Background paper, World Bank, Washington, DC.

Dorosh, Paul, and James Thurlow. 2013. "Agriculture and Small Towns in Africa." *Agricultural Economics* 44 (4-5): 449–59. doi: 10.1111/agec.12027.

Duflo, Esther, Pascaline Dupas, Michael Kremer, and Samuel Sinei. 2006. "Education and HIV/AIDS Prevention: Evidence from a Randomized Evaluation in Western Kenya." Policy Research Working Paper 4024, World Bank, Washington, DC.

Eriksen, Michael, Judith Mackay, and Hana Ross. 2012. *The Tobacco Atlas.* 4th ed. Atlanta: American Cancer Society.

Falco, Paolo, William F. Maloney, Bob Rijkers, and Mauricio Sarrias. 2012. "Heterogeneity in Subjective Well-Being: An Application to Occupational Allocation in Africa." Policy Research Working Paper 6244, World Bank, Washington, DC. doi: 10.1596/1813-9450-6244.

Fox, Louise, Katie Kibbuka, Jorge Huerta Munoz, and Thomas Pave Sohnesen. 2011. "Small Is Big: Development of the Household Enterprise Sector in Ghana; a Quantitative Look at Household Enterprises." World Bank, Washington, DC.

Holla, Alaka, Sibomana Leonard, and Wema Wilson. 2010. "The Secret Lives of Economically Empowered Women: Qualitative Evidence on Sensitive Issues from Female Entrepreneurs in Dar es Salaam." World Bank, Washington, DC.

ILO (International Labour Organization). 2012. *Global Employment Trends for Women, 2012.* Geneva: ILO.

LISGIS (Liberia Institute of Statistics and Geo-Information Services). 2011. "Report on the Liberia Labor Force Survey 2010." LISGIS, Monrovia.

Lundberg, Mattias, and Alice Wuermli, eds. 2012. *Children and Youth in Crisis: Protecting and Promoting Human Development in Times of Economic Shocks.* Washington, DC: World Bank.

McKenzie, David. 2007. "A Profile of the World's Young Developing Country Migrants." IZA Discussion Paper 2948, Institute for the Study of Labor, Bonn.

McLeod, D., R. Ramirez, M. Davalos, and W. Gruben. 2005. "Apparel Jobs: Ladder Up or Poverty Trap?" Paper presented at the 2005 meeting of the Latin America and Caribbean Economics Association, Paris, October 27–29.

Pasquier-Doumer, Laure. 2013. "Intergenerational Transmission of Self-Employed Status in the Informal Sector: A Constrained Choice or Better Income Prospects? Evidence from Seven West African Countries." *Journal of African Economies* 22 (1): 73–111. doi: http://dx.doi.org/10.1093/jae/ejs017.

Petesch, P., and Rodríguez Caillava, I. 2012. "Voices of Young Villagers in Sub-Saharan Africa." Background paper, World Bank, Washington, DC.

Ruiz Abril, Maria Elena. 2008. "Liberia: Girls Vulnerability Assessment." Government of Liberia, Nike Foundation, and World Bank, Washington, DC. https://docs.google.com/document/d/1FvEgQNMsZHVfMLYxfp62DUly8nY1850lh2vGmiYHk_0/edit?hl=en_US&pli=1.

Sander, Cerstin, and Samuel Munzele Maimbo. 2003. "Migrant Labor Remittances in Africa: Reducing Obstacles to Developmental Contributions." Africa Region Working Paper 64, World Bank, Washington, DC.

Simkins, Charles. 2013. "Urbanization in Africa and Its Relation to the Demographic Dividend." Background paper for the Africa Regional Study on the Demographic Dividend, World Bank, Washington, DC.

Sneeringer, Stacy E. 2009. "Fertility Transition in Sub-Saharan Africa: A Comparative Analysis of Trends in 30 Countries." DHS Comparative Reports 23, ICR Macro, Calverton, MD.

United Nations. 2007. "Age-Specific Fertility Rate." United Nations, Statistics Division, New York. http://data.un.org/Data.aspx?d=GenderStat&f=inID%3A13.

UNWomen. 2012. "Breaking the Cycle of Violence and HIV in Liberia." http://www.unwomen.org/en/news/stories/2012/7/breaking-the-cycle-of-violence-and-hiv-in-liberia/.

Uteng, Tanu Priya. 2011. "Gender and Mobility in the Developing World." Background paper for the *World Development Report 2012: Gender Equality and Development*, World Bank, Washington, DC.

Warren, Charles W., Samira Asma, Juliette Lee, Veronica Lea, and Judith Mackay. 2009. *Global Tobacco Surveillance System: The GTSS Atlas.* Atlanta, GA: CDC Foundation.

Wietzke, Frank-Borge, and Catriona McLeod. 2012. "Jobs, Well-Being, and Social Cohesion: Evidence from Value and Perception Surveys." Background paper for *World Development Report 2013*, World Bank, Washington, DC. https://openknowledge. worldbank.org/bitstream/handle/10986/12138/ WDR2013_bp_Jobs_Wellbeing_SocialCohesion. pdf?sequence=1.

World Bank. 2003. *World Development Report 2004: Making Services Work for Poor People.* New York: Oxford University Press.

———. 2006. *World Development Report 2007: Development and the Next Generation.* New York: Oxford University Press.

———. 2008. *World Development Report 2009: Reshaping Economic Geography.* New York: Oxford University Press.

———. 2011. *World Development Report 2012: Gender Equality and Development.* New York: Oxford University Press.

———. 2012a. "Kenya at Work: Energizing the Economy and Creating Jobs." *Kenya Economic Update* 7 (December).

———. 2012b. *World Development Report 2013: Jobs.* New York: Oxford University Press.

Chapter 3

Skills for Productive Employment

A critical part of the policy agenda for youth employment in Africa is to strengthen human capital. Although training alone will not deliver more and better jobs for youth—much also depends on policies to strengthen the business environment, as discussed elsewhere in this report—the education that young people receive and the skills they acquire can expand the spectrum of employment opportunities they can access and the earnings they are likely to command. Skills strongly influence where people work and how much they earn. A key problem is that across Africa rapid increases in school participation and educational attainment have come at the cost of quality, contributing to a serious shortfall in the skills for productive employment. Those skills include basic and higher-order cognitive skills, behavioral and socioemotional skills, technical or vocational skills, and business skills.

To facilitate entry, improve productivity, and raise earnings across the range of employment in agriculture, household enterprises (HEs), and the modern wage sector, the most pressing priority is to increase the quality of schooling and ensure that it delivers actual learning and skills. Other important priorities are to identify and directly build the socioemotional and behavioral skills that contribute to productivity, including

the skills demanded by employers, and to build the evidence needed to guide specific programs to improve skills for youth employment. Governments must also bear in mind that a dynamic private market exists for training and avoid introducing undue distortions in this market. Priority areas for government intervention are to provide information and facilitate access to existing training for disadvantaged youths (such as young women or the poorest) as well as to ensure the availability of better-quality training options. In the presence of active training markets, public interventions need to be selective, performance driven, and evidence based.

Low educational achievement and limited skills contribute to difficult transitions into work and limited employment mobility among African youth. Education and skills open pathways into productive employment. Schooling is a good predictor of an individual's eventual occupation, but the quality of education also matters for productivity. In Africa more children attend school than ever before. Yet the generally poor quality of the education they receive means that schooling has relatively small effects on productivity, earnings, and poverty reduction. Rapid improvements in the quality

Figure 3.1 Primary school completion rates have risen substantially in Sub-Saharan Africa, 1990–2011

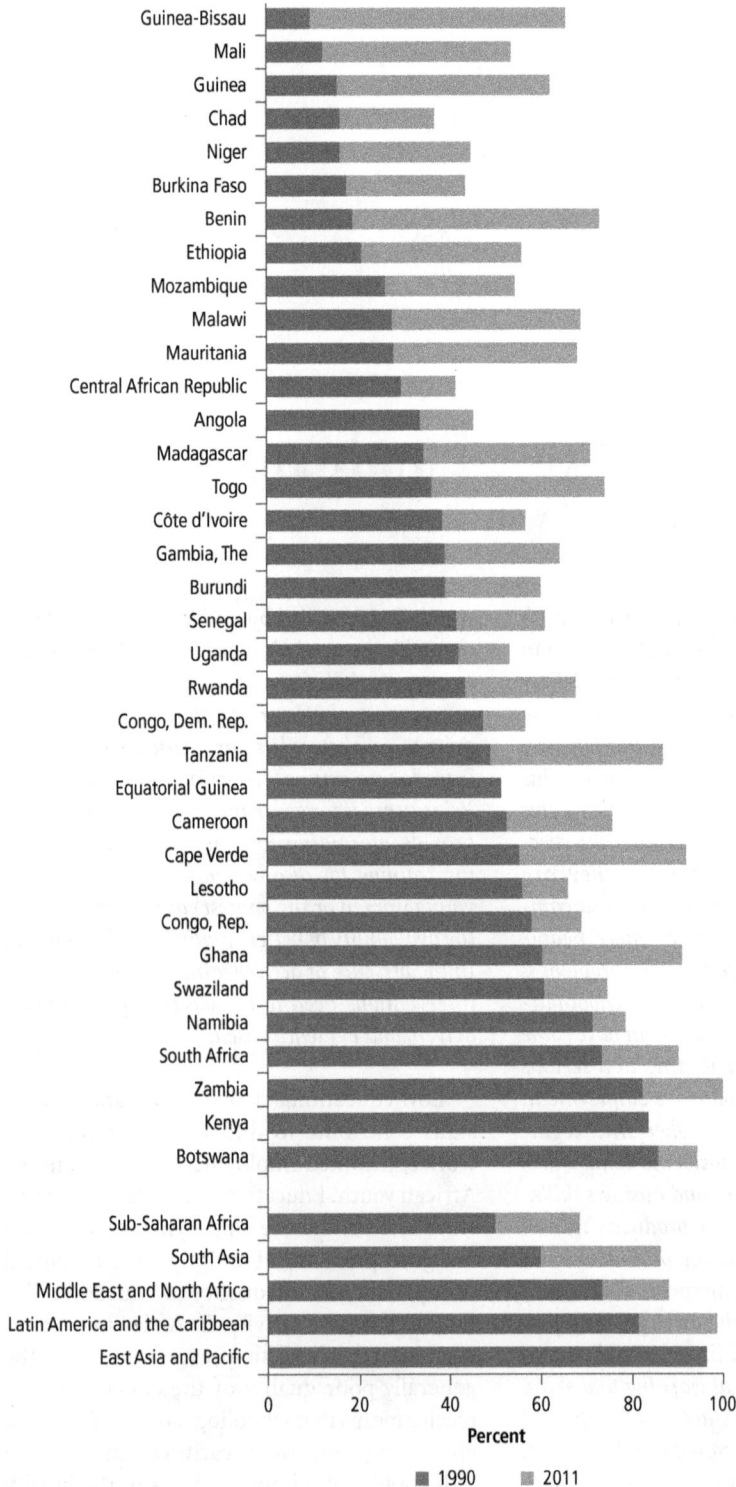

Source: World Bank various years.

of learning provided in school are critical to increase the productivity and earnings of Africa's youth.

Schooling, Educational Attainment, and Work

Measured against the objective set by the Millennium Development Goal for education—"ensure that all boys and girls complete a full course of primary schooling"—Sub-Saharan Africa has made remarkable progress. Across the region, the share of children completing primary school rose from 51 percent in 1990 to 70 percent in 2011. Some countries made exceptional progress (figure 3.1). Burkina Faso, Chad, Ethiopia, Madagascar, Malawi, Mauritania, Mozambique, and Niger *more than doubled* their primary completion rates; Benin, Guinea, Guinea-Bissau, and Mali *more than tripled* theirs. These achievements rival those of countries with the best historical increases, such as the Republic of Korea, and far exceed those typical of most developing countries since 1960 (Clemens 2004). An average young Ghanaian or Zambian today has more schooling than an average French or Italian person in 1960 (Pritchett 2013).

Nevertheless, these improvements started from a very low base, and Sub-Saharan Africa lags behind other world regions in primary school completion. The young people entering Africa's labor force right now have more schooling than any previous generation, but they still have little overall schooling. Nearly 60 percent of 15- to 24-year-olds have completed only primary school (figure 3.2). Among the group that is most likely to have exited school for good—those who are 25–34 years old—30 percent have no education, 21 percent have completed only some primary schooling, and 14 percent have completed only primary education. About 35 percent have continued beyond primary school, and 19 percent have gone beyond lower-secondary school. Educational attainment is higher in urban areas, although more than 40 percent of 25- to 34-year-olds in those areas have not completed lower-secondary school.

Figure 3.2 Africa's young people have more education than ever before, but average education attainment is still low

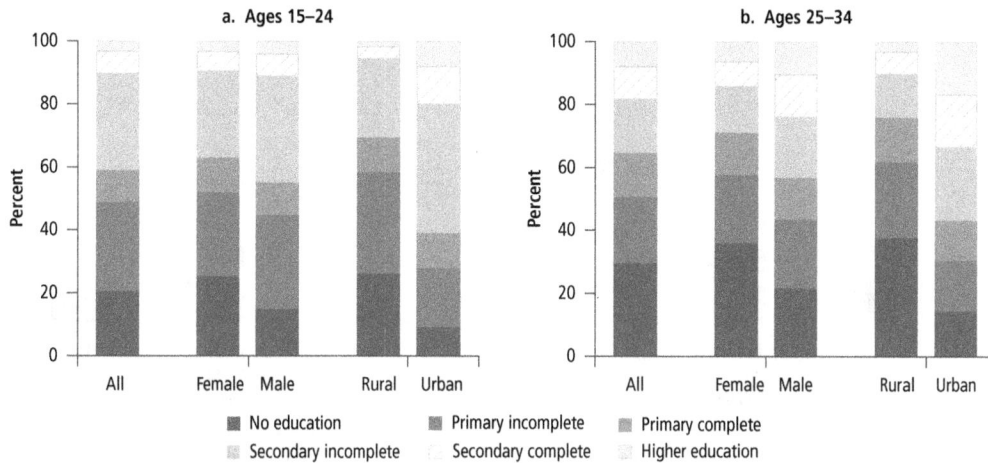

Source: Based on demographic and health surveys in 30 countries (see appendix).

Figure 3.3 Educational attainment in Sub-Saharan Africa is projected to rise substantially

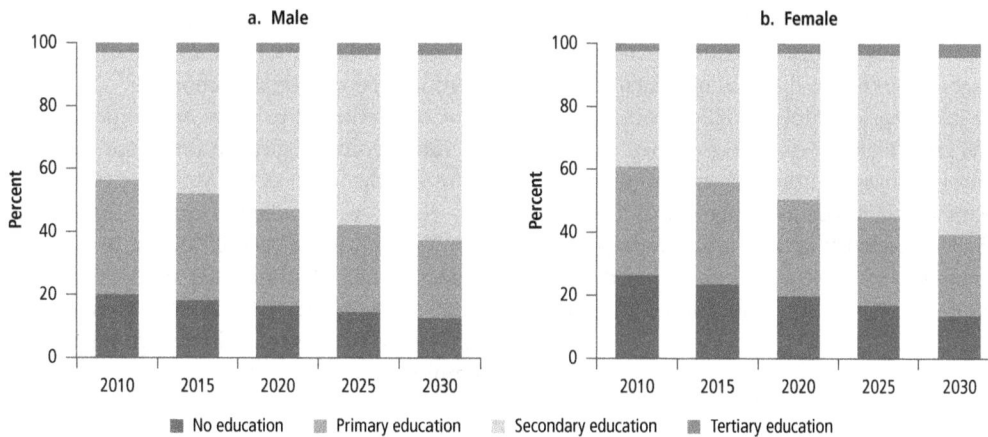

Source: Based on International Institute for Applied Systems Analysis data.

Younger generations are likely to do better. Thanks to recent progress in getting children into school, incoming cohorts should have substantially higher levels of education than past cohorts—in fact, they will be the most highly educated cohort ever in Africa. By 2020, more than half of men ages 15–24 are projected to have attained secondary education; women will cross that threshold in 2025 (figure 3.3). Of course these projections depend on policies to come, and they are only a rough guide to actual outcomes. Moreover, greater access to school-

ing has come at the cost of learning outcomes, as discussed later.

Schooling and Sector of Employment

The links between educational attainment and sector of employment are very clear. Most people who never finish primary school work in agriculture. Those with a primary or lower-secondary education work in nonfarm household enterprises (HEs), whereas those with higher levels of education are more likely to enter the modern wage sector.

Figure 3.4 **Schooling maps to sector of employment**

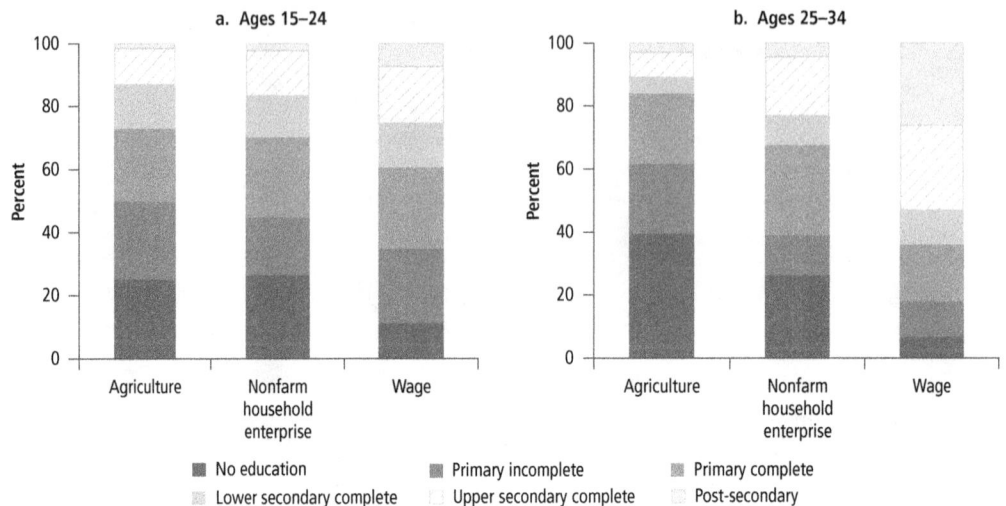

a. Ages 15–24

b. Ages 25–34

No education · Primary incomplete · Primary complete · Lower secondary complete · Upper secondary complete · Post-secondary

Source: Based on standardized and harmonized household and labor force surveys (see appendix).

Since schooling strongly influences the sector in which people work, the educational profile of wage earners is very different from that of workers in the agricultural and HE sectors in Africa. The great majority of youths and young adults working in agriculture never completed primary school. Close to 80 percent of those ages 25–34 who work in agriculture have primary schooling or less; 40 percent have no education at all (figure 3.4). The educational attainment of youths and young adults who work in HEs is only somewhat better, but about half have not completed even primary schooling.

Completion of primary or additional education becomes the norm only among young adults in the wage sector. Almost 65 percent of 15- to 24-year-olds who work for wages have completed primary school. Because youths who transition out of school later are more likely to enter the wage sector, the share of young adults (25–34) who finished primary school and are employed in that sector increases to over 80 percent. Wage employees are significantly more likely to have a secondary or a tertiary education: among 25- to 34-year-olds, wage employees are more than twice as likely as the self-employed to have completed secondary schooling.

Wage workers with more schooling are also more likely to work under contract—an indicator that they perform more formal modern wage work (figure 3.5). Close to 70 percent of wage employees without primary schooling lack a contract, compared to less than 40 percent of those with upper-secondary schooling.

The relationships between schooling and work in each sector are broadly similar across various subgroups of the population, with two main distinctions. First, women are substantially more likely to work in the nonfarm HE

Figure 3.5 **Wage workers with more schooling are more likely to work under contract**

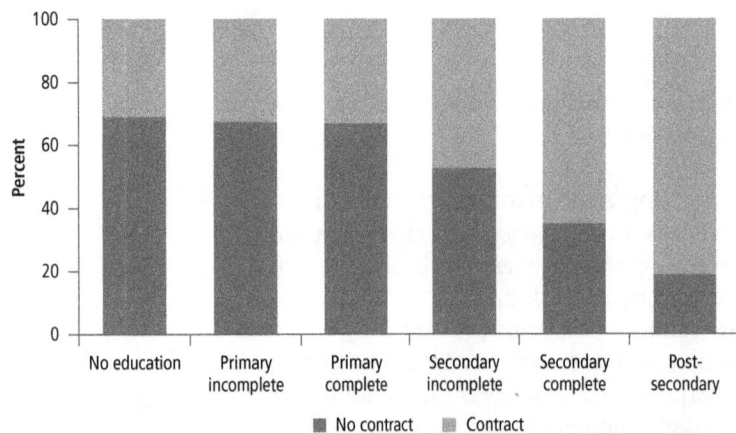

No contract · Contract

Source: Based on standardized and harmonized household and labor force surveys (see appendix).

Figure 3.6 Relationships between schooling and work vary depending on gender and urbanization

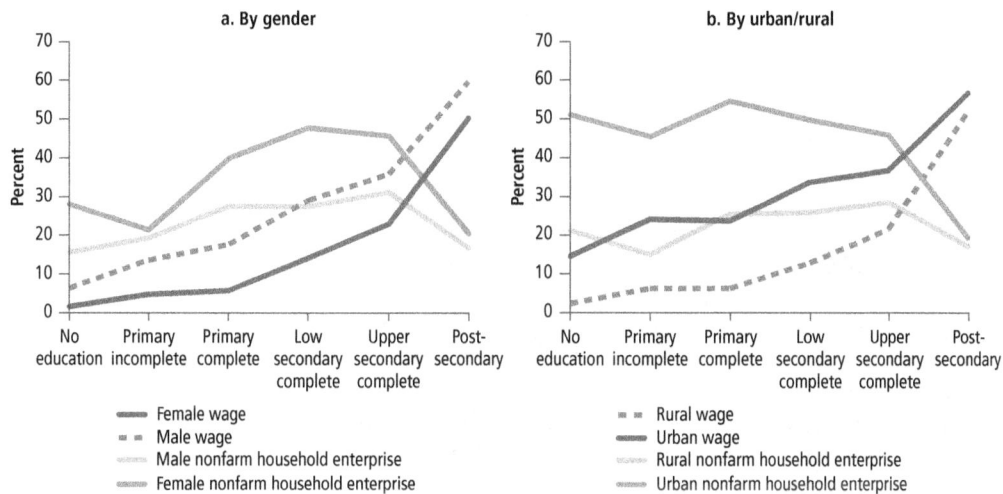

a. By gender

b. By urban/rural

Source: Based on standardized and harmonized household and labor force surveys (see appendix).

sector as their educational attainment rises, suggesting that education facilitates women's transition out of agriculture (figure 3.6). Second, participation in the wage sector begins at lower levels of educational attainment in urban areas, reflecting the larger pool of educated youth in urban areas as well as the greater availability of jobs for relatively unskilled workers in the modern wage sector.

Will Workers' Increasing Educational Attainment Change Employment Patterns?

There is potential for employment patterns to shift, if current patterns in educational attainment and sector of work persist in Africa and if educational attainment improves as projected. Africa is positioned for a large shift of workers out of the farm sector and into HEs, along with an increase in modern wage sector employment.

Analysis of past trends in four countries (Al-Samarrai and Bennell 2007) suggests that increasing shares of secondary school graduates are working in self-employment (Malawi, Tanzania, and Zimbabwe, for example), except where economic growth has led to the creation of substantially more self-employment and wage jobs (Uganda). The employment projections in chapter 1 suggest that even a growing

modern wage sector cannot absorb the incoming cohorts of youth. The majority of young people will still create their own livelihoods. As a result, a growing share of workers in agriculture and nonfarm HEs will probably have higher levels of schooling.

Shifts in employment patterns will not occur automatically. Additional years of schooling that impart actual competencies will be needed for young people to develop the skills that can promote such a shift. Research has suggested that higher levels of educational achievement and cognitive skills are associated with overall economic growth (Hanushek and Woessmann 2012) as well as with the employment of a larger share of youth in modern wage jobs outside of agriculture (Lee and Newhouse 2012). If increases in educational attainment are not associated with a greater accumulation of skills, schooling will have a limited effect on overall growth and composition of employment. Then there is the demand side of the labor market to consider. The economy will need to generate new employment opportunities to make use of the learning and skills acquired by young people. As discussed throughout this report, policies to address human capital are not sufficient in themselves to address the youth employment challenge; improvements in the business environment are needed as well.

"Education guarantees a better job and a stable life."
Togo

Schooling Increases Productivity and Earnings

Schooling is associated not only with the sector in which youth—and older workers—work, but also with greater productivity and earnings. Therefore, in addition to facilitating entry into nonfarm HEs and modern wage jobs, education is also essential to tackle the policy challenge of increasing workers' productivity across the spectrum of employment.

The education level of household members is a strong determinant of standards of living. Households where adults have attained higher levels of schooling have substantially higher consumption levels per capita than households where members have less schooling. This difference partly reflects the selection of workers into sectors described previously.

Considerable research in the agricultural sector indicates that farmers with primary schooling tend to have higher profits than farmers without schooling, even for those holding similar assets. Educated farmers generally are the first to adopt new seeds, tillage practices, fertilizer, and animal breeds (see, for example, Welch 1970; Huffman 1977; Besley and Case 1993; Foster and Rosenzweig 1995; Abdulai and Huffman 2005). The benefit of education is particularly pronounced in environments undergoing rapid technical change (Foster and Rosenzweig 2010). More educated farmers are more likely to adopt new agricultural technologies first, either because they initially have more information about the technology or because they are able to learn more than less educated farmers exposed to the same information. Schooling enhances the capacity to learn throughout life. The introduction of new technologies is a learning opportunity that reveals the complementarity between schooling and the adoption of profitable new technology.

Outside of agriculture, in the HE and wage sectors, the link between education and earnings is strong. Figure 3.7 shows that higher levels of education among HE owners are associated with higher earnings in Ghana, Rwanda, Tanzania, and Uganda. Figure 3.8 shows the average wage increment associated with increasing levels of education by comparing wage workers at each education level to uneducated workers in a sample of nine African countries. In both figures, earnings differentials are adjusted for the age, gender, and rural or urban location of the worker. The figures should not be understood as indicating "returns to education." They merely capture an association between education and earnings and may not fully control for factors that confound the analysis (box 3.1 discusses the challenges in estimating returns to education).

Earnings Tend to Increase Little with Only a Few Years of Primary Schooling

A review of rates of return to education across several developing countries finds that the mean rate of return to an additional year of education is almost 9 percent (Banerjee and Duflo 2005). In other words, six years of primary schooling yield an increment of almost 70 percent. Although figures 3.7 and 3.8 do not necessarily represent estimates of rates of return to education (box 3.1), they illustrate an association between earnings and education that is substantially lower than the link documented in other developing countries. A few years of basic education appear to yield much lower productivity gains in Africa than in other regions.

For instance, owners of HEs who have not completed primary education do not earn sig-

Figure 3.7   Education is associated with higher earnings in household enterprises

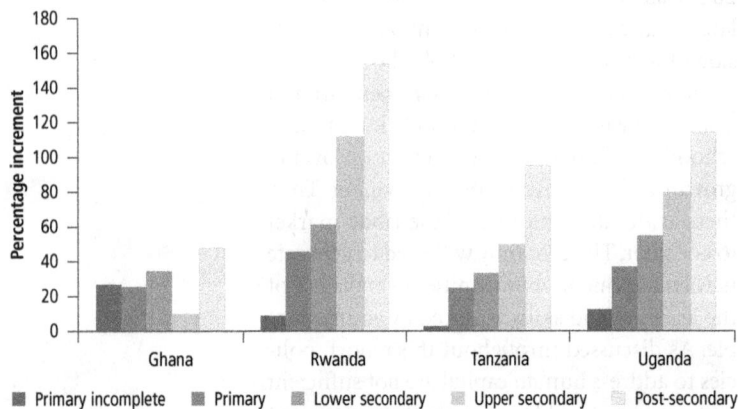

Source: Based on standardized and harmonized household and labor force surveys (see appendix).
Note: Figure displays net average earnings (sales minus expenditures per month) for a sample of self-employed owners of HEs by level of education (relative to HE owners without education).

nificantly more than owners of HEs without any education—suggesting that minimal productivity gains are associated with a few years of primary school (figure 3.7).[1]

In contrast, HE owners who have completed primary education earn significantly more than HE owners who have no education. The earnings increment associated with primary school completion ranges from 25 percent in Ghana to 46 percent in Rwanda. Low earnings differentials at low levels of education are a serious issue, because most young people in the HE sector have not completed primary school.[2]

In the wage sector, workers with incomplete primary schooling earn a modest premium (10–25 percent on average) compared to workers with no education, and often the difference is not even statistically significant (Ghana, Mozambique, and Sierra Leone).[3] In contrast, wage workers who have completed primary education earn consistently more than uneducated wage workers. The wages of primary school completers typically are more than 20 percent higher than the wages of workers without education; the gap reaches as much as 52 percent in Cameroon. Wage workers with upper-secondary education typically earn wages that are 100–150 percent higher than those without education.

Earnings Increase Faster with Education beyond Primary School

In contrast with the limited earnings gains associated with a few years of basic education, earnings and wages increase faster when education extends beyond primary school. For owners of HEs, the increment in earnings associated with completing lower-secondary education ranges from around 35 percent in Ghana and Tanzania to around 60 percent in Rwanda and Uganda. Upper-secondary and postsecondary education are associated with even higher increments to earnings, although few individuals in the HE sector acquire that much education.[4]

These descriptive patterns are consistent with more robust econometric evidence tackling the selection issues involved in estimating returns to education (Fasih et al. 2012), particularly in Africa and in the HE sector.[5] An

Figure 3.8 Education is associated with higher wages

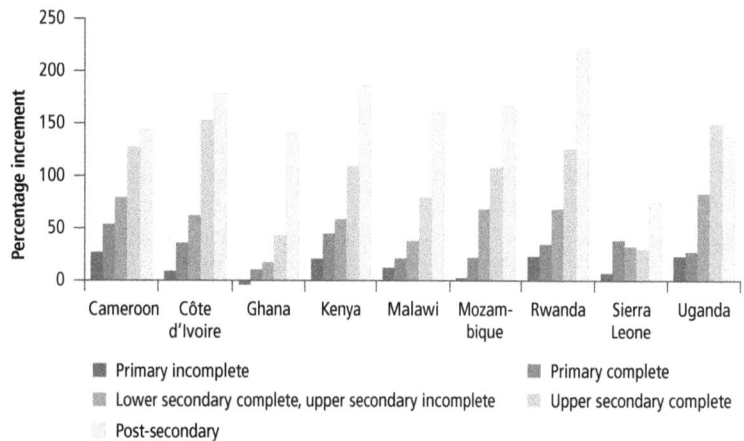

Source: Based on standardized and harmonized household and labor force surveys (see appendix).
Note: Based on a regression of hourly wages (in logs) by education level, adjusted for age, gender, and whether the workplace is urban or rural. Figure displays hourly wages among wage workers by level of education (relative to workers without education). The dependent variable is ln (wage/hours) using information from the last seven days. Wages were adjusted for local consumer price index (2005 = 100) and purchasing power parity. This dependent variable was run against the dummy level of education variables listed above, and the "no education" dummy was excluded. As the mean wage among those with no education is normalized to zero, the wages shown are not absolute but are depicted in comparison to workers with no education. Workers are ages 20–64.

analysis of seven cities in West Africa found evidence of strong associations between education and earnings in HEs as well as evidence of an increase in the earnings premium across education levels (figure 3.9; Kuepie, Nordman, and Roubaud 2009). In particular, the study found that marginal returns for an additional year of postprimary education are higher than marginal returns associated with an additional year of primary education.

As seen in figure 3.8, individuals in the wage sector who have completed upper-secondary school earn 30–155 percent more than individuals without any schooling. Postsecondary education is associated with a premium of 70–200 percent over no schooling. As in the HE sector, the increment in earnings is substantially higher at higher levels of education (Teal 2010; Söderbom, Teal, and Harding 2006; Bigsten et al. 2000). Each additional year of schooling in Kenya, for example, is estimated to increase earnings by 3 percent among those with only 1–7 years of schooling, 9 percent among those with 8–11 years, and 24 percent among those with 12 years or more (Söderbom, Teal, and Harding 2006). A review of studies concludes

Box 3.1

Estimating the returns to education

When the more educated differ inherently from the less educated, the relationship observed between earnings and education levels ceases to be a reliable guide to the causal impact of schooling on earnings and productivity. For instance, when the more educated are of higher-than-average innate ability, the earnings gap observed between individuals with high and low levels of education partly reflects the higher-than-average ability of the more educated group. An individual of average ability and an individual of above-average ability should not expect the same outcome from the same education. If those who are more educated are also more likely to come from advantaged backgrounds, then the measured returns to education would be overstated, since they include returns to family background. In the wage sector, they can also reflect connections in labor markets, particularly because job referrals from family members appear to be particularly important in developing countries.

Concerns about bias arising from omitted factors or selection effects have motivated an entire field of research focused on correctly measuring the causal impact of education on earnings. One approach is to adjust the estimates for omitted factors by including their proxy measures in a regression analysis (for example, by using measures of cognitive skills to proxy for innate ability). However, this approach may not correct for all omitted factors. For that reason, some of the best-regarded studies have chosen to take advantage of "natural experiments"—instances in which policies or

supply-side factors have influenced levels of schooling independently of confounding factors such as ability. A surprising finding is that the estimates of the returns to schooling from such natural experiments are not much lower than unadjusted estimates. Although quasi-experimental methods relying on "natural experiments" or other econometric techniques cannot eliminate all bias resulting from omitted variables, the typically high estimates emerging from these careful studies make it much harder to reject the idea that schooling leads to substantial earnings gains.

Developed countries have produced a vast body of evidence on the adjusted returns to schooling. The studies use a range of econometric techniques to correct for the problems just mentioned. Estimates from studies in developing countries tend to be higher than those from developed countries, but developing countries rarely provide opportunities to use panel data or natural experiments to identify causal effects. One of the best-cited examples concerns the impact of a program to build schools in Indonesia (Duflo 2001). The study benefited from the fact that the program, launched in 1974, differentially increased school opportunities among children from different cohorts and different regions. Looking at wages in 1995, the study found returns to education in the range of 6.8–10.6 percent, approximately similar to returns found in previous studies. A recent review of rates of return to education across multiple countries found that the mean rate of return to an additional year of education was almost 9 percent (Banerjee and Duflo 2005).

that while the wage gains associated with an additional year of secondary or higher education are in the 10–15 percent range, gains associated with an additional year of primary schooling are only 3–10 percent (Bigsten et al. 2000; Schultz 2004). Here again, patterns are consistent with more robust econometric results of increasing returns to education, including evidence from urban West Africa (figure 3.9).

Returns to Education Change with Educational Attainment

Returns to education change over time as the relative shares of the population with no, primary, and secondary schooling change. In other regions of the world, these shifts were

often accompanied by a decline in the earnings increment associated with being a primary or secondary school graduate. In India in 1994, for example, the wage increment for a primary school graduate versus someone with no education was 50 percent, but by 2010 it had fallen to 30 percent. The wage increment for a university graduate versus an upper-secondary graduate was 10 percent in 1994, but had risen to 36 percent by 2010. Similar changes occurred in other South Asian countries (Nayar et al. 2012). In Latin America between the mid-1990s and the late 2000s, the wage increment associated with completing secondary relative to primary schooling declined systematically—for example, from around 40 percent to about 30 percent in Brazil and Peru—while the increment

Figure 3.9 **The convex relationship between earnings and education: Schooling and earnings in urban West Africa**

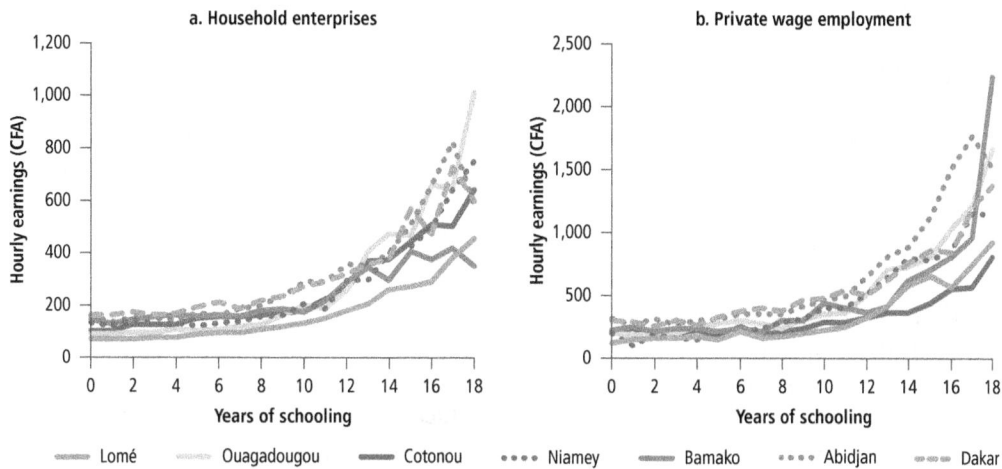

Source: Kuepie, Nordman, and Roubaud 2009, based on 1-2-3 surveys on employment and earnings in urban West Africa. Reproduced with permission of the authors.
Note: In the study, household enterprises are defined as "production units with no fiscal or statistical identity or without any formal accountancy" and labeled as "informal sector" by the authors. We use the term "household enterprises" for consistency with terminology used in this report.

associated with being a tertiary graduate rose (Aedo and Walker 2012).

All else being equal, the rising share of Africa's population with completed primary schooling should put downward pressure on the earnings increment to schooling. However, all else is not necessarily equal. The returns to schooling depend on the quality of schooling and the skills it supplies, as discussed in the remainder of this chapter. Returns also depend on the demand side of the labor market. The productivity of the work done by individuals with a given level of schooling, in the particular economic environment where they put their skills to work, will determine how effectively their schooling turns into earnings. Chapters 4, 5, and 6 elaborate on how to improve employment opportunities and the business environment on the demand side of the labor market.

Building a Foundation: Cognitive, Socioemotional, and Behavioral Skills

Many types of skills are needed for productive employment. Weak education systems are contributing to a critical shortfall in two key sets of skills—cognitive skills as well as socio-emotional and behavioral skills. These shortfalls can prevent youth from reaching their full potential. Cognitive, socioemotional, and behavioral skills create the foundation for acquiring higher-order cognitive and technical skills, whether through more formal education, training, or on-the-job learning. Improvements in the quality of basic education are urgently required to ensure that incoming youth acquire the necessary foundational skills.

Schooling aims to develop an assortment of skills, including literacy and numeracy as well as higher-order cognitive, socioemotional, and behavioral skills. The skills shaped by the education system explain part of the gains in earnings that are associated with more schooling. The fact that a few years of education confer only a small increase in earnings is related to the low quality of basic education in Africa as well as other economywide factors beyond the education system. Moreover, the pattern of increasing marginal returns to education in Africa suggests that productivity increases faster at higher levels of education—consistent with the notion that skills can complement one another and that "skills produced at one stage raise the productivity of investment at subsequent stages" (Cunha and Heckman 2007). The fundamental issue is that many African children never acquire the skills that are the foundation for a productive life because of the low quality of basic education systems.

This section discusses how skills are built through the education system, in early childhood, and through other avenues for learning. Productivity-enhancing skills can be categorized as follows:[6]

- *Basic cognitive skills,* such as numeracy and literacy
- *Higher-order cognitive skills,* such as problem solving and critical analysis
- *Behavioral and socioemotional skills* (also called *soft skills* or *life skills*), including a broad range of skills, such as social skills, self-regulation, self-confidence, and conscientiousness
- *Technical or vocational skills,* often specific to each occupation
- *Business skills,* such as entrepreneurship skills, managerial skills, and financial literacy.

The track record of the education system in producing these skills, including basic cognitive skills, has been abysmal in Africa. If the quality of education does not improve rapidly, productivity and earnings are likely to remain low—a problem that will only become more acute as new generations of Africans enter and graduate from school in larger numbers. Without substantial improvements in quality, the rewards that graduates of primary and lower-secondary school can expect to reap in the labor market will surely fall as more graduates enter the workforce. To some extent, such outcomes can be mitigated by urgent improvements in the education system that enable young people to develop more productivity-enhancing skills. Of course, education is only a starting point; graduates will also need an economic and business environment where they can use their skills productively.

The relevance of the range of productivity-enhancing skills can vary by sector of employment as well as across occupations. For instance, the mix of skills required for productivity in wage employment will depend on the complexity of the job. Higher-order cognitive skills matter more when jobs are more complex. Analytical thinking is an absolute requirement for professors and scientists, but less so for entry-level or "semi-skilled" workers. Technical and vocational skills matter in technical occupations. Other characteristics of personality, such as "openness to experience" and "agreeableness," have been shown to matter for particular career paths (Cobb-Clark and Tan 2010). Still, the first step is a basic education of sufficient quality that lays the foundations for young people to acquire a range of relevant skills later in life—through additional formal education, training, on-the-job learning, or other means.

Education Systems in Africa Are Failing to Produce Critical Foundational Skills

Rapid increases in school participation and educational attainment have undoubtedly come at the cost of quality. Empirical evidence confirms that poor learning outcomes—a few years of low-quality education, producing individuals who are barely literate and numerate—are hampering the potential for education to increase productivity, even in African economies that have been performing well. Learning assessments in Africa show that most primary students still lack basic proficiency in reading at the end of second or third grade. In several countries, a very large proportion of primary school students are illiterate. For example, more than 80 percent of Malian third-graders and more than 70 percent of Ugandan third-graders cannot read a single word (figure 3.10). Household surveys that measure numeracy and literacy are consistent with these troubling results. In Tanzania, for example, a 2011 assessment of children's abilities revealed that 70 percent of students complete standard two without meeting the numeracy standards of that level (Uwezo Tanzania 2011). Assessments in Kenya and Uganda revealed similar shortfalls in students' cognitive skills.

Even children who complete primary school have low levels of basic skills. In the regionally benchmarked Southern Africa Consortium for Measuring Educational Quality (SACMEQ) in 2007, 43 percent of sixth-graders in Tanzania and 74 percent in Mozambique did not get beyond the "basic numeracy" level, while 44 percent in Mozambique could not "read for meaning" (figure 3.11). The results from an

Figure 3.10 The ability to read in early grades is alarmingly low

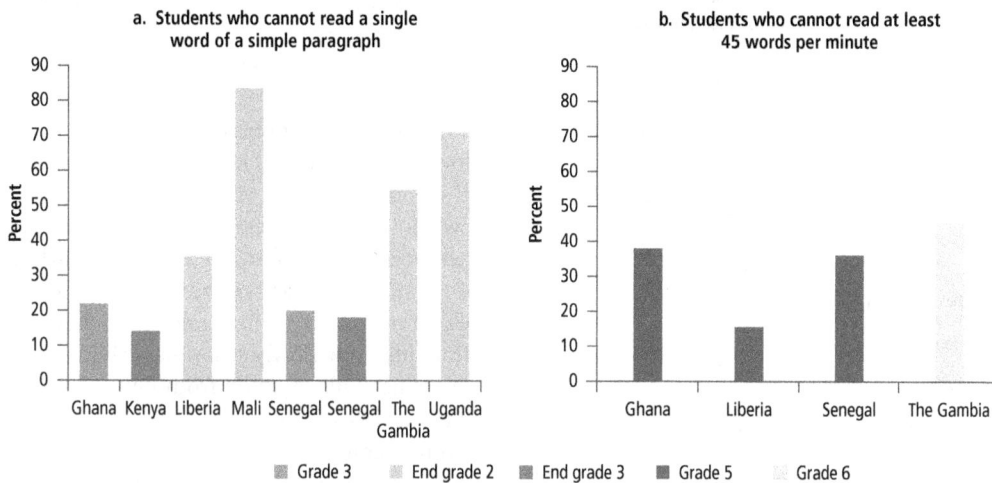

a. Students who cannot read a single word of a simple paragraph

b. Students who cannot read at least 45 words per minute

Grade 3 · End grade 2 · End grade 3 · Grade 5 · Grade 6

Sources: Cloutier, Reinstadtler, and Beltran 2011; Gove and Cvelich 2010.
Note: These findings refer only to students who have stayed in school. Those who have dropped out—who would have scored even lower on these assessments—are excluded from these calculations. The many primary school dropouts who lack the most basic skills, including simple numeracy or literacy, are largely young people who will find work in agriculture and HEs.

Figure 3.11 By the end of primary school, many students have not mastered even basic competencies: 2007 SACMEQ results for math and reading proficiency

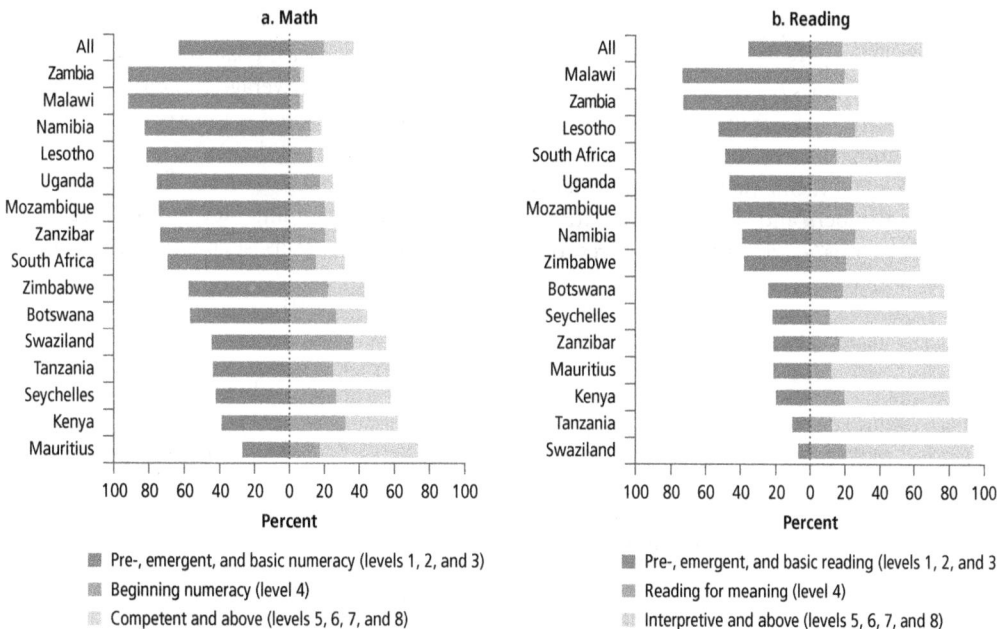

a. Math

b. Reading

Pre-, emergent, and basic numeracy (levels 1, 2, and 3)
Beginning numeracy (level 4)
Competent and above (levels 5, 6, 7, and 8)

Pre-, emergent, and basic reading (levels 1, 2, and 3
Reading for meaning (level 4)
Interpretive and above (levels 5, 6, 7, and 8)

Source: Hungi et al. 2010.

earlier round of SACMEQ (in 2003) were generally similar.

Beyond primary school, learning outcomes remain a cause for concern. Botswana, Ghana, and South Africa all participated in the lat-

est round (in 2011) of globally benchmarked learning assessments, the Trends in Math and Science Study (TIMSS). Among the eighth-grade (Ghana) and ninth-grade (Botswana and South Africa) students tested, 79 percent

Figure 3.12 Secondary school students in Sub-Saharan Africa perform poorly on internationally comparable assessments: TIMSS results for math proficiency, 2011

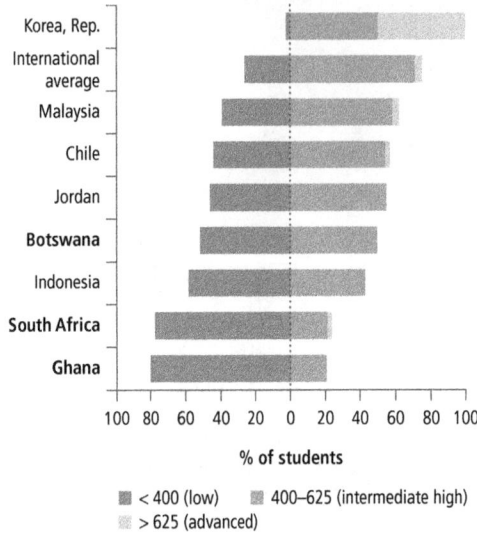

% of students

- ■ < 400 (low)
- ▨ 400–625 (intermediate high)
- ▨ > 625 (advanced)

Source: Mullis et al. 2012.
Note: Students tested in grade eight in Ghana and grade nine in Botswana and South Africa.

of Ghanaians and 76 percent of South Africans did not surpass the lowest benchmarked level of mathematics proficiency (figure 3.12).[7] In other words, all of those students failed to meet the proficiency criterion for this level— for example, "students have some knowledge of whole numbers and decimals, operations, and basic graphs"—which is a low threshold,

especially given the grade in which this test is administered. (The international mean was 25 percent; the result was 67 percent for Indonesian students and 45 percent for Jordanian students.)

School-age children are building skills too slowly. The amount of learning that takes place in schools from one year to the next is very low. Household surveys that include the same measures of skills for all children, regardless of the grade they are attending, illustrate this phenomenon. Learning trajectories demonstrate just how slowly school-age children are acquiring skills. A study from Guinea-Bissau that mapped performance in basic literacy and numeracy by children's ages (figure 3.13) shows that only half of 8-year-olds recognize single digits, while less than half of 9-year-olds recognize letters of the alphabet (Boone et al. 2013). Literacy and numeracy performance improves only very slowly with age. An average 16-year-old still cannot read a paragraph and cannot subtract a single-digit number from a two-digit number. These low learning trajectories are widespread: 351 schools were visited as part of the Guinea-Bissau study, but in only 6 of them could an average student read a paragraph. In none of the schools could an average student multiply or divide.

Learning trajectories are flat not only for basic literacy or numeracy but for a range of other cognitive skills, such as language, math-

Figure 3.13 Learning trajectories by age are flat in Guinea-Bissau

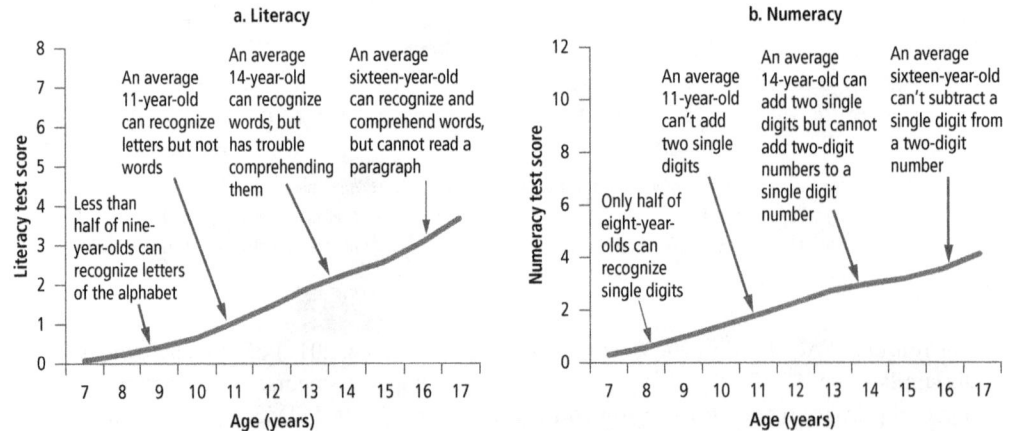

Source: Boone et al. 2013. Reproduced with permission of the authors.

Figure 3.14 Learning trajectories by grade are flat: Performance on test scores in selected African countries, by educational achievement

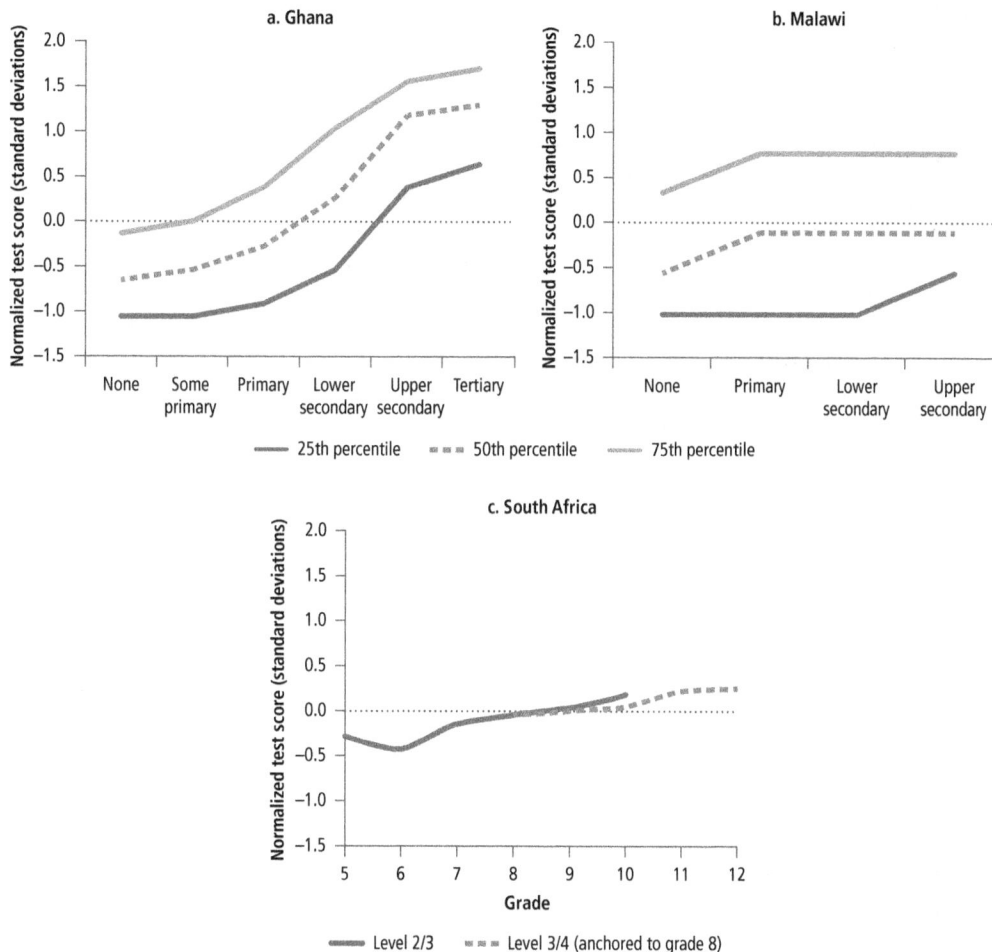

Sources: Calculations from Ghana 2004 living standards survey, Malawi Zomba Pilot control group, and South Africa 2008 national income dynamics study survey.
Note: Standardized score tests are different and cannot be compared across countries. In South Africa, different tests were administered at different grades; scores on the two tests have been anchored at grade eight.

ematics, and problem solving. Figure 3.14 illustrates how problem-solving skills are associated with education in samples from Ghana, Malawi, and South Africa. Learning trajectories from Ghana show that the median level of problem-solving skills is higher for individuals who have completed more schooling. Nevertheless, the increases are very slow. The poorest-performing students in lower-secondary school (the twenty-fifth percentile) perform roughly the same as the median performer among those with incomplete primary school. This finding is consistent with the results of another analysis using TIMMS data to infer learning trajectories, which shows that they are very flat in Ghana (Pritchett 2013). The learning trajectories for problem-solving skills in Malawi or South Africa are likewise very flat (figure 3.14). Overall, students at each level vary greatly in their problem-solving skills, but across levels of schooling, the accumulation of skills varies little around a generally low level. Africa's schools are not effectively imparting basic numeracy or literacy skills, nor are they imparting other cognitive skills such as problem solving or critical analysis.

Poor Cognitive Skills Contribute to Poor Employment Outcomes

Because returns to schooling depend considerably on the quality of education (Card 1999), returns to basic education will remain low as long as new cohorts of young people enter the labor force with more schooling but limited skills. Studies seeking to disentangle the returns to cognitive skills from other effects that schooling might have on earnings have demonstrated a strong association—including in Africa.[8] For example, one careful study of wage earners in Ghana found that cognitive skills have significant positive effects on wages. An earlier study of urban wage earners in Kenya and Tanzania produced similar findings (Glewwe 2002).

Recent evidence from Kenya documents the chain of causation from schooling to cognitive skills to employment outcomes.[9] Secondary school graduates were shown to perform significantly better than comparable nongraduates on vocabulary and reasoning tests in adulthood. Test scores were higher by 0.6 standard deviation, which is a large effect. By their mid-20s, school completers had a roughly 50 percent lower probability of low-skilled self-employment compared to noncompleters. They were about 30 percentage points more likely to be in formal employment.

How can African countries overcome the problem of limited accumulation of cognitive skills? For those who have already dropped out, especially younger workers, one option is to expand access to second-chance education. Second-chance education is an option to assist the large stock of young workers who have already dropped out of school, but it is potentially expensive and has had mixed success (see boxes 3.2 and 3.3).

For current and future schoolchildren to become productively employed, however, an immediate priority is to address the lack of learning in basic education. Improving the quality of basic education will not be easy. Surveys of schools reveal substantial failures in service delivery. For example, absenteeism among teachers is on the order of 16 to 20 percent on a given day in Kenya, Senegal, and Tanzania; primary school students in those countries experience only about two to three hours of

learning a day.[10] Reforming the accountability framework that allows such poor performance to persist is key (World Bank 2003; Bruns, Filmer, and Patrinos 2011). Better information on performance must be complemented by targeted approaches that increase oversight by the people who are most affected: students and their parents. Steps to ensure that teachers are well prepared for teaching and supported in their tasks are critical for creating a cadre of high-performing professionals. What teachers know and what they do is the cornerstone of good teaching and learning. The rise of private schools in Africa—schools that deliver superior performance often at lower costs—should not be stifled; rather they should be encouraged and channeled to give more students the opportunity to learn. Such strategies would need to be undertaken in tandem with efforts to ensure that children are prepared for learning when they attend school.

Children Acquire Limited Cognitive and Socioemotional Skills before Entering School

There are strong signs of cognitive delays among African children even before they enter school. Data from the Democratic Republic of Congo, Nigeria, Sierra Leone, and Togo show that young children acquire cognitive skills more slowly than expected (figure 3.15). Signs of delays are already apparent at age 36 months and get worse as children grow older (Naudeau et al. 2010). Some children acquire skills faster than others, however. For instance, the accumulation of cognitive skills in early childhood is associated with household socioeconomic status. Children from poorer households score worse on measures of cognitive skills such as receptive language or memory than children in better-off households. In addition, the gap in cognitive skills between the poor and nonpoor widens with age. These results are consistent across the region, including detailed studies in Madagascar and Mozambique as well as other parts of the world.[11] Delays in early childhood development can affect children throughout their lives, limit school readiness, and contribute to the slow accumulation of skills in school (Shonkoff and Phillips 2000).

Box 3.2

A second chance at education for African youth

Many young people in Africa have not completed basic education and lack numeracy and literacy skills. In the school year ending in 2010, it is estimated that 23 percent (31 million) of 132 million primary school–age children (5–14 years) in Sub-Saharan Africa were out of school or not enrolled.[a] A large proportion of children never attend school (28 percent of young people ages 25–34 never started school). Many who manage to start school drop out after just a few years (figure B3.2.1). As learning achievement tests demonstrate, when the quality of education is poor, even formal schooling is no guarantee that students will master basic literacy and numeracy skills.

Figure B3.2.1 Proportion of 15- to 19-year-olds who have completed each grade

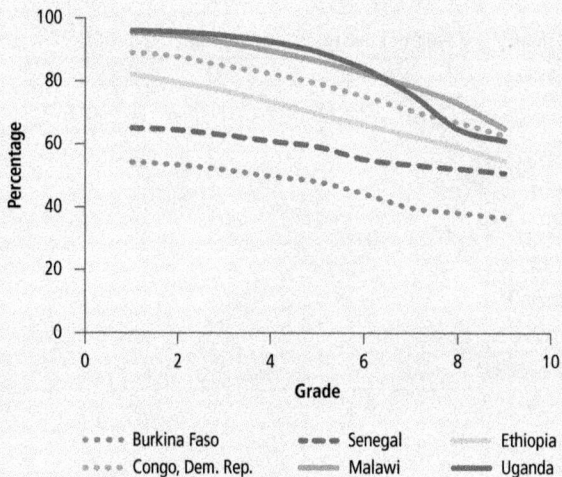

Source: Based on demographic and health survey data, except for the Democratic Republic of Congo, which is from the Multiple Indicator Cluster Survey. Data are for 2010 or 2011 (http://econ.worldbank.org/projects/edattain).

Second-chance education programs have the potential to bring school-age children back to school as well as to equip youth with the basic literacy and numeracy skills needed for productive employment. They enable individuals to complete general primary or secondary education, either by substituting for formal education or by offering "bridges" to return to the formal education system (Mattero 2010). The main types of second-chance programs are (1) accelerated learning programs, (2) nonformal education programs, and (3) education equivalency programs. Although adult nonformal education as well as programs providing technical, vocational, and life skills are sometimes referred to as second-chance education programs, this report considers them separately.

Accelerated learning programs (ALPs) give children and youth an opportunity to catch up on missed education in a short period (Mattero 2010). They use intensive, flexible methods or schedules to complete the curriculum faster than in traditional education and help youth to reenter the formal primary or secondary school system. Such programs are common in countries where children's schooling was interrupted by armed conflict or other kinds of social upheaval:

- *Republic of South Sudan.* ALPs provide basic education to those who missed the opportunity during the civil war. The eight primary grades are reduced to four years of learning. The programs are part of a broader alternative education system that reaches more than 165,000 students (mostly ages 12–18), roughly equal to the number of fourth-grade students in primary schools nationwide (Government of South Sudan 2011).
- *Sierra Leone.* The Complementary Rapid Education Programme for Schools, implemented in three districts, reduced the traditional curriculum and introduced teaching strategies, thereby shortening the six-year primary cycle to three years.
- *Northern Ghana.* The School for Life Program, described in box 3.3, was implemented to address a shortage of teachers in areas where literacy among 12- to 18-year-olds was only 5 percent. The program recruited volunteer teachers with some secondary education and gave them modest incentives along with a short induction training to teach out-of-school youth.

Nonformal education programs provide youth with instruction equivalent to formal education, focusing on essential learning needs and basic skills such as literacy, oral expression, numeracy, and problem-solving skills (Delors 1996). Most nonformal education courses range from a few months to years and can be offered on a part-time or full-time basis. They are normally delivered face-to-face in formal school facilities and learning centers but can also be provided through e-learning and radio. Community schools are a well-known example of nonformal education programs in Africa. In Zambia, community schools enroll individuals who are 14 and older and are vulnerable, orphaned, or unable to meet the costs associated with formal schooling. In Mali, community schools originally designed for adults have been extended to rural children, offering primary school education up to sixth grade. In Eritrea, to ensure basic education for all (especially girls), a UNICEF-supported Complementary Elementary Education Program provided nonformal education to children and young adults (ages 10–14 years old)

(continued)

Box 3.2

(continued)

who missed an opportunity to complete a five-year primary school curriculum.

Equivalency degree programs are nonformal education programs leading to qualifications equivalent to those gained through formal education programs. Equivalency degree programs target primary or secondary school dropouts and provide corresponding degrees, signaling that the recipient has demonstrated the ability to read, write, think, and compute at the level for which the degree was offered (Boesel, Alsalam, and Smith 1998). Equivalency programs vary in terms of admission, age, place, and pace, and they are delivered either via face-to-face learning or distance education.

Systematic evidence on the effectiveness of second-chance programs is quite limited and mixed. In Sierra Leone, students in ALPs performed consistently better than students in traditional schools, with a 91 percent passing rate on primary school achievement tests. Students progressed to secondary schooling at similar rates (Nicholson 2006). For students in Ghana's School for Life, the transition back into the formal system is close to 90 percent (DeStefano et al. 2006). However, in the Republic of South Sudan the dropout rates for ALPs during the 2010–11 school year were 52 percent for females compared to around 20 percent in formal schools (Government of South Sudan 2011). Results are better for males; only 5 percent dropped out of the ALP versus around 25 percent in formal schools. In Zambia students in community schools performed well on math and English

proficiency tests compared with students in public schools. Students who attended community schools in Mali outperformed their public school counterparts in school completion examinations (DeStefano et al. 2006).

Studies suggest that the costs per learner can be higher in second-chance programs than in traditional public schools (table B3.2.1), but the limited information on the ultimate outcomes of interest makes it hard to evaluate their cost-effectiveness. Much more data are needed to understand how these programs can cost-effectively build skills and increase youth productivity and earnings.

Table B3.2.1 Costs per pupil in second-chance education programs and formal public schools

Country and type of education	Annual cost per pupil (US$)
Ghana	
School for Life	39
Public	27
Mali	
Community schools	47
Public	30
Zambia	
Community schools	39
Public	67

Source: DeStefano et al. 2006.

a. UNESCO 2012.

Box 3.3

Northern Ghana's School for Life second-chance education program

School for Life (SfL) offers a nine-month literacy cycle in the mother tongue for children ages 8–14. The curriculum aims to meet the first three years of the formal school system's requirements and transition participants into the formal system on graduation. Facilitators—volunteers selected by the community—receive an initial three-week intensive training, supplemented with follow-up workshops and training. Communities provide their own teachers or facilitators, who are literate in the community's language; the mother tongue is both the language of literacy and the medium of instruction; the community is actively involved; the school calendar and hours are flexible and adapted to local conditions, allowing

children to maintain daily duties; and training takes place in primary school classrooms after school, which provides a link with formal education.

The program's reach is broad and growing. Approximately 800 facilitators served 20,000 learners in 17 districts in 2012–13, up from 10,000 in 9 districts the previous year. The vast majority complete the program—the graduation rate was 97 percent in 2011–12—and most join the formal schooling system. As many as 90 percent of the 2011–12 cohort entered primary school on leaving SfL.

Sources: CREATE 2010; DFID 2012.

Figure 3.15 Cognitive skills increase slowly, especially for the poorest

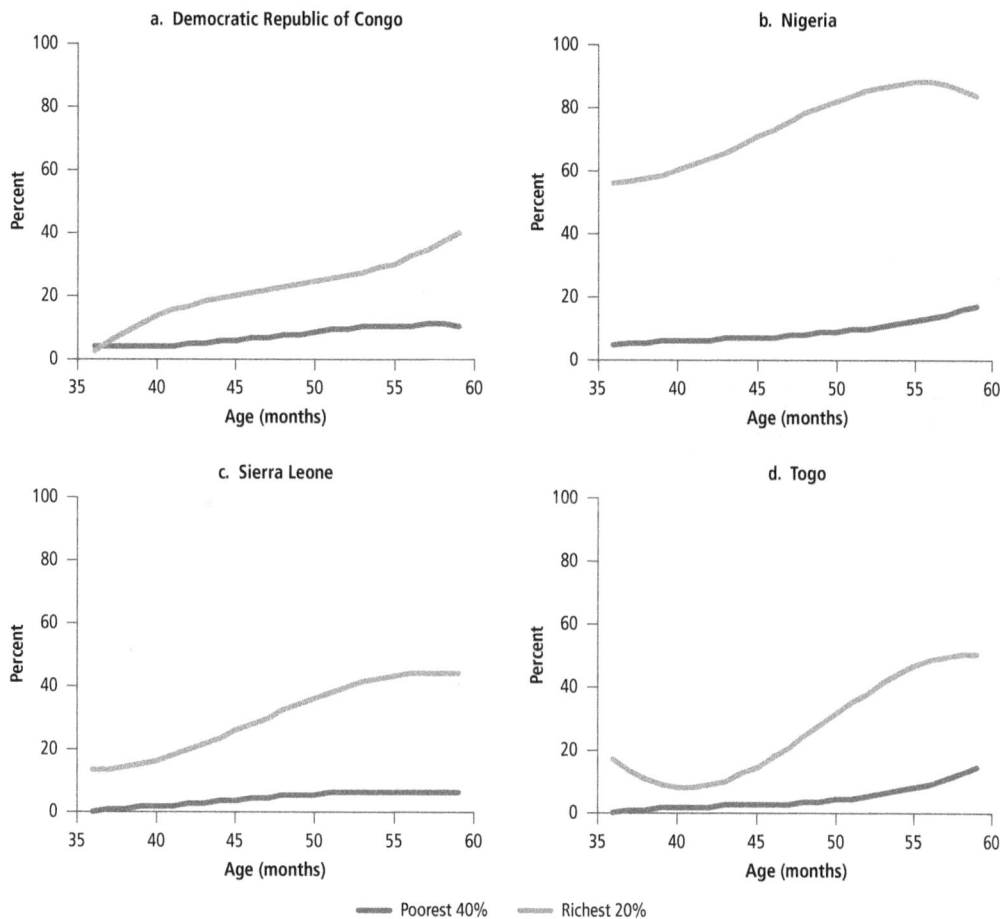

a. Democratic Republic of Congo

b. Nigeria

c. Sierra Leone

d. Togo

Poorest 40%   Richest 20%

Source: Based on Multiple Indicator Cluster Survey 4 data.
Note: Graphs show the proportion of respondents who can perform two of the following three tasks: identify or name at least 10 letters of the alphabet; read at least four simple, popular words; know the name and recognize the symbols of all numbers from 1 to 10.

Multiple factors contribute to the slow acquisition of skills in early childhood. Nutrition is one factor, but parenting practices and stimulation also matter greatly. Poor nutrition in early childhood can hinder the accumulation of cognitive skills[12] and affect reading or problem-solving skills in adulthood (Maluccio et al. 2009). Parenting practices and psychosocial stimulation also shape cognitive and socioemotional skills. Programs that encourage stimulation as well as nutrition have been shown to be more effective than programs that only aim to improve nutrition. They increase skills as well as earnings in adulthood (Grantham-McGregor et al. 2007; Gertler et al. 2013). In Mozambique, a recent preschool program led to gains in school readiness and improvements in a range of cognitive skills. Similar effects on skills in early childhood have been found in other developing countries for interventions focusing on improving parenting practices and stimulation through home visits, community-based centers, or preschools.[13]

Early childhood is also a critical window for the development of socioemotional and behavioral skills, including skills involved in forming relationships, communication or socialization, and self-regulation of behaviors and emotions (table 3.1; Lundberg and Wuermli 2012; Tubbs and McCoy 2012; Aber and Jones 1997). Stressful experiences such as conflicts or other shocks can trigger behavioral

Table 3.1 Developmental tasks, by age

Age	Period of life	Developmental task
0–1	Early childhood	Establishing (secure) attachment relationships
1–3	Early childhood	Learning to explore and communicate
3–5	Early childhood	Learning to self-regulate thoughts, behaviors, and emotions
6–12	Middle childhood	Learning and reasoning, developing interpersonal and social problem-solving skills
13+	Adolescence and emerging adulthood	Establishing autonomy (renegotiating relationships), forming identity, setting and achieving goals

Source: Wuermli et al. 2012.

problems and affect socioemotional development through depression, anxiety, or self-esteem. Parenting practices and psychosocial stimulation contribute to shaping these socioemotional skills—as shown recently in Mozambique, where children participating in a preschool program showed improved emotional maturity, including self-regulation (Martinez, Naudeau, and Pereira 2012).

Socioemotional and Behavioral Skills Are a Neglected Part of the Skill Set for Productivity

Socioemotional and behavioral skills complement and extend cognitive skills to improve productivity, but they are often neglected. Socioemotional skills develop through early and middle childhood. Social competencies are consolidated through increasing interactions and socialization in school and in communities (Lundberg and Wuermli 2012). As children reach adolescence, they further hone their social skills, become increasingly autonomous, and forge a sense of identity (see chapter 2). Depending on the context in which they live, including the social expectations surrounding them, adolescents shape aspirations and set goals for themselves. Concurrently, they experience deep socioemotional changes that can challenge their self-confidence or self-regulatory skills and make them vulnerable to depression, anxiety, or risky behaviors (Lundberg and Wuermli 2012). Long after cognitive skills have been acquired, socioemotional and behavioral skills remain malleable, reflecting the many changes and transitions characteristic of adolescence. Cognitive skills are largely acquired

by the time individuals are 15 years old, whereas many behavioral skills are acquired between the ages of 15 and 30 (figure 3.16).

Psychology has a long history of studying domains of human functioning. In practice, socioemotional and behavioral skills are often taken to encompass a broad set of "soft skills" or "life skills," which have come to include a mix of skills and less well-defined individual characteristics such as social skills, self-regulation, goal-setting behavior, personal initiative, achievement orientation, proactivity, action planning, deliberate practice, or self-confidence. Sometimes behavioral skills also include life skills linked with avoiding risky behavior or more general measures of psychological well-being, attitudes, or aspirations. They are sometimes linked to personality characteristics such as the "big five": extraversion, emotional stability, agreeableness, conscientiousness, and openness to experience. These traits can continue to change in adulthood (Roberts and Mroczek 2008).

Socioemotional and behavioral skills such as self-regulation have been linked to educational achievement and those such as self-confidence, social skills, or emotional stability have been shown to affect employment outcomes (Heckman, Stixrud, and Urzua 2006). In fact, employer surveys and qualitative research from

Figure 3.16 Behavioral skills take longer to develop than cognitive skills

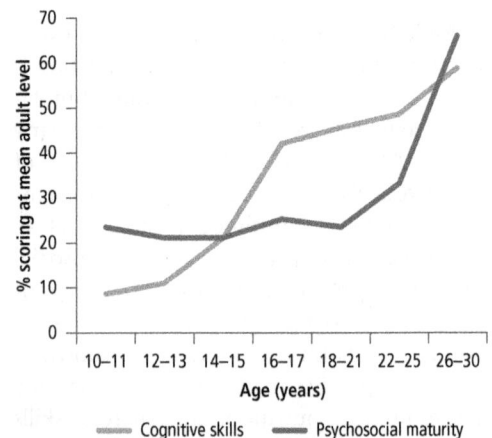

Source: Steinberg et al. 2009. Reproduced with permission of the authors.

various African countries suggest that employers are looking for soft skills in young hires. In Botswana, employers report that they seek workers with skills such as "honesty, commitment and hard work, reliability and punctuality, communication, and team working skills" (World Bank 2012a). In Lesotho, employers rate soft skills (the "appropriate personal characteristics") as among the hardest to find in prospective employees. Of the soft skills they seek when recruiting professionals or skilled workers, employers rate "punctuality and reliability" and "honesty and trustworthiness" as the most important.[14] In Sierra Leone, focus group discussions revealed that the young are perceived to lack "work attitudes" appropriate for formal jobs, such as punctuality and the ability to follow instructions (Peeters et al. 2009).

Behavioral skills also matter for HEs for many reasons, including the firm's dependence on the skills of the owner, who is often the sole worker (chapter 5). In South Africa and Zimbabwe, for example, the owner's "entrepreneurial orientation"—measured by personal initiative (proactivity and persistence) and achievement orientation (taking responsibility for one's own performance, taking on challenges, and setting high goals for oneself)—are positively associated with success in operating a small business.[15] A similar link between personal initiative and business success was found in Uganda (Koop, De Reu, and Frese 2000, quoted in Krauss et al. 2005). Other work has emphasized how the "deliberateness" of business owners is linked to success. Examples include the role of "elaborate and proactive planning" skills in Namibia, South Africa, and Zimbabwe (Frese et al. 2007) and "deliberate practice" (self-regulated and effortful activities showing a willingness to learn) in South Africa (Unger et al. 2009). Self-control—a behavioral skill that builds on cognitive capacity—also appears to be an important influence on the savings and investment behavior of HE owners in Kenya (Dupas and Robinson 2013).

Despite the recognized importance of behavioral skills, it is not yet well understood which ones matter most or the extent to which different behavioral skills are required for different occupations and sectors. New research from the United States suggests that not all behavioral skills matter in the same way across different types of work or even across relatively unskilled tasks. For example, sociability (or "extraversion") has higher returns in the service sector—specifically in sales jobs—than in unskilled manual work (Almlund et al. 2011; Fletcher 2012).

The relative importance of behavioral and cognitive skills is also not well established. Fundamentally, many behavioral and cognitive skills are interconnected. For instance, the ability to regulate one's behavior or emotions also depends on cognitive abilities. Research suggests that for less complex tasks, such as those required for relatively "unskilled" work, the role of behavioral skills can be relatively larger. For more complex tasks, the contribution of cognitive skills can be relatively higher, although soft skills matter there as well (Almlund et al. 2011). For wage jobs, two personality characteristics, in particular, seem to have strong predictive power for job performance and wages: conscientiousness (the tendency to be organized, responsible, and hardworking) and emotional stability. Almost all such evidence comes from developed countries, although similar findings are emerging from developing countries. A recent study in Peru shows that cognitive skills and perseverance—a behavioral skill—have similar effects on earnings in wage employment (box 3.4).

Overall, socioemotional and behavioral skills matter for productivity. Such skills can be shaped through experience in early childhood, through education, as well as through a range of experiences and programs in adolescence and adulthood. The relative effectiveness of different approaches to building these skills needs to be better understood, and this is an area that warrants policy attention.

Schooling Can Contribute to Building Socioemotional and Behavioral Skills

The link between education and behavioral skills is complex. Part of the association between behavioral skills and employment

Box 3.4

Returns to behavioral skills in wage employment: Evidence from Peru

A survey of micro and small enterprises in Peru found that employers seek workers with a range of skills. About half of the firms said that the main problem in hiring suitable workers is the lack of qualified or competent workers (in this case, "qualifications" and "competence" reflect perceived cognitive and technical skills). At the same time, about 40 percent cited the lack of skills such as a strong work ethic, ability to work in teams, persistence, adaptability, initiative, and other socioemotional skills. Other data from the national public employment service show that, in addition to cognitive skills, employers seek employees with traits related to work ethic, reliability, and interpersonal relations—regardless of formal schooling. Moreover, the results also suggest that behavioral skills may be more important for the less educated.

The study also set out to measure the supply of skills directly. In addition to traditional measures such as years of education, the study applied a range of standardized and specifically designed instruments. The Peabody Picture Vocabulary Test was used to measure receptive vocabulary—the ability to comprehend specific words. Additional cognitive tests were designed to measure verbal ability, working memory, and numeracy or problem-solving skills. Socioemotional skills were measured with self-reported tests for personality characteristics related to behaviors. They were measured with scales of the big-five personality factors (openness to experience, conscientiousness, extraversion, agreeableness, emotional stability), factors that are considered in psychology as characterizing differences in broad personality traits (and associated behaviors), and "grit," a narrower trait capturing a person's inclination and motivation to achieve long-term goals (through perseverance of effort and consistency of interest). The study measured these skills in the context of a household survey that collected information on multiple topics, including a range of other individual and household characteristics.

Analysis of those data reveals that measures of cognitive skills correlate with higher earnings. An increase of 1 standard deviation in receptive language, numeracy, working memory, or verbal fluency was associated with 9–18 percent higher hourly earnings. Behavioral skills were also associated with higher earnings. Workers scoring 1 standard deviation higher in the perseverance facet of grit earned 13 percent more; those scoring 1 standard deviation higher in three of the big-five scores (extraversion, emotional stability, and openness to experience) earned 8 percent more. Not all behavioral skills necessarily correlate positively with earnings. A score for "agreeableness-cooperation" that was 1 standard deviation higher was associated with 10 percent lower earnings.

Schooling, cognitive skills, and behavioral skills affect earnings through multiple pathways, both direct and indirect. When the role of each factor is evaluated while controlling for the other factors, years of schooling, years of work experience, and cognitive skills all have significantly positive effects. This finding suggests that measured cognitive skills affect earnings over and above years of schooling alone, suggesting that what is *learned* in school matters. The behavioral skills that significantly affect earnings (even after accounting for schooling, experience, and cognitive skills) are emotional stability and perseverance. Perseverance matters as much as cognitive skills. A score that is 1 standard deviation higher on either the cognitive skill or the perseverance scale led to a similar increase in earnings (of 8 and 9 percent, respectively).

Source: World Bank 2011b.

outcomes stems from their effect on higher educational achievement—and the cognitive skills that underlie higher educational achievement. Behavioral skills such as perseverance or personal initiative are correlated with success in school. It could be that people who are inherently more conscientious both acquire more schooling and perform better at work (Almlund et al. 2011). Recent work on China found a positive association between behavioral skills and educational achievement, even after accounting for cognitive skills (Glewwe, Huang, and Park 2011).

Education systems have scope for developing skills other than cognitive skills. Research in the United States suggests that elementary or even preschool programs that enrich the early learning environment can have lasting effects on later-life outcomes through positive impacts on behavioral and socioemotional skills (Almlund et al. 2011). Increased attention to imparting behavioral skills through schooling may take several forms, including modes of instruction as well as the modeling of appropriate behaviors, including teachers' behavior, in the school environment.

Schooling imparts behavioral skills in several ways. First, school success itself increases self-esteem and confers a greater sense of self-determination, as shown in research among high school and college graduates in the United States.[16] Second, the way that teaching and learning are delivered may influence behavioral skills. Teaching approaches that encourage participation, group activities, and exploration instill different mind-sets among students than approaches that emphasize rote learning. Third, the experience of education and the habits learned in school matter. Teacher absenteeism on the order of 20 percent, with little or no consequence to teachers, has been documented in several African countries (World Bank 2003).[17] Students' exposure to such an environment will likely instill a sense that punctuality (one of the skills that some employers say they are seeking) is not important.

There are little data on the extent to which education builds socioemotional and behavioral skills, including the soft skills demanded by employers. The education system could be leveraged to build further behavioral skills and reach a large number of children and young people. Policies that aim to improve the quality of education—for instance, by decreasing teachers' absenteeism and improving their behavior—might also contribute to improving students' behavioral skills through their demonstration effect. Teaching approaches that are more interactive and group based may facilitate the acquisition of both cognitive and behavioral skills, for instance. Curricular reforms that explicitly seek to improve behavioral skills may also be considered. However, such reforms may entail a trade-off requiring a decision about what to prioritize. Curriculum reforms introducing behavioral skills should not come at the cost of neglecting urgent improvements in the acquisition of basic literacy and numeracy skills. Reforms might be more relevant for higher grades where potential trade-offs with other teaching may be more limited. Given the limited evidence on the effectiveness of such approaches and the importance of their development in local contexts, they should be introduced in an experimental setup and rigorously tested before being rolled out widely.

Beyond education, other more focused approaches are showing promise in reaching youths and building behavioral skills. They include targeted interventions in postconflict settings (box 3.5). Programs that integrate behavioral skills into more comprehensive youth employment programs can also improve behavioral skills (box 3.6). Chapter 5 (for the

---

Box 3.5

Developing socioemotional and behavioral skills in postconflict settings

Children exposed to violence such as rape or killing can develop conditions such as depression or anxiety that might lead to behavioral problems. In Sierra Leone, where the long civil war has had deep psychosocial consequences, a Youth Readiness Intervention has focused on rebuilding skills related to anger management, interpersonal relations, and goal setting. The intervention is delivered to groups of young people. The groups meet for weekly sessions over two months. The intervention seeks to "increase adaptive coping, health-promoting behavior, and the development of life skills, such as goal setting and positive self-efficacy; decrease maladaptive coping strategies, such as high-risk sexual behavior and substance use; decrease trauma-related distress, including aggression, depressive symptoms, social isolation, and poor interpersonal skills; [and] increase prosocial behavior, including community involvement and success-

ful integration into educational or livelihoods initiatives, and positive peer, family, and community relationships."

The Sierra Leone pilot intervention was developed through an approach building on rigorous use of qualitative methods to ensure that the training modules and intervention strategy were culturally appropriate and could be delivered by local providers. A randomized control trial is under way to test the intervention's effectiveness. Such pilots have yet to be tested at scale, and the employment outcomes remain to be documented. Still, this type of well-designed model to foster socioemotional and behavioral skills is an example of potential interventions that could be integrated more systematically into youth employment programs.

Source: Draws from FXB Center for Health and Human Rights 2012, including quoted material.

Promoting socioemotional and behavioral skills

Employment programs in Malawi and Uganda that focused on female empowerment and life skills improved psychosocial well-being and reduced risky behaviors (Bandiera et al. 2013; Cho et al. 2013). A program integrating training in technical and life skills in Uganda resulted in a self-reported increase in routine condom use of almost 50 percent and a 29 percent reduction in the likelihood of becoming a mother (Bandiera et al. 2013). Positive impacts on behaviors was seen in programs in Tanzania and Uganda aiming to increase personal initiative and develop a more entrepreneurial mind-set (Glaub 2009; Berge et al. 2011). These results are consistent with others outside of Africa. Programs in countries as diverse as Chile, Jordan, Nicaragua, and Peru have produced graduates who have greater self-esteem, measured empowerment, mental health, or positive attitudes about the future (Carneiro, Galasso, and Ginja 2010; Valdivia 2011; Macours, Premand, and Vakis 2013; Premand et al. 2012; Groh et al. 2012).[a]

a. These effects are corroborated by an ongoing evaluation of a comprehensive youth training program—Juventud y Empleo—in the Dominican Republic. Preliminary evidence indicates significant effects on future expectations, job satisfaction, and job search attitudes.

HE sector) and chapter 6 (for the modern wage sector) discuss the extent to which programs aiming to shape behavioral skills are effective in improving employment outcomes.

Skills Build on Each Other

A growing body of research documents how cognitive and socioemotional skills build on each other, starting in early childhood (Helmers and Patnam 2011). Cognitive skills such as literacy and numeracy form the foundation for acquiring higher-order and technical skills later in life, whether through more formal education, training, or on-the-job learning. Basic cognitive skills are necessary for learning more advanced concepts, and better foundational skills lower the costs of any additional investments.

One way to understand how skills build on each other is to observe that the productivity returns to investments in further schooling are higher when foundational skills are stronger. Figure 3.17 presents an example from Ghana, Kenya, South Africa, and Tanzania. Returns to schooling tend to be lower for individuals with lower ability compared to those with

higher ability—with the pattern being starkest in Kenya and Tanzania. This finding suggests that education has the greatest benefit among people who start with greater ability or better foundational skills.

Basic cognitive skills also underlie the development of business skills, which are often particularly low for young people and women (Xu and Zia 2012). A study of small HEs in Ghana found that owners with more schooling are more likely to keep written records: Only 23 percent of HE owners who had not completed basic education kept accounts, compared to 52 percent of owners who had completed basic education (Fafchamps et al. 2011). Low business skills are observed even among more formal firms. In a survey of owners of small and medium enterprises in Ghana, only 27 percent of owners were found to keep business records (Mano et al. 2012). Throughout the world, financial literacy is associated with higher educational attainment (Xu and Zia 2012).

Another study from Ghana measured a range of business practices among HE owners, such as whether "the owner keeps written business records, has a written budget, has a sales target, visits competitors' business to observe prices, asks existing customers if they had interest in other products." The number of management practices adopted by the owners of micro and small enterprises was found to

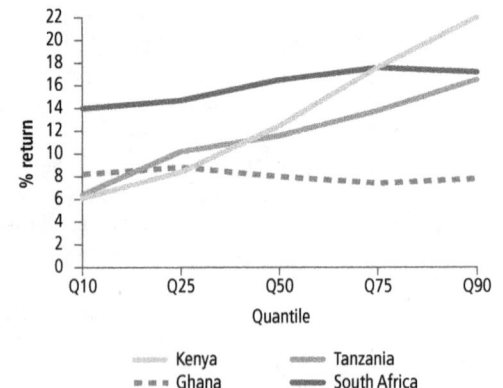

Figure 3.17 The returns to schooling are higher for those with greater ability: Returns of an additional year of schooling by quantile

Source: Fasih et al. 2012. Reproduced with permission from the authors.

vary substantially. In addition, these business practice scores also predicted business performance (Fafchamps and Woodruff 2012). The adoption of better management practices was significantly higher among respondents who scored better on various cognitive tests.

Although business skills are not taught in school, they are correlated with education, because they are rarely acquired without basic cognitive skills. A more direct measure of this effect, however, is the interaction between education and the effectiveness of interventions to build business skills. A program to provide business training to small-scale entrepreneurs in Tanzania found larger impacts among participants with higher initial cognitive (math) test scores (Bjorvatn and Tungodden 2010).

Basic cognitive skills also complement on-the-job learning for wage workers, including learning through the use of instructions. Although literate workers can be trained in job specifications and procedures partly through detailed and complex written instructions, such training is rare in Africa, where literacy is low. Among firms surveyed in Ghana, Kenya, and Zimbabwe, 80 percent said that they rarely use technical documentation or procedural manuals (Biggs, Shah, and Srivastava 1995). A recent study in Ghana found that, in a job involving the handling of money, more educated workers were more likely to pick up math skills while working (Aslam and Lehrer 2012). Perhaps because of the complementarity between basic education and on-the-job learning, firms in Africa (as in other parts of the world) are more likely to provide formal on-the-job training to more educated workers (Rosholm, Nielsen, and Dabalen 2007).

Beyond the complementarities between basic skills and business skills, there may be potential for incorporating entrepreneurship education or financial literacy education into school curricula. Yet it remains unclear whether the education system can provide such skills effectively. Some developed countries have attempted to include entrepreneurship training at the primary and tertiary level (see Rosendahl Huber, Sloof, and van Praag 2012 for efforts in primary school; Oosterbeek, van Praag, and Ijsselstein 2008 for efforts in tertiary education).

In Tunisia, a middle-income country, entrepreneurship training was introduced in the university curriculum and led to changes in behavioral skills (Premand et al. 2012). Initial evidence on a pilot financial education program provided through the schools in Brazil suggests some positive impacts: 59 percent of students who benefited from the program saved, compared to 55 percent among the control group, and knowledge about savings increased (Bruhn et al. 2013). Similar efforts are under way in some African countries (for example, in secondary education in Uganda). An important challenge is that soft skills for self-employment and wage employment may differ, requiring careful attention to curriculum development and program effectiveness.

Building Skills through Post-School Training

A wide array of institutions throughout Africa offer skills training for nonfarm employment. This array of institutions and programs can be described as a market, since it involves those who supply training coming together with those who demand training. Informal training is normal. Most training is offered by private providers, and the offerings vary in price and quality. The rationale for public investment in training needs to be made in the context of this existing market, based on careful analysis of its added value and cost-effectiveness.

Pathways from Training to Sectors of Employment

Four main kinds of youth training provide skills for employment outside agriculture: apprenticeships, public formal technical vocational education and training (TVET), private formal and informal TVET ("formal" meaning integrated into the formal education system; "informal" meaning outside of the formal education system), and stand-alone programs. Training is delivered through a mix of private and public institutions, and each type of training tends to lead to a different type of work (nonfarm HE or modern wage sector).

Figure 3.18 Many young people, especially in West Africa, have been an apprentice, whereas experience with TVET is less prevalent

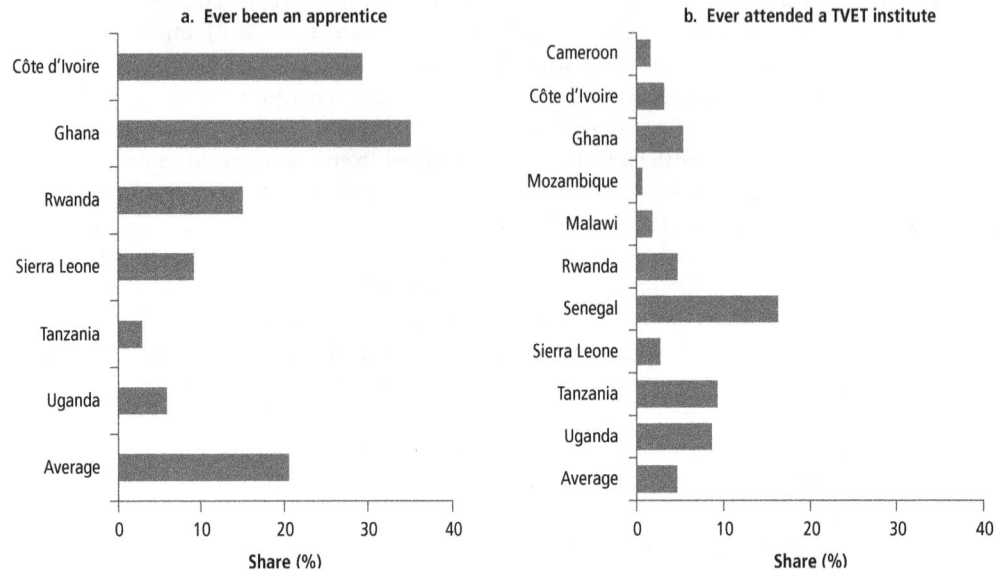

Source: Based on standardized and harmonized household and labor force surveys, latest data available (see appendix).

Two of the most common forms of training pursued by young people are apprenticeships and TVET. Apprenticeships are the more prevalent type of training, particularly in West Africa. Detailed survey data on apprenticeship are limited, but in five countries with comparable data, 20 percent of young adults ages 24–35 have had experience as an apprentice (figure 3.18), although there is variation across countries, from 6 percent in Uganda to 35 percent in Ghana.

Enrollment in formal TVET, delivered in the classroom and leading to a formal degree after two to three years, is low throughout Africa. Overall, around 4 percent of young people between 25 and 34 have ever attended formal TVET,[18] and only 1 percent currently attend.[19] Because most TVET requires some secondary schooling, the majority of young people lack the general qualifications even to enroll in a technical or vocational institute.

The prevalence of apprenticeship in Ghana is well documented (for example, see Atchoarena and Delluc 2001; Frazer 2006; Monk, Sandefur, and Teal 2008). A 2006 urban labor market survey found that one-third of respondents between ages 16 and 65 had some form of training (Monk, Sandefur, and Teal 2008).

Apprenticeship was by far the most common form (55 percent had been an apprentice), followed by on-the-job formal training in a firm (25 percent), and formal vocational training (16 percent). An earlier study estimated that traditional or informal apprenticeships supply 80–90 percent of all basic skills training in Ghana, while public training institutions supply 5–10 percent (Atchoarena and Delluc 2001). Ghana may have as many as four informal apprentices for every trainee in either a formal public or a private training center (Darvas 2012; Haan and Serrière 2002; Monk, Sandefur, and Teal 2008). Apprenticeships are widespread elsewhere in West Africa as well, including in Benin and Côte d'Ivoire (AfDB and OECD 2008).

Traditional apprenticeship can also be the dominant form of training for nonfarm occupations in East Africa. In Kenya, enrollment in traditional apprenticeships delivered by master craftsmen is much higher than enrollment in formal TVET.[20] A small survey of 350 informal enterprises in Dar es Salaam found that more than half of the operators had apprentices, on average about two per firm (Nell and Shapiro 1999).

Beyond the more traditional apprenticeship and formal TVET models, a broad range of private providers offers various types of skills training. Private providers of informal vocational training (in other words, training outside the formal education system) include for-profit private institutes and firms, nongovernmental organizations (NGOs), and community organizations. While the distinction with master craftsmen providing apprenticeships can be fuzzy, the vast majority of providers of informal vocational training are self-financing and operate with little government oversight or support. Many informal private providers are not registered (World Bank 2003). Many operate at a very small scale; these micro training providers provide short, intensive training based on a curriculum of their own design and may offer certificates (Johanson and Gakuba 2011). Assessing their reach is challenging. Household surveys rarely ask respondents about training other than apprenticeships, on-the-job training, or formal TVET. A recent tracer study of cohorts of secondary and university graduates suggests that the use of private post-school training may be rising (Al-Samarrai and Bennell 2007).

Apprenticeships (as well as other types of informal training) are typically geared toward individuals who have completed primary school or less, while formal TVET is geared toward individuals with at least some secondary schooling (figure 3.19). For example, among young adults ages 25–34 in Uganda who had done an apprenticeship, 95 percent had no more than a primary education. A study in Ghana found that apprenticeships are undertaken primarily by persons with a junior high school or lower level of education (Monk, Sandefur, and Teal 2008). Among those who had entered a TVET program, almost all had some education beyond primary.

The type of training pursued maps closely to the subsequent sector of employment. Apprenticeship is mainly a pathway to work in an HE, since apprentices are most likely to become self-employed. By contrast, formal TVET is mostly a pathway to wage employment.

As a result, the training experience of workers in different sectors is quite different. For young adults ages 25–34 working in the HE sector, apprenticeships are the most common form of post-school training: 32 percent have been an apprentice at some point, compared to 30 percent of young adults in the modern wage sector and 13 percent in the agricultural

Figure 3.19 **Apprenticeships are geared toward youths with lower levels of education**

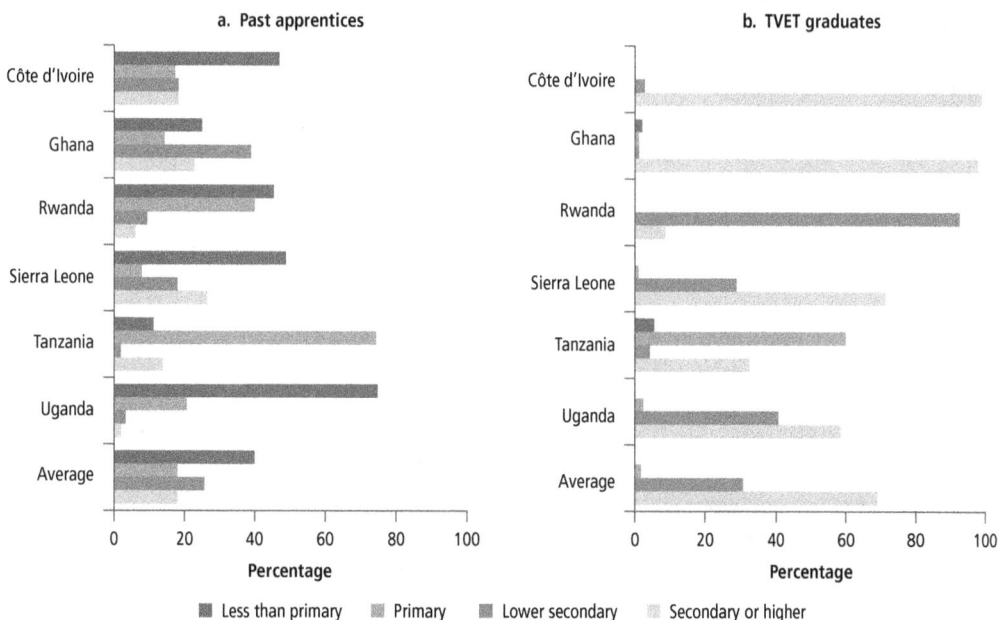

Source: Based on standardized and harmonized household and labor force surveys, latest data available (see appendix).

Figure 3.20 TVET is geared toward wage work, whereas apprenticeships lead to working in either a household enterprise or wage work

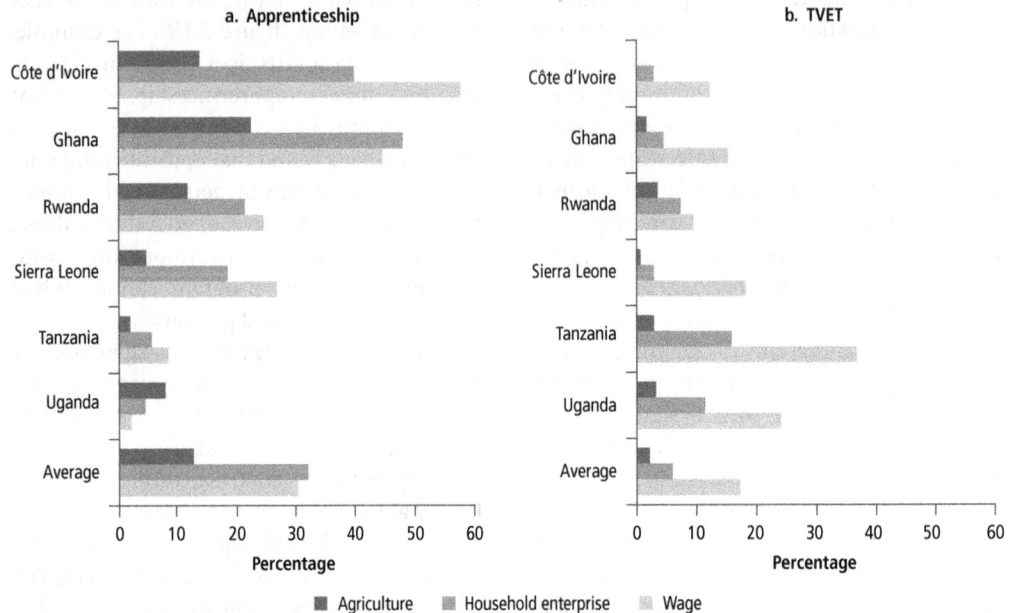

Source: Based on standardized and harmonized household and labor force surveys, latest data available (see appendix).

sector (figure 3.20).[21] Returns to apprenticeships may be particularly high in HEs. A study from Ghana found that former apprentices earn about 49 percent more a year being self-employed than working as a wage worker, despite having slightly fewer years of schooling and being slightly younger.[22] Relatively few young workers enter the HE sector after obtaining formal technical or vocational training. Only 6 percent of individuals between 25 and 34 in the HE sector have attended a formal TVET institution (figure 3.20). The share of workers in the wage sector who have attended formal TVET is much higher (17 percent).

Apprenticeships and Informal Private Training

The distinction between apprenticeship and informal private training (two of the most prevalent forms of youth training) is fuzzy. Both types of training encompass a range of offerings delivered by private providers.

Apprenticeships in Africa overwhelmingly occur in small informal firms with a master craftsman. They are private arrangements between an apprentice and a master craftsperson or another relatively skilled person, who

provides practical training in the workplace over a period of a few weeks or months to as much as three or four years. Many apprenticeships build technical skills in a narrow range of traditional vocations or crafts, such as metalworking, carpentry, mechanics, or tailoring. Some offer certification, but most do not. Apprenticeships can be offered in return for a fee or reduced earnings while learning.

In an apprenticeship program in Malawi, master craftsmen were primarily in carpentry and joinery (19 percent), tailoring (18 percent), auto mechanics (11 percent), and fabrication and welding (11 percent). A large share of the observed apprenticeship training in Rwanda was concentrated in tailoring (Johanson and Gakuba 2011).

The duration of apprenticeships can vary greatly. Many youths only spend a few months as an apprentice. In Rwanda, 56 percent of HE owners with experience as an apprentice reported that their apprenticeship lasted less than a month (Johanson and Gakuba 2011). In Malawi, participants in an apprenticeship program reported that apprenticeships lasted on average 3.3 months; training for auto mechanics spanned more than three months, whereas training for hairdressers lasted only three weeks (Cho et al. 2013). By contrast, in countries such as Côte d'Ivoire or Ghana, where the institution of apprenticeship is more established, apprenticeships can last several years and can be hard to leave.

The range of private informal training in Africa is quite wide. Many micro training providers develop their own teaching programs, market their services, and deliver a mix of theoretical and applied training to individuals in small groups. For example, in Rwanda, 97 percent of all training providers are private, and they account for 90 percent of enrollment (figure 3.21; Johanson and Gakuba 2011). Individuals own about half of all private training enterprises, and associations and cooperatives own the other half. Just over half of all providers are micro training providers, such as associations, cooperatives, or training centers, enrolling 12 or fewer trainees. Micro training providers enroll only 8 percent of private trainees, but total enrollment in micro training still exceeds enrollment in all public, formal vocational training in Rwanda (figure 3.21). In Tanzania, private training institutions, including faith-based organizations and NGOs, produce about three-fourths of all vocational graduates, even though most of those institutions do not operate at capacity (Cojocaru 2011).[23]

Like apprenticeships, informal training programs are often concentrated in a limited set of areas. Youth eligible for vocational train-ing vouchers in Kenya, for example, enrolled mainly in informal training in tailoring (37 percent), mechanics (18 percent), hairdressing (9 percent), driving (7 percent), and masonry (6 percent; Hicks et al. 2011). In northern Uganda, youth groups eligible for cash grants chose training heavily concentrated in a few trades: tailoring (38 percent), carpentry (24 percent), metalwork (13 percent), hairdressing (8 percent), and business or management (5 percent).[24]

The duration of informal training can be quite short. In Northern Uganda, where youths engaged in informal training for an average of about 321 hours over two years, they increased their investment in training to 560 hours after receiving a cash grant. When grant recipients enrolled with private formal TVET providers, the training was substantially longer, ranging up to two years (Hicks et al. 2011).

Formal TVET

Formal TVET runs parallel to general schooling at the secondary or tertiary level and meets the need for intermediate or advanced technical skills. Entry requirements often include having completed primary or secondary school. Therefore, participants in formal TVET have substantially more schooling than participants in other forms of post-school training.

In Nigeria, technical colleges at the secondary level produce craftsmen and master craftsmen, focusing on traditional technical vocations (electricians, vehicle mechanics, and

"For many long years, I worked as an apprentice and had to follow the masons.... It wasn't until I turned 30 that I got my license." Madagascar

Figure 3.21 **Africa has a wide range of informal private training providers, 2009**

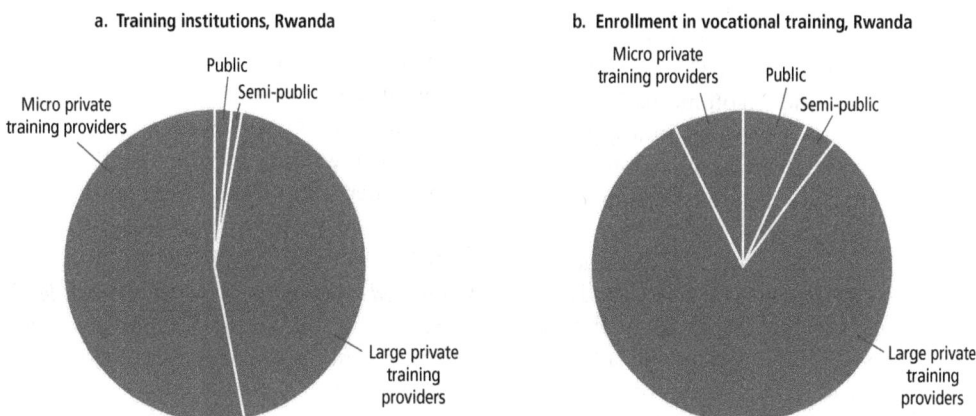

Source: Johanson and Gakuba 2011.

masons). At the tertiary level, vocational institutions (polytechnics) produce technicians, professionals, and engineers. Business-oriented vocational training is prevalent. Nearly half of all polytechnic graduates pursue qualifications in accounting, business studies, marketing, and banking and finance (World Bank 2011a). In Rwanda, technical secondary schools prepare students for entering the labor market at roughly the same level as an upper-secondary school graduate. Vocational training centers prepare basic education graduates or dropouts to enter the labor market (World Bank 2011a).

Several types of nongovernmental entities also provide technical and vocational training, including for-profit private institutes and firms as well as NGOs. However, data on the extent to which the private sector provides formal TVET are scarce; household surveys rarely ask respondents to identify whether they attended a public or a private TVET institute.[25] Nevertheless, studies suggest that the private sector is a large and increasingly important provider of pre-employment TVET. In some countries, the majority of trainees are enrolled in nongovernmental institutions. Examples include Mali (where nongovernmental training accounts for two-thirds of all TVET), Tanzania (90 percent), and Zambia (82 percent). Private technical institutes in Ghana enroll about six times as many trainees as public institutes (Haan 2001 for Tanzania; Atchoarena and Esquieu 2002 for Mali; Kitaev 2003 for Ghana and Zambia). A recent study in Ethiopia estimates that 30–50 percent of TVET students are enrolled in private institutions (Shaorshadze and Krishnan 2013). A recent World Bank report, using statistics from 33 countries in the region, found that the private sector currently accounts for about 35 percent of formal TVET enrollment (Mingat, Ledoux, and Rakotomalala 2010).

Compared with public institutes, private training providers tend to focus on "light" vocational skills such as business, commercial, and service skills, possibly owing to the high fixed costs of providing more industry-oriented sorts of skills. Private providers in Uganda, for instance, focus on office qualifications and various business skills that require only a limited investment (Haan 2001). Private providers also tend to be concentrated in specific regions—

often those with larger populations and greater demand for training (Ghana and Zambia are examples).

Besides pre-employment TVET, post-employment formal training paid for by employers can also be a source of technical or vocational skills. About 30 percent of African firms provide formal on-the-job training, a rate comparable to other developing regions (box 3.7).

Government Interventions and the Post-school Training Market

Governments the world over are active in skills development, but before designing public policy, it is essential to assess the rationale for government intervention. Given the large array of training already provided by the private sector, the rationale for governments to invest in specific programs is not obvious. As a general principle, public interventions need to be based on clearly identified "market failures" and weighted against "government failures."

Market failures for skills development take specific forms—all of which can lead to underinvestment in training (see the discussion in Almeida, Behrman, and Robalino 2012; World Bank 2011a). These failures can be grouped into four main categories:

1. *Imperfections in labor markets,* such as "poaching externalities," whereby the firm that trains an employee loses the benefits of that training if the worker moves to another firm, or information and signaling failures, whereby a potential worker cannot effectively show her level of skills to a potential employer

2. *Imperfections in credit markets,* whereby it is hard to get financing to pay for training

3. *Coordination failures,* occurring, for example, when workers and firms need to make investments, but those investments pay off only if both parties invest, which can lead to neither side making the first move

4. *Limited information at the individual level,* which can lead to too little or too much investment in particular types of skills development

Box 3.7

On-the-job training varies by country and type of firm, and it is not for everyone

In the United States, one-quarter to half of human capital accumulation occurs through on-the-job training (Heckman, Lochner, and Taber 1998). Even in developing countries (including African countries), many firms provide training to their workers. Estimates from the World Bank's enterprise surveys indicate that, on average, about 30 percent of formal firms in Africa provide training (figure B3.7.1), only slightly below the average for low- and middle-income countries. In Africa, the percentage of firms training workers varies

Figure B3.7.1 On-the-job training in African firms varies by country

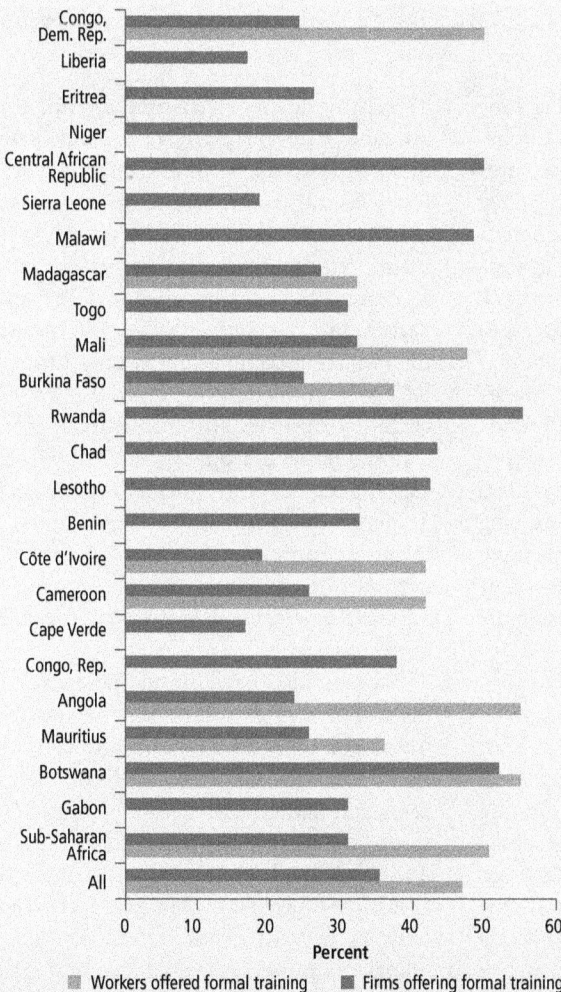

Source: Based on World Bank enterprise surveys.
Note: Countries ordered by GDP per capita.

between 15 and 30 percent in most countries, but in some (such as Botswana, Malawi, and Rwanda), the incidence is as high as 50 percent.

Variations in the rates of on-the-job training across Africa do not appear to be related to per capita income levels. Since firm surveys tend to focus on formal, officially "registered" firms and often miss unregistered firms, some of the variation might arise from differences in the share of firms that are registered. In most countries around the world, the incidence of training in firms is strongly related to firm characteristics such as size and export orientation. Smaller firms are less likely to provide formal training to employees. So are nonexporters. This pattern is borne out in Africa as well (figure B3.7.2). Thus African countries with larger, more outwardly oriented firms may have more on-the-job training.

Figure B3.7.2 On-the-job training in African firms varies by firm size and export orientation, 2006

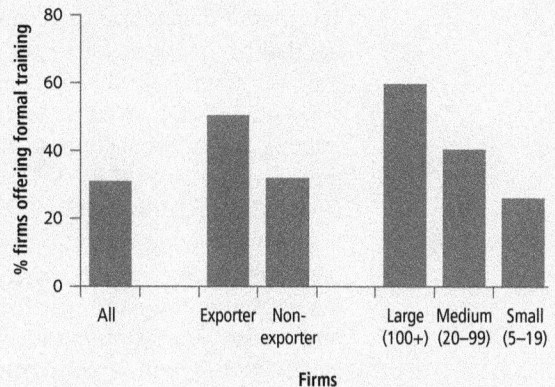

Source: World Bank enterprise surveys (average for African countries surveyed in 2006).

Firms providing on-the-job training do not train all of their workers. As figure B3.7.2 suggests, African firms that provide on-the-job training rarely provide it to more than half of the workforce, perhaps because levels of education are low. As in the rest of the world, in Africa workers with more education and skills are much more likely to receive formal training on the job. A 1980 survey of formal training in enterprises in Dar es Salaam, Tanzania, and Nairobi, Kenya, found that unskilled and semi-skilled manual workers are significantly less likely to have received formal training from their current employer than skilled production, cleri-

(continued)

Box 3.7

(continued)

cal, and supervisory workers (De Beyer 1990). Surveys conducted in Kenya and Zambia in 1995 found that workers with no formal education do not receive on-the-job training (Rosholm, Nielsen, and Dabalen 2007).

There are scarce data on the content of on-the-job training in African firms or on how it may differ from the training that a young job seeker might receive at a training institute. It is likely that the content of on-the-job training has an element of firm-specificity. In Dar es Salaam workers who had previously been in another firm were almost as likely to get formal on-the-job training as those who were on their first job (De Beyer 1990), suggesting that the training was at least

partly specific to their current firm. On-the-job training is also specific to the technology used in the firm.

The typical worker is more likely to get training through on-the-job learning than from classroom training paid for by employers. Firm surveys in Kenya and Zambia found that, in the 12 months prior to the survey, the most common forms of learning among employees were "instructions from a supervisor or coworker" and "watching others or learning on your own" (Rosholm, Nielsen, and Dabalen 2007). Courses paid for by the employer were less common and about as likely as training at a school or technical or vocational institute.

These various forms of market failure provide general rationales for government intervention, but their prevalence needs to be carefully assessed in specific country contexts. They also provide guidance as to the range of activities that the public sector might want to support. For example, credit constraints may provide a rationale for policies to improve access to training. Limited or inaccurate information at the individual level has also led to underinvestment in training or suboptimal choice of training and can provide a case for public intervention. Governments need to recognize that there is a market for training and avoid introducing undue distortions in this market. Overall, there are two broad areas for government intervention: (1) providing information and facilitating access to training and (2) intervening to ensure the availability of better-quality training options. Those two areas are discussed next.

Facilitating Access to Training

Public policy should facilitate access to existing training opportunities, including those available in the private market. One strategy, for example, is to provide information or incentives to young people who have the least access to training, starting with individuals from the poorest households, women, and individuals in rural areas. Better provision of information about employment and training opportunities can start in school.

Existing forms of training are not equally available to everyone (figure 3.22). Patterns of training across income groups suggest that financial constraints reduce access to training among the poorest households. Among youth from households in the top income quintile, 11 percent have ever enrolled in TVET and 2.7 percent are currently enrolled. By contrast, in the bottom income quintile, only 1.6 percent have ever enrolled in TVET and 0.1 percent are currently enrolled. This inequality in access to training holds not only for formal vocational training but also for informal apprenticeships: 25 percent of youth in the top quintile have taken an apprenticeship and 7.6 percent are currently in an apprenticeship, compared with 7.3 and 2.5 percent, respectively, of youth in the bottom quintile.

Women also have limited access to training opportunities, and when they do receive training, it often focuses on a limited range of occupations. Women are less likely than men to be enrolled in formal TVET or apprenticeships (see also Atchoarena and Delluc 2002). Across the region, 18 percent of individuals ages 15–34 have ever been an apprentice, but only 12 percent of women.[26] Women who manage to pursue informal technical training or apprenticeships tend to end up in heavily concentrated sectors with limited demand, such as tailoring or hairdressing. In Uganda, 91 percent of training hours taken by females who were not involved in the Youth Opportunities Program were in tailoring (Blattman, Fiala, and Martinez 2011). In Kenya, the most popular courses for women were tailoring, hairdressing, and computer packages, whereas men preferred training to become mechanics, drivers, or masons (figure 3.23).

Youths in rural areas also have less access to training, since more training providers are located in urban areas and distance to training centers is a constraint for access. Across Sub-Saharan Africa, 25 percent of 15- to 34-year-olds living in an urban area have ever been an apprentice, compared with only 11 percent of those living in a rural area. In Kenya, women were significantly more likely than men to cite proximity to training opportunities as a determining factor (50 and 43 percent, respectively), suggesting that female participants are more geographically constrained than their male peers (Hicks et al. 2011).

In the presence of financial and other constraints on access to training, there is scope for policies to facilitate access to training among youth, particularly women and the poor. Interventions that provide targeted financial incentives to increase participation in training have been shown to help. In northern Uganda, a program providing large cash grants to self-created groups increased the proportion of youth enrolled in vocational training from 15 to 74 percent, and recipients also engaged in more intensive training. Some training opportunities were already available in the community, but the young people participating in the project had not purchased much of this training before. Although youths in the program did not *have* to buy training, most chose to spend a large part of their cash grants on training prior to starting a business. This finding suggests that programs that help to finance access to training might be effective. Among those who did not get a grant (the control group), some participants did acquire training on their own, but it was of much shorter duration. Of the 15 percent of individuals who took training without the program, only 6 percent paid for it.

Voucher programs can be effective when recipients have the option to choose a private training provider. In Kenya, the Technical and Vocational Vouchers Program offered

Figure 3.22 **There are stark differences between rich and poor in experience with apprenticeships and TVET**

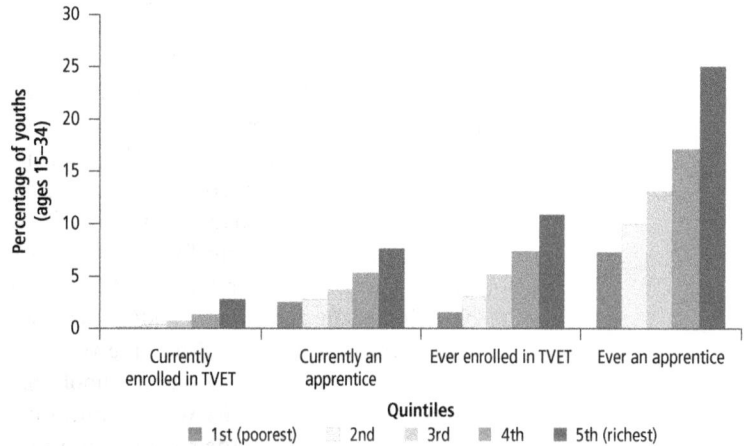

Source: Based on standardized and harmonized household and labor force surveys (see appendix).

Figure 3.23 **Men and women take up different types of vocational training in Kenya**

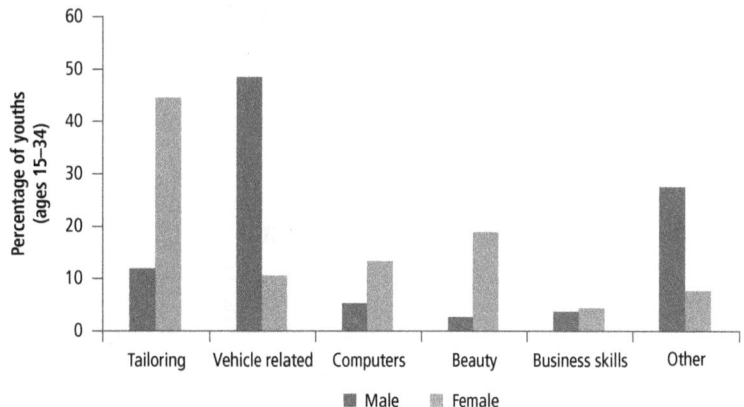

Source: Hicks et al. 2011.

young people vouchers worth approximately US$460 to encourage them to enroll (Hicks et al. 2011). Voucher winners who were closer to private schools were more likely to take up training compared to winners who were farther away. Among voucher winners, a random half received a voucher that could be used only in a public (government) vocational institution, while the other half received a voucher that could be used in either a private or a public school.[27] The broader choice and access to private providers increased the use of training: 69 percent of individuals who were awarded the restricted vouchers attended vocational training, compared with 79 percent of individuals who were awarded unrestricted vouchers. Winners of unrestricted vouchers were also more likely to complete training.

Voucher programs can also have an effect on skill providers and stimulate the supply of training available. In Kenya, a large program that provided vouchers to workers in the informal sector (called Jua Kali) not only increased access to training but also led to the emergence of new training providers relevant for the HE sector, such as master craftsmen (see box 3.8; Adams 2001; Johanson and Adams 2004). Evidence from a smaller-scale pilot of training vouchers in Kenya suggests that programs or schools that received voucher students were significantly more likely to expand their course offerings (Hicks et al. 2011). Although such programs have not been scaled up yet and would likely require some prior identification of eligible providers, they have the potential to be effective, given the vast diversity of existing providers.

There might also be scope for interventions that provide information on employment and training opportunities to help young people to decide which training to undertake. Research in Kenya has shown that young people have inaccurate perceptions about the returns to vocational training (including misconceptions about which trades provide the highest earnings) and that their perceptions have a strong gender bias (Hicks et al. 2011). In such a context, there is a role for interventions to increase participation in training by providing information to better match trainees to training. In Kenya, young people changed their training choices after receiving information on actual labor market returns—including differences in expected earnings for trades dominated by men (such as electrician) and women (such as seamstress)—and viewing inspirational videos about successful female car mechanics. In particular, the provision of information caused more women, especially young and more educated girls, to take up training in male-dominated trades.

Such information failures have long been recognized, but public policy has rarely been able to address the issue successfully at scale. Many employment programs aim to improve information on the labor market, but most focus almost exclusively on formal training providers and wage employment. Despite the lack of evidence and thorough testing of such approaches, the cost of providing information is low and the potential for impact is high. Governments could systematically disseminate and communicate data on labor market earnings or training options collected through household surveys or surveys of training providers. Schools could also provide information on employment and training opportunities.

Intervening to Ensure Better Training Options

Given that governments have often stumbled in their efforts to promote skills development, interventions to address market failures must be assessed against the risks of government failures in the provision of training or training subsidies. Inefficiencies in public interventions usually involve challenges in the policy-making process, governance, and institutional arrangements—especially as they relate to accountabil-

---

Box 3.8

Kenya's Jua Kali voucher program

In the mid-1990s, Kenya's Jua Kali Program (Kiswahili for "work under the hot sun") offered training vouchers to HEs operating small fabrication or repair workshops. Eligible participants had to pay 10 percent of the training cost and received vouchers to cover the remainder. The vouchers produced a positive supply response, predominantly from NGOs and master craftsmen in the informal sector. These suppliers developed new programs tailored to the needs of voucher recipients and offered the programs at times that suited participants' work schedules. Public institutions showed little interest in adapting their traditional programs to respond to this new source of demand (Adams 2001). In its pilot stage, the Jua Kali Program successfully expanded the supply and reduced the cost of training for workers in the informal sector. There is evidence that the training had a positive effect on participants' earnings and strengthened the capacity of the local Jua Kali associations responsible for distributing the vouchers. When the program was scaled up, problems in governance led to high administrative costs (Adams 2001; Riley and Steel 2000). Ghana offered a similar voucher program targeted at informal sector enterprises in the early 1990s, but it failed largely because of flaws related to the marketing and distribution of vouchers (Johanson and Adams 2004).

Source: Reproduced from Adams, Johanson de Silva, and Razmara 2013.

ity—and mismatches between the rationale for government intervention and the ways governments actually intervene (such as limited attempts to incorporate the role of information in an effective way). Examples of wasteful institutions abound. Training is often provided in a fragmented way by a large number of ministries with limited accountability, creating substantial inefficiencies and distortions. Many TVET systems are inefficient and create distortions by subsidizing the supply of technical training of similar or inferior quality to the types of training widely delivered by the private sector. Given this experience, public intervention should not only be based on a clear understanding of market failures but also emphasize efficiency and quality service delivery. Whenever public provision or financing is considered, the efficiency of the institutions involved and the quality of service delivered require careful attention.

Given the large number of training institutions and wide range of private providers, the training available to Africa's young people varies greatly in price and quality. In the presence of active training markets, public interventions need to be selective, performance driven, and evidence based.

Measuring the Cost of Training

Large variations in training costs, as well as in the share of costs borne by participants, prevail across types of training—although systematic data are hard to come by. Data from Kenya, illustrated in figure 3.24, give some idea of patterns in training costs.[28] The data include formal TVET (postsecondary TVET, postsecondary National Youth Service, and postprimary youth polytechnics) as well as informal training delivered through faith-based institutions, private TVET providers, or apprenticeships. Training costs range from US$113 for the cheapest private TVET to US$204 for apprenticeships, US$1,942 for National Youth Service, and US$1,704 for the most expensive private TVET. The share paid by participants ranges from all (in private TVET or apprenticeships) to nothing (National Youth Service). The vouchers supplied in the Technical and Vocational Vouchers Program were approximately US$460, which the program designers calculated was "sufficient to fully (or almost

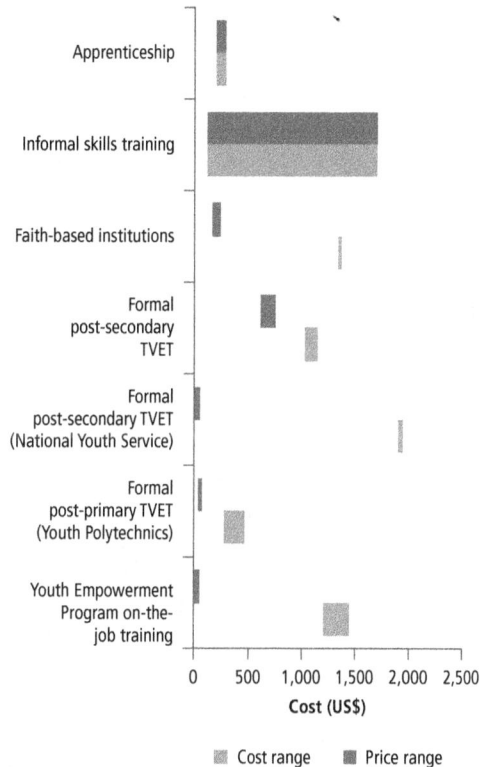

Figure 3.24 **Training costs and the price paid by participants vary by type of training in Kenya**

Source: Franz 2011.
Note: Approximate training cost and price in U.S. dollars.

fully) cover tuition costs for both government and private vocational programs" (Hicks et al. 2011).

The data from Kenya reflect three patterns in training costs that appear to be common in other countries:

- *Formal TVET is very expensive.* In Ghana, the cost of TVET per pupil is about five times the cost of primary education and almost three times the cost of senior secondary education, in line with international averages, in which TVET costs range from two to three times the cost of secondary education (Adams et al. 2009). In Mozambique, TVET costs four times more than secondary school (Fox et al. 2012).

- *The cost of private training varies substantially.* The median cost of private training in northern Uganda, for example, ranges from US$24 to US$444, depending on the type

"Even if training was available for free, it would be hardly possible for me to get time to attend, lest I lose the little income that I get daily in order to survive."
Tanzania

of training (Blattman, Fiala, and Martinez 2011).

- *Informal apprenticeship is often among the cheaper training options.* Sometimes payment is not even required. Among Rwandan owners of HEs who have been trained through apprenticeships, only 40 percent paid for the apprenticeship (Johanson and Gakuba 2011).

Measuring the Quality and Effectiveness of Training

The quality of various training providers is rarely measured directly. A survey of training providers in Kenya found few differences in observable quality between public, private formal, and private informal training providers (Hicks et al. 2011). When young people were offered vouchers to take vocational training, they had a slight preference for public training centers (56 percent) compared to private providers (44 percent). Instructors in public institutions were more likely to have taken the secondary school exam and completed college, yet the profiles of instructors in all institutions were similar in many respects (they had the same practical experience, for example). Differences in infrastructure also appear limited. Urban and formal private institutions were more likely to have flush toilets and electricity than their public, rural, and informal counterparts, but they had comparable instructional capital per student.

Systematic evidence on the quality of TVET institutions is hard to compile. Key indicators of the quality of training are attendance, dropout rates, and graduation rates. Better attendance leads to better learning (Bjorvatn and Tungodden 2010), and high-quality programs have fewer dropouts. Many providers do not track the percentage of participants who complete training, however; when data are available, it is common to find that 25–50 percent of participants do not complete training. Yet high dropout rates are not inevitable (box 3.9).

The share of enrollees who graduate from a training program (in other words, complete and pass the final exam) is often reported to be very low. For example, the pass rates for the Malawi craft and advanced craft examinations are less than 70 percent. For the trades, the pass rate is closer to 50 percent, and it is even lower (on the order of 10–20 percent) in the trades for which delivery is more complex, such as the electrical and mechanical trades (World Bank 2013). Moreover, the constraints facing young women tend to lead to even higher dropout rates for them (Cho et. al. 2013).

Box 3.9

Can incentives improve training quality and participation?

Beneficiary assessments consistently highlight serious issues with the quality of training. For example, a qualitative assessment of the Youth Empowerment Project in Kenya found that the implementation of various training modules varied substantially in quality, and those variations played a key role in participants' evaluation of the modules and decisions to drop out (KEPSA 2012).

Dropout rates can be limited by motivating training participants as well as providers. In Liberia, the Economic Empowerment of Adolescent Girls and Young Women (EPAG) Program used innovative strategies to ensure high participation and training quality (Word Bank 2012b). Participants signed commitment forms, received small stipends contingent on attendance, were offered free child care, and were assigned to small teams with mentors. In addition to those incentives, trainees participated in a variety of contests and competitions. All of the measures contributed to a retention rate surpassing 95 percent and an attendance rate of 90 percent.

Incentives to provide good-quality training can also improve attendance. In a business skills program in Tanzania, attendance, subjective evaluations of course quality, and self-reported knowledge were higher when professional trainers did the teaching (Berge et al. 2011). A qualitative assessment of training in life skills under the Liberia Youth Employment Project found large variations in quality among community trainers (World Bank and Republic of Liberia 2012). In the EPAG Program, training providers were incentivized through performance bonuses, and frequent and unannounced visits to monitor the quality of training also helped to make the training program effective (World Bank 2012b)

Box 3.10

Impact evaluation to build the evidence base on youth employment programs

Impact evaluations provide rigorous evidence of a program's effectiveness by estimating the program's effects on final outcomes, based on an estimate of the counterfactual (the outcomes that would have prevailed for program beneficiaries if they had not participated in the program; see Gertler et al. 2010). The hallmark of sound impact evaluations is that they ensure that the counterfactual is credible—that the only difference between treatment and control groups is participation in the program.

Randomized assignment is the gold standard for impact evaluation. It generates fully comparable treatment and comparison groups by assigning program benefits randomly (for example, by lottery) among equally eligible individuals, households, or communities. Impact evaluations can rely on other methods, although those methods typically require additional (often untestable) assumptions. Most impact evaluations require baseline data as well as a solid comparison group, and they are best designed before a program is implemented, to ensure that baseline data are collected and valid comparison groups identified.

Impact evaluations are often implemented at the scale of pilots, with the result that the scalability and ultimate affordability of the evaluated programs remain a matter of debate, even when the results are positive. Moreover, it may not always be possible to achieve similar positive results in other contexts. Despite these caveats, impact evaluations provide critical information about whether a program can work. When scaled-up programs are evaluated rigorously, the results provide evidence on their effectiveness in "real-world" conditions.

Few interventions to support young workers in Africa have been subject to impact evaluations over the years (Betcherman, Olivas, and Dar 2004; Cho and Honorati 2012). The impacts of a small number of programs targeting the self-employed were evaluated between 2002 and 2012, and recent studies add somewhat to this tally, but more high-quality impact evaluations are greatly needed. Such studies would specifically evaluate the best ways of designing youth employment programs (including the best components to package together), the cost-effectiveness of those programs at scale, and their general equilibrium effects.

Another indicator of quality is the probability of securing a job after graduation. A 2008 study from Nigeria (Billetoft 2010), for example, estimates that less than 30 percent of polytechnic graduates secure a paid job within their area of competence after completing their education. Polytechnic graduates with technical or scientific training do better, however, than those with more general training oriented toward white-collar jobs. A study of public TVET graduates in Tanzania in 1996 found that only 14 percent had found work upon graduation (Fluitman 2001). Studies in the mid-1990s in Mali and Madagascar estimated employment rates of 44 and 45 percent, respectively, one to three years after graduation (Johanson and Adams 2004). In Uganda, although two-thirds of TVET graduates were working, only 31 percent had a "permanent" job (Johanson and Adams 2004).

Aside from tracking employment outcomes among graduates more systematically, impact evaluations are required to compare employment outcomes among graduates to counterfactual employment outcomes, as well as to assess cost-effectiveness by comparing measured impacts to costs. Overall, the evidence from Africa to guide specific programs for improving skills remains thin. Building that evidence base is an urgent priority for action (box 3.10).

Given the large array of skills training available in the private sector, public financing or direct provision of training needs to be selective, performance driven, and evidence based. Governments need to have rationales for the value-added of public intervention in the market for skills, and they must be sure not to displace privately provided training. In addition, the objectives of funding or providing training need to be clear; it is particularly important to clarify whether such training aims to provide pathways to productive employment in HEs or wage employment.

Conclusion: A Skills Agenda for Youth

This chapter has reviewed aspects of the skills agenda that cut across the three sectors of employment: agriculture, HEs, and the modern wage sector. The most urgent policy action is to ensure that children and youths acquire foundational skills through quality basic education. The abysmal performance of education systems throughout Africa results in low worker productivity, and the lack of foundational skills prevents youths from acquiring additional skills and reaching their full potential. It is a pressing priority to improve substantially the quality of schooling so that it results in actual learning and skills acquisition for the growing cohorts of youth who will enter the labor force in the next 10 years. Early childhood development and nutrition must also be promoted actively to ensure that children are more ready to learn when they enter school.

Having a range of skills, beyond cognitive and technical skills, matters for productive employment. Behavioral and socioemotional skills are often a neglected skill set. More attention is required to identify and build the behavioral skills that contribute to productivity—including the skills that employers demand. There is room to leverage education systems to impart behavioral skills as well as to consider including a behavioral skills component in youth employment programs.

Skills "markets" are active in Africa, operating through the private provision of apprenticeships in the HE sector, on-the-job training in the modern wage sector, and other channels. In this context, there is a role for governments to provide information to youth about training and occupational choices as well as to facilitate greater access to existing training opportunities among disadvantaged groups, such as women and the poor.

The scope for direct government intervention in the skills market is more limited. It needs to be well motivated by clearly identifying the rationale for public sector engagement, and it needs to be evidence based. Chapters 4–6 review the evidence for each sector and identify interventions and approaches that are more

promising and worthy of public investment. More evidence on what works in improving employment outcomes among youth, including careful evaluations, is clearly needed across the board.

Chapter 4 discusses the scope and priorities for skills training in the agricultural sector. Traditional agricultural TVET and extension have had a mixed record. However, new models of service delivery that empower farmers and allow them to choose across a range of providers appear promising. These models include participatory farmer field schools as well as beneficiary-driven models to deliver extension services, build skills, and facilitate access to information among young people.

Chapter 5 reviews the evidence on the effectiveness of training for the HE sector. Young people often face multiple constraints in starting a business. Programs attempting to build one skill at a time (such as technical skills, business skills, or behavioral skills alone) have had limited impacts. "Integrated" interventions that build a range of complementary skills together are more promising. Especially promising are "bundled interventions" that deliver integrated skills training along with assistance with accessing start-up capital. Finally, informal training delivered by private providers is normal in the HE sector, so there is scope for governments to leverage NGOs and private providers to support youth through demand-driven, performance-based models.

Chapter 6 outlines specific policy recommendations to build skills for the modern wage sector. Overall, the experience with TVET has been disappointing. Governments in Africa should focus on support for public goods in TVET, such as quality assurance and information, and they should facilitate access to training for poor and disadvantaged youths. Post-school vocational training should only be provided selectively, based on careful targeting and demand-driven models that link employers and training providers. To the extent that governments support specific training options, those options should emphasize portable skills rather than the firm- or job-specific skills that employers should already have an incentive to provide. Programs for disadvantaged youths that integrate training with internships show promise—but the challenge is to make them cost-effective.

Overall, education and skills matter. The starting point in meeting the youth employment challenge is to improve human capital by providing education and allowing youths to acquire the skills needed for productive work. At the same time, it is only the starting point. Governments cannot solely "train their way" to more and better jobs for youth. Policies addressing the economic and business environment have a critical role to play, and chapters 4–6 examine the relative roles of policies that promote skills and those that promote the business environment for the agricultural sector, the HE sector, and the modern wage sector.

Notes

1. Only in Ghana do self-employed workers with incomplete primary education earn significantly more (20 percent) than self-employed workers without education.

2. Low differentials in earnings premiums cannot be explained by the recent surge in primary school enrollment and completion in Africa. Most of that surge happened in the late 2000s, when the cohorts benefiting from increased enrollment had not reached the labor force.

3. In Ghana, the mean wage for workers with incomplete primary schooling was lower than the mean wage of workers without any education, but the difference was not statistically significant.

4. The general patterns for earnings increments hold for both men and women, as well as across urban and rural areas. In Rwanda, Tanzania, and Uganda, earnings differentials tend on average to be higher and steeper for women. In Rwanda and Uganda, earnings differentials are higher in urban areas, while in Ghana and Tanzania, differentials are higher in rural areas.

5. See Aromolaran (2006); Rankin, Sandefur, and Teal (2010). For example, Rankin, Sandefur, and Teal (2010) find clear evidence of convexity in the returns to education for the self-employed in urban Ghana and Tanzania, along with low average returns. Söderbom, Teal, and Harding (2006) find convex earnings functions in both Ghana and Tanzania. They suggest that "convexity may be part of the explanation as to how rapid expansion of education in Africa has generated so little growth if expansion has

been concentrated at lower levels of education." As Teal (2010) finds, "Returns to education, measured both by macro production functions and by micro earning functions, are highest for those with higher levels of education." He argues, "Growth has been more closely linked to investment in physical capital than in education, and this may well reflect the fact that education is most valuable when it is linked to technology which requires higher skills." See also Moll (1996); Appleton, Hoddinott, and Krishnan (1999); Schultz (2004); and Lassibille and Tan (2005).

6. This categorization is only indicative, and many skills are interconnected. For instance, self-control is a behavioral skill that also builds on cognitive ability.

7. In Botswana form-two and in South Africa grade-nine students were tested, corresponding to nine years of schooling; in Ghana form-two students were tested, corresponding to eight years of schooling.

8. Other studies find that differences in a range of cognitive skills explain part of the earnings. See, for example, Glewwe (1991) in Ghana; Moll (1998) for computational skills in South Africa; Denny, Harmon, and O'Sullivan (2003) for functional literacy; Boissiere, Knight, and Sabot (1985) in Kenya and Tanzania; Heckman and Vytlacil (2000) in the United States; or Azam, Chin, and Prakash (2010) in India.

9. Ozier (2010) is based on the fact that in Kenya the probability of admission to a government secondary school rises sharply at a score close to the national mean on a standardized eighth-grade examination. The causal effect of schooling is estimated by comparing those who score just below the national mean to those who score just above it.

10. See www.sdindicators.org.

11. For Madagascar, see Fernald et al. (2011); for Mozambique, see Naudeau et al. (2010); for other parts of the world, see Paxson and Schady (2007); Case, Lubotsky, and Paxson (2002).

12. Walker et al. (2007); Engle et al. (2007). See also the Maternal and Child Undernutrition Series of *The Lancet*, http://www.thelancet.com/series/maternal-and-child-undernutrition.

13. For home visits, see Attanasio et al. forthcoming; Macours et al. forthcoming. For community-based centers, see Martinez, Naudeau, and Pereira (2012). For preschools, see Attanasio and Vera-Hernández (2004); Behrman, Cheng, and Todd (2004); Berlinski, Galiani, and Gertler

(2006); Berlinski, Galiani, and Manacorda (2008).

14. Based on World Bank, Lesotho skills and employment survey, 2011.

15. See Krauss et al. (2005), who study a sample of owners of firms employing seven persons on average. All had been active for more than a year, and half had started with less than US$1,000; 37 percent of the firms were informal. Krauss and her co-authors measure business success as business growth or number of employees. They find that other skills (learning orientation, autonomy orientation, competitive aggressiveness, innovative orientation, risk-taking orientation) are less strongly associated with business success than entrepreneurial and achievement orientation.

16. Heckman, Stixrud, and Urzua (2006). The Rotter Scale measures the degree of control that individuals feel they possess over their lives.

17. www.sdindicators.org.

18. The remainder of this discussion focuses on young adults ages 25–34, because younger individuals may still be in school, and results including them would not reflect the apprenticeship or TVET experience accurately.

19. In Ghana, only 12.7 percent of students who advance beyond lower-secondary education enroll in a TVET institution (World Bank 2009). Low enrollment partly reflects limited capacity; only 5 percent of junior secondary students could have expected to obtain a place in a public TVET institution. If private TVET capacity is included, the percentage rises to 7.2 percent. In Nigeria, less than 1 percent of university enrollment is in a technical college and about 20 percent is in a more advanced polytechnic (World Bank 2011b). Rwanda's vocational training centers enroll just over 10,000 trainees; of these, about 4,700 are enrolled in a public training center—a modest number compared to the roughly 260,000 students enrolled at the secondary level (World Bank 2011a).

20. An estimated 100,000 youths are enrolled in formal TVET, compared with 150,000 in traditional apprenticeships (Franz 2011).

21. Other studies point to similar patterns. In Nigeria, it is estimated that more than half of small business operators acquired their skills in the informal sector from master craftsmen or master trainers (Billetoft 2010). In Rwanda, 25 percent of HE owners report having been trained as an apprentice (Johanson and Gakuba 2011).

22. Frazer (2006) finds that apprenticeship training increases an individual's productivity in the current firm but not in any other firm. Still,

individuals are willing to fund apprenticeships because they can reap the returns to the specific training if they manage to acquire the capital to start their own firm and replicate the technology and business practice of the apprenticeship firm. Apprentices are constrained only by capital from becoming apprenticed entrepreneurs.

23. In northern Uganda, when youth groups were provided cash to pay for training as part of the Youth Opportunities Program, 33 percent chose to obtain training from local artisans and 32 percent chose to obtain it from informal training institutions. In Nigeria, the volume of informal training far exceeds that of formal TVET. Despite being short and of varying quality, informal training is in great demand (Billetoft 2010, 185). Kenya also has a remarkably large, diverse array of private training providers (Hicks et al. 2011; Franz 2011).

24. Youths who did not receive cash grants chose a slightly different mix of training. Short courses on business and management (27 percent) or agribusiness and farming (7 percent) were more common.

25. In the statistics based on household surveys used in this chapter, for example, it is not possible to apportion TVET enrollment between public and private providers or even to know with certainty whether the numbers correspond to both public and private TVET or to public TVET alone.

26. A recent review of training in Malawi estimates that, over the past 10 years, female enrollment in apprenticeships was 21–35 percent of male enrollment (World Bank 2013).

27. While the program was mainly for "industrial courses," it also allowed students to enroll in more academic courses (for example, computer training) and to cover fees up to the level of the average two-year industrial course.

28. These costs exclude opportunity costs, which can be large for training of long duration.

References

Abdulai, Awudu, and Wallace E. Huffman. 2005. "The Diffusion of New Agricultural Technologies: The Case of Crossbreeding Technology in Tanzania." *American Journal of Agricultural Economics* 87 (3): 645–59.

Aber, Lawrence, and Stephanie Jones. 1997. "Indicators of Positive Development in Early Childhood: Improving Concepts and Measures." In *Indicators of Children's Well-being*, edited by Robert Hauser, Brett Brown, and William Prosser, 395–427. New York: Russell Sage Foundation.

Adams, Arvil V. 2001. "Assessment of the Jua Kali Pilot Voucher Program." World Bank, Washington, DC.

Adams, Arvil V., Sara Johansson de Silva, and Setareh Razmara. 2013. *Improving Skills Development in the Informal Sector: Strategies for Sub-Saharan Africa.* Direction in Development Series. Washington, DC: World Bank.

Adams, Arvil V., Harold Coulombe, Quentin Wodon, and Setarah Razmara. 2009. "Education, Employment, and Earnings in Ghana." In *Ghana: Job Creation and Skills Development,* Vol. 2. Washington, DC: World Bank.

Aedo, Christian, and Ian Walker. 2012. *Skills for the 21st Century in Latin America and the Caribbean.* Washington, DC: World Bank. doi: 10.1596/978-0-8213-8971-3.

AfDB (African Development Bank) and OECD (Organisation for Economic Co-operation and Development). 2008. *African Economic Outlook 2008.* Paris: AfDB and OECD. doi: 10.1787/aeo-2008-en.

Al-Samarrai, Samer, and Paul Bennell. 2007. "Where Has All the Education Gone in Sub-Saharan Africa? Employment and Other Outcomes among Secondary School and University Leavers." *Journal of Development Studies* 43 (7): 1270–300.

Almeida, Rita, Jere Behrman, and David Robalino, eds. 2012. *The Right Skills for the Jobs? Rethinking Training Policies for Workers.* Washington, DC: World Bank.

Almlund, Mathilde, Angela Lee Duckworth, James J. Heckman, and Tim Kautz. 2011. "Personality Psychology and Economics." IZA Discussion Paper 5500, Institute for the Study of Labor, Bonn.

Appleton, Simon, John Hoddinott, and Pramila Krishnan. 1999. "The Gender Wage Gap in Three African Countries." *Economic Development and Cultural Change* 47 (2): 289–313.

Aromolaran, Adebayo B. 2006. "Estimates of Mincerian Returns to Schooling in Nigeria." *Oxford Development Studies* 34 (2): 265–92.

Aslam, Monazza, and Kim Lehrer. 2012. "Learning by Doing: Skills and Jobs in Urban Ghana." CSAE Working Paper 2012-15, Centre for the Study of African Economies (CSAE), Oxford.

Atchoarena, David, and Andre Delluc. 2001. "Revisiting Technical and Vocational Education in Sub-Saharan Africa." Report for the World Bank, International Institute for Educational Planning, Paris.

———. 2002. "Revisiting Technical and Vocational Education in Sub-Saharan Africa: An Update on Trends, Innovations, and Challenges." International Institute for Educational Planning (IIEP) and the United Nations Educational, Scientific, and Cultural Organization (UNESCO), Paris.

Atchoarena, David, and Paul Esquieu. 2002. "Private Technical and Vocational Education in Sub-Saharan Africa: Provision Patterns and Policy Issues." International Institute for Educational Planning (IIEP) and the United Nations Educational, Scientific, and Cultural Organization (UNESCO), Paris.

Attanasio, Orazio, Emla Fitzsimons, Sally Grantham-McGregor, Costas Meghir, and Marta Rubio-Codina. Forthcoming. "Stimulation and Childhood Development in Colombia: The Impact of a Scalable Intervention." Institute for Fiscal Studies, University College, London.

Attanasio, Orazio, and Marcos Vera-Hernández. 2004. "Medium- and Long-Run Effects of Nutrition and Child Care: Evaluation of a Community Nursery Program in Rural Colombia." Working Paper EWP04/06, Institute for Fiscal Studies, University College, London.

Azam, Mehtabul, Aimee Chin, and Nishith Prakash. 2010. "The Returns to English-Language Skills in India." IZA Discussion Paper 4802, Institute for the Study of Labor, Bonn.

Bandiera, Oriana, Robin Burgess, Narayam Das, Selim Gulesci, Imran Rasul, and Munshi Sulaiman. 2013. "Can Basic Entrepreneurship Transform the Economic Lives of the Poor?" IZA Discussion Paper 7386, Institute for the Study of Labor, Bonn.

Banerjee, Abhijit V., and Esther Duflo. 2005. "Growth Theory through the Lens of Development Economics." In *Handbook of Economic Growth,* edited by Philippe Aghion and Steven N. Durlauf, 473–52. Amsterdam: Elsevier.

Behrman, Jere, Yingmei Cheng, and Petra Todd. 2004. "Evaluating Preschool Programs When Length of Exposure to the Program Varies: A Nonparametric Approach." *Review of Economics and Statistics* 86 (1): 108–32.

Berge, Lars Ivar Oppedal, Kjetil Bjorvatn, and Bertil Tungodden. 2011. "Human and Financial Capital for Microenterprise Development: Evidence from a Field and Lab Experiment." NHH Department of Economics Discussion Paper 1/2011, Chr. Michelsen Institute (CMI), Bergen.

Berlinski, Samuel, Sebastian Galiani, and Paul Gertler. 2006. "The Effect of Pre-Primary Education on Primary School Performance." Working Paper WP06/04, Institute for Fiscal Studies, University College, London.

Berlinski, Samuel, Sebastian Galiani, and Marco Manacorda. 2008. "Giving Children a Better Start in Life: Preschool Attendance and School-Age

Profiles." *Journal of Public Economics* 92 (5–6): 1416–40.

Besley, Timothy, and Anne Case. 1993. "Modeling Technology Adoption in Developing Countries." *American Economic Review* 83 (2): 396–402.

Betcherman, Gordon, Karina Olivas, and Amit Dar. 2004. "Active Labor Market Programs: New Evidence from Evaluations with Particular Attention to Developing and Transition Countries." Social Protection Discussion Paper 04012, World Bank, Washington, DC.

Biggs, Tyler, Manju Shah, and Pradeep Srivastava. 1995. "Technological Capabilities and Learning in African Enterprises." Technical Paper 288, World Bank, Washington, DC.

Bigsten, Arne, Anders Isaksson, Mans Soderbom, Paul Collier, Albert Zeufack, Stefan Dercon, Marcel Fafchamps, and Jan Willem. 2000. "Rates of Return on Physical and Human Capital in Africa's Manufacturing Sector." *Economic Development and Cultural Change* 48 (4): 801–27.

Billetoft, Jorgen. 2010. "Labor Market Trends and Skills Development." In *Putting Nigeria to Work: A Strategy for Employment and Growth,* edited by Volker Treichel, 167–202. Washington, DC: World Bank.

Bjorvatn, Kjetil, and Bertil Tungodden. 2010. "Teaching Business in Tanzania: Evaluating Participation and Performance." *Journal of the European Economic Association* 8 (2–3): 561–70.

Blattman, Christopher, Nathan Fiala, and Sebastian Martinez. 2011. "Can Employment Programs Reduce Poverty and Social Instability? Experimental Evidence from a Ugandan Aid Program." Columbia University, New York.

Boesel, David, Nabeel Alsalam, and Thomas M. Smith. 1998. *Research Synthesis: Education and Labor Market Performance of GED Recipients.* Washington, DC: U.S. Department of Education, January.

Boissiere, M., J. B. Knight, and R. H. Sabot. 1985. "Earnings, Schooling, Ability, and Cognitive Skills." *American Economic Review* 75 (5): 1016–30.

Boone, Peter, Ila Fazzio, Kameshwari Jandhyala, Chitra Jayanty, Gangadhar Jayanty, Simon Johnson, Vimala Ramachandrin, Filipa Silva, and Zhaoguo Zhan. 2013. "The Surprisingly Dire Situation of Children's Education in Rural West Africa: Results from the CREO Study in Guinea-Bissau (Comprehensive Review of Education Outcomes)." NBER Working Paper 18971, National Bureau of Economic Research, Cambridge, MA.

Bruhn, Miriam, Luciana de Souza Leão, Arianna Legovini, Rogelio Marchetti, and Bilal Zia. 2013.

"Financial Education and Behavior Formation: Large-Scale Experimental Evidence from Brazil." World Bank, Washington, DC.

Bruns, Barbara, Deon Filmer, and Harry Anthony Patrinos. 2011. *Making Schools Work: New Evidence on Accountability Reforms.* Washington, DC: World Bank. doi: 10.1596/978-0-8213-8679-8.

Card, David. 1999. "The Causal Effect of Education on Earnings." In *Handbook of Labor Economics,* Vol. 3, edited by Orley Ashenfelter and David Card, 1802–59. Amsterdam: Elsevier.

Carneiro, Pedro, Emanuela Galasso, and Rita Ginja. 2010. "The Impact of Providing Psycho-Social Support to Indigent Families and Increasing Their Access to Social Services: Evaluating Chile Solidario." Evaluation report, University College, London.

Case, Anne, Darren Lubotsky, and Christina Paxson. 2002. "Economic Status and Health in Childhood: The Origins of the Gradient." *American Economic Review* 92 (5): 1308–34.

Cho, Yoonyoung, and Maddalena Honorati. 2012. "Entrepreneurship Programs in Developing Countries: A Meta Regression Analysis." Policy Research Working Paper 6202, World Bank, Washington, DC.

Cho, Yoonyoung, Davie Kalomba, Ahmed Mushfiq, and Victor Orozco. 2013. "Gender Differences in the Effects of Vocational Training: Constraints on Women and Drop-Out Behavior." Policy Research Working Paper 6545, World Bank, Washington, DC.

Clemens, Michael. 2004. "The Long Walk to School: International Education Goals in Historical Perspective." CGD Working Paper 37, Center for Global Development, Washington, DC.

Cloutier, Marie-Hélène, C. Reinstadtler, and Isabel Beltran. 2011. "Making the Grade: Assessing Literacy and Numeracy in African Countries." DIME Brief, World Bank, Washington, DC. http://go.worldbank.org/15Y7VXO7B0.

Cobb-Clark, Deborah A., and Michelle Tan. 2010. "Noncognitive skills, occupational attainment, and relative wages" *Labour Economics* 18 (1): 1–23.

Cojocaru, Alexandru. 2011. "Tanzania: Skills and the Informal Sector." World Bank, Washington, DC.

CREATE (Consortium for Research on Educational Access, Transitions, and Equity). 2010. "Complementary Education and Access to Primary Schooling in Northern Ghana." CREATE Ghana Policy Brief 2, September. http://www.create-rpc.org/pdf_documents/Ghana_Policy_Brief_2.pdf.

Cunha, Flavio, and James Heckman. 2007. "The Technology of Skill Formation." *American Economic Review* 97 (2): 31–47.

Darvas, Peter. 2012. "Demand and Supply of Technical and Vocational Skills in Ghana." World Bank, Washington, DC.

De Beyer, Joy. 1990. "The Incidence and Impact on Earnings of Formal Training Provided by Enterprises in Kenya and Tanzania." *Economics of Education Review* 9 (4): 321–30.

Delors, Jacques. 1996. *Learning: The Treasure Within.* Report to UNESCO of the International Commission on Education for the Twenty-first Century. Paris: United Nations Educational, Scientific, and Cultural Organization.

Denny, Kevin J., Colm P. Harmon, and Vincent O'Sullivan. 2003. "Functional Literacy, Educational Attainment, and Earnings: A Multi-Country Comparison." School of Economics, University College, Dublin.

DeStefano, Joseph, Audrey-Marie Schuh Moore, David Balwanz, and Ash Harwell. 2006. "Meeting EFA: Reaching the Underserved through Complementary Models of Effective Schooling." EQUIP 2 Working Paper, U.S. Agency for International Development and Academy for Education Development, Washington, DC.

De Wolf, Stefan, Yves Rolland Rakotoarisoa, Laurence Vanpaeschen, and Honoré Rabekoto. 2008. *Madagascar: Le Grand Livre des Petits Métiers: Portraits of Daily Life Professions.* Belgium: Snoek Publishers.

DFID (Department for International Development, UK). 2012. "School for Life 'Literacy for Change.'" *DFID Annual Review* (December).

Duflo, Esther. 2001. "Schooling and Labor Market Consequences of School Construction in Indonesia: Evidence from an Unusual Policy Experiment." *American Economic Review* 91 (4): 795–813.

Dupas, Pascaline, and Jonathan Robinson. 2013. "Savings Constraints and Microenterprise Development: Evidence from a Field Experiment in Kenya." *American Economic Journal: Applied Economics* 5 (1): 163–92.

Engle, Patrice, Maureen Black, Jere Behrman, Meena Cabral de Mello, Paul Gertler, Lydia Kapiriri, Reynaldo Martorell, Mary Young, and the International Child Development Steering Group. 2007. "Strategies to Avoid the Loss of Developmental Potential in More Than 200 Million Children in the Developing World." *The Lancet* 369 (9557): 229–42.

Fafchamps, Marcel, David McKenzie, Simon Quinn, and Christopher Woodruff. 2011. "When Is Capital Enough to Get Female Microenterprises Growing? Evidence from a Randomized

Experiment in Ghana." CSAE Working Paper 2011-11, Centre for the Study of African Economies, Oxford.

Fafchamps, Marcel, and Christopher Woodruff. 2012. "Identifying and Relaxing Constraints to Employment Generation in Small-Scale African Enterprises." University of Oxford.

Fasih, Tazeen, Geeta Kingdon, Harry Anthony Patrinos, Chris Sakellariou, and Mans Soderbom. 2012. "Heterogeneous Returns to Education in the Labor Market." Policy Research Working Paper 6170, World Bank, Washington, DC.

Fernald, Lia C. H., Ann Weber, Emanuela Galasso, and Lisy Ratsifandrihamanana. 2011. "Socioeconomic Gradients and Child Development in a Very Low Income Population: Evidence from Madagascar." *Developmental Science* 14 (4): 832–47.

Fletcher, Jason M. 2012. "The Effects of Personality Traits on Adult Labor Market Outcomes: Evidence from Siblings." IZA Discussion Paper 6391, Institute for the Study of Labor, Bonn.

Fluitman, Fred. 2001. "Working, But Not Well: Notes on the Nature and Extent of Employment Problems in Sub-Sahara Africa." ITC Occasional Paper, International Training Centre, International Labour Organization, Turin.

Foster, Andrew D., and Mark R. Rosenzweig. 1995. "Learning by Doing and Learning from Others: Human Capital and Technical Change in Agriculture." *Journal of Political Economy* 103 (6): 1176–209.

———. 2010. "Microeconomics of Technology Adoption." Yale University, Economic Growth Center, New Haven, CT.

Fox, Louise, Lucrecia Santibañez, Vy Nguyen, and Pierre André. 2012. "Education Reform in Mozambique: Lessons and Challenges." World Bank, Washington, DC.

Franz, Jutta. 2011. "Realizing the Youth Dividend in Kenya through Skills for the Informal Sector: Institutional Assessment of Skills Development and Youth Employment Promotion Programmes and Projects." World Bank, Washington, DC.

Frazer, Garth. 2006. "Learning the Master's Trade: Apprenticeship and Human Capital in Ghana." *Journal of Development Economics* 81 (2): 259–98.

Frese, Michael, Stephanie I. Krauss, Nina Keith, Susanne Escher, Rafal Grabarkiewicz, Siv Tonje, T. Luneng, Constanze Heers, Jens Unger, and Christian Friedrich. 2007. "Business Owners' Action Planning and Its Relationship to Business Success in Three African Countries." *Journal of Applied Psychology* 92 (6): 1481–98.

FXB Center for Health and Human Rights. 2012. "Building Youth Readiness: An Integrated Approach to Promoting Healthy Functioning among War-Affected Youth in Sierra Leone." Harvard University, Cambridge, MA.

Gertler, Paul, James Heckman, Rodrigo Pinto, Arianna Zanolini, Christel Vermeersch, Susan Walker, Susan M. Chang, and Sally Grantham-McGregor. 2013. "Labor Market Returns to Early Childhood Stimulation: A 20-Year Follow-up to an Experimental Intervention in Jamaica." NBER Working Paper 19185, National Bureau of Economic Research Cambridge, MA.

Gertler, Paul, Sebastian Martinez, Patrick Premand, Laura B. Rawlings, and Christel M. J. Vermeersch. 2010. *Impact Evaluation in Practice*. Washington, DC: World Bank.

Glaub, Matthias E. 2009. *Training Personal Initiative to Business Owners in Developing Countries: A Theoretically Derived Intervention and Its Evaluation*. Ph.D. thesis, Justus-Liebig University, Giessen.

Glewwe, Paul. 1991. "Schooling, Skills, and the Returns to Government Investment in Education: An Exploration Using Data from Ghana." Living Standards Measurement LSM76, World Bank, Washington, DC.

———. 2002. "Schools and Skills in Developing Countries: Education Policies and Socioeconomic Outcomes." *Journal of Economic Literature* 40 (2): 436–82.

Glewwe, Paul, Qiuqiong Huang, and Albert Park. 2011. "Cognitive Skills, Non-Cognitive Skills, and the Employment and Wages of Young Adults in Rural China." Paper presented at the annual meeting of the Agricultural and Applied Economics Association, July 24–26, Pittsburgh.

Gove, Amber, and Peter Cvelich. 2010. "Early Reading: Igniting Education for All: A Report by the Early Grade Learning Community of Practice." Research Triangle Institute, Research Triangle Park, NC.

Grantham-McGregor, Sally, Yin Bun Cheung, Santiago Cueto, Paul Glewwe, Linda Richter, and Barbara Strupp. 2007. "Developmental Potential in the First Five Years for Children in Developing Countries." *The Lancet* 369 (9555): 60–70.

Groh, Matthew, Nandini Krishnan, David McKenzie, and Tara Vishwanath. 2012. "Soft Skills or Hard Cash? The Impact of Training and Wage Subsidy Programs on Female Youth Employment in Jordan." Policy Research Working Paper 6141, World Bank, Washington, DC.

Haan, Hans Christian. 2001. "Training for Work in the Informal Sector: Fresh Evidence from Eastern and Southern Africa." International Training Centre, International Labour Organization, Turin.

Haan, Hans Christian, and Nicholas Serrière. 2002. "Training for Work in the Informal Sector: Fresh Evidence from West and Central Africa." International Training Centre, International Labor Organization, Turin.

Hanushek, Eric A., and Ludger Woessmann. 2012. "Do Better Schools Lead to More Growth? Cognitive Skills, Economic Outcomes, and Causation." *Journal of Economic Growth* 17 (4): 267–321.

Heckman, J., L. Lochner, and J. Taber. 1998. "Explaining Rising Wage Inequality: Explorations with a Dynamic General Equilibrium Model of Earnings with Heterogeneous Agents." *Review of Economic Dynamics* 1 (1): 1–58.

Heckman, James A., Jora Stixrud, and Sergio Urzua. 2006. "The Effects of Cognitive and Noncognitive Abilities on Labor Market Outcomes and Social Behavior." *Journal of Labor Economics* 24 (3): 411–82.

Heckman, James, and Edward Vytlacil. 2000. "Identifying the Role of Cognitive Ability in Explaining the Level of and Change in the Return to Schooling." *Review of Economics and Statistics* 83 (1): 1–12.

Helmers, Christian, and Manasa Patnam. 2011. "The Formation and Evolution of Childhood Skill Acquisition: Evidence from India." *Journal of Development Economics* 95 (2): 252–66.

Hicks, Joan Hamory, Michael Kremer, Isaac Mbit, and Edward Miguel. 2011. "Vocational Education Voucher Delivery and Labor Market Returns: A Randomized Evaluation among Kenyan Youth." Report for Spanish Impact Evaluation Fund (SIEF) Phase II, World Bank, Washington, DC.

Huffman, Wallace E. 1977. "Allocative Efficiency: The Role of Human Capital." *Quarterly Journal of Economics* 91 (February): 59–79.

Hungi, Njora, Demus Makuwa, Kenneth Ross, Mioko Saito, Stéphanie Dolata, Frank van Cappelle, Laura Paviot, and Jocelyne Vellien. 2010. "SACMEQ III Project Results: Pupil Achievement Levels in Reading and Mathematics." Working Document 1, Southern Africa Consortium for Measuring Educational Quality (SACMEQ), Harare. http://www.sacmeq.org/downloads/sacmeqIII/WD01_SACMEQ_III_Results_Pupil_Achievement.pdf.

Johanson, Richard K., and Avril V. Adams. 2004. *Skills Development in Sub-Saharan Africa*. Washington, DC: World Bank.

Johanson, Richard, and Theogene Kayiranga Gakuba. 2011. "Rwanda: Training for the Informal Sector." World Bank, Washington, DC.

KEPSA (Kenya Private Sector Alliance). 2012. "Beneficiary Assessment of Kenya Youth Empowerment Project (KYEP) Training and Internship Component." KEPSA, March.

Kitaev, Igor, with contributions from J. Glover, A. Melomey, Th. Coleman, and B. Kaluba. 2003. "Phase II: Synthesis of Main Findings from Two Case Studies Carried out in Ghana and Zambia on Private Technical and Vocational Education and Training (TVET)." International Institute for Educational Planning (IIEP) and UNESCO, Paris.

Koop, Sabine, Tamara De Reu, and Michael Frese. 2000. "Sociodemographic Factors, Entrepreneurial Orientation, Personal Initiative, and Environmental Problems in Uganda." In *Success and Failure of Microbusiness Owners in Africa: A Psychological Approach*, edited by M. Frese, 55–76. Westport, CT: Quorum.

Krauss, Stefanie I., Michael Frese, Christian Friedrich, and Jens M. Unger. 2005. "Entrepreneurial Orientation: A Psychological Model of Success among Southern African Small Business Owners." *European Journal of Work and Organizational Psychology* 14 (3): 315–44.

Kuepie, Mathias, Christophe J. Nordman, and Francois Roubaud. 2009. "Education and Earnings in Urban West Africa." *Journal of Comparative Economics* 37 (3): 491–515.

Lassibille, Gerard, and Jee-Peng Tan. 2005. "The Returns to Education in Rwanda." *Journal of African Economies* 14 (1): 92–116.

Lee, Jean N., and David Newhouse. 2012. "Cognitive Skills and Youth Labor Market Outcomes." Background paper for *World Development Report 2013: Jobs*. World Bank, Washington, DC.

Lundberg, Mattias, and Alice Wuermli, eds. 2012. *Children and Youth in Crisis: Protecting and Promoting Human Development in Times of Economic Shocks*. Washington, DC: World Bank. doi: 10.1596/978-0-8213-9547-9.

Macours, Karen, Patrick Premand, Norbert Schady, and Renos Vakis. Forthcoming. "Experimental Evidence from an Early Childhood Parenting Intervention in Nicaragua." World Bank, Washington, DC.

Macours, Karen, Patrick Premand, and Renos Vakis. 2013. "Demand Versus Returns? Pro-Poor Targeting of Business Grants and Vocational Skills Training." Policy Research Working Paper 6389, World Bank, Washington, DC.

Maluccio, John A., John Hoddinott, Jere R. Behrman, Reynaldo Martorell, Agnes R. Quisumbing, and Aryeh D. Stein. 2009. "The Impact of Improving Nutrition during Early Childhood on Education among Guatemalan Adults." *Economic Journal* 119 (537): 734–63.

Mano, Yukichi, Alhassan Iddrisu, Yutaka Yoshino, and Tetsushi Sonobe. 2011. "How Can Micro and Small Enterprises in Sub-Saharan Africa Become More Productive? The Impacts of Experimental Basic Managerial Training." *World Development* 40(3):458–68.

Martinez, Sebastian, Sophie Naudeau, and Victor Pereira. 2012. "The Promise of Preschool in Africa: A Randomized Impact Evaluation of Early Childhood Development in Rural Mozambique." World Bank and Save the Children, Washington, DC.

Mattero, Minna. 2010. "Second Chance Education for Out-of-School Youth: A Conceptual Framework and Review of Programs." World Bank, Washington, DC.

Mingat, Alain, Blandine Ledoux, and Ramahatra Rakotomalala. 2010. *Developing Post-Primary Education in Sub-Saharan Africa: Assessing the Financial Sustainability of Alternative Pathways*. Washington, DC: World Bank.

Moll, Peter G. 1996. "The Collapse of Primary Schooling Returns in South Africa, 1960–90." *Oxford Bulletin of Economics and Statistics* 58 (1): 185–209.

———. 1998. "Primary Schooling, Cognitive Skills, and Wages in South Africa." *Economica* 65 (258): 263–84.

Monk, Courtney, Justin Sandefur, and Francis Teal. 2008. "Does Doing an Apprenticeship Pay Off? Evidence from Ghana." CSAE Working Paper 2008-08, Centre for the Study of African Economies, Oxford.

Mullis, Ina V.S., Michael O. Martin, Pierre Foy, and Alka Arora. 2012. *TIMSS 2011 International Results in Mathematics*. TIMSS & PIRLS International Study Center, Lynch School of Education, Boston College, Chestnut Hill, MA, and International Association for the Evaluation of Educational Achievement (IEA) IEA Secretariat, Amsterdam, the Netherlands.

Naudeau, Sophie, Sebastian Martinez, Patrick Premand, and Deon Filmer. 2010. "Cognitive Development among Young Children in Developing Countries." In *No Small Matter: The Impact of Poverty, Shocks, and Human Capital Investment in Early Childhood Development*, edited by Harold Alderman, 9–50. Washington, DC: World Bank.

Nayar, Reema, Pablo Gottret, Mitra Pradeep, Gordon Betcherman, Yue Man Lee, Indhira Santos, Mahesh Dahal, and Maheshwor Shrestha. 2012. "More and Better Jobs in South Asia." South Asia Development Matters Report 66229, World Bank, Washington, DC.

Nell, Marian, and Janet Shapiro. 1999. "Traditional Apprenticeship Practice in Dar es Salaam: A

Study." Consultancy report prepared for GTZ/VETA, GTZ/VETA, Dar es Salaam.

Nicholson, Sue. 2006. "Accelerated Learning Programs in Post Conflict Settings: A Discussion Paper." Save the Children US, Westport, CT.

Oosterbeek, Hessel, Mirjam van Praag, and Auke Ijsselstein. 2008. "The Impact of Entrepreneurship Education on Entrepreneurship Competencies and Intentions: An Evaluation of the Junior Achievement Student Mini-Company Program." IZA Discussion Paper 3641, Institute for the Study of Labor, Bonn.

Ozier, Owen. 2010. "The Impact of Secondary Schooling in Kenya: A Regression Discontinuity Analysis." Development Research Group, World Bank, Washington, DC.

Paxson, Christina, and Norbert Schady. 2007. "Cognitive Development among Young Children in Ecuador: The Roles of Wealth, Health, and Parenting." *Journal of Human Resources* 42 (1): 49–84.

Peeters, Pia, Wendy Cunningham, Gayatri Acharya, and Arvil Van Adams. 2009. "Youth Employment in Sierra Leone: Sustainable Livelihood Opportunities in a Post-Conflict Setting." World Bank, Washington, DC.

Premand, Patrick, Stefanie Brodmann, Rita Almeida, Rebekka Grun, and Mahdi Barouni. 2012. "Entrepreneurship Training and Self-Employment among University Graduates: Evidence from a Randomized Trial in Tunisia." Policy Research Working Paper 6285, World Bank, Washington, DC.

Pritchett, Lant. 2013. *The Rebirth of Education: From 19th-Century Schooling to 21st-Century Learning.* Washington, DC: Brookings Institution Press.

Rankin, Neil, Justin Sandefur, and Francis Teal. 2010. "Learning and Earning in Africa: Where Are the Returns to Education High?" CSAE Working Paper 2010-02, Centre for the Study of African Economies, Oxford.

Riley, Thyra A., and William F. Steel. 2000. "Kenya Voucher Programme for Training and Business Development Services." In *Business Development Services: A Review of International Experience,* edited by Jacob Levitsky, ch. 12. London: Intermediate Technology Publications.

Roberts, Brent W., and Daniel Mroczek. 2008. "Personality Trait Change in Adulthood." *Current Directions in Psychological Science* 17 (1): 31–35.

Rosendahl Huber, Laura, Randolph Sloof, and Mirjam van Praag. 2012. "The Effect of Early Entrepreneurship Education: Evidence from a Randomized Field Experiment." IZA Discus-

sion Paper 6512, Institute for the Study of Labor, Bonn.

Rosholm, Michael, Helena Skyt Nielsen, and Andrew Dabalen. 2007. "Evaluation of Training in African Enterprises." *Journal of Development Economics* 84 (1): 310–29.

Schultz, T. Paul. 2004. "Evidence of Returns to Schooling in Africa from Household Surveys: Monitoring and Restructuring the Market for Education." *Journal of African Economies* 13 (supplement 2): ii95–148.

Shaorshadze, Irina, and Pramila Krishnan. 2013. "Technical and Vocational Education and Training in Ethiopia." Working Paper, International Growth Centre, London School of Economics, February.

Shonkoff, Jack P., and Deborah Phillips, eds. 2000. *From Neurons to Neighborhoods: The Science of Early Childhood Development.* Washington, DC: National Academy Press.

Söderbom, Måns, Francis Teal, and Alan Harding. 2006. "The Determinants of Survival among African Manufacturing Firms." *Economic Development and Cultural Change* 54 (3): 533–55.

South Sudan, Government of, Ministry of General Education and Instruction. 2011. *Education Statistics for the Republic of South Sudan: National Statistical Booklet, 2011.* Juba.

Steinberg, Laurence, Elizabeth Cauffman, Jennifer Woolard, Sandra Graham, and Marie Banich. 2009. "Are Adolescents Less Mature Than Adults? Minors' Access to Abortion, the Juvenile Death Penalty, and the Alleged Apa 'Flip-Flop.'" *American Psychologist* 64 (7): 583–94.

Teal, Francis. 2010. "Higher Education and Economic Development in Africa: A Review of Channels and Interactions." CSAE Working Paper 2010-25, Centre for the Study of African Economies, Oxford.

Tubbs, Carly, and Dana Charles McCoy. 2012. "Early Childhood Development: An Introduction." In *Children and Youth in Crisis: Protecting and Promoting Human Development in Times of Economic Shocks,* edited by Mattias Lundberg and Alice Wuermli, 106–15. Washington, DC: World Bank.

UNESCO (United Nations Educational, Scientific and Cultural Organization). 2012. *EFA Global Monitoring Report: Youth and Skills: Putting Education to Work.* Paris: UNESCO.

Unger, Jens M., Nina Keith, Christine Hilling, Michael M. Gielnik, and Michael Frese. 2009. "Deliberate Practice among South African Small Business Owners: Relationships with Education, Cognitive Ability, Knowledge, and Success." *Jour-*

nal of Occupational and Organizational Psychology 82 (1): 21–44.

Uwezo Tanzania. 2011. "Are Our Children Learning? Annual Learning Assessment Report." Uwezo Tanzania, Dar es Salaam. http://www.uwezo.net/wp-content/uploads/2012/08/TZ_2011_AnnualAssessment-Report.pdf.

Valdivia, Martin. 2011. "Training or Technical Assistance? A Field Experiment to Learn What Works to Increase Managerial Capital for Female Microentrepreneurs." Grupo de Análisis para el Desarrollo (GRADE), Lima.

Walker, Susan P., Theodore D. Wachs, Julie Meeks Gardner, Betsy Lozoff, Gail A. Wasserman, Ernesto Pollitt, and Julie A. Carter. 2007. "Child Development: Risk Factors for Adverse Outcomes in Developing Countries." The Lancet 369 (9556): 145–57.

Welch, F. 1970. "Education in Production." Journal of Political Economy 78 (1): 35–59.

World Bank. 2003. World Development Report 2004: Making Services Work for Poor People. New York: Oxford University Press.

———. 2009. Ghana: Job Creation and Skills Development. Vol. 1: Main Report. Washington, DC: World Bank.

———. 2011a. "Challenges and Options for Technical and Post-Basic Education in South Africa." World Bank, Washington, DC.

———. 2011b. "Raising Productivity and Reducing the Risk of Household Enterprises." Ghana Country Study, Policy Note, World Bank, Washington, DC.

———. 2012a. "Botswana: Policy Note 2: Labor Market Signals on Demand for Skills." World Bank, Africa Region, Human Development Department, Washington, DC.

———. 2012b. "Preliminary EPAG Midline Report: Economic Empowerment of Adolescent Girls and Young Women (EPAG) Project in Liberia." World Bank, Washington, DC.

———. 2013. "The Skills Development System in Malawi." World Bank, Washington, DC.

———. Various years. World Development Indicators. Washington, DC: World Bank. http://wdi.worldbank.org.

World Bank and Republic of Liberia. 2012. "Community Works Life Skills Training Assessment: Youth, Employment, Skills Project Mid-Term Review." World Bank, Washington, DC.

Wuermli, Alice, Rainer K. Silbereisen, Mattias Lundberg, Michele Lamont, Jere R. Behrman, and Larry Aber. 2012. "A Conceptual Framework." In Children and Youth in Crisis: Protecting and Promoting Human Development in Times of Economic Shocks, edited by Mattias Lundberg and Alice Wuermli, 29–102. Washington, DC: World Bank.

Xu, Lisa, and Bilal Zia. 2012. "Financial Literacy around the World: An Overview of the Evidence with Practical Suggestions for the Way Forward." Policy Research Working Paper 6107, World Bank, Washington, DC.

Chapter 4

Agriculture as a Sector of Opportunity for Young Africans

Efforts to accelerate agricultural growth and improve food security have often been separated conceptually from efforts to create jobs for young people. This damaging compartmentalization, if it persists, will limit Africa's ability to reap the benefits of its youth dividend. Agriculture, already Africa's largest employer, is the most immediate means of catalyzing economic growth and employment for young people. To realize this potential, farming must shift rapidly from its present status as occupation of last resort and low productivity to one of technical dynamism and recognized opportunity. With higher priority accorded to accelerated implementation of well-designed programs of public investment in agriculture, continued progress on regulatory and policy reform, and further specific measures to include young people, agriculture will absorb the large numbers of new job seekers and offer meaningful work with large public and private benefits.

Agriculture—once the predominant sector in most of the world's economies—has historically played a lesser role as economies developed the accumulated wealth, innovations in technology, and connections through trade that spurred diversification and structural change. Faster growth in nonagricultural sectors has drawn enough labor out of agriculture to cause the share of employment in agriculture to fall. Labor shifted out of agriculture because productivity gains on the farm saved labor (push factors), and higher productivity and earnings opportunities off the farm attracted labor (pull factors).[1]

Africa is not following that trajectory. In many African countries, income generated through the extraction of natural resources and urban construction and services has raised gross domestic product (GDP) without drawing significant numbers of workers out of agriculture. Even under optimistic assumptions, the cohort of young Africans now entering the labor force is likely to exceed the number that can be absorbed into jobs in manufacturing and services (see chapter 1). Over the next few decades, young people will continue to apply their energies and talents to agriculture, on or near the farmstead of their birth (Proctor and Lucchesi 2012). The critical question is how African youths and their countries can benefit from agricultural employment. The answer depends on whether governments take the policy and investment decisions that will lift the constraints on agricultural productivity.

The reasons for Africa's slow growth in agricultural productivity are known. Cropping systems based on wheat and irrigated rice, which registered spectacular productivity gains in South and East Asia, are not suited for most environments south of the Sahara. Africa's complex agro-ecologies and highly diverse production systems demand a level of original research comparable to that undertaken elsewhere in the world, but Africa is only beginning to reverse decades of neglect and underinvestment in agricultural research. It will take time for the benefits to be felt in earnest. The effects of low productivity in African agriculture are also well known. Low productivity is partially responsible for the high food prices prevalent in much of Africa, where expenditures on primary food products can account for as much as half of consumers' expenditures (OECD and FAO 2012). High food prices also curtail competitiveness by increasing the cost of labor.

In the interim and until research specific to Africa's environments is available, growth in agricultural productivity will need to come from wider use of superior technologies that have worked elsewhere—improved seeds, breeds, cropping methods, conservation practices, and equipment. Over the past decade, more farmers across Africa have started to adopt such technologies,[2] although not as rapidly as farmers in other regions. Recent investments and policy reform may catalyze more rapid adoption, but the levels of investment, pace of implementation, and quality of programs in Africa have not yet sufficed to deliver a large shift in productivity.

Agriculture: Potential Opportunity, Room to Grow

The opportunity that farming represents in Sub-Saharan Africa is clearly evident in the region's trade accounts. The value of Africa's food markets is projected to increase from US$313 billion in 2010 to US$1 trillion in 2030 (World Bank 2013). Food imports surged ahead of exports as recently as 2003, and they have continued to climb. The growth in imports has been variously attributed to the failure of agricultural production to keep up with population growth (which is incorrect, as per capita production has risen over this period), climate change, and other supply-side factors. Supply matters, but the fundamental point is that rapid growth in population, incomes, and urbanization is increasing the demand for imported food faster than the supply of domestically produced substitutes is growing.

Rapidly growing demand creates opportunities for suppliers. For example, urbanization could be good news for local agriculture. The denser patterns of settlement seen as rural communities grow and merge[3] can reduce marketing costs for agricultural producers in the hinterlands and raise the returns to investments in processing raw products. Nor is growth in demand limited to Africa's expanding domestic markets. Global food prices are at their highest point in several decades, and, barring significant changes in policies related to biofuels, food prices are expected to remain high for at least the rest of the decade.

The opportunities presented by this growing local and international demand for food are likely to be as varied as African agriculture itself. On average agriculture is a sector of low labor productivity and high employment, but in reality it is exceptionally heterogeneous. Even in developed countries, agriculture is sufficiently heterogeneous to raise questions about what constitutes a farm. In Africa every farm lies somewhere along wide continuums of farm size, capital intensity, use of mechanical and biological technology, and degree of commercialization. The first requirement for creating good opportunities for young people in African agriculture is to gain a detailed understanding of the sector by peeling back the averages to reveal the dispersion of participants' activities, command of assets, and use of skills. This task demands close, continuous attention to gender issues, given the importance of women and girls in Africa's agricultural labor force (box 4.1).

New opportunities for African agriculture to benefit from changes in local and national markets will emerge from segments of the farming structure that have been underdeveloped in the past but now have room to grow. For example, in many African capitals, rice is twice as expensive as it is in Asian exporting countries. The price of maize, the main food staple in Eastern and Southern Africa, is 30–40 percent above export prices in South Africa, the United States, and the Black Sea region (table 4.1). If local producers become more competitive, they can capture thriving domestic and regional markets. Measures that reduce the costs of production (such as the dissemination of improved technology) and marketing (such as investments in transportation and infrastructure) can increase profitability and reduce food costs. Even in countries that are relatively well linked to world markets, increased local production can lower food prices, because international prices do not translate directly into local market prices (Minot 2011). Lower food prices not only help consumers but also temper demands for higher wages in the nonfarm sector, which attracts new investment in manufacturing and services. New investment creates new jobs, fueling a virtuous cycle (box 4.2).

Box 4.1

Women and girls: A major force within Africa's agricultural labor force

African women and girls work in agriculture as farmers on their own land, as unpaid workers on family farms, and as paid laborers on other farms and in agricultural enterprises. They are involved in both crop and livestock production at subsistence and commercial levels.

Across developing countries, women comprise 43 percent of the agricultural labor force, on average; this figure ranges from around 20 percent in Latin America to 50 percent in parts of Africa and Asia. Some Sub-Saharan African countries have seen women's share of the agricultural labor force rise significantly in recent decades due to conflict, the human immunodeficiency virus/acquired immune deficiency syndrome (HIV/AIDS), migration, and livelihood diversification, but regional data conceal wide differences. The share of women in the agricultural labor force ranges from 36 percent in Côte d'Ivoire and Niger to more than 60 percent in Lesotho, Mozambique, and Sierra Leone (FAO 2011). Nevertheless, one regional trend is clear—it is usually the male member of the agricultural household who moves into a nonfarm activity first (Fox and Sohnesen 2012).

How countries choose to increase agricultural productivity will influence whether this virtuous cycle is sustained, with benefits to young people and the economy as a whole, or

Table 4.1 Wholesale prices of unprocessed maize and rice in selected countries (average, January–April 2012)

Maize		Rice	
Market	Wholesale price (US$ per ton)	Market	Wholesale price (US$ per ton)
Africa			
Ethiopia	390	Benin	1,055
Kenya	393	Burkina Faso	738
Malawi	400	Madagascar	593
Mozambique	378	Mali	690
Rwanda	318	Mozambique	865
South Africa	293	Niger	850
Tanzania	334	Senegal	810
Togo	453	Togo	1,097
Uganda	334	Uganda	1,368
Zimbabwe	300	*International benchmark*	
International benchmark		India	378
Black Sea region	267	Thailand	556
United States	276	Vietnam	434

Source: FAO Global Information and Early Warning System.

Box 4.2

When agriculture is more productive, economies can grow

Despite differences in the global context and national economic circumstances, the effects of agriculture on the U.S. economy over the past 45 years may provide useful lessons for Africa at this juncture, when so many young people are poised to enter the agricultural workforce. From 1960 to 2005, the United States produced more agricultural commodities more cheaply than ever. The real prices of most agricultural commodities declined 20–50 percent (see table B4.2.1). Even though the cost of food was rising throughout the world, most food prices were still lower in 2010 (in constant U.S. dollars) than they were in 1960. For the economy as a whole, low prices of primary food products meant that it was much cheaper to process food into an array of consumer products (an activity that generated new jobs). The low prices enabled consumers to spend more money on items other than food. Higher agricultural productivity contributed to broad-based income growth in the United States.

Figure B4.2.1 Higher total factor productivity helped U.S. farmers to compensate for declining terms of trade, 1975–2009

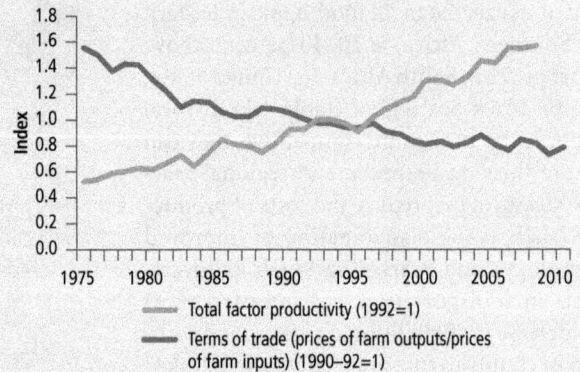

Legend:
- Total factor productivity (1992=1)
- Terms of trade (prices of farm outputs/prices of farm inputs) (1990–92=1)

Source: Executive Office of the President 2011.

Even while the prices of commodities they produced declined, farmers and other agricultural workers preserved their livelihoods. As real agricultural prices fell and the cost of inputs and factors of production rose, farmers in the United States and other developed countries still managed to profit (and so did agricultural wage earners) by increasing their productivity. They used inputs more efficiently and changed their mix of outputs. In the United States between 1975 and 2010, total factor productivity rose 2.2 percent a year, which was low by historic standards but sufficient to maintain profitability (see figure B4.2.1).

Table B4.2.1 Percentage change in prices of selected food products in the United States, 1960–2010

Period	Wheat	Maize	Sugar	Beef
1960–2005	−43	−52	−19	−23
2006–2010	8	41	50	22
1960–2010	−24	−18	24	−10

Source: World Bank Pink Sheets.

whether it is short-lived. As demand for food rises, growth in total factor productivity will be necessary to keep real food prices in check and maintain the capacity to create jobs.[4] Unless serious attention is paid to interventions that can truly sustain productivity, such as agricultural research, the development of farming skills, and the adoption of new and better varieties, growth in output will come through increased use of purchased inputs such as fertilizer and agro-chemicals. The resulting growth in output may be rapid for a short period if the inputs boost yields, but it will be costly, increase the real price of food, and ultimately erode potential gains to producers, consumers, and society at large (box 4.3).

African leaders who are framing strategies for agriculture now should be aware that the circumstances they face are quite different from those that shaped traditional experiences of development and structural change. African agriculture is developing in a context of high global food prices, potential for growth in area and yield, few nontradable manufactured goods, and shifts in comparative advantage in the developed world in favor of technology-intensive services and products (Losch, Fréguin-Gresh, and White 2012). In this context, if African farmers change the technology they use and the mix of commodities they produce, agriculture's share in African GDP could remain larger than has historically been the case or even grow with development. Furthermore, the cost of withdrawing labor from agriculture seems to have increased over time around the world, and this is another factor arguing that Africa's experience may be different (Timmer and Akkus 2008). Over the past 50 years, the point at which wages in agriculture converge with those in nonagricultural jobs has been reached at later and later stages in the transformation of successful economies, perhaps suggesting that globally industry is becoming less and less able to absorb labor.

Recent cautiously optimistic trends suggest that the sources of agricultural growth in Africa may be changing. Between 1960 and 2008, cultivated area grew faster than yields (Fuglie 2011). About 40 percent of the growth in yield came from greater use of purchased inputs and 60 percent from changes in total factor productivity. Between 2006 and 2008, when African governments began to give greater attention to agriculture,[5] yield growth dominated area growth, and total factor productivity rose. These recent developments suggest that if governments would intensify and sustain their efforts to raise factor productivity, they could secure lower prices for consumers, higher earnings for farmers, and good opportunities for young people to enter farming.

Recognizing the Opportunity in Agriculture for Young People

Many young people know little of the opportunities and dynamism possible in farming today. When young rural Africans in 32 focus groups were asked about the best and worst ways to earn a living in their community, they rarely mentioned agriculture as the "best job" (although it was not considered the worst). Participants described good jobs as those that command good pay and respect, two features not typically associated with farming under the conditions most familiar to young Africans. They described bad jobs as those that offer poor, insecure returns and are physically damaging or demanding or illegal.

Even so, the focus groups gave mixed messages regarding the desirability of farming as a

> ### Box 4.3
>
> ### Compromising growth and job creation without improving long-term food security
>
> Since 2008, several African countries have introduced subsidy programs that encourage farmers to use fertilizer on staple crops without supporting the use of more productive varieties and better management practices. As a result, farmers have devoted much of their land to staple crops, crowding out higher-value, more labor-intensive crops and slowing the pace at which agriculture creates jobs and expands productivity. In some cases, the production of staple crops surged briefly, only to drop off sharply once the expensive (and often politicized) distribution of subsidized fertilizer came to an end. Early evidence suggests that, even while the subsidies were in place, the yield response of varieties in use was considerably less than anticipated. Much can be done to improve the production of staple food crops without compromising growth and job creation in this way. The lesson is that fertilizer use should be one part of a broader program to promote gains in productivity and encourage diversification into higher-valued and more labor-intensive products.

livelihood, and their perceptions varied widely across Africa. Within three broad categories of jobs (nonfarm wage, nonfarm nonwage, and agriculture), "family farming" was the desirable job named most often. Yet with the exception of a women's group in North Darfur, none of the focus groups from South Africa, Sudan, or Togo mentioned any farming activities as a good job (Petesch and Caillava 2012). Within the same broad categories, farming followed only illegal and antisocial jobs as the "worst job." Focus group interviews with urban young people suggest that agriculture virtually disappears from mention as the "best job." To attract young people, agriculture will need to be more dynamic and appealing than it is now, and young people will need to view the sector more positively (IDS 2012). The farms that offer attractive opportunities will have to be quite different from those that most young Africans know.

Patterns of Land Use, Farm Size, and Profitability

The farms that many young Africans know from childhood are small and worked with back-breaking labor and little mechanization.

"Farming is a good job because it is where I can get food to eat and live well."
Liberia

Figure 4.1 The young do not typically own land

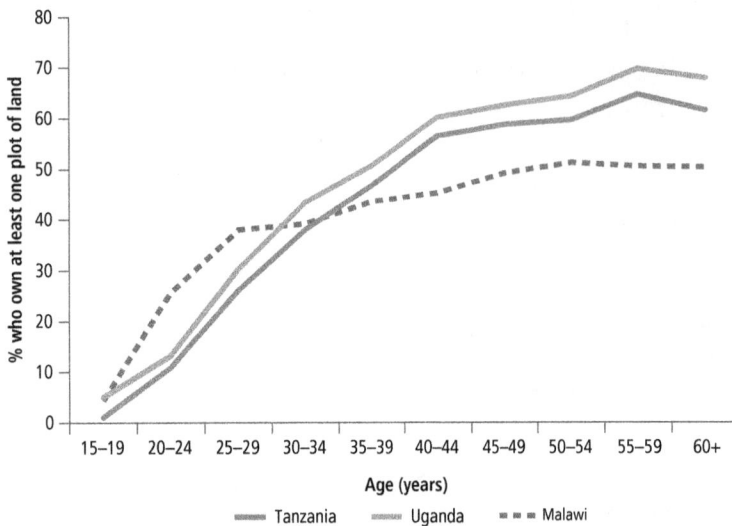

Source: Based on data from the Living Standards Measurement Study–Integrated Survey on Agriculture.

"If you have only a small parcel for eight people, not everyone can eat." Madagascar

Holdings of 1 to 2 hectares predominate, and the most common implements are the hand hoe and machete (Nagayets 2005). According to World Bank data from three countries, owned land increases with age of the farmer (figure 4.1)—the average plot size, even for older farmers, often remains well under 1 hectare.

This pattern of land use is seen whether land is scarce or abundant, although for different reasons. Where settlement is dense and land is scarce, as in Rwanda and Malawi, holdings per household and per worker are small and shrinking with population growth. Under these circumstances, investments in irrigation, application of purchased inputs, improved varieties, high-valued crops, double and triple cropping, terracing, and other practices can increase the productivity of land and incomes. Investments that make it easier to reach markets increase the demand for agricultural products and reduce the cost of transporting them. The returns to intensification rise, and more such investments take place.

But why are farms so small in areas where land is abundant, as in much of Africa? Farm size is often limited to the amount of land that a household can farm manually, because machinery is expensive, cannot be purchased without financing, and can be challenging to own and use collectively. Animal traction makes it possible to farm larger areas, but trypanosomiasis and other animal diseases constrain the use of draft animals in many parts of Africa.

Alternatively, land may be abundant but virtually impossible to acquire because of ambiguities in the transactability of land through purchase, sale, leasing, inheritance, assignment under traditional rules, and mortgage (World Bank 2012b). When constraints on the operation of land markets raise the cost of accessing new land, a young person reaching adulthood may simply farm a portion of the family's original holding rather than secure a new allotment. It is not unusual for the continuous fragmentation of small holdings to persist alongside the acquisition of large tracts by outside investors, whether domestic or foreign.

A third consideration is that small, labor-intensive farms can be economically appropriate, efficient, and profitable under certain conditions. Recent evidence based on a geographically wide and heterogeneous set of data confirms an inverse relationship between maize yield and farm size, supporting the premise documented in earlier studies that small farms are often productive in the African context and that smallholders do not necessarily forgo economies of scale (Larson et al. 2012). Historically, primary production of staple commodities has not exhibited increasing returns to scale, and smallholders who voluntarily form producer groups can capture scale economies where they do exist—for example, in the marketing of their produce and access to information (see box 4.4; Morris, Binswanger-Mkhize, and Byerlee 2009).

The most desirable farm size, however, is an economic issue and not a matter of principle or ideology. Where relevant costs of production are readily divisible, smallholders will do as well as or better than others. Where costs are not divisible for whatever reason, smallholders will be at a disadvantage but will still be very numerous. In that case, programs that facilitate adjustments in farm size or address the indivisible costs will be constructive.

Getting Young Africans the Farms They Need

Even where small farms are demonstrably efficient, agricultural productivity cannot grow if more family labor crowds onto them. The income that 1 or 2 hectares can generate is rarely sufficient to pull all members of a household out of poverty. For agricultural productivity and incomes to grow, young people will need to be able to acquire more land, and young workers will need to be able to leave the farm of their birth for other forms of employment.

Since mobility out of farming has been low in Africa, much of the land is now held by aging farmers despite the large cohort of potential new entrants. Constraints to intergenerational transfers of land are particularly costly when land is scarce or young people have difficulty acquiring holdings to start farming on their own. Where old-age pensions do not exist and rental markets are poorly developed, elderly farmers often retain control over holdings that would be managed more efficiently by younger, more innovative, and energetic farmers (box 4.5).

More fluid land markets would create better opportunities for young people to practice more productive and managerially demanding agriculture. As processors and urban consumers demand quality and traceability in agricultural produce and as changing weather patterns undermine the validity of traditional "rules of thumb" for the agricultural cycle, agriculture requires a more sophisticated level of management. Young people are well suited to acquire and exercise managerial expertise, and they can do so in many ways, but the managerial acumen of an individual farmer is as indivisible as a tractor. Each creates economic pressures to amalgamate very small farms into larger units or develop new networks of producers to share costs. For this reason, increased fluidity of land markets, in particular through land rentals, is essential for a new generation of African farmers to take advantage of opportunities emerging in agriculture. Producer organizations may need to innovate in the delivery of managerial services, an area in which they have not been active in the past.

When factor endowments and the characteristics of technology and markets imply that the optimal farm size is larger than what is observed, constraints on capital and land markets impose a high burden of inefficiency on rural people. Although smallholders may not

---

Box 4.4

Producer organizations and the transition to modern supply chains

Rural productive alliances can bring producer organizations and commercial buyers together to increase income and employment via participation in modern supply chains. These alliances have been shown to bring about higher agricultural incomes and increased rural employment, especially for agricultural workers and women working in postharvest activities (World Bank 2012a). Farmers have also benefited from employment opportunities generated by public-private partnerships that enhance agricultural productivity. For example, a successful model in Latin America that sought to increase competitiveness along the entire value chain for cassava (production, processing, and utilization) worked with farmer groups and cooperatives (among many others) and ultimately expanded training and jobs for farmers in cassava-based agro-industries.

Source: World Bank 2012a.

Box 4.5

Options for establishing or leaving a farm in Kenya

Kenya's young people have great difficulty establishing themselves as farm operators. According to a large national sample drawn from participants in the Kenya Agricultural Productivity and Agribusiness Project, people whose primary economic occupation is farming are in their late 50s, on average. In most cases, these people are also the principal decision makers on the farm.

Men who identify themselves primarily as farmers usually farm as their first occupation; they have a spouse who works in the household and on the farm but does not earn significant outside wages. Women who identify themselves primarily as farmers may or may not have an adult male in the household contributing wage earnings to the household income. Women farmers with wage-earning adult males in their household do very well in farming—in most cases, better than men. In contrast, single women who manage farms are, on average, about 10 years older than other farmers, and their earnings are the lowest. These women probably retain control of land because the cost of holding it is low in the absence of land tax, and they have no other way to feed themselves as they age. This information suggests that elderly women and land-hungry young farmers could benefit from participating in a program that eases intergenerational land transfers while providing some kind of social safety net for elderly landholders.

Source: Torkelsson 2012.

have the skills or appetite for risk to manage as much as 100 hectares, many could probably handle 5–10 hectares if they had access to machinery to work it, particularly if public investments were made in infrastructure that would make farming more profitable. The incentives for young people to remain in school and acquire basic numeracy and literacy skills would increase if intermediate-size farms were among the possible options and were known to require those basic skills for successful operation. Intermediate-size farms can emerge only if land markets are more active.

One concern is that an expansion of farm size in Africa could displace labor precisely when demography requires agriculture to absorb labor. In parts of the world where farms have expanded from very small (2 hectares and less) to mid-size holdings (5–100 hectares), labor has often been displaced. This displacement need not occur in Africa because underused land can be brought into production—Africa can still expand at the extensive margins of farming without compromising forest area. Larger farms need not be less labor intensive than small ones when both area and employment can expand simultaneously. However, if farm size grows through consolidation on land that is already farmed and is accompanied by a capital subsidy that reduces the cost of mechanization, as occurred in Brazil, then bigger farms could be expected to displace labor. If the change is occasioned by shifts in technology and markets that require greater managerial skill, formerly independent farm operators might become hired workers or outgrowers on larger, technically more sophisticated holdings. Thus the effects of changing farm size on employment are specific to the factor endowment in a given market and to the forces triggering the change. The conditions in Africa offer ample opportunities for simultaneous increases in average farm size and in employment. The fact that average farm size in Africa is now declining is a worrisome indicator that constraints on land markets are already damaging the prospects for young people and becoming stronger (Djurfeldt and Jirström 2013).

Agricultural Career Paths for the Future

The young people who will look to agriculture for employment are familiar with traditional agriculture, but given the changes under way in the sector, they are likely to experience their working years in ways different from their parents. They will also have different requirements for support if they are to succeed. Young farmers will face four generic paths to agricultural employment: continuing on the family plot but with a different mix of enterprises; establishing their own operations on new land; combining farming with part-time other work; or taking wage work on large or mid-size commercial holdings. Although these four basic paths cover many options, the diversity of African agriculture ensures that some young people will face other choices. For example, young people in pastoral areas confront a different set of challenges and opportunities.

The four basic pathways to employment in agriculture vary in their requirements for land, capital, and skills (table 4.2). The first two—full-time employment on the family farm and full-time farming on a new holding—are the most prevalent. Among households surveyed in nine African countries in 2008, 51 percent reported that inheriting land already under cultivation was the most common means for young people to obtain land, while 16 percent would be allocated land not previously cultivated, 9 percent would rent or borrow land, and 12 percent would buy land (Proctor and Lucchesi 2012).

For each pathway to become a more productive source of employment, policy makers will need to use a range of approaches to improve young people's acquisition of land, capital, and

Table 4.2 Pathways for agricultural employment and their requirements

Type of employment	Need for land	Need for capital	Need for skills
Full-time on existing family holding	None	Medium	Medium
Full-time on new holding	High	High	High
Part-time combined with household enterprise (processing, trading, sales of services)	Low	Medium	High
Wage work off the family farm	None	None	Medium or high

skills. Evidence from various African countries suggests some approaches that show promise.

Pathway 1: Full-Time Employment on an Existing Family Holding

For young people with no other options, the default outcome is to remain on the family holding and simply farm a portion, essentially subdividing an already small parcel. Others choose not to leave. Eventually many can expect to inherit a portion of the land, but if siblings are in the same position, the holding will be small. These youths need capital and skills to make the most of their small holdings through higher-value agriculture. Young people who foresee this as their future, however, may have little incentive to invest in skills, since they will not have the power to use them as long as the parental generation retains recognized rights of decision.

Families in this situation may find themselves in increasingly difficult circumstances, with alienated young people resentful of their elders' continued control over resources. With some guidance and mentoring, however, families could turn this situation to advantage by managing the household as an enterprise with a portfolio of activities. Many households already support small natural resource–based enterprises (selling eggs and poultry, processing cassava or grain, collecting reeds, making bricks) as adjuncts to their primary farming enterprise. The difference here is that the household takes a strategic approach enabling the small household farm to evolve and support multiple generations and families. In this way, pathway 1 resembles pathway 3, but the emphasis is on full-time agriculture as part of a diversified, multigenerational family business.

In this pathway, the skills and labor of multiple young adults in the household could allow for specialization. If there is demand for their labor, those capable of earning off-farm wages could do so, thus easing the household's capital constraints. Those with sufficient skill to manage higher-value agriculture could sharpen the specific skills required through short courses or focused training. Some superior technologies, such as conservation tillage, require high investment of labor at peak periods, and a household with several young adults should be able to undertake the required work.

Thus even if young people are absorbed into the farm of their birth as a young adult, a change in management of the household enterprise could make this absorption more rewarding for the individuals and the family. A combination of pooled off-farm earnings, a shift in farming technology to higher-value and more commercial products, and aggregation of household labor at peak periods could allow small farms to absorb young adults constructively. An emphasis on extension programs that focus on the household as an enterprise and do not just offer technical and economic advice on crops or livestock could help this group.

The view sketched above of the small household farm evolving as young adults become economically active provides an important perspective on the conceptual understanding of youth employment. A young person in, for example, northern Uganda who is a member of such a household and has also benefited from the Youth Opportunities Program of the northern Uganda Social Action Fund might have acquired vocational skills as a hairdresser (see discussion in chapter 3). She might see her primary occupation as "hairdresser," but she would also be an equity holder in a small farm enterprise (if her earnings were applied in part to investment on the farm) and an occasional laborer at times of peak demand. Her economic security would come from the farm earnings as well as from her trade. To create space for the contributions of young people like this, the parental generation would need to view the farm as an enterprise.

Pathway 2: Full-Time Employment on New Farm Starts

A second group of young people will succeed in leaving the farm of their childhood and establishing a new and separate holding, ideally larger than the parcel they left. Those more likely to succeed in such an undertaking would probably be relatively experienced in farming and hence on the older end of the age range for "youth." They would also have the highest potential returns in the form of increased productivity. These young farmers would

"Two [of our children] have become farmers as well . . . the others took another direction. It is best that we are not in the same profession; that way we can help out one another."
Madagascar

have the greatest need for land, start-up capital, and advisory services or training to assist with technical and managerial challenges. Few young farmers will be able to assemble the elements required to establish a new farm without assistance.

New holdings may be in the localities where young people already live and on land newly available for cultivation through clarification of ownership, conversion of marginal or grazing land, or public investment in irrigation and improvement. Alternatively, new holdings may be farther away, in which case establishing the new farmstead will require relocation.

Resettlement is often controversial. Experience globally and in Africa attests to the importance of strict adherence to voluntary decision making on the part of participants, careful selection, full information for all stakeholders, effective support services for new arrivals, and adequate investment in infrastructure. An assessment of several decades of public support for resettlement in Indonesia found mixed results tending toward the negative. Improvements in the incomes and access to public services of settlers were offset by disappointing outcomes in agricultural production, environmental degradation, and resentment against newcomers on the part of indigenous inhabitants (World Bank 2012a). Preliminary results regarding a program of market-assisted land reform in Malawi, in contrast, indicate more positive outcomes (Chirwaa 2008). If local young people can secure access to land in or near their community, this approach is clearly simpler. If relocation is required, lessons of past experience should be fully weighed.

Pathway 3: Part-Time Farming and Household Enterprises

A third group of young people may be independent part-time farmers, either managing their own holdings or contributing to family operations described under pathway 1, with enough capital to establish themselves as a seller of services, a trader, or an occasional wage worker. Higher-value agriculture will use services more intensively and create employment for those who can provide them (box 4.6). Demand for transport, plant protection, veterinary services,

mechanized field operations, and advice can be met by young men and women with the capital and skills to start a small business. These young people may not have the capital to acquire a full array of farm machinery, but they could offer services on a paid basis by purchasing or leasing a limited selection of equipment. Young people would also need the particular skills to deliver the services and maintain the machinery.

Pathway 4: Wage Work off the Family Farm

The seasonal nature of agriculture creates demand for part-time wage work at peak periods even on small farms. In a heterogeneous farm structure with significant numbers of large holdings, wage work on a regular basis is also observed. Most of this work pays relatively little and requires very little skill, and few young people aspire to be low-skilled day laborers. For the very poorest, however, paid work, even if undesirable, is a better option than no work. Therefore, it is anticipated that a fourth group of young people will take wage work, whether formal or informal, on large commercial farms or in the processing and service sectors. These young people need skills to handle a range of tasks and equipment. At a minimum, for the most basic low-skilled work, they need good health to withstand often grueling working conditions. Such wage work could fit into the livelihood strategies described above in combination with other activities, or it could be a temporary option until better opportunities appear.

Not all wage work is poorly paid or low skilled. Some very large enterprises, both in primary production and in processing, require a range of skills depending on the technical sophistication of the production process and types of machinery used. Drivers, machine operators, mechanics, quality testing technicians, and others will be required in increasing numbers in the future, and these jobs are often better paid than unskilled day labor. For example, Red Fox Ethiopia, a floriculture firm located outside of Addis Ababa, draws labor from the surrounding rural areas and towns and offers employer-provided transport to work, life and health insurance, and a subsidized cafeteria (box 4.7).

"My first job was a contract job that paid 300 [Liberian] dollars per day . . . I didn't enjoy it. I just did it for the money, worked on someone else's farm . . . I just forced myself because of food . . . I'm still doing it. It was my first job." Liberia

High-value agriculture and opportunities for employment off the farm

The labor market effects of high-value agriculture are documented in several countries in Africa. In 1985, just 14 percent of the agricultural and food exports from African countries consisted of high-value agricultural products; by 2005, the share had risen to 30 percent, with many jobs created along the way. In Madagascar, the export of vegetables has relied on about 10,000 smallholders contracted for procurement of primary produce. In other instances, production of primary produce has been vertically integrated with large estate farms, as is the case with tomato and bean exports in Senegal; the jobs created are for wage earners in processing units and pack houses. Table B4.6.1 gives several examples of employment created in export horticulture chains. Horticultural work is generally labor intensive and effective at alleviating poverty, especially among women.

Processing food for local markets is another growth area for rural employment. As new towns proliferate through in situ urbanization, demand for processed foods increases, along with investment in processing. Greater attention to food safety in public policy will improve conditions within processing plants, since the conditions that assure safe products also contribute to improved hygiene and safety for workers. The regulatory bar for wages and working conditions cannot be set so high that it stifles investment, eliminates jobs, and depresses demand for primary production. The surge in food imports in Africa since 2003 reflects the underdevelopment of local food-processing capacity. Remedying this underdevelopment will create jobs and raise returns to investments in primary agriculture.

Table B4.6.1 Employment in horticultural supply chains in Sub-Saharan Africa

Country	Commodity	Year of survey	Number of employees in the fresh fruit and vegetable agro-industry	Percentage of female employees
Cameroon	Bananas	2003	10,000	—
Côte d'Ivoire	Bananas and pineapples	2002	35,000	—
Kenya	Flowers	2002	40,000–70,000	75
	Fruits and vegetables	2002	2,000,000	
Senegal	Cherry tomatoes	2006	3,000	60
	French beans	2005	12,000	90
South Africa	Deciduous fruit	1994	283,000	53
Uganda	Flowers	1998	3,300	75
Zambia	Flowers	2002–03	2,500	35
	Vegetables	2002–03	7,500	65

Source: Maertens, Minten, and Swinnen 2009.
Note: — = not available.

Lifting Key Constraints on Capital, Land, and Skills

Constraints on the acquisition of capital, land, and skills block young people's progress along the four basic pathways to employment in agriculture. To create opportunities commensurate with the number of young people who will need employment, those constraints must be removed or relieved, as discussed next. The removal of other constraints—from the lack of agricultural research and infrastructure to the weak rural investment climate—is also integral to raising agricultural productivity and creating jobs, but those constraints are not specific to opportunities for young people and are not addressed here.

Financial Services

Access to capital and credit for smallholders has been a perennial problem and the subject of analysis for decades.[6] Small farmers in Africa,

Box 4.7

Red Fox Ethiopia: More technically sophisticated wage work

Red Fox Ethiopia was established in 2003 by a German entrepreneur with long experience in the flower business. Red Fox Ethiopia produces and exports more than 150 varieties of unrooted young plants, mainly to France, Germany, Italy, and the United States. In 2009, it exported 127 million cuttings valued at US$10 million.

The firm started on 8 hectares in Koka, 95 kilometers from Addis Ababa. The factory's area increased incrementally to 35 hectares in 2009, and the firm is acquiring additional land to bring its area to 65 hectares. The firm has 1,300 employees, 450 of whom are hired on a seasonal basis for three to four months at a time. Expatriate professionals currently run the operation, but the owners plan to replace them slowly and smoothly with local professionals.

Red Fox controls the end-to-end supply chain by having its own importing company, transportation services, and distribution networks in the international market. The company imports its fertilizer and other agro-chemicals and sources packaging materials and plastic bags locally. The presence of a well-established customer network enables the firm to book orders in advance and produce accordingly, resulting in minimal wastage and risks of price fluctuations.

Red Fox plans to strengthen its market leadership and consolidate its special expertise in producing unrooted young plants. In addition, it plans to diversify into fruit production, in partnership with another firm that has knowledge and experience of the sector.

Source: Sutton and Kellow 2010.

"You may have innovative ideas, but there is nothing you can do if you can't afford to get a loan from the bank. It is difficult getting a loan from the bank, as you have to have security. It's hard." Rwanda

like their counterparts elsewhere, work in risky environments that are expensive for financial institutions to serve. Most such farmers have little or no usable collateral and little experience with financial services. A history of public intervention in credit markets has created expectations that defaults on agricultural loans will carry little penalty to the borrower. All of these challenges for financial institutions seeking to serve smallholders are relevant for young farmers and compounded by their lack of experience. Not everyone will be able to access credit, although many farmers can benefit from a wider array of financial services such as insurance and money transfer. Yet small farmers, particularly if they are young, need capital to adopt the technologies and secure the land and equipment that will allow them to become more commercially active. Because finance is so important and the potential client base is so large, banks and nongovernmental organizations (NGOs) continue to experiment with innovations to overcome the barriers to providing sustainable financial services to large numbers of smallholders. A brief review of some of these new products and services follows. Many of the innovations discussed are still being tested; their performance and sustainability on a large scale are unknown. They warrant close attention nonetheless to identify, replicate, and scale up the successful approaches.

Institutions and Organizations

Various actors offer financial services, including bank and nonbank financial institutions, insurers, and payment service providers. As commercial banks tend to limit their outreach in rural areas, alternative institutions such as self-help groups, savings and credit associations, and cooperatives have emerged to fill the gap and to address both credit risk (usually higher in agriculture than in other sectors) and covariant risks specific to agriculture—weather and other climatic risks, pest and disease epidemics, and so on (see focus note 3).

Access to Credit

Allowing alternative forms of collateral, such as chattel mortgages, warehouse receipts, and the future harvest, can ease the credit market. The OHADA[7] Uniform Act on Secured Transactions, in effect in 17 Sub-Saharan African countries, was amended at the end of 2010 to allow borrowers to use a wide range of assets as collateral, including warehouse receipts and movable property such as machinery, equipment, and receivables that remain in the hands of the debtor (AgriFin 2012). Even where the regulatory framework allows collateralization, however, assets may not be attractive for various reasons, and banking practices require time for adjustment.

Leasing also offers young farmers some relief, as it requires either no or less collateral than typically required by loans. Most rural leases are financial (unlike operating leases); the price of the asset is amortized, and the lessee can purchase the asset at the end of the lease period for a small price (IFPRI and World Bank 2010, brief 6). A notable example is DFCU Leasing in Uganda, which provided more than US$4 million in farm equipment leases in 2002 for items such as rice hullers, dairy processing equipment, and maize milling equipment. CECAM in Madagascar[8] leased more than US$2.8 million in 2002–03 to rural microenterprises, with an average US$945 per lease (Kloeppinger-Todd, Nair, and Mulder 2004). Individuals in pathways 2 and 3, who may need new equipment to start their venture, would particularly benefit from leasing. Despite leasing's clear potential to relieve constraints on access to mechanical technology, few firms have chosen to enter this business.

Young farmers' simultaneous needs for finance and information can be addressed by linking agricultural credit to extension services, an approach followed by BASIX Social Enterprise Group, a livelihood promotion institution based in India. Initially established to provide microcredit to the rural poor, BASIX now provides rural households with financial services and advice in managing crop and livestock enterprises. Almost 1,000 service providers work with more than 25,000 villages in India under the program. BASIX's research has shown that farmers prefer cost-saving and risk-reducing interventions to yield-enhancing ones that require more investment. The combination of financial services and information or mentoring allows the financial institution to identify the products in greatest demand, such as savings, money transfer, and insurance rather than credit (IFPRI and World Bank 2010, brief 13).

Grants

Matching grants can promote employment and employability among young people.[9]

Many governments and development partners use matching grants in a variety of schemes, including efforts to promote improved technologies, empower farmers to hire service providers, strengthen linkages with private firms through productive partnerships, and provide rural infrastructure for common use (AgriFin 2012). Grant schemes carry well-known risks of diversion and elite capture, and their success depends crucially on their design, including transparent rules for participation, checks and balances in monitoring at the local level, and clear expectations regarding accounting and auditing. The expectation and encouragement of savings should be a key feature of grants to individual beneficiaries. Africa has widespread experience with grant programs, yet few have focused specifically on the needs of young participants. In Sri Lanka, the Gemi Diriya Program allocates a portion of its Livelihood Fund for one-time grants of US$46–US$92 to generate income and help clients to start an economic activity without incurring the risk of a loan (World Bank 2007b). Young people are one of the program's target groups. Just over 10 percent of participants are destitute young people (World Bank n.d.).

Contracting Arrangements

Some outgrower arrangements offer prefinancing of inputs and assured marketing channels. In Mozambique, Rwanda, Tanzania, and Zambia, Rabo Development (a subsidiary of Rabobank) provides management services and technical assistance to financial institutions, which, in turn, finance supply chains with a range of agricultural clients. Participants include commercial farmers, farmers with little commercial presence, and an intermediate group of farmers with ambitions to grow commercially. Rabo takes particular interest in linking this last group to finance through contract farming under financial arrangements that limit the risk of default or side selling.[10] Kenya's DrumNet Project is piloting a similar supply-chain approach to promote agricultural lending among 3,000 farmers in the horticultural and oilseed subsectors. Risks of default are reduced through cashless direct payment to the input supplier via a bank transfer once the product is delivered to the buyer (IFPRI and World Bank 2010, brief 14).

E-Transfers and Payments

Electronic and mobile technology are rapidly bringing banking services to rural areas (where the regulatory environment permits). For example, Kenya's M-PESA service has transformed rural banking there. This service allows users to transfer money safely via their mobile phone without requiring a bank account. Initially intended to enable wage earners to send money home to families in rural areas, M-PESA now allows customers to pay bills (utilities, school fees, and others), repay loans, and pay insurance and microinsurance premiums. A new business feature allows companies to pay employees via M-PESA. Equity Bank in Kenya recently offered all M-PESA users the option to open a savings account, using M-PESA to deposit and withdraw funds (IFPRI and World Bank 2010, brief 8). Young people are especially quick to adopt innovations based on mobile phones when they have access.

The use of biometrics is being explored in the context of credit markets in countries where unique identification systems do not exist (making it difficult for banks to spot repeat defaulters). Biometric identification allows lenders to withhold new loans from known defaulters and to grant loans to known responsible borrowers. An experiment in Malawi linked higher repayment rates with the use of fingerprint scanning among paprika farmers (IFPRI and World Bank 2010, brief 9). Biometric tools that reduce the costs of identifying borrowers and diminish default rates can enhance outreach to hard-to-serve clients. Such measures are unlikely to be introduced solely to foster the employment of young people, but they are yet another example of how measures that generally facilitate agricultural growth have specific, significant benefits for the young.

Insurance

Innovations in microinsurance are also under way. The International Labour Organization (ILO) estimates that microinsurance in Africa almost doubled between 2006 and 2009 from a very small base. Microinsurance differs from traditional insurance by being available through well-trusted yet innovative channels and by offering low premiums, products with simple designs, flexible payments for premiums, and prompt settlement of claims. For example, more than 11,000 Kenyan maize farmers, some with as little as 1 acre, have obtained insurance policies that cover significant losses when drought or excess rain destroys their harvest. Similarly, BASIX and a commercial insurer in India provide weather insurance based on a rainfall index to smallholders to improve their access to credit. Payments are triggered when rainfall at local weather stations exceeds a minimum threshold; insurance contracts secure the repayment of loans (IFPRI and World Bank 2010, brief 9).

Loan Guarantees

Banks reluctant to enter the business of agriculture can sometimes be induced to do so through partial guarantee schemes that protect their losses in cases of default. The Alliance for a Green Revolution in Africa has established an innovative financing initiative operating in Kenya, Mozambique, and Tanzania. The initiative provides partial guarantees that result in lower interest rates on loans to smallholders. Since 2009, it has provided US$160 million in financing to smallholder agriculture. Rabobank's Rabo Sustainable Agriculture Guarantee Fund issues partial credit guarantees and provides other financial products to mitigate the risks of financial intermediaries, allowing them to offer better prices and terms for commercial finance to grow and export agricultural produce.[11]

Rural Finance Targeted to Young People

None of these innovations in rural finance is relevant exclusively to young people. Nor should young people be segregated as a group and offered financial services designed specifically for them. The risks of working with this client base are high, and separating young people from a larger pool for sharing risks would make them even less attractive to financial institutions. Rather, any and all innovations in finance that facilitate sustainable outreach to small farmers and rural entrepreneurs should be supported. When necessary, additional features should be added to enable these programs to serve young people.

Land Policies That Benefit the Young

Of the many aspects of land administration that require attention in Africa, the two that matter most to young entrants to the labor force are the need to improve security of tenure and the need to relax controls on rental. Land redistribution will also influence young people's access to land. In general, policies and measures that help the poor to gain access to land will also help young people.

High food prices and the resulting spike in demand for land add urgency to the challenges of improving land governance for all citizens and applying appropriate safeguards to protect the land rights of the poor. When arrangements for governance are weak, the rights of traditional users may be overlooked or abused, consultation with communities about impending transactions may be limited, and transparency may be constrained (IDS 2012).

Decentralized land administration can empower local communities, expedite decisions on land management and uses (highly desirable for individuals pursuing pathways 1 and 2), and help to clarify the legal rights of landowners and tenants amid the surge in demand for land.[12] Various models for decentralization exist (see Bruce and Knox 2009, for example). Their success depends on their design, implementation, and prevailing local conditions.

The *Land Governance Assessment Framework*[13] and the *Voluntary Guidelines on the Responsible Governance of Tenure of Land, Fisheries, and Forests in the Context of National Food Security*[14] have been developed to assist decision makers at the country level and guide the formulation of land tenure projects and policies.[15] According to the World Bank (2012b),

> Sound land policies can safeguard the livelihoods of the very vulnerable by giving them access to land and income-earning opportunities through rental markets or redistribution

of land. Accelerated land registration facilitates land rental markets, which make it easier for the poor to access land on rental terms . . . Land access for the poor can also be improved by redistributing underused and unused agricultural land to them.

Policies and programs to improve access to land can include special provisions to assist young people. Several are described next.[16]

Systematic Inventory and Registration of Land

Systematic land registration is a prerequisite for creating employment in agriculture through any of the four pathways. Notable efforts are yielding results for various categories of tenure, but the pace of activity does not reflect the urgency of the problem.

Only 10 percent of occupied land in Africa is formally registered (World Bank 2012b). State ownership of land is widespread, but even state-owned land is not fully documented, and long-term use and occupancy by individuals or groups blur ownership claims and limit investment. For example, in Ghana in 2000, the state owned about 40 percent of urban and periurban land, most of it undeveloped (Kasanga and Kotey 2001). Periurban land is often in transition from agricultural to nonagricultural use. It is well placed to offer high returns in intensive horticulture, tank aquaculture, and pig or poultry production, but it requires significant investment. Holders of periurban land often have other income streams and are linked to the financial system, so they can, in principle, make the required investments. They will not do so, however, if their ownership or the duration of their tenure is ambiguous.

Inventory and registration of individual land rights. Several countries are making progress in formally documenting individual land-ownership. By the end of 2012, Rwanda had demarcated all 10.5 million land parcels in the country and registered and prepared leases for at least 83 percent of them. Of the almost 1 million leases collected as of March 2012, 7 percent were claimed by women, 5 percent by men, 83 percent by married couples, and 1 percent by other legal entities (World Bank

Box 4.8

Documenting land rights: Encouraging investment and reducing the cost of land transfers

The economic literature has long held that more secure tenure will increase investments in land. Evidence from Ethiopia and Rwanda appears to confirm this finding and to highlight improvements in environmental management as well. Other estimates suggest that certification-induced investment increased output in Ethiopia by about 9 percentage points (Deininger, Ali, and Alemu 2011). Investment and productivity improvements were also found in Benin, where households participating in rural land use plans planted more perennial crops than nonparticipants (Selod 2012).

The same documentation of rights that strengthens tenure can reduce the cost of transactions. By 2010, both Ghana and Rwanda had reduced the cost of transferring property to less than 1 percent of property value (World Bank 2010b).

2012b). Ethiopia used a participatory public process to award certificates for more than 25 million parcels in rural areas throughout the country, with noted benefits, including "reduced conflicts, empowerment of women, increased individual and community investment, and improved security" (World Bank 2012b). Madagascar has issued 75,000 certificates akin to traditional land titles; Tanzania issued about 27,000 certificates of customary rights of occupancy in two districts. A pilot program in Ghana registered nearly 10,000 land parcels in periurban areas, and a similar program in Uganda registered 10,000 parcels in three districts. Benin, Burkina Faso, and Côte d'Ivoire have been piloting various rural land use plans—*plans fonciers ruraux*—as another way to establish individual land use rights. While methods have differed and success has varied, these efforts have done much to establish smallholders' land rights (box 4.8).

Inventory and registration of communal land. Where legal provisions recognize customary tenure and communal land, it may be more appropriate to register communal land than individual holdings. Registration of communal land can be an important first step in securing an agreement with an outside investor (that will generate jobs within the community) or allocating a portion of communal land to young people for new farm starts. As noted in a recent World Bank review (World Bank 2012b), registration can be very slow if there are no clearly defined community owners of land and if new formal entities have to be developed. Demarcation of communal land boundaries requires time and financial resources. Registration needs to be followed up with resources to plan for land use and to delineate common property resources (such as grazing land).

Inventory of state land. The extent of state landownership in Africa is largely unknown, as most lands have not yet been surveyed and registered. Some governments have started inventorying state-owned land, including recent efforts in Ghana and Uganda. Underused or poorly used state land can be auctioned to the private sector in ways that combine large-scale operators and small and medium farmers in innovative relationships—with care to avoid disenfranchising indigenous users such as herders and subsistence communities. Long-term occupants can be formally (legally) recognized as owners (as in Kenya), and land can be made available to land-poor farmers (as in Malawi), including the young (for Kenya, see United Republic of Kenya 2010; World Bank 2011; for Malawi, see World Bank 2004; Tchale 2012). Individuals in pathway 2 are most likely to benefit from these programs, and underused state-owned land is a clear source of supply for young people showing promise in farming.

Reforms in Land Rental Markets

For the very poor, the landless, the young, and migrants, land rental is the gateway to agricultural employment and eventual landownership. For those pursuing pathway 1 (perhaps hoping to acquire additional land to expand family holdings) and pathway 2, rental is a workable approach to gain access to land. Worldwide, evidence demonstrates that introducing long-term leases or certifying land rights can increase land rental activity,[17] because people with secure rights are more likely to offer temporary use of their land to others. In turn, well-functioning land rental markets can facilitate labor mobility, increase efficiency by transferring land to more productive users, increase equality, and enhance structural transformation. Rental can be particularly helpful in easing the intergenerational transfer of land while still providing income to elderly owners (box 4.9). The most common restrictions on rental markets, such as ceilings on rental rates or prohibitions against absentee landownership, are often introduced to safeguard smallholders' interests, but instead they may lock land into inefficient patterns of use, greatly disadvantaging prospective young users (Deininger 2003).

Land rental markets have promoted commercial farming in Ghana and created new opportunities elsewhere in West Africa (for Ghana, see Amanor and Diderutuah 2001; for elsewhere in West Africa, see Estudillo, Quisumbing, and Otsuka 2001). In Sudan land rental markets facilitated the transfer of land to smaller producers (Kevane 1996). In contrast, Uganda's rental markets largely ceased to function in the 2000s due to severe ceilings on rent and controls on the eviction of tenants. In Ethiopia, restrictions on land rental markets in all regions except Amhara not only reduced opportunities to use land more productively but also may have inhibited development of the nonfarm sector, as individuals who took nonfarm jobs perceived that the risk of losing their land through redistribution was high (Deininger et al. 2003).

Redistribution of Agricultural Land

Land redistribution programs can profoundly and positively affect the poor, but their success depends critically on their objectives and design. If operated at sufficient scale, they can change the income distribution and increase the incentives and opportunities for investment by poor households. If poorly designed, they can transfer land to persons poorly suited to farm it and can discourage investment by heightening uncertainty about future redistribution. As individuals in pathway 2 have the greatest need for new land, they will have the most to gain or lose from approaches to redistribution. Examples of approaches to land redistribution can

Box 4.9

Mexico's program to speed intergenerational land transfers

Most land in Mexico was held in common under unclear tenure arrangements until reforms initiated in the 1990s. Heavy restrictions on the transfer of rights to common land from one generation to another limited young farmers' access to land. In the early 2000s, with support from the World Bank and as part of a wider set of reforms in land administration, the Government of Mexico initiated its Young Rural Entrepreneurs and Land Fund Program (Programa para Jóvenes Emprendedores Rurales y Fondo de Tierra) to accelerate the intergenerational transfer of land. This successful program provided credit for rural youths without land to acquire underused common land. The young people were trained and received technical assistance in setting up their farming activities. The program also helped older landowners who transferred land to young farmers to gain access to social welfare schemes for their retirement.

Source: FAO, IFAD, and MIJARC 2012.

be seen in Malawi, South Africa, and Zambia, and each of which has drawn on lessons from programs in Brazil.

Malawi's pilot land reform program. Malawi recently piloted a land reform program in four districts in which underused land from former tea estates was made available to smallholders wishing to relocate from densely settled areas.[19] Patterned after Brazil's market-based approach to land reform, the pilot had three key elements: (1) communities voluntarily acquired land from estate owners, the government, or private donors; (2) resettlement and on-farm development included transportation of settlers, establishment of shelter, and purchase of basic inputs and advisory services; and (3) redistributed land was surveyed and registered, initially under group title, with the expectation that individual titles would be provided to beneficiaries on demand in the future. A cap on the maximum amount of a grant that could be spent to acquire land improved the bargaining power of beneficiaries in relation to land sellers,[20] and access to advisory services significantly lowered the failure rate.

"But even for a farmer, without education, forget about good production."
Tanzania

Although the program did not focus explicitly on attracting young people, most participants were young. They preferred to relocate within or close to their original home, which preserved sociocultural ties and supported young people when they were forming families and needed links to the older generation. The program distributed an average of more than 1.5 hectares to each of 15,142 rural households, increased agricultural incomes 40 percent a year on average for beneficiaries between 2005–06 and 2008–09, and had positive effects on surrounding communities.

South Africa's land reform program. Despite having had programs in place for a decade and a half, South Africa has made little progress in providing growing numbers of underemployed rural young people with land that they can farm.[18] At the end of apartheid in 1994, South Africa's new government introduced tenure reform, restitution, and redistribution of land. The redistribution program was designed to transfer land through market-mediated transactions to historically disadvantaged South Africans who wanted to enter farming. After disappointing results, a new program launched in 2001 provided graduated areas of land and start-up grants depending on the amount of the beneficiary's contribution. Those who could contribute little (and most of that in kind) received a base allotment of land and a grant of R 20,000 (almost $3,000). Those who could contribute more or leverage a bank loan could receive larger holdings and a grant of up to R 100,000 (about $14,000). Although the goal was to redistribute 30 percent of the land by 2014, as of March 2011, only 6.27 million hectares (7.2 percent of land owned by white African farmers) had been redistributed to black African farmers, and many recipients struggled to manage that land well. The program had limited success because allocations of land and start-up capital were not accompanied by advisory services or technical assistance. Those who received land through the program were prohibited from subdividing it, even though repeal of the prohibition was announced several times. Beneficiaries of small allotments were forced into group structures similar to collective farms and experienced the deficiencies in internal management that are common under such arrangements.

Zambia's irrigation development and support project. In this project (approved in 2011 and receiving just over US$200 million from all funding sources), smallholders can exchange small parcels for holdings of 3–5 hectares as part of a larger scheme that will join small producers, large commercial operators, and mid-size farmers in a shared area. Management of irrigation services for the entire scheme will be contracted to a concession. To ensure that small and mid-size farmers earn enough to pay irrigation fees, professional farm management services will be available to assist with production and marketing. The selection of smallholders taking on the mid-size parcels is not complete, so the age distribution of participants is unknown, but this opportunity is expected to appeal to young people with prior experience in farming.

Enhancing Skills and Building a Better Educational Foundation

Rural children need to go to school and learn. Better-educated farmers are more likely to adopt modern farm inputs and technologies, make better use of purchased inputs and labor, choose technologies more effectively, and respond rapidly to changes in markets or to natural calamities (Schultz 1988). Basic education can significantly improve the efficacy of agricultural training. The relationship between education and agricultural development cuts both ways, and the two are mutually reinforcing, with demand for schooling rising as rural incomes increase.

To equip young Africans with the skills to thrive in all four pathways to agricultural employment, schools must do a better job of providing the basic skills for any endeavor. Foremost among these are reading, writing, numeracy, and the ability to use digital technology to access and interpret information (box 4.10). Beyond these basics, the skills required for individuals in pathways 1 and 2

Box 4.10

Information and communication technologies: Altering the flow of agricultural information

For African farmers operating in an environment of rapid climatic and economic change, the age-old questions of what to plant, when to plant, and how to plant have assumed immense importance. Answers are proliferating, as rural radio, television, the Internet, and mobile services offer an expanding array of information about specific technologies and practices, climate change, disaster management, early warning (for drought, floods, and diseases), prices, natural resource management, production efficiency, and market access (World Bank 2012a).

Researchers are rigorously testing the effectiveness of different information and communication technologies (ICTs) at reaching and benefiting farmers, focusing primarily on the transmission of price information.[a] Radio, a long-standing method of communicating with farmers, has helped them to obtain better farm-gate prices by providing information on commodity prices. Internet stations with agricultural market information (e-Choupals) have done the same in Madhya Pradesh, India. Mobile phones have allowed fishermen and onshore buyers in Kerala, India, to communicate supply and price information, resulting in higher profits, lower consumer prices, and less waste. Among grain traders in Niger, the introduction of mobile phone coverage in two markets reduced the price variation between the two, ultimately increasing traders' profits, decreasing prices paid by consumers, and increasing total welfare. Cell phone coverage also reduced within-year price variation for producers.

Actors in the public and private sector are interested in using mobile phones to deliver information to farmers in developing countries. A rigorous evaluation of one program found that text messages provided by Reuters Market Light did not have a robust effect on producer prices or input use among farmers of five crops in Maharashtra, India (Fafchamps and Minten 2012).Similar interventions to supply price and weather information in Colombia and India failed to have a substantial impact on crop choices, revenues, or profits (Camacho and Conover 2011 on Colombia; Cole and Hunt 2010 on India). These findings suggest the need to experiment with different content and methods of delivery. More attention should be given to the underinvestigated, distinct, and potentially complex issue of using ICT to support agricultural production and production technologies, as distinct from marketing information.

For newer ICTs such as mobile phones and the Internet to convey agricultural information effectively, the content and mode of delivery may need to change, but what about the users themselves? Much has been made of young people's ready adoption of newer ICTs, as well as the capacity of ICTs (newer and older) to break through barriers to the acquisition of information and skills, such as distance, the inability to read and write, or the expense of producing and disseminating audiovisual information. Much has also been made of the potential for interactive ICTs to provide agricultural recommendations tailored to an individual farmer's circumstances. Yet much depends on whether the individual user of ICTs is able to frame relevant questions based on learning acquired in good primary schools, coupled with practice in imagining states of the world other than those already experienced. As discussed in chapter 3, most African educational systems are not delivering high-quality basic education, even though enrollment is increasing. Among rural youths who lack a basic cognitive foundation on which they can build, the benefits of ICTs may be slower to emerge.

a. See Svensson and Yanagizawa (2009) on radio and farm-gate prices; Goyal (2010) on Internet stations in India; Jensen (2007) on fishers in Kerala; Aker (2008) on traders in Niger; and Aker and Fafchamps (2010) on phone coverage and variation in producer prices.

may differ from the skills required in pathways 3 and 4. The majority of farmers, who will have little more than a primary school education, will need access to effective agricultural extension services to sharpen their skills and clearly convey their requirements for information and technology to service providers. Finally, a growing and diversifying agricultural sector will create jobs that demand increasingly advanced technical and professional skills, from processing and marketing to agricultural research.

This section describes recent initiatives and changes in "schools of thought" regarding the role and delivery of both basic and agricultural education, agricultural extension, and other innovative models of training and research and development. As with some of the finance mechanisms discussed earlier, many of these programs are experimental. They have not been rigorously evaluated or tested for their effectiveness or sustainability on a larger scale.

Schooling and Learning

To the extent that schooling raises literacy and numeracy skills and enhances the ability to process agricultural information, an education effect can exist independent of the design of school curriculum. Returns to such skills are particularly magnified in a modernizing agricultural sector, where access to advanced technology complements an understanding of how to use it. The decision to adopt new technologies is an investment decision if significant costs are incurred in obtaining information and learning about the performance of one or more new technologies, while the returns are distributed over time. Furthermore, only a small share of new technologies will be profitable for any given farmer to adopt. Given the degree and multiple sources of uncertainty facing farmers, effective schooling may help them to make better decisions to increase farm profitability.

Returns to schooling in rural areas depend, in part, on the pace of technological innovation in farming. A large body of literature has shown that more educated farmers are the first to adopt new seed, tillage practices, fertilizer, and animal breeds (for example, see Welch 1970; Huffman 1977; Besley and Case 1993; Foster and Rosenzweig 1996; Abdulai and Huffman 2005). Moreover, farmers with primary education tend to earn higher profits than farmers

"I decided to get married after my stepmother refused to pay school fees for me, and the job I could find there was only farming."
Tanzania

without schooling, assuming that both have access to the same assets, and this effect is magnified in environments undergoing rapid technical change (Rosenzweig 2010). Schooling thus enhances learning, and a dynamic agricultural sector provides opportunities to apply it.

Education offers spillover effects when uneducated farmers are able to observe the choices and outcomes of their better-educated neighbors. This type of social learning is usually inferred from observed behavior or outcomes over time. For example, in Ghana, social learning played an important role in diffusing knowledge on pineapple cultivation among farmers. In this case, the experiences of the farmers and their neighbors influenced profitability and adoption rates (Conley and Udry 2010).

The importance of female labor in agriculture brings into sharp focus the urgency of improving access to schooling for girls and women. There is widespread recognition of the need to improve both basic education and agricultural vocational education for women and to enhance rural women's access to extension services.

Postsecondary Education in Agriculture

Alongside jobs in primary production, a growing and diversifying agricultural sector creates demand for skilled labor in rural areas inside and outside of the sector. Africa's existing agricultural vocational schools can play a constructive role in training skilled personnel for jobs in processing, marketing, machinery operation and repair, transport, logistics, and quality control—provided that students have sufficient preparation to benefit from that training (box 4.11).

The number and quality of trained technical and professional personnel in agriculture are critical factors in agricultural development, because a sector undergoing structural transformation has an expanding need for skills. In addition to gaining technical skills, workers need to master teamwork, communication, diligence, creativity, and entrepreneurship. In many cases, these behavioral "soft skills" are learned through mentoring and through the standards of performance set in the formal workplace.

Box 4.11

Vocational agricultural education: A poor substitute for general education

To remedy gaps in skills, many African governments and their development partners in past years focused on vocational agricultural training, often at the expense of primary, secondary, or postsecondary education. More often than not, attempts to substitute vocational education in agriculture for general education have failed. The returns to such training have been mixed at best, largely because the individuals undertaking the training and the neighbors who could learn from their example lacked sufficient basic education to make use of more advanced, specific skills.

As formal nonfarm employment increases, a larger cohort of young people can be expected to acquire behavioral skills in this way.

Institutional infrastructure for agricultural higher education and training has been in place in Africa since the 1960s but has not strengthened sufficiently over time to meet the enormous demands evident now. Sub-Saharan Africa now has more than 200 public universities (compared with 20 in 1960), about 100 of which teach agriculture and natural resource management. Private universities complement this public capacity (World Bank 2007a). Much stronger national and regional institutions are needed to train future professionals and leaders with appropriate technical and functional skills.

Women face particular obstacles in obtaining the education and training to become more successful in agriculture, whether as farmers, entrepreneurs, providers of extension information, or leaders in agricultural research and education. Few women graduate from agricultural education programs, few women become agricultural extension workers, and women are often marginalized during agricultural events, activities, and programs. These problems are widely evident, although detailed gender-disaggregated data are only available sporadically or are not reported at all (World Bank 2009). Efforts are under way to give stronger recognition to the role of women in agriculture, to increase the number of female students in agricultural schools and colleges, and to provide resources for extension services directed to women farmers. An innovative program was launched in 2008 by the Gender and Diversity Program of the Consultative Group on International Agricultural Research. The African Women in Agricultural Research and Development Program seeks to strengthen the research and leadership skills of African women in agricultural science, empowering them to contribute more effectively by establishing mentoring partnerships, building science skills, and developing leadership capacity.

Agricultural Extension

Agricultural extension arose to address farmers' needs for information in a wide array of settings around the world. Their needs then were quite similar to those of young Africans now entering the labor force in rural and urban areas. Much of what has been learned about effective extension methods may be used to design advisory services and mentoring programs for young people generally, in farming and in other spheres of activity.

Early models of agricultural extension were centralized, public, and linear. The basic model was one in which a trained extension worker traveled over a large area to convey messages to farmers, who then applied the advice to improve their operations. The deficiencies of this model became clear over the years, especially in Africa. The foremost deficiencies involved cost, quality, and relevance. Traditionally designed agricultural extension programs are now a rarity, although the term is still used and applied to nontraditional approaches. Newer programs empower farmers to specify the information they require and to select the provider (box 4.12; see Davis 2008). The provision of information is still recognized as a public good, and the government assumes a share of the cost, particularly for small farmers and the poor. The advice may be delivered by public officials, private advisers, NGOs, or the media, depending on farmers' needs. The new systems are decentralized, integrated with the private sector, coordinated with agricultural research, and tailored to local contexts. Extension is understood to be part of a broader innovation system.

Agricultural extension services can contribute significantly to young farmers' success, but the design of successful programs is still an open empirical question. Several approaches have been tried and reviewed in different contexts, but rigorous assessment is elusive (Davis 2008). For example, participatory and group-based approaches are gaining traction. These methods have the potential to overcome barriers to participation, foster inclusiveness, and lead to more demand-driven services. Many African countries have pluralistic extension services (which have a variety of service providers), including Kenya, Mozambique, and Uganda.

Many factors in addition to the mode of providing extension services affect agricultural

"Many who received training commented that their farming efforts are now 'more efficient and sustainable.'" Ethiopia

Box 4.12

Innovations in agricultural extension: Relying on farmers to improve service delivery

The question of whether agricultural extension services are best provided by the public sector (the traditional model), the private sector, or a range of providers continues to generate debate in light of the mixed results obtained with the traditional model.[a] This uncertainty has complicated efforts to widen the adoption of improved agricultural technologies and increase agricultural productivity. Newer models of extension, which are driven by farmers and reinforce the quality of service delivery through incentives and other innovations, are proving more effective than traditional methods, but they, too, encounter difficulties and constraints to effectiveness.

The impact of innovative approaches that mobilize farmers to improve returns to agricultural extension was recently evaluated on a large scale. In Malawi and Mozambique, randomized controlled trials tested multiple modalities for implementing peer and lead farming. In both experiments, communities nominated lead or peer farmers, who were trained to use sustainable land management techniques and mandated to communicate those techniques to other farmers in their village through demonstrations.

In Malawi, the social status (peer versus lead) and gender of the communicator were subject to random assignment, and a small performance-based material incentive was given to a subset of the communicators. The project designated "shadow" communicators in control villages to provide a counterfactual. In Mozambique, lead farmers—mostly men—were already designated by the project team in all project villages at baseline. The intervention trained a random subset of these lead farmers in sustainable land management. To add a gender variation, a woman lead farmer was added to a random subset of treatment villages, since it was not possible to demote the previously chosen communi-

cator. Small performance-based material and social incentives were distributed to a subset of the treatment villages.

The results from these large pilots suggest that female farmers can be as productive as male farmers in teaching their peers about a new technology and getting them to adopt it. Adding a woman communicator to a male-centered model for delivering extension advice can add value and change the numbers of male and female beneficiaries. Evidence on the use of performance-based incentives suggests that providing service to the community is more costly for women leaders, as they are more responsive to incentives. Finally, despite performing as well as, and in some cases better than, male communicators, female communicators still suffer from discrimination and are rated as worse teachers than men.

Overall, these results suggest that development projects that place the adoption of new agricultural techniques at the center of their theory of change may consider using peer and lead farming interventions to boost their returns. Given that female leaders appear to be as productive as male leaders in getting farmers to learn about and adopt new techniques, empowering women to take on leadership roles may not only increase equity but also add value. Performance-based incentives can play an important role in getting women leaders to devote additional time and effort to working with their community.

a. For example, Birkhaeuser, Evenson, and Feder (1991) found no significant relationship between the provision of traditional extension services and farm productivity in Africa, whereas Evenson (2001) and Dercon et al. (2009) identified some successes. Anderson and Feder (2003) propose an organizational inquiry into which model of extension (public or private) can deliver superior results.

performance. Spillover effects are hard to capture or isolate. Selection bias may enter even in controlled environments, and programs performing well at scale can be subverted by clientelism and patronage (Anderson and Feder 2004). While most experts would agree that advisory services or extension of some kind are vital, particularly in light of the challenges faced by young people entering agriculture in Africa, the profession does not have a clear view on the best approach to program design.

Each pathway to agricultural employment has particular needs for advice and training that may determine which approach will work best. For example, programs of competence-based training in Ethiopia and Uganda in high-value export crops (horticulture and floriculture, respectively) are providing a workforce for these demanding subsectors. Individuals in pathways 3 and 4 (engaged in wage work either part or full time) might benefit most from such training. For those in pathways 1 and 2, farmer field schools may be useful. They exist in many countries and are "a participatory method of learning, technology development, and dissemination based on adult-learning principles such as experiential learning" (World Bank 2012a). A recent study in East Africa found that farmer field schools are especially beneficial for women, people with low literacy levels, and farmers with medium-size landholdings. Field school participants had significant differences in outcomes with respect to the value of crops produced per acre, the livestock value gained per head, and agricultural income per capita (Davis et al. 2010). For those in pathway 1 who adopt a more corporate approach to family farming, the shift to entrepreneurial family farms can be aided by local agribusiness development services, which are advisory services with a business orientation. Although the provision and use of these services are still relatively new, anticipated impacts for smaller-scale farmers and entrepreneurs include enhanced rural income (both directly and through employment) and enhanced small-scale entrepreneurial activity (World Bank 2012a). Such services could also assist young people seeking to combine self-employment with part-time farming (pathway 3).

Producer organizations can be a highly effective means of building members' skills and entrepreneurial expertise by improving access to advice and training. Once again, however, the ability to self-organize and participate effectively in such organizations requires the fundamentals of a solid education.

Priorities for a Diverse Skills Agenda

The skills agenda to meet the needs of Africa's young people is diverse, and the resources to address that agenda are highly constrained. Priority should be accorded to improving the quality of basic education and keeping young people in school long enough for them to acquire basic skills. Agricultural programs in tertiary education must be strengthened to produce a new generation of scientists and teachers in all fields. In the intermediate arena of extension and outreach, emphasis should be placed on providing resources to the final users of information, so that they can seek out the

help they need, coupled with careful evaluation and transparent display of user satisfaction with the various channels of information. The alternative approach of seeking a new, highly structured, unitary style of extension system, widely applicable to all, is not likely to deliver good results. In designing a skills agenda for Africa's rural young people, distinctions should be made between the needs of the stock of young adults in the labor force today—whose elementary education is incomplete—and the children who will flow into the labor force in the future. The very young need better schools with more learning as a matter of highest urgency. Those who are already beyond school age will need a mix of short-term remedial programs for applied literacy and numeracy and access to mentoring, apprenticeships, and flows of "just-in-time" information, perhaps delivered through electronic media.

Current Agricultural Programs Deliver Too Little, Too Slowly, to Meet the Needs of Africa's Young People

As early as 2003, African heads of state met in Maputo, Mozambique, and pledged to give renewed attention and resources to agriculture. The pledge was made under the rubric of the Comprehensive African Agriculture Development Programme (CAADP) of the African Union and the New Partnership for Africa's Development.[21] The CAADP framework recognizes the breadth of the agricultural agenda and the corresponding need for multiple entry points and complementary public investments in several areas (box 4.13).

Until food prices spiked in 2008, the commitment to increase public spending on agriculture was not implemented widely, but between 2003 and 2008, the technical work to design a framework for reinvestment in agriculture under CAADP proceeded. When rising food prices caught the attention of global and African leaders, the conceptual framework was available to address the long-standing neglect of key public goods and services. The framework does not specifically recognize the unique

When asked how their days differ from their parents' generation, one young man offers, "Those days were days for farming and that is it. Now we do farming, we do business, we even go to school in great numbers." Tanzania

Box 4.13

Overview of the Comprehensive African Agriculture Development Programme (CAADP)

CAADP's four pillars are complementary. The first pillar, land and water, addresses the design of programs and investment required to improve land administration, sustainability of land use, and management of water through irrigation and water harvesting and storage.

The second pillar identifies investment and reforms in policy and regulations needed to improve smallholders' access to markets. Many of these interventions focus on rural infrastructure, including roads, rail transport, and power (both on- and off-grid), but important regulatory measures also require attention, such as regulation of the trucking industry and food safety standards. These measures aim to reduce marketing costs to make farming more profitable, while reducing food prices for net buyers to accelerate job creation.

The third pillar addresses measures that will make agriculture less risky for those with a commercial orientation and strengthen the resilience of the very poor when shocks hit. Diversification, affordable insurance products, and rural safety nets can help people to manage risks, and higher income levels associated with growth in productivity and profitability provide a cushion of savings for hard times.

Finally, the agricultural technology pillar underpins the other three. Modern agriculture is science based, and producers at all levels of sophistication benefit from improved systems to generate and spread improved technologies. Some of these entail breeding improved crops and animals to address changing demand or agro-ecological conditions or to allow producers to select a desired level of risk. Others emphasize new systems of management and rotation, to reduce costs of inputs, enhance soil health, and capture carbon for additional revenue streams.

The CAADP framework is applied to help countries and regions to improve the quality of their agricultural planning and policy making and to use them as the basis for scaled-up investment in the sector. CAADP offers political, technical, and financial support for countries and regions that engage in this process, through a partnership of continental and regional African institutions in collaboration with other stakeholders, including civil society, the private sector, and Africa's development partners.

demography of Africa, nor does it make specific provisions for young farmers, but its key features can be enriched to address a youth agenda.

Complementing the largely public elements of CAADP, local and international private investors are expressing growing interest in the opportunities in agriculture. The African Union has declared a "Decade on Youth Development in Africa 2009–2019." The United Nations General Assembly has called for member states to prepare a "National Review and Action Plan on Youth Employment," and the African Union, Economic Commission for Africa, African Development Bank, and the ILO have recently proposed a "Joint Initiative on Job Creation for Youth in Africa." The initiatives demonstrate the level of attention being given to the youth employment issue (Proctor and Lucchesi 2012). Each of these organizations also emphasizes agriculture.

Thus efforts to reach out to Africa's young farmers can draw on resources from the public and private sectors, domestically and internationally, under strategic initiatives already in place. No new or separate strategy is required, but the current slow pace of implementation, if continued, will fail young people and compromise Africa's future. Existing commitments must be accorded focused attention, with improved quality of public spending, more efficient approaches to increasing production of food staples, more attention to meeting demand for high-quality products by the growing urban middle classes, continued progress on policy and regulatory reforms, and improved data and tracking of progress. With better-implemented public programs, private investment will accelerate, and opportunities for young people will increase. Some proactive additional attention to meet the specific needs of the large group of young people may be required, but doing so without more effective programs in general will be counterproductive. Successfully mobilizing the talents of young people will increase the likelihood that

CAADP and other ongoing initiatives will meet their ambitious goals.

Harnessing Agriculture's Youth Dividend

Agriculture—already Africa's largest employer—is changing, and the large numbers of young people entering the sector will accelerate the pace of change. Africa's leaders recognize that agriculture is a source of growth, an instrument for improved food security, and a means to steward valuable natural resources. As the potential for the sector to absorb the large numbers of new job seekers and to offer meaningful work with public and private benefits becomes clearer, agriculture will gain even more attention from policy makers.

This attention will be necessary, because the sector's ability to create jobs will not be realized without modifications to public programs. Present levels of public investment are not sufficient. The quality of investment is inadequate to yield high returns. Too much has gone into short-term palliatives, such as fertilizer subsidies, without complementary attention to improved technologies and management practices and long-term investments in research and infrastructure. The investment climate still cannot attract the private firms needed in marketing, processing, input supply, and finance. Public policies governing trade, the introduction of new varieties, licensing and intellectual property rights, and taxation offer weak incentives to producers and innovators.

Detailed agendas in each of these areas are beyond the scope of this chapter, but the future of Africa's young people is at present hostage to the wide gap between rhetorical commitment to the importance of agriculture and actual, effective attention accorded to it by Africa's leaders. Efforts to address constraints to land, capital, and skills will have to be redoubled and accelerated, and features to make programs friendly to the needs of the young introduced.

Although farming is often done by the elderly, the profession's requirements for energy, innovation, and physical strength make it ideally suited for persons who are 25–45 years old—the "mature young." Energy, creativity, and strength are attributes that Africa's young people have in abundance. The agriculture that attracts them will have to be profitable, competitive, and dynamic. These same characteristics are needed for agriculture to deliver growth, to improve food security, and to preserve a fragile natural environment. With much higher priority accorded to the implementation of well-designed programs of public investment in agriculture, continued progress on regulatory and policy reform, and a modest overlay of attention to assure the inclusion of young people in Africa's agricultural renaissance, the sector's youth dividend can be collected and widely shared.

Notes

1. Whether an economy's agricultural labor force rose or fell in absolute numbers as the relative share of the sector declined depended on birth and death rates in rural areas, migration, and the size and labor intensity of sectors that were growing more rapidly than agriculture. See Timmer and Akkus (2008).

2. For example, farmers grow modern improved varieties of food crops on an estimated 35 percent of all planted area, compared to just 23 percent in 1998 (Renkow and Byerlee 2010).

3. A band of settlements of 10,000 or more inhabitants now stretches from Djibouti to Dakar, with few gaps in between. Another rings Lake Victoria, and another marks the Kinshasa-Brazzaville corridor.

4. Agricultural total factor productivity is growing at just over and under 3 percent annually in Southeast Asia and South America, respectively. Since 2000, total factor productivity in Sub-Saharan Africa has been higher than the average in the four prior decades but is still short of being transformative. Estimates range from just under 1 percent annually to just over 2 percent annually, owing to severe deficiencies in the underlying data; see Fuglie (2011); Nin-Pratt, Johnson, and Yu (2012).

5. After food prices spiked in 2007–08, governments began to set ambitious growth targets for agriculture. At 8–10 percent, those rates exceed the 6 percent target set by the African Union through the Comprehensive Africa Agriculture Development Programme and the rates recently observed for the entire region (3.8–4.0 percent; World Bank 2012c).

6. This section draws heavily on AgriFin (2012) and IFPRI and World Bank (2010).

7. Organisation pour l'Harmonisation en Afrique du Droit des Affaires (Organization for the Harmonization of Business Law in Africa).

8. Caisses d'Epargne et de Crédit Agricole Mutuelles, a cooperative agricultural financial institution.

9. This section draws from World Bank (2010a).

10. IFPRI and World Bank (2010, brief 4); see also http://www.rabobank.com/content/products_services/business_clients/professionalproducts/raboagrifund/index.jsp.

11. See http://www.rabobank.com/content/products_services/business_clients/professionalproducts/raboagrifund/index.jsp.

12. For a perspective on equity issues arising from heightened global interest in Africa's farmland, see Deininger and Byerlee (2011).

13. See Deininger, Selod, and Burns (2011) for more on this relatively quick and innovative tool.

14. Endorsed by the Committee on World Food Security in May 2012, the *Voluntary Guidelines* promote secure tenure rights and equitable access to land, fisheries, and forests as a means of eradicating hunger and poverty, supporting sustainable development, and enhancing the environment. They set out principles and internationally recommended standards for responsible practices. They are a framework that actors can use when developing their own strategies, policies, legislation, and programs, allowing government authorities, the private sector, civil society, and citizens to judge whether their proposed actions and the actions of others constitute acceptable practices.

15. Encouraging collaboration with the Sustainable Commodity Roundtables can also help to increase the extent to which crop production systems meet voluntary environmental and social criteria, including those of the Roundtable for Responsible Soy, the Roundtable on Sustainable Palm Oil, the Better Sugarcane Initiative, and a variety of forest certification processes.

16. The following sections draw heavily from World Bank (2012b).

17. For example, in China, the Dominican Republic, Ethiopia, Nicaragua, and Vietnam.

18. This section is adapted from Lahiff and Li (2012); World Bank (2012b).

19. Adapted from Tchale (2012); World Bank (2012b).

20. Each family received a grant of US$1,050, managed directly by the beneficiary; up to 30 percent was for land acquisition, and the rest was for transportation, water, shelter, and farm development.

21. See http://www.nepad-caadp.net/.

References

Abdulai, Awudu, and Wallace E. Huffman. 2005. "The Diffusion of New Agricultural Technologies: The Case of Crossbreeding Technology in Tanzania." *American Journal of Agricultural Economics* 87 (3): 645–59.

AgriFin. 2012. "Making Finance Work for Africa: Policy Brief on Agricultural Finance in Africa." Report sponsored by the African Union, GIZ, and BMZ. Washington, DC.

Aker, Jenny C. 2008. "Does Digital Divide or Provide? The Impact of Cell Phones on Grain Markets in Niger." CGD Working Paper 154, Center for Global Development, Washington, DC.

Aker, Jenny C., and Marcel Fafchamps. 2010. "How Does Mobile Phone Coverage Affect Farm-Gate Prices? Evidence from West Africa." Working Paper, Tufts University, Department of Economics and the Fletcher School; Center for Global Development; University of Oxford, Center for the Study of African Economies. http://www.aeaweb.org/aea/2011conference/program/retrieve.php?pdfid=629.

Amanor, Kojo S., and Maxwell K. Diderutuah. 2001. "Share Contracts in the Oil Palm and Citrus Belt of Ghana." International Institute for Environment and Development, London.

Anderson, Mary, Dayna Brown, and Isabella Jean. 2012. "Time to Listen: Hearing People on the Receiving End of International Aid." CDA Collaborative Learning Project, Cambridge, MA.

Anderson, Jock, and Gershon Feder. 2003. "Rural Extension Services." Policy Research Working Paper 2976, World Bank, Washington, DC.

———. 2004. "Agricultural Extension: Good Intentions and Hard Realities." *World Bank Research Observer* 19 (1): 41–60.

Besley, Timothy, and Anne Case. 1993. "Modeling Technology Adoption in Developing Countries." *American Economic Review* 83 (2): 396–402.

Birkhaeuser, Dean, Robert Evenson, and Gershon Feder. 1991. "The Economic Impact of Agricultural Extension: A Review." *Economic Development and Cultural Change* 39 (3): 607–50.

Bruce, John W., and Anna Knox. 2009. "Structures and Stratagems: Decentralization of Authority over Land in Africa." *World Development,* special issue on the limits of state-led land reform 37 (8): 1360–69.

Camacho, Adriana, and Emily Conover. 2011. "The Impact of Receiving Price and Climate Information in the Agricultural Sector." Working Paper IDB-WP-220, Inter-American Development Bank, Washington, DC.

Chirwaa, Ephraim W. 2008. "Land Tenure, Farm Investments, and Food Production in Malawi." Discussion Paper 18, prepared for Institutions and Pro-Poor Growth (IPPG).

Cole, Shawn, and Stefan. Hunt. 2010. "Information, Expectations, and Agricultural Investment: Evidence from a Field Experiment in India." Working Paper, Harvard University, Cambridge, MA.

Conley, Timothy, and Christopher Udry. 2010. "Learning about a New Technology: Pineapple in Ghana." *American Economic Review* 100 (1): 35–69.

Davis, Kristin. 2008. "Extension in Sub-Saharan Africa: Overview and Assessment of Past and Current Models and Future Prospects." *Journal of International Agricultural and Extension Education* 15 (3): 15–28.

Davis, Kristin, Ephraim Nkonya, Edward Kato, Daniel A. Mekonnen, Martins Odendo, Richard Miiro, and Jackson Nkuba. 2010. "Impact of Farmer Field Schools on Agricultural Productivity, Poverty, and Farmer Empowerment in East Africa." IFPRI Discussion Paper, International Food Policy Research Institute, Washington, DC.

Deininger, Klaus. 2003. *Land Policies for Growth and Poverty Reduction.* Washington, DC: World Bank.

Deininger, Klaus, Daniel A. Ali, and Tekie Alemu. 2011. "Impacts of Land Certification on Tenure Security, Investment, and Land Market Participation: Evidence from Ethiopia." *Land Economics* 87 (2): 312–34.

Deininger, Klaus, and Derek Byerlee. 2011. "Rising Global Interest in Farm Land: Can It Yield Sustainable and Equitable Benefits?" World Bank, Washington, DC.

Deininger, Klaus, Songqing Jin, Berhanu Adenew, Samuel Gebre-Selassie, and Mulat Demke. 2003. "Market and Non-Market Transfers of Land in Ethiopia: Implications for Efficiency, Equity, and Nonfarm Development." Policy Research Paper 2992, World Bank, Washington, DC.

Deininger, Klaus, Harris Selod, and Anthony Burns. 2011. "The Land Governance Assessment Framework: Identifying and Monitoring Good Practice in the Land Sector." ARD Series, World Bank, Washington, DC.

Dercon, Stefan, Daniel O. Gilligan, John Hoddinott, and Tassew Woldehanna. 2009. "The Impact of Agricultural Extension and Roads on Poverty and Consumption Growth in Fifteen Ethiopian Villages." *American Journal of Agricultural Economics* 91 (4): 1007–21.

De Wolf, Stefan, Yves Rolland Rakotoarisoa, Laurence Vanpaeschen, and Honoré Rabekoto. 2008. *Madagascar: Le Grand Livre des Petits Métiers: Portraits of Daily Life Professions.* Heule, Belgium: Snoek Publishers.

Djurfeldt, Agnes Andersson, and Magnus Jirström. 2013. "Urbanization and Changes in Farm Size in Sub-Saharan Africa and Asia from a Geographical Perspective: A Review of the Literature." A Foresight Study of the Independent Science and Partnership Council, Consultative Group on International Agricultural Research, Washington, DC. http://www.sciencecouncil.cgiar.org/file admin/templates/ispc/documents/Strategy_and_ Trends/2013/Foresight.Andersson.pdf.

Estudillo, Jonna P., Agnes R. Quisumbing, and Keijiro Otsuka. 2001. "Gender Differences in Land Inheritance and Schooling Investments in the Rural Philippines." *Land Economics* 77 (1): 130–43.

Evenson, Robert. 2001. "Economic Impacts of Agricultural Research and Extension." In *Handbook of Agricultural Economics.* Vol. 1a: *Agricultural Production*, edited by Bruce L. Gardner and Gordon C. Rausser, 573–628. Amsterdam: Elsevier.

Executive Office of the President. 2011. "Economic Report of the President 2011." U.S. Council of Economic Advisers, Washington, DC.

Fafchamps, Marcel, and Bart Minten. 2012. "Impact of SMS-Based Agricultural Information on Indian Farmers." *World Bank Economic Review* 26 (3): 383–414.

FAO (Food and Agriculture Organization). 2011. *Women in Agriculture: Closing the Gender Gap in Agriculture.* State of Food and Agriculture Report. Rome: FAO.

FAO (Food and Agriculture Organization), IFAD (International Fund for Agricultural Development), and MIJARC (Mouvement International de la Jeunesse Agricole et Rurale Catholique). 2012. "Facilitating Access of Rural Youth to Agricultural Activities." Farmers' Forum Youth Session, Rome, February 18.

Foster, Andrew D., and Mark R. Rosenzweig. 1996. "Technical Change and Human-Capital Returns and Investments: Evidence from the Green Revolution." *American Economic Review* 86 (4): 931–53.

Fox, Louise, and Thomas Pave Sohnesen. 2012. "Household Enterprises in Sub-Saharan Africa: Why They Matter for Growth, Jobs, and Livelihoods." Policy Research Working Paper 6184, World Bank, Washington, DC.

Fuglie, Keith. 2011. "Agricultural Productivity in Sub-Saharan Africa." In *The Food and Financial Crises in Sub-Saharan Africa: Origins, Impacts, and Policy Implications*, edited by David R. Lee and Muna Ndulo. Cambridge, MA: CABI.

Goyal, Aparajita. 2010. "Information, Direct Access to Farmers, and Rural Market Performance in Central India." *American Economic Journal: Applied Economics* 2 (3): 22–45.

Huffman, Wallace E. 1977. "Allocative Efficiency: The Role of Human Capital." *Quarterly Journal of Economics* 91 (February): 59–79.

IDS (Institute of Development Studies). 2012. "Young People and Agriculture in Africa." *IDS Bulletin,* special issue 43 (6).

IFPRI (International Food Policy Research Institute) and World Bank. 2010. "Innovations in Rural and Agriculture Finance: Focus 18." Washington, DC.

Jensen, Robert. 2007. "The Digital Provide: Information (Technology), Market Performance, and Welfare in the South Indian Fisheries Sector." *Quarterly Journal of Economics* 122 (3): 879–924.

Kasanga, Kasim, and Nii Kotey. 2001. "Land Management in Ghana: Building on Tradition and Modernity." International Institute for Environment and Development, London.

Kevane, Michael. 1996. "Agrarian Structure and Agricultural Practice: Typology and Application to Western Sudan." *American Journal of Agricultural Economics* 78 (1): 236–45.

Kloeppinger-Todd, Renate, Ajai Nair, and Annabel Mulder. 2004. "Leasing: An Underutilized Tool in Rural Finance." ARD Discussion Paper 7, World Bank, Washington, DC.

Lahiff, Edward, and Guo Li. 2012. "Land Redistribution in South Africa: A Critical Review." Working Paper for the "Land Administration and Reform in SSA" study, World Bank, Washington, DC.

Larson, Donald, Keijiro Otsuka, Tomoya Matsumoto, and Talip Kilic. 2012. "Should African Rural Development Strategies Depend on Smallholder Farms? An Exploration of the Inverse Productivity Hypothesis." Policy Research Working Paper 6190, World Bank, Washington, DC.

Losch, Bruno, Sandrine Fréguin-Gresh, and Eric Thomas White. 2012. *Structural Transformation and Rural Change Revisited: Challenges for Late Developing Countries in a Globalizing World.* African Development Forum series. Washington, DC: World Bank.

Maertens, Miet, Bart Minten, and Jo Swinnen. 2009. "Growth in High-Value Export Markets in Sub-Saharan Africa and Its Development Implications." LICOS Discussion Paper 245, Katholieke Universiteit, Leuven.

Minot, Nicholas. 2011. "Transmission of World Food Price Changes to Markets in Sub-Saharan Africa." IFPRI Discussion Paper 01059, International Food Policy Research Institute, Washington, DC.

Morris, Michael, Hans Binswanger-Mkhize, and Derek Byerlee. 2009. *Awakening Africa's Sleeping Giant.* Washington, DC: World Bank.

Nagayets, Oksana. 2005. "Small Farms: Current Status and Key Trends." Information brief prepared for the Future of Small Farms Research Workshop, Wye College, June 26–29.

Nin-Pratt, Alejandro, Michael Johnson, and Bingxin Yu. 2012. "Improved Performance of Agriculture in Africa South of the Sahara: Taking Off or Bouncing Back?" IFPRI Discussion Paper 01224, International Food Policy Research Institute, Washington, DC.

OECD and FAO (Organisation for Economic Co-operation and Development and Food and Agriculture Organization). 2012. *Agricultural Outlook 2012–2012.* Annex B, Table B.1. Paris: OECD; Rome: FAO.

Petesch, Patti, and Ines Rodríguez Caillava. 2012. "Voices of Young Villagers in Sub-Saharan Africa." Background paper, World Bank, Washington, DC.

Proctor, Felicity J., and Valerio Lucchesi. 2012. "Small-Scale Farming and Youth in an Era of Rapid Rural Change." International Institute for Environment and Development, London.

Renkow, Mitch, and Derek Byerlee. 2010. "The Impact of CGIAR Research: A Review of Recent Evidence." *Food Policy* 35 (5): 391–402.

Rosenzweig, Mark. 2010. "Microeconomic Approaches to Development: Schooling, Learning, and Growth." *Journal of Economic Perspectives, American Economic Association* 24 (3): 81–96.

Schultz, T. Paul. 1988. "Education Investments and Returns." 1988. In *Handbook of Development Economics,* Vol. 1, edited by Hollis Chenery and T. N. Srinivasan, ch. 1, 543–630. Amsterdam: Elsevier.

Selod, Harris. 2012. "Formalizing Rural Land Rights in West Africa: Results from an Impact Evaluation in Benin." Paper prepared for the conference "Land and Poverty 2012," World Bank, Washington, DC, April 23–26.

Sutton, John, and Nebil Kellow. 2010. *An Enterprise Map of Ethiopia.* London: International Growth Centre.

Svensson, Jakob, and David Yanagizawa. 2009. "Getting Prices Right: The Impact of the Market Information Service in Uganda." *Journal of the European Economic Association* 7 (2–3): 435–45.

Tchale, Hardwick. 2012. "Pilot Redistributive Land Reform in Malawi: Innovations and Emerging Good Practices." Working Paper for the "Land

Administration and Reform in SSA" study, World Bank, Washington, DC.

Timmer, Peter, and Selvin Akkus. 2008. "The Structural Transformation as a Pathway out of Poverty: Analytics, Empirics, and Politics." Working Paper 150, Center for Global Development, Washington, DC.

Torkelsson, Asa. 2012. "Sex Disaggregated Data on Agriculture, Water, and Food Security: Lessons from Kenya." World Water Week Seminar on Global Practice in Promoting Gender Equality in the Water Sector, Stockholm, August 30.

United Republic of Kenya. 2010. "The Constitution of Kenya 2010." National Council for Law Reporting, Nairobi.

Welch, Finis. 1970. "Education in Production." *Journal of Political Economy* 78 (1): 35–59.

World Bank. n.d. "Sri Lanka Community Development and Livelihood Improvement Gemidiriya Project: Analysis of Youth Inclusion and Participation in Gemidiriya." World Bank, Washington, DC.

———. 2004. "Malawi Community-Based Rural Land Development Project." Project Appraisal Document, World Bank, Washington, DC.

———. 2007. "Cultivating Knowledge and Skills to Grow African Agriculture: A Synthesis of an Institutional, Regional, and International Review, 2007." Report No. 40997-AFR. Agriculture and Rural Development Department and Africa Region Human Development Department, World Bank, Washington, DC.

———. 2007b. "South Asia: Livelihoods Learning: Community-Managed Microfinance: A New Model from Sri Lanka." Series 1, Note 5, World Bank, Washington, DC.

———. 2009. *Gender in Agriculture Sourcebook.* Washington, DC: World Bank.

———. 2010a. "Designing and Implementing Agricultural Innovation Funds: Lessons from Competitive Research and Matching Grant Projects." Report 54857-GLB, World Bank, Washington, DC.

———. 2010b. *Doing Business 2011: Making a Difference for Entrepreneurs.* Washington, DC: World Bank.

———. 2011. "Kenya Informal Settlements Improvement Project." Project Appraisal Document, World Bank, Washington, DC.

———. 2012a. *Agricultural Innovation Systems: An Investment Sourcebook.* Washington, DC: World Bank.

———. 2012b. "Land Administration and Reform in Sub-Saharan Africa: From Piloting to Scaling Up." World Bank, Washington, DC.

———. 2012c. World Development Indicators 2012. Washington, DC: World Bank.

———. 2013. "Growing Africa: Unlocking the Potential of Agribusiness." AFTFP/AFTAI Report, World Bank, Washington, DC.

Safety Nets and Pathways to Productive Employment

Social safety nets are programs that aim to increase households' consumption of basic commodities and facilitate access to basic services (Grosh et al. 2008; Monchuk 2014). They can also help households to cope with shocks such as an economic crisis, drought, or illness. The coverage of safety net programs targeted to poor and vulnerable households is growing rapidly in Africa (Monchuk 2014; Subbarao et al. 2013; McCord and Slater 2009). The most common safety nets include public works and cash transfer programs. Participants in public works programs receive cash or food in exchange for engaging in labor-intensive work to build or maintain public goods such as local infrastructure. Some longer-term public works programs ensure temporary employment to the poor at critical junctures, such as lean periods in the agricultural cycle. Cash transfers provide temporary relief to households to reduce poverty. These traditional safety nets can improve productivity in the long term through a range of channels (Alderman and Yemtsov 2013). For instance, safety nets have been shown to increase human capital by improving nutrition and access to education and health services.[1] Such improvements for today's children can contribute to higher labor productivity for tomorrow's youth.

Because safety net programs explicitly target the poor or vulnerable, they often reach the core of the population engaged in low-productivity employment, particularly in agriculture and household enterprises. Many governments also deliver complementary productive interventions through safety net programs, with the explicit objective of fostering productive employment in the short to medium term. The intention is to allow poor households to build pathways to raise productivity in the farming sector, diversify livelihoods, or enter into non-farm household enterprises. If complementary productive interventions are targeted to youth, they can pave a pathway to productive employ-

ment at a critical period when youth may be completing their education, transitioning to work, or already working on their own account in low-productivity occupations. As such, safety nets with these complementary components have the potential to improve productive employment for the current generation of youth.

Short-Term Benefits of Safety Net Programs

African governments rely extensively on public works programs to provide short-term employment. Public works programs are common throughout the region and typically offer temporary employment for periods ranging from 10 days to 6 months.[2] For example, the Malawi Social Action Fund has offered temporary employment to more than 800,000 individuals for 12 days on average since 1995 (World Bank 2011). The Tanzania Social Action Fund offers cash transfers through short-term employment in a labor-intensive public works program, which has offered an average of 75 days of employment to more than 200,000 beneficiaries since 2000 (World Bank 2010). One public works program of longer duration is Ethiopia's Productive Safety Net Program. Participants, who can remain in the program for up to five years, work during the lean season on labor-intensive projects building community assets, such as soil and water conservation structures. The program reaches more than 7 million people and operates with an annual budget of nearly US$500 million (Gilligan, Hoddinott, and Taffesse 2009).

Public works programs have well-documented short-term benefits, including on participants' income. To work the hours required by these labor-intensive programs, beneficiaries usually forgo other income-earning opportunities (Subbarao et al. 2013). For this reason, beneficiaries' earnings generally increase less than the actual wages they receive (which are usually based on estimated market rates for wage employment or a minimum wage). Argentina initiated a public works program in 2002 after a severe economic crisis pushed unemployment and poverty to record heights. Net earnings (after subtracting income forgone from other activities) were estimated to be two-thirds of the benefits offered by the public works program during the crisis and only one-third of those offered after the crisis had dissipated (Galasso and Ravallion 2004).

In low-income African countries, nearly all individuals are working, and very few are unemployed (see discussion in chapter 1). In this context, public works do not necessarily substantially increase overall employment. At the same time, public works programs tend to be oversubscribed despite paying low wages and can strongly increase the earnings of beneficiaries. Few evaluations measure net earnings gains from participating in public works programs in Africa.

Overall, public works programs are first and foremost social protection programs that provide temporary employment. They are generally not designed to foster sustainable productive employment beyond beneficiaries' participation in the program. Some evidence suggests that traditional public works programs can open pathways to employment in new activities, even if that is not their primary goal. In Liberia, participants reported using 14.2 percent of the income from public works for farm and nonfarm investments (Andrews et al. 2011). In Ethiopia, beneficiaries from the public works program were more likely to enter in nonfarm business activities and less likely to work as day laborers (Gilligan, Hoddinott, and Taffesse 2009). Evidence from an impact evaluation in Sierra Leone shows that participation in a cash-for-works program increased participation in informal saving groups, led to accumulation of assets such as livestock, and fostered the creation of new household enterprises (Rosas and Sabarwal 2013).

Cash transfer programs also primarily focus on immediate poverty relief, and there is solid evidence documenting their short-term impacts on reducing poverty, improving a range of outcomes such as food security or nutrition, and increasing the use of health or education services (see Fiszbein and Schady 2009 for a review). There is also growing evidence showing that cash transfer beneficiaries are able to save and enter into more productive activities, even if these programs were not designed with that objective in mind.[3] For instance, in Malawi, cash transfers facilitated investments in agricultural assets and livestock and reduced adults' participation in low-skilled labor (Covarrubias, Davis, and Winters 2012). In Mexico, cash transfers led poor rural households to invest in productive assets such as farm animals and land for agricultural production, increasing agricultural income by 10 percent (Gertler, Martinez, and Rubio-Codina 2011). Beneficiaries were also more likely to start non-agricultural household enterprises, particularly the production of handcrafts for sale.

A new generation of safety net programs is trying to be more explicit about maximizing their productive potential in the short to medium term.

Safety Nets Plus Explicit Productive Components

A growing number of safety net programs attempt to create the conditions for beneficiaries to access pathways to more productive employment or sustainable livelihoods in the short to medium term. Policy makers start with the proven ability of safety net programs to stabilize household consumption and add productive interventions that may lead to sustainable, productive employment for the current generation. For example, "public works plus" delivers complementary services such as links to financial services or training in a range of skills. Some "cash transfer plus" programs take a similar approach.

Financial Services
A growing number of public works programs aim to strengthen financial inclusion or build linkages to other intermediate services. Participants in Rwanda's Vision Umurenge Programme are given access to bank accounts and encouraged to save some of their earnings.

Beneficiaries of Tanzania's Productive Safety Net Program can participate in small groups that promote community savings to increase their ability to save for future needs and investments; a similar approach is being considered for a public works program in Mozambique. A public works program in Côte d'Ivoire includes a component that fosters saving by delivering payments to a bank account (during its pilot phase, the program awarded a matching grant to participants who had saved a certain amount). For more discussion on financial services, see focus note 3.

Capital

Participants in Ethiopia's public works program are linked to the Household Asset Building Program to help them to make their farms more productive and to increase their long-term food security. They obtain "at least one of several productivity-enhancing transfers or services, including access to credit, agricultural extension services, technology transfer (such as advice on food crop production, cash cropping, livestock production, and soil and water conservation), and irrigation and water harvesting schemes" (Gilligan, Hoddinott, and Taffesse 2009).

Skills Training

Many public works programs also provide short-term training in basic literacy, skills for microenterprise development, technical skills, or life skills. In South Africa's Expanded Public Works Program, beneficiaries receive two days of training each month in literacy and numeracy, vocational skills, and business skills. In Côte d'Ivoire, the public works program implemented by the national roads agency includes sensitization in basic life skills, training in basic business skills to help participants to set up a household enterprise, and sensitization to wage employment opportunities to help youth to prepare themselves and search for a wage job. In Liberia, the community works component of the Youth Employment and Skills Project provides eight sessions of life skills training during the 40-day works program. Each of these sessions lasts two to three hours and is led by 1 trainer for every 25 trainees. The life skills training has six main sections: Myself and My Community, Making a Living, Managing Money, My Workplace, My Health, and My Future.

Some programs deliver a package of benefits including cash transfers together with a range of complementary productive interventions. For instance, the "targeting the ultra-poor" or "graduation model" is currently being tested in 10 countries around the world including Ethiopia and Ghana (Hashemi and Montesquiou 2011). The intervention targets the poor and offers basic consumption support similar to a safety net program. It also facilitates savings, transfers assets to allow the poor to enter into higher-productivity farming activities (for example, livestock) or start a household enterprise, and provides skills training and regular technical assistance to beneficiaries. The stated objective of this approach is to help households to graduate from extreme poverty through productive employment.

Do Complementary Interventions Open Pathways toward Productive Employment for Youth?

Despite their potential to increase productivity and facilitate entry into new employment opportunities, few rigorous evaluations have shown that expanded safety net programs lead to employment or productivity gains.[4] In Ethiopia, households with access to the public works program and complementary interventions are "more likely to be food secure and are more likely to borrow for productive purposes, use improved agricultural technologies, and operate nonfarm own business activities" (Gilligan, Hoddinott, and Taffesse 2009). Their incomes grow, and distress sales of assets decline. Elsewhere in Africa, evidence on the productive impacts of "public works plus" programs is limited, especially evidence on the effectiveness of short training modules and links to financial services. An evaluation testing alternative complementary training targeted to young beneficiaries of a public works program is under way in Côte d'Ivoire.

Figure F2.1 Impacts of conditional cash transfers plus business grants or conditional cash transfers plus skills training in Nicaragua

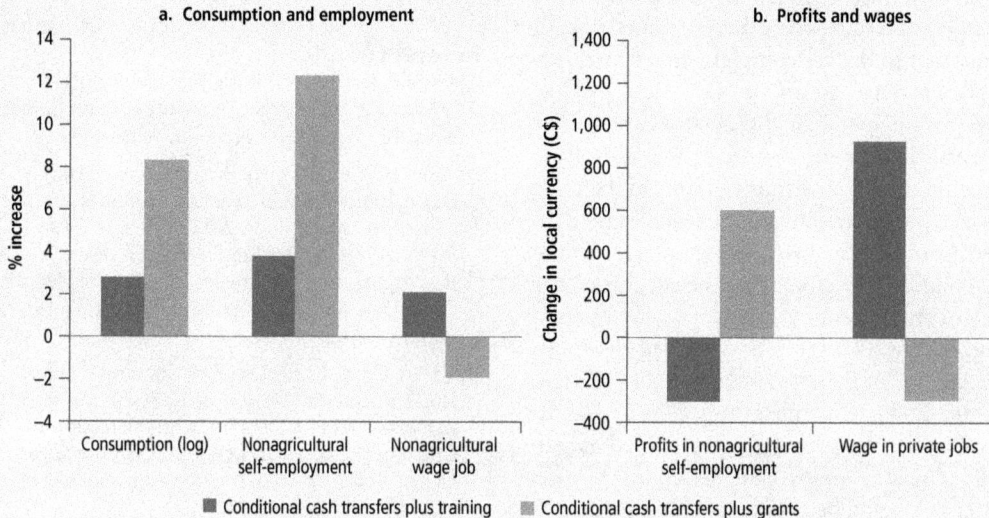

a. Consumption and employment

b. Profits and wages

■ Conditional cash transfers plus training   ▨ Conditional cash transfers plus grants

Source: Macours, Premand, and Vakis 2012.
Note: Impacts are measured as differences between beneficiaries and a control group. The impact on consumption and entry in a nonagricultural wage job is not significant for beneficiaries of the "conditional cash transfers plus training" package, while the impact on entry in a nonagricultural wage job and on wages in a private sector wage job is not significant for beneficiaries of the "conditional cash transfers plus grant" package.

Evidence is also thin on the effectiveness of productive components embedded in cash transfer programs. In Niger, monitoring data suggested that beneficiaries save a substantial share of their earnings through savings groups created by the program. A new cash transfer program in Cameroon encourages beneficiaries to participate in awareness and training activities to learn about generating income, understand how to access microfinance, and acquire business skills. Impact evaluations are under way in both countries.

Although the effectiveness of complementary productive interventions has not been ascertained in Africa, promising evidence is emerging elsewhere. In rural areas of Nicaragua, an evaluation tests the relative effectiveness of complementing a cash transfer program with business grants or vocational training (see figure F2.1; Macours, Premand, and Vakis 2012). Two years after the end of the program, results show that the business grant enabled cash transfer recipients to enter nonagricultural self-employment and increased profits in household enterprises as well as overall income and consumption. The main effect of the vocational

training delivered to cash transfer recipients was to increase wages in private wage jobs. But overall the average impact on income and consumption across all beneficiaries was not significant.

Early results from impact evaluations of the "graduation model" also suggest substantial productive impacts. For instance, a program that targets the ultra-poor with a package including large asset transfers and intensive training was effective in inducing entry into self-employment in Bangladesh. The combined intervention was successful in inducing a change from agricultural wage labor to small businesses, raising annual income 36 percent on average (Bandiera et al. 2012). These results are consistent with evidence emerging from similar programs in Honduras, Pakistan, and West Bengal.

Safety Nets as Vehicles to Deliver Interventions Aimed at Improving Youth Employment Outcomes

Traditional safety nets do not seek primarily to foster productive employment for the current generation of youth, but they have the potential to do so. These programs target the very households that are engaged in low-productivity activities. As such, safety net programs have the potential to deliver complementary interventions opening pathways toward more productive employment for the poor. There are not necessarily any equity-efficiency trade-offs in targeting productive interventions to the poor: in fact, poor households often would benefit the most from productive interventions (Macours, Premand, and Vakis 2013). The effectiveness of these complementary interventions for opening such pathways is yet to be evaluated rigorously in Africa, but their potential to help individuals to "graduate" to more productive and secure livelihoods deserves to be considered as part of inclusive employment strategies. Greater attention could be paid to targeting productive interventions to youth within poor households benefiting from such programs.

Notes

1. Safety nets can also create positive externalities on the local economy.
2. See Subbarao et al. (2013) for a review. For instance, Liberia and Sierra Leone rolled out cash-for-work programs in 2008 to cushion the impacts of soaring food prices (Wodon and Zaman 2010). In its first phase, the program in Sierra Leone reached 16,000 beneficiaries, who worked for approximately 50 days, for six to eight hours a day, on road rehabilitation, reforestation, soil conservation, and cultivation of rice and alternative crops (Andrews et al. 2012). The program in Liberia offered, on average, 40 days of temporary employment to 17,000 households, which mostly rehabilitated public agricultural land and cleaned and cleared roads, drains, and public spaces (Andrews et al. 2011). The program was later scaled up to cover 45,000 beneficiaries.
3. Cash transfers can contribute to raising growth through channels other than their direct impact on beneficiaries (Alderman and Yemstov 2013). For instance, simulations also suggest that they have productive impacts on the local economy (Asfaw et al. 2012).
4. Pilots delivering cash grants to beneficiaries have had large impacts on employment and earnings (for example, Blattman, Fiala, and Martinez 2011). It remains unclear how the impacts from a public works program would compare to those of a program delivering cash to beneficiaries amounting to the labor and capital costs of a public works program.

References

Alderman, Harold, and Rusla Yemstov. 2013. "How Can Safety Nets Contribute to Economic Growth?" *World Bank Economic Review*.

Andrews, Collin, Prospère Backiny-Yetna, Emily Garin, Emily Weedon, Quentin Wodon, and Giuseppe Zampaglione. 2011. "Liberia's Cash for Work Temporary Employment Project: Responding to Crisis in Low-Income, Fragile Countries." Social Protection and Labor, World Bank, Washington, DC.

Andrews, Colin, Mirey Ovadiya, Christophe Ribes Ros, and Quentin Wodon. 2012. "Cash for Works in Sierra Leone: A Case Study on the Design and Implementation of a Safety Net in Response to a Crisis." Social Protection Discussion Paper 1216, World Bank, Washington, DC.

Asfaw, Solomon, Silvio Daidone, Benjamin Davis, Josh Dewbre, Alessandro Romeo, Paul Winters, Katia Covarrubias, and Habiba Djebbari. 2012. "Analytical Framework for Evaluating the Productive Impact of Cash Transfer Programmes on Household Behaviour? Methodological Guidelines for the From Protection to Production Project." Working Paper 101, International Policy Centre for Inclusive Growth, Brasilia.

Bandiera, Oriana, Robin Burgess, Selim Gulesci, Imran Rasul, and Munshi Sulaiman. 2012. "Can Entry-Level Entrepreneurship Transform the Economic Lives of the Poor?" Mimeo, London School of Economics.

Blattman, Christopher, Nathan Fiala, and Sebastian Martinez. 2011. "Employment Generation in Rural Africa: Mid-Term Results from an Experimental Evaluation of the Youth Opportunities Program in Northern Uganda." Social Protection Discussion Paper 66523, World Bank, Washington, DC.

Covarrubias, Katia, Benjamin Davis, and Paul Winters. 2012. "From Protection to Production: Productive Impacts of the Malawi Social Cash Transfer Scheme." *Journal of Development Effectiveness* 4 (1): 50–77.

Fiszbein, Ariel, and Norbert Schady. 2009. *Conditional Cash Transfers: Reducing Present and Future Poverty*. Washington, DC: World Bank.

Galasso, Emanuela, and Martin Ravallion. 2004. "Social Protection in a Crisis: Argentina's Plan Jefes y Jefas." *World Bank Economic Review* 18 (3): 367–99.

Gertler, Paul J., Sebastian W. Martinez, and Marta Rubio-Codina. 2011. "Investing Cash Transfers to Raise Long-Term Living Standards." *American Economic Journal: Applied Economics* 4 (1): 164–92.

Gilligan, Daniel O., John Hoddinott, and Alemayehu Seyoum Taffesse. 2009. "The Impact of Ethiopia's Productive Safety Net Programme and Its Linkages." *Journal of Development Studies* 45 (10): 1684–706.

Grosh, Margaret, Carlo del Ninno, Emil Tesliuc, and Azedine Ouerghi. 2008. *For Protection and Promotion: The Design and Implementation of Effective Safety Nets.* Washington, DC: World Bank.

Hashemi, Syed M., and Aude Montesquiou. 2011. "Reaching the Poorest: Lessons from the Graduation Model." CGAP Focus Note 69, Consultative Group to Assist the Poor, Washington, DC.

Macours, Karen, Patrick Premand, and Renos Vakis. 2012. "Transfers, Diversification, and Household Risk Strategies: Experimental Evidence with Implications for Climate Change Adaptation." Policy Research Working Paper 6053, World Bank, Washington, DC.

———. 2013. "Demand Versus Returns? Pro-Poor Targeting of Business Grants and Vocational Skills Training." Policy Research Working Paper 6389, World Bank, Washington, DC.

McCord, Anna, and Rachel Slater. 2009. "Overview of Public Works Programmes in Sub-Saharan Africa." Overseas Development Institute, London.

Monchuk, Victoria. 2014. *Reducing Poverty and Investing in People: The New Role of Safety Nets in Africa.* Washington, DC: World Bank.

Rosas, Nina, and Shwetlena Sabarwal, 2013. "Public Works as a Productive Safety Net in a Post-Conflict Setting? Evidence from a Randomized Evaluation of Sierra Leone's Cash for Work Program." World Bank, Washington, DC.

Subbarao, Kalanidhi, Carlo del Ninno, Colin Andrews, and Claudia Rodríguez-Alas. 2013. "Public Works as a Safety Net: Design, Evidence, and Implementation." World Bank, Washington, DC.

Wodon, Quentin, and Hassan Zaman. 2010. "Higher Food Prices in Sub-Saharan Africa: Poverty Impact and Policy Responses." *World Bank Research Observer* 25 (1): 157–76.

World Bank. 2010. "Project Paper on Second Additional Financing Credit in the Amount of SDR 23.1 Million (US$35 Million Equivalent) in Pilot Crisis Response Window Resources to the United Republic of Tanzania for the Second Social Action Fund Project." World Bank, Africa Region Social Protection Unit, Human Development, Washington, DC.

———. 2011. "Implementation Status and Results of Malawi Third Social Action Fund (MASAF3) APL II (P110446)." Report ISR7009, World Bank, Washington, DC.

Chapter 5

Creating Productive Employment for Youth in the Household Enterprise Sector

Despite the large share of employment in household enterprises (HEs) and the potential for substantial growth, few governments recognize that "the informal will be normal" or develop effective policies and programs to help youth to create productive enterprises. Young people who lack the education for a wage job recognize the potential in HEs, but they often struggle to amass the savings, skills, and market know-how to enter and consistently succeed in the HE sector. At a time when the formal wage sector is just beginning to gain ground, supportive national strategies are needed to facilitate entry into the HE sector, provide an environment to make it more productive, and realize the corresponding benefits for youth employment and economic growth.

"Because I am not educated, I could not be employed. Therefore, I had no other option than employing myself."
Tanzania

In Africa today, most employment in low-income households comes from household-based activities. These activities include family farming and very small nonfarm enterprises, which we call household enterprises (HEs; see box 5.1). As countries have become richer, the labor force has shifted out of agriculture, but it has not left the household economy. Employment in HEs is growing especially rapidly for those who have not completed a secondary education—the majority of new entrants into Africa's overwhelmingly young, burgeoning workforce. These young people generally lack the education for a wage job but can pursue the economic opportunities that HEs offer—as a full-time activity or together with agriculture in a mixed-livelihood strategy.

Development processes in other regions have included HEs in parallel with large-scale manufacturing, so the growth of HEs in Africa is not surprising (figure 5.1). Such enterprises are still an important source of employment in low-income countries where nonfarm wage jobs have grown rapidly, such as in Bangladesh and Cambodia. In Asia and Latin America, HEs provided an important pathway for surplus labor to move out of agriculture as farm productivity improved. In Africa's low- and middle-income countries, where the modern wage sector has not grown fast enough to absorb everyone who is prepared to leave agri-

Box 5.1

What is a household enterprise?

Household enterprises (HEs) are unincorporated, nonfarm businesses owned by households. From an employment perspective, they include *self-employed people* running unincorporated businesses and *family members* working in those businesses. When employment in the HE sector is tabulated, employees from outside the family are not included in this category; they constitute wage workers. The owners themselves account for most of the employment in the sector. Family helpers make up only 11 percent of employment in the sector (not counting wage workers). From an enterprise perspective, they follow the same pattern. Most HEs in Africa today are pure self-employment, and only 10 percent have hired someone outside of the family (see figures B5.1.1 and B5.1.2). Therefore, employment in the sector grows primarily through the creation of new enterprises.

HEs may also be referred to as own-account workers (another term for self-employed) or as contributing or unpaid family workers, indicating that the family members work in the enterprise but receive no cash payment based on hours worked or output, although they may share in the profits. Some call these enterprises microenterprises, but the term is not used uniformly (for example, in Grimm, Knorringa, and Lay 2012). Some authors categorize both self-employment and larger, more substantial businesses as microenterprises (and may include partnerships and firms that employ workers regularly). In this report, only HEs that hire workers (less than 4 percent of all owners) are classified as microenterprises.

Some refer to HEs as informal enterprises. The International Labour Organization (ILO) considers everyone working in an unincorporated business with less than five employees as having informal sector employment (ILO 1993; see Fox and Pimhidzai 2013 for a discussion). The label "informal sector" ignores the household nature of these businesses, however, and the ILO definition does not distinguish between the family (which gets the profits from the enterprise and absorbs the losses) and outside wage workers (who are paid for a task but not expected to share in profits or losses).

Figure B5.1.1 Most people working in the HE sector are owners

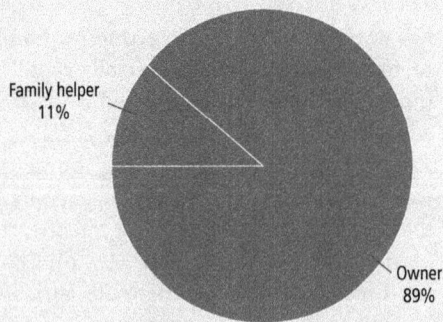

Source: Fox and Sohnesen 2012.

Figure B.5.1.2 Most HEs are family operations

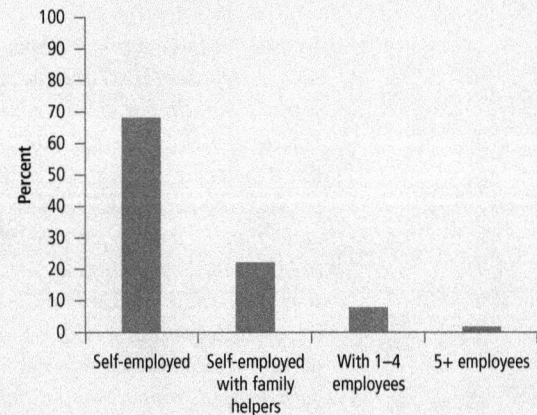

Source: Fox and Sohnesen 2012.

culture, the HE sector is larger than in comparator countries. The HE sector has generated the majority of new nonfarm jobs in most low- and lower-middle-income countries of Africa, even during times of high economic growth (figure 5.2). This trend is expected to continue.

HEs are an important way for households to move out of poverty. Strong correlations between higher rural HE income and lower poverty have been observed in several Asian countries (Haggblade, Hazell, and Reardon 2010; Lanjouw, Quizon, and Sparrow 2001). The shift in primary economic activity out of agriculture—including day labor—and into running a nonfarm business contributed substantially to poverty reduction in Bangladesh

Figure 5.1 Household enterprises are an important share of nonfarm employment in low- and middle-income countries

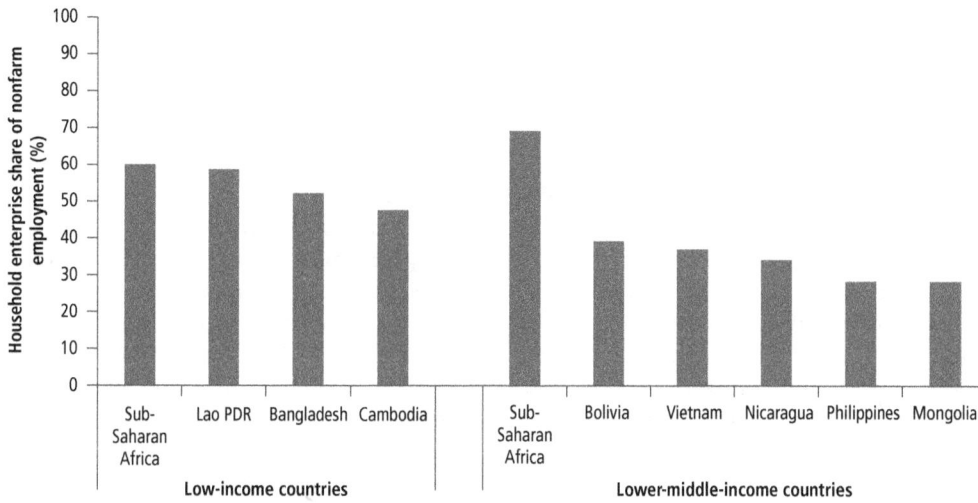

Source: Based on standardized and harmonized household and labor force surveys for Sub-Saharan Africa (most recent data available) and on household and labor force surveys for countries in other regions (see appendix).

Figure 5.2 In Africa, as labor moved out of agriculture, more people moved into the HE sector than into private wage employment

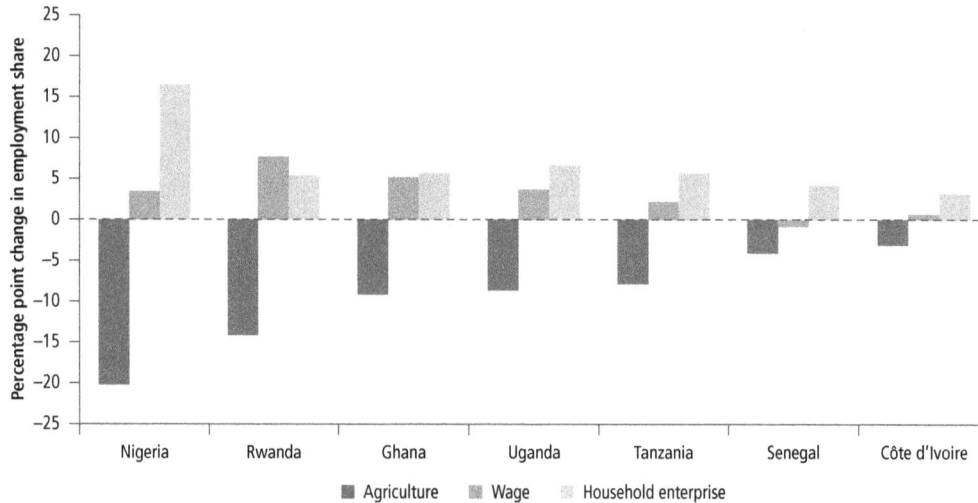

Source: Based on standardized and harmonized household and labor force surveys (see appendix).

and Uganda over the last decade (see Inchauste and Olivieri 2012 on Bangladesh; Fox and Pimhidzai 2012 on Uganda).

In Africa, most government strategies overlook the HE sector, partly because policy makers may know little about the sector or its role in creating youth employment and supporting economic growth. Urban policies often actively discourage HEs, making it challenging

for youth to take advantage of the opportunities these businesses present. Youth often lack even the small amount of savings needed to start a trading business, and banks and microfinance entities rarely lend to start-ups. A small-scale processing or service venture could require more capital than a trading venture, as well as some technical skills that school leavers may not have. Young people may also need to develop business and behavioral skills, if they have not acquired them in school or through experience. In short, it is difficult for youth to find pathways into the HE sector.

Facilitating entry into the HE sector and providing an enabling environment to make it more productive are fundamental policy challenges. Research across Africa and other regions shows that these challenges can be met; *the key is to recognize the potential.* By changing the fragmented approach to the HE sector into a coherent, coordinated approach—with a strong focus on sustainable employment for youth—government, donors, nongovernmental organizations (NGOs), and other stakeholders could lift the constraints on productivity and open opportunities for sustainable employment for everyone in this sector.

This chapter outlines the opportunities and challenges facing HE owners in Africa today. It explores why young people often struggle to enter the sector and describes policies and programs that could change this reality and make the sector more productive.

The Household Enterprise Sector Today

HEs have been an important part of the recent shift of value added and employment out of agriculture and into the services sector, as the majority of HEs engage in trading (figure 5.3). At the same time, HEs have contributed to employment in the industrial sector, where they engage in manufacturing (primarily transforming agricultural goods or natural resources into products such as charcoal, flour, roof thatching, or bricks) and artisanal activities (producing custom furniture and ironwork, dressmaking and tailoring, or construction). In the services sector, HEs engage in food services (making and selling snacks or meals), transport, and personal services (barbering and hairdressing). Partly because of local opportunities to process agricultural products, manufacturing is a common activity for rural HEs. Although street vendors and local markets are the most visible signs of HE activity, many businesses operate out of the owner's home.

HEs survive and grow because they provide low-cost goods and services demanded in a growing but less developed economy that lacks a modern services sector. In urban areas, mobile retail traders and HEs in market stalls provide the services found in convenience stores and malls in richer countries. The lower-quality goods manufactured by HEs typically will not be demanded as incomes rise and mass-produced or higher-quality goods enter the market. For this reason, services tend to dominate the sector and to persist longer than manufacturing.

"One who does not have a nonagricultural enterprise stays idle for most of the dry season when agricultural activities are few. Therefore, I started my enterprise of selling soft and alcoholic drinks."
Tanzania

Figure 5.3 **Most HEs are in the trading sector**

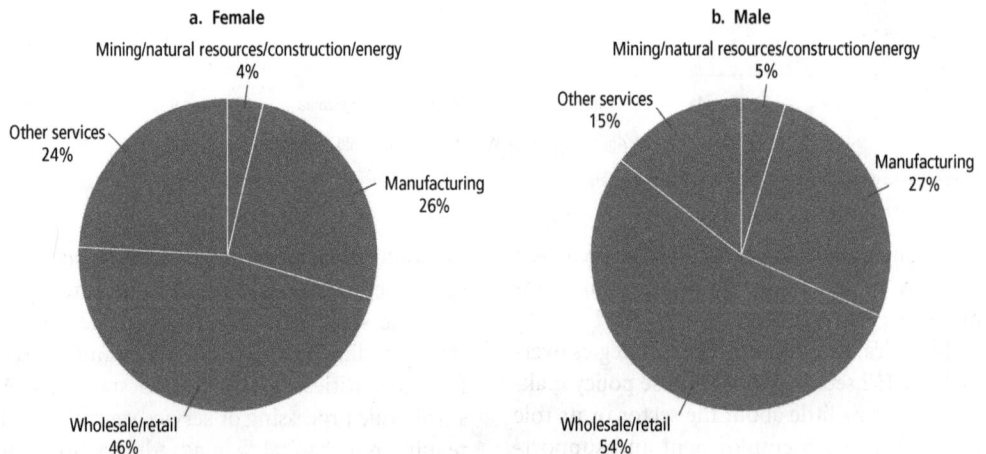

a. Female

Mining/natural resources/construction/energy
4%

Other services
24%

Manufacturing
26%

Wholesale/retail
46%

b. Male

Mining/natural resources/construction/energy
5%

Other services
15%

Manufacturing
27%

Wholesale/retail
54%

Source: Fox and Sohnesen 2012.

Although HEs account for a larger share of employment in urban areas, 60 percent of HEs in Sub-Saharan Africa are located where the population is—in rural areas. HEs are different in rural and urban areas (table 5.1).[1] It is quite common for rural households with an HE to operate a farm, either for subsistence and food security or as a commercial venture. The majority of these households consider the HE to be a secondary activity. Most HEs in rural areas operate during at least 10 months of the year, but for less than 30 hours a week. Often rural HE owners can do business only on weekends, when markets are open and foot traffic is heavier. Owners in rural areas are more likely to operate their business at home; in rural areas without electrification, HEs usually cannot operate after sunset.

Urban HEs are almost always the primary activity of the owner, but some owners have multiple businesses or lines of work. When HEs are a secondary activity, the primary activity is usually a wage job. As a result, urban owners work long hours; 47 percent work more than 50 hours a week. Almost all of those who hire paid labor are based in urban areas. Women are as active in the urban HE sector as men, but they are slightly underrepresented in rural HEs. Women and men clearly gravitate toward different types of enterprises. For example, females are more likely to do tailoring, and men are more likely to work in construction (Fox and Sohnesen 2012). The result of this gender segregation is that women are less likely to work in the sectors where earnings are higher (box 5.2).

Basic education is a key pathway for youth to transition into the HE sector. Individuals who enter the labor force with a completed primary education are the most likely to become an HE owner, and primary education is the main formal opportunity for developing skills that most young people now entering the HE sector will ever have. Whereas 35 percent of young adults (ages 25–34) who work in agriculture have never been to school, 79 percent of those in the nonfarm HE sector have at least some schooling. Although the majority of HE owners in Africa do not have primary education (reflecting the low levels of education among the older generations), as the level of education has risen

Table 5.1 Rural versus urban household enterprises

Indicator	Urban	Rural
Share of households owning an HE	53	36
Share of HEs as primary activity for owner	82	42
Share of HE owners working more than 30 hours a week	79	45
Share of HE owners operating their own business at least 10 months a year	69	61
Share of HE owners operating their business at home	30	43
Share of HE owners who are female	55	47
Share of HE owners with hired labor	8	11

Source: Fox and Sohnesen 2012, based on data from Cameroon (2001), the Republic of Congo (2009), Ghana (2005), Mozambique (2008), Rwanda (2005), and Tanzania (2005).

in the labor force, so has the level of education among HE owners. Figure 5.4 shows that the youngest owners are much less likely than their parents' generation to have no education. Still, only 29 percent of young adults (ages 25–34) employed in the HE sector have completed more than primary school, much less than the 59 percent in the modern wage sector.

The Business: Constraints and Opportunities

As businesses, Africa's HEs are quite heterogeneous. Even in the trading sector, some are very small-scale operations, using little human or physical capital, whereas others sell higher-value products, have a substantial inventory, and provide a much higher income. For example, a study of female HE owners in Accra, Ghana, found "high-profit" females, who had much higher average profits and capital stock, working in roughly the same sectors as low-profit females (Fafchamps et al. 2011).

Profits vary by sector as well. An analysis of data from seven capital cities in West Africa found monthly profits ranging from US$70 for petty traders to US$107 for construction workers (Grimm, Krüger, and Lay 2011). That same analysis found very high returns to capital for many self-employed and family businesses, especially at low levels of investment (Fafchamps et al. 2011 found similarly high rates in Accra). Monthly marginal returns on capital are estimated to be about 70 percent for those with capital stock valued at less than US$150. Although most businesses report capital con-

"All of us have the maximum of primary education, and this cadre represents the majority who are roaming in the streets. It is impossible for such people to get employment because there are better educated individuals." Tanzania

Box 5.2

Why do females earn less? Occupational segregation in the household enterprise sector

Gender segregation is common among HE owners. Both women and men are likely to engage in trading, but women are much more likely to do tailoring or catering (lower-paying activities) and men to engage in carpentry, metalworking, and repair (higher-paying activities). For example, owners of HEs surveyed in the Kassida workshop area of Kampala, Uganda, indicated that even in metalworking, males almost completely dominate the higher-earning fabrication activities, while more females engage in scrap metal processing, where earnings are lower. One of the sectors with the lowest earnings—selling drinks—is almost completely dominated by females.

The reasons for this gender segregation are complex. They include social norms, the lack of female role models who have entered occupations traditionally performed by men, and constraints on time and money, which can be more binding for women than for men. For example, studies in South Asia and Kenya found that when women choose to work outside the home, they spend more time traveling on slower modes of transport, which limits them to employment options that are closer to home (Uteng 2011; Gulyani, Talukdar, and Jack 2010). Regardless of the cause, women tend to earn less than men from HEs (Fox and Sohnesen 2012).

Evidence also suggests that men and women have different information or expectations about particular enterprises. In Kenya, a recent experiment with vocational training vouchers found that prior to enrollment males overwhelmingly preferred traditionally "male-dominated" courses such as motor vehicle mechanics, whereas women almost exclusively chose traditionally "female-dominated" courses such as hairdressing (Hicks et al. 2011). The program administrators randomly provided half of the participants with information on the actual returns to training, highlighting the higher returns in male-dominated trades and using "soft persuasive" methods, such as a video of female auto mechanics, to encourage females to pursue more traditionally male-dominated trades. Females exposed to the information were almost 9 percentage points more likely to express a preference for a male-dominated course, and they were 5 percentage points more likely to enroll in one. Younger and more educated females were especially likely to prefer male-dominated fields. This experiment suggests that efforts to provide information and encouragement have potential to reduce occupational segregation and increase women's earnings.

Figure B5.2.1 Earnings are higher in male-dominated subsectors than in female-dominated subsectors

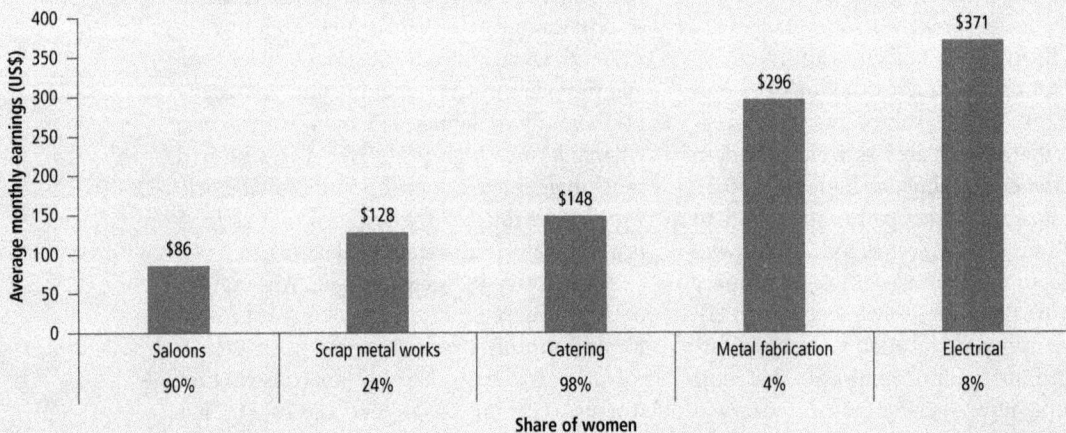

Source: Campos et al. 2013.

straints, returns do not appear to increase with the level of capital stock.

People need savings to start an HE, because it is virtually impossible for them to get credit.

Banks and microfinance institutions in Africa rarely lend to start-ups. Almost all owners report that they started their business with their own savings and a loan or grant from their fam-

Figure 5.4 Younger HE owners tend to have more education than older ones

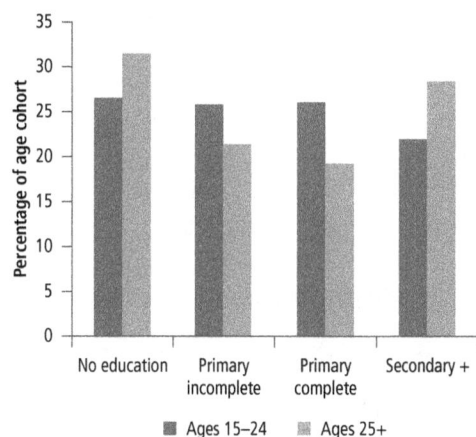

Source: Fox and Sohnesen 2012.

ily or friends (table 5.2). Very few applied for a loan after starting their enterprise. To the extent that these enterprises have access to financial services, those services tend to be informal. Suppliers' credit (informal loans at high interest rates) is common for trading enterprises. Other sources include informal local systems such as rotating savings and credit associations and village savings and loan associations, which pool savings within a village and lend small amounts for a short term, usually no more than one year (see focus note 3). Microfinance has not yet reached this sector, even for working capital. Despite the high returns to capital, current owners, those who did not start a business, and those who closed a business all reported that limited access to capital is the most important business constraint they face.

Completing primary education is a key driver of profits for HE owners. Compared to having no schooling at all, having only a few years of education does not add to earnings in the HE sector. This outcome reflects the fact that in many African countries a few years of basic education fail to provide basic skills such as literacy and numeracy. Because 45 percent of young adults in the HE sector have not completed basic education, the lack of basic skills contributes to their low earnings. By contrast, youth who have completed primary school and reached functional levels of literacy and numer-

acy can add as much as 40 percent to their earnings, controlling for sector, location, and other characteristics (see the discussion in chapter 3; Fox and Sohnesen 2012). While some of this earnings premium probably reflects other characteristics of primary school completers, it suggests that the basic skills acquired in primary school—such as literacy and numeracy—matter for productivity in HEs. Development policies and programs often confuse HEs with small and medium enterprises (SMEs) or micro, small, and medium enterprises. This is a mistake (box 5.3 explains why). Even though there is substantial heterogeneity among HEs, a fundamental difference between HEs and SMEs is that while HEs often persist for a long time (more than five years), they are not oriented toward employment growth (Fox and Sohnesen 2012). Even if productivity improves, these businesses rarely grow beyond HE status. Data from West Africa show that capital grows quickly to a steady state, and even after 10 years of operation, the capital stock of the business

Table 5.2 Sources of capital for household enterprises: Start-up and credit for operations

Source	Male	Female	All
Start-up capital[a]			
Personal savings	79.9	71.6	75.1
Official or formal	1.3	0.8	1.0
Relative or friends	6.6	13.9	10.8
Microfinance, NGO, cooperative	1.3	1.3	1.3
Informal	3.0	3.2	3.1
Other	7.9	9.2	8.7
Total	100.0	100.0	100.0
Credit for business operation[b]			
Official or formal	17.0	15.8	16.3
Relative or friends	39.9	43.0	41.7
Microfinance, NGO, cooperative	28.7	21.4	24.7
Informal	10.3	13.1	11.9
Other	4.0	6.6	5.5
Total	100.0	100.0	100.0

Source: Fox and Sohnesen 2012, based on World Bank harmonized household surveys.
Note: "Official or formal" includes commercial banks and public programs. "Other" includes loans from employers and other unspecified loans. "Informal" includes credit from customers or suppliers, informal moneylenders, rotating savings and credit associations, village savings and loan associations, and savings and credit cooperatives.
a. Includes Cameroon (2001), the Republic of Congo (2009), Ghana (2005), Rwanda (2005), and Uganda (2005).
b. Includes Ghana (2005), Rwanda (2005), Tanzania (2005), and Uganda (2005).

Box 5.3

Small and medium enterprises are not the same as household enterprises

Policies and programs to encourage business start-ups often place HEs and SMEs under one umbrella, often called micro, small, and medium enterprises. But HEs and SMEs have important differences.

Differences in where they locate:

- HE are usually not located in a building (establishment) in a business or commercial area. They may locate in a regular market stall, on a usual corner, or in the owner's house. Many have no fixed location.
- SMEs operate from a fixed location. They may be a sole proprietorship or have multiple owners, but they usually do not operate from the household, and they separate the business from the household accounts.

Differences in number of employees:

- Most HEs do not hire labor.
- SMEs by definition hire labor. Definitions of size vary, but in Sub-Saharan Africa a business with 5–20 employees is considered small, and a business with 21–50 is considered medium. However, some global studies classify businesses with less than 250 employees as small (see, for example, Ayyagari, Demirgüç-Kunt, and Maksimovic 2011). Differences in classification often lead to confusion in policy discussions.

Relationships between the enterprise and the state with respect to registration and payment of taxes depend in part on the rules and practices in each country.

Differences in registration and taxation requirements:

- In many countries, it is legal to run HEs without any business registration or license. However, local governments may require HEs to get a trading permit or license or to register for a place in a public market stall.
- Most countries require SMEs to have a business license, and their hiring is subject to national labor laws. At the same time, SMEs are known for hiring workers informally—that is, without paying payroll taxes or enrolling them in a mandatory social insurance system. In part this practice reflects the lower labor productivity in the SME sector, which calls for lower real wages.

Differences in access to financial services:

- HEs usually combine household and business finances. The HE is part of the household's livelihood portfolio, in which funds move back and forth between the HE and other activities (such as purchasing farm inputs).
- SMEs are likely to have a relationship with a bank or microfinance institution (as a saver or borrower), but they depend on their own and their family's savings for capital as well.

remains the same (Grimm, Knorringa, and Lay 2012). Most enterprises never hire another worker (Fox and Sohnesen 2012).

This steady state is not simply the result of capital constraints. It arises for multiple reasons. First, consistent with their growth-oriented approach, SMEs tend to start not as HEs but as SMEs, with more assets and employees at the beginning. From the start, they are a different type of business. The owners have demonstrated that they have an important skill—the ability to hire and manage labor outside the family. Managerial skill is often considered a key indicator of entrepreneurial potential (De Mel, McKenzie, and Woodruff 2012b; Gelb et al. 2009).

Second, almost all HEs rely on households, not other businesses, as their customers. HEs are rarely connected to larger value chains. The exception occurs when large wholesalers use informal retail networks, including HEs, as vendors to reach consumers (for example, selling bottled beverages or mobile phone cards). Depending on location and sector, the market for their product may be limited, which restricts growth.

Third, HEs tend to operate in sectors that are relatively easier to enter, so they face a lot of competition. Expansion would require more capital and constitute a big risk. HE owners report having to work hard to keep customers and stay ahead of the competition. In a West Africa study, 60 percent of HEs reported that competition and lack of customers are major threats to their existence (Grimm, Knorringa, and Lay 2012).

Fourth, even if the market for their product has growth potential, expansion for a self-employed HE owner means taking on employees, with associated management costs that owners usually do not want to handle. HEs are likely to take on apprentices, but not full-time employees.

Fifth, HEs operate in a risky environment, with limited opportunities to hedge their risk. Given the retail nature of their sales, HEs depend on growth in income both from agriculture and from wages and salaries to survive. This dependence means that their incomes are pro-cyclical; a negative shock to the local agricultural sector can hurt them as well. Expansion may only increase risk.

Seventh, in addition to business risk, HEs face household risk. In surveys, business risk tends to be listed as more important, although females tend to cite household events such as an illness in the family as a reason for exiting the HE sector. In addition, HEs rarely separate the business accounts from the household accounts.

Finally, HE owners have other responsibilities (in farming or the household, for example), so they do not have additional time to devote to their business. In their risky environment, giving up subsistence farming to devote more time to the business may not make sense for the household.

For creating employment, the implication of these differences is that employment grows in the HE sector because an individual or household seizes a business opportunity and creates a new enterprise, not because HEs hire a young person looking for work.

Even though HEs will not transform themselves into SMEs, they are often a good business opportunity in Africa. In African countries they tend to be found in richer areas, and households with these enterprises are less likely to be poor—they tend to be clustered in the middle quintiles (Fox and Sohnesen 2012). Stronger evidence from recent panel data in a few Eastern and Southern African countries indicates that adding an HE does make household income and consumption grow faster regardless of wealth level, suggesting that HEs help to reduce poverty.

For many rural households, the hourly income from an HE is higher than the hourly income from the agricultural sector. One reason for this discrepancy is that agriculture in Sub-Saharan Africa is still mostly rain-fed, resulting in substantial seasonal underemployment. Another reason is that farmers still use very basic production techniques, which make it hard for them to get ahead.

In urban areas, some HE owners earn more than they could expect to make in a wage job, either because their lower education and skills limit their access to a wage job or because wage rates are still low in Africa. It is usually the roughly 10 percent of HE owners who have the managerial skills to hire workers whose earnings exceed those from wage employment (Fox and Sohnesen 2012). Other benefits cited by HE owners include the opportunity to be their own boss and flexible hours (Falco et al. 2012).

Constraints for Young People to Enter the HE Sector

Owners of HEs tend to range between the ages of 25 and 40 (figure 5.5). Despite having more education than older workers, young people struggle to enter the HE sector. They are held back by multiple constraints, including insufficient capital or savings, inadequate information on markets and input supply, and the lack of a range of skills, such as literacy, numeracy, and business, behavioral, and technical skills. Often the most important constraint is lack of capital. Young people may leave school with the aspiration to start a business, but without savings, they find it very difficult to start a business.

Many young people, including those still in school, work in the HE sector, but not as business owners. They contribute work to a family business without receiving a regular wage. This experience can be a pathway to sustainable employment in the sector (see chapter 2). Working in a family business can provide essential on-the-job training—in business or technical skills—and build the informal networks necessary for success. These young people may also be earning the trust of their family, who might eventually supply start-up capital for an enterprise. Studies in West African capital cities show a strong correlation between having a

"Despite the difficulties … in a day's work, I make as much as a civil servant does in a month."
Madagascar

Figure 5.5 Household enterprise owners tend to be over 25 years of age

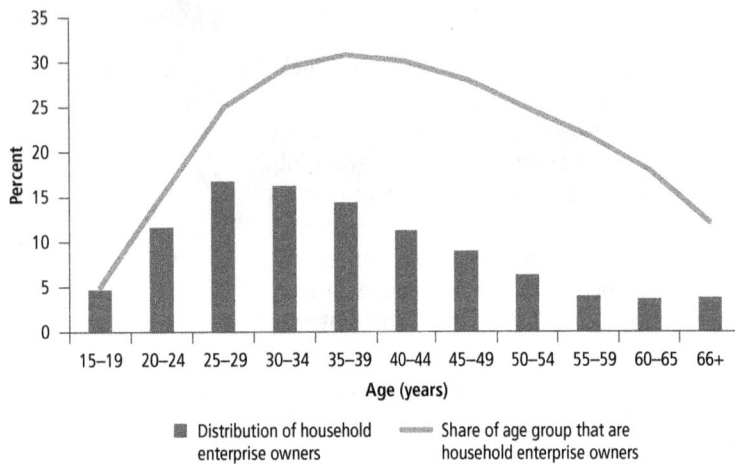

Source: Fox and Sohnesen 2012.

HE. Some occupations, including trading (the most common business), do not require specific technical skills, but some do (for example, construction, manufacturing, repair, and personal services such as hairdressing). Young people acquire these skills through training or apprenticeships, mostly supplied by private providers rather than public institutions. Governments need to recognize that, just as *informal employment* is normal, *informal training* is normal for youth in the HE sector. Most such training consists of private courses and apprenticeships, as discussed extensively in chapter 3 and summarized in box 5.4.

Two issues related to apprenticeship have a bearing on young people's ability to enter and remain in the HE sector. First, the skills offered through apprenticeships are often quite narrow, limited to a specific production technology, and difficult to transfer to another occupation. Second, the time spent in an apprenticeship can make it challenging for young people to accumulate the savings they will need to apply their new skills in an enterprise of their own.

self-employed parent and being self-employed (Pasquier-Doumer 2013).

Another common way for youth to enter the sector is to gain skills and experience. Technical skills are not a prerequisite for starting an

Box 5.4

Informal training is normal for youths seeking to operate a household enterprise

Young people working in HEs are substantially more likely to have gone through informal skills training or an apprenticeship than formal vocational training. Among 25- to 34-year-olds employed in the HE sector, 32 percent have been an apprentice at some point, but only 6 percent have gone through formal vocational training.

Private, informal training is the primary source of technical skills for HEs. The spectrum of providers includes for-profit private institutes and firms, NGOs, religious and community organizations, and individuals. The vast majority of these providers develop their own teaching programs, are self-financing, and operate on a very small scale with little government oversight or support. Training is generally short and intensive, and it may offer a certificate. In some countries, informal private training providers enroll more trainees than public institutes providing formal vocational training.

Apprenticeship, in which an experienced enterprise owner (master) teaches skills on the job, is by far the most common and important institution providing training. Apprentices generally have at most a junior high school education. The scope and content of apprenticeships are heavily focused on a basic,

narrow set of technical skills—such as tailoring, carpentry, vehicle repair, or hairdressing—that are used primarily in the HE sector. In addition to being specific to the sector of activity, such skills may be specific to the technology used by the master (Frazer 2006). Ghana's highly developed apprenticeship system is a good example (Monk, Sandefur, and Teal 2008).

Apprenticeships take many forms and vary in duration. If a family lacks cash to compensate the master, the master may take on the apprentice for a lower fee but require more time (labor) from the apprentice in return. Many apprenticeships are informal, although some are based on a contract. To enforce this contract, the first year of the apprenticeship often involves little training, just unskilled labor. The time spent in an apprenticeship without earning money may account for the lower payoff to apprenticeship that is observed in countries such as Ghana, where this practice is common. Unless young people can save money during their apprenticeship, they still face barriers to entering the sector. After completing an apprenticeship, youth often report that a lack of capital prevents them from applying their newly acquired skills.

In addition to capital and skills, a third barrier to entry is young people's general lack of information about opportunities in the HE sector, especially relative to wage and salary jobs. Young people participating in a small survey in urban Tanzania in 2005 reported that they had spent an average of five years idle or doing odd jobs while seeking a wage or salary job in an enterprise. Three-fourths of the respondents ended up self-employed (Bridges et al. 2013). Could this search time be reduced by providing better information about opportunities for self-employment or programs to help young people to enter the HE sector?

The short answer is that the large number of public and nongovernmental projects undertaken in Africa to help young people to enter and remain in the HE sector have provided little evidence on the best ways to facilitate entry and raise the earnings of HEs (box 5.5 presents examples from Rwanda). In particular, there is little guidance on which interventions could work on a large scale—that is, beyond small-scale pilots. What is clear is that, although young people encounter specific constraints in the HE sector, reducing the multiple obstacles that all HE owners encounter in entering and earning a living in the sector can generate productive employment for many. The next section focuses on how governments and policy makers can support productive employment for the large numbers of people who will spend their working lives outside of the wage economy in the HE sector.

Creating and Sustaining Productive Employment in Household Enterprises

The HE sector has developed with little public support. Public policy has neglected this sec-

---

Rwanda: Many programs to support household enterprises, but little information on results

In 2010 the World Bank and Government of Rwanda inventoried the major public and nongovernmental programs to support HEs and then conducted focus group discussions around the country to elicit HE owners' perceptions of the programs. Of 19 NGO and 7 government programs identified, most government programs targeted SMEs, not HEs; most NGO programs targeted HEs and emphasized training. Some NGO programs combined training with small grants to start a business. NGO programs tended to support specific groups, such as women, youths, people with human immunodeficiency virus/acquired immune deficiency syndrome (HIV/AIDS), and so on, which meant that many participants felt excluded. Few participants had received any support, but those who had were generally appreciative. Most programs focused on providing support to set up a business; participants felt that assistance is also needed after a business is started.

Given the huge number of HEs operating in Rwanda, the demand for assistance is high, but support is relatively modest because funding is limited, as reported by many nongovernmental and civil society organizations. These limitations partly reflect the tremendously fragmented effort to support

HEs. While this fragmentation is common in low-income countries, it means that the whole is less than the sum of its parts.

Several organizations contacted for the inventory complained that their products were not being taken up. Programs directed at women noted that social attitudes limiting the scope of women's activities hindered participation. Some NGOs may not be providing a product appropriate for the majority of the clients or government policies may not be supportive of their efforts. Training cannot be effective if it cannot be used productively.

Since systematic evaluation of many of these projects is rare, it is difficult to measure their effectiveness. Some programs could not even provide assessments of beneficiaries or basic monitoring data. A few had evidence on outcomes, however. The literacy programs had data on the number of women who passed the test. Better monitoring and evaluation would help the government to identify which programs might be scaled up effectively and to help the NGO or agency involved obtain financing to do so.

Source: World Bank and IPAR 2012.

tor—both by failing to support youth to enter it and by failing to provide the business climate to sustain incomes and productivity. Government strategies tend to identify the SMEs as a source of employment, but not the HE sector.

Often the main obstacle to supporting the HE sector is an implicit bias against HEs, which are not necessarily attractive in the eyes of public authorities, who sometimes even chase them out of business areas in capital cities. The perception of HEs as unworthy of public support renders systematic efforts to support them politically challenging. In some development circles, HEs have been criticized for not offering the income and benefits of wage and salary employment, so national governments hesitate to include them in their strategies, despite the evidence that they contribute to growth, reduce poverty, and provide better opportunities than other occupations such as agriculture. Recognizing that "the informal will be normal" is the first step in developing effective policies and programs to help youth to create sustainable enterprises.

Analysis of the sector and its multiple constraints yields five key areas where public policy can be effective in supporting the creation and growth of HEs:[2]

- *National strategies* that recognize HEs, encourage the sector, and give HEs a voice in developing national and local strategies
- *Urban policies* that provide adequate locations where HEs can work and sell their products, along with essential support services such as lighting, water, sanitation, and security
- *Financial sector policies and programs* that encourage private providers and NGOs to improve household access to financial services, including savings and credit
- *Support for programs* that tackle multiple constraints, either by building a range of skills (technical, business, and behavioral skills) or by combining skills with capital
- *Support for programs* that improve access to markets by integrating HEs into value chains

In many cases, public support is needed only to facilitate entry and to encourage the private initiatives that already serve the sector. In other cases, information gaps or market failures indicate a need for public intervention in the form of regulation or targeted financial support.

National Strategies

Employment policy, including youth employment, is embedded in national growth strategies. In Africa, most national strategies explicitly recognize that private enterprise is the key agent in economic growth and job creation, but they focus on farms, SMEs, and larger firms, despite the large share of employment in HEs and the potential for substantial growth. Limited national support for the HE sector as an agent of economic development trickles down to subnational governments, which often exclude HEs from local development (box 5.6). Mechanisms to organize the sector and give its constituents a voice are not developed, and national institutions lack channels to provide support to HEs. Because national and local policies, programs, and projects that could support productive HEs are not designed with the sector in mind, governments miss opportunities to improve the incomes and prospects of HEs and encourage entry into the sector for many who could benefit from it. The result is that HEs and the employment they provide are invisible to policy makers.

To the extent that HEs are even on the strategic radar screen, they are seen as entities to be transformed into SMEs and "formalized." In Tanzania, a law from 1972 outlawing businesses that operate without a fixed premise is still on the books. This law effectively makes more than 80 percent of HEs illegal (a fact conveniently ignored when the government collects taxes or fees from HE owners). The objective of national economic policy (2008)—"to empower the informal sector to become formal in order for them to access finance, training, or any other business development service"—runs directly counter to HEs' own aspiration *not* to be transformed into an employer, but rather to survive and bring sufficient cash income into the household. It is not clear how a sector that is virtually regulated out of business by law could become "formal" in the sense of complying with the law.

Rwanda's development strategies (Vision 2020 and the Economic Development and Poverty Reduction Strategy), while supportive of the informal sector in general, do not recognize HEs as key economic actors. HEs either are not differentiated from SMEs or are excluded entirely from government support (for example, the SME policy is limited to enterprises with hired labor). The disconnect between Rwanda's national strategies and the characteristics of the HE sector creates a poor business environment in which HEs are largely overlooked and their specific needs are not addressed. Even so, the fact that HEs are legal in Rwanda gives the government large scope to broaden national policies specifically to include them.

Ghana, where HEs have been included in the national strategy and institutions for many years, provides a positive example of what can be achieved (box 5.7). Its rich history as a trading economy, dating back before colonization, is one of the reasons why it has some of the most developed public and private institutions to support informal enterprises. For example, one objective detailed in the national Poverty Reduction Strategy Paper of 2006 is to "enhance productivity and income/wage, with equal opportunities for men and women in all sectors of the economy, including the informal economy" (Republic of Ghana 2006). The National Board for Small Scale Industries (NBSSI) explicitly includes the self-employed within its mandate and has used technical assistance and donor funding to pilot, refine, and scale up locally developed programs to support this sector. Rather than shunning HEs, the trade union movement in Ghana opened its doors to them, taking in nascent organizations such as the Ghana Traders Association (which at the time primarily covered Accra City) to give a collective voice to this important economic group. In 1996, the Ghana Trade Union Congress adopted a policy to encourage the organization of informal enterprises and informal economy workers and to support their integration into the organized consul-

Box 5.6

Need for a comprehensive approach

In 2007 Victor Tokman, one of the first researchers on informal enterprises, published a seminal article called "Modernizing the Informal Sector" (Tokman 2007). He observed,

> There is general agreement over the need to pay attention to the informal sector because of its importance to employment and poverty issues. There are also an increasing number of programmes aimed at supporting similar informal activities in highly diverse national contexts . . . Nevertheless, to the extent that it fails to embrace a shared strategic vision, this is a limited consensus that hinders the effectiveness of policies implemented in this area. While often adequate on an individual basis, they are insufficient and produce limited effects by failing to respond to a more comprehensive approach.

tative mechanisms between the government and the private sector. Aside from providing mechanisms for dialogue at the strategic level, the development of HE associations helps to improve information flows and access to technologies and markets, allowing national and international distributors to integrate informal agents into their value chains.

Urban Policies and the Household Enterprise Sector

HEs are much more common in urban areas, and urban residents are more likely to identify their business as their primary and only activity (although rural HEs are an important pathway out of agriculture, as detailed in chapters 2 and 4). Youth unemployment and idleness are also more frequent in urban areas. Yet the business climate for HEs in urban areas is rarely supportive and often hostile. The most frequent complaint relates to the lack of functional space in which to do business. Other complaints refer to authorities' petty corruption in the context of enforcing regulations or collecting taxes and the lack of services such as security.

Urban authorities have five responsibilities that affect the entry and productivity of HEs:

- Controlling the use of public space (sidewalks, streets, parks, and the like)

Box 5.7

Ghana's integrated approach to HE development

Ghana's development strategy explicitly acknowledges the contribution of HEs to employment absorption, income growth, and local economic development. The strategy places a growing emphasis on enabling youths and women to obtain the skills and capital they need to succeed in business. The approach is sustainable because it is decentralized. Local officials support HEs' growth because they recognize that their political survival and the generation of internal revenue depend on a vibrant local economy that includes HEs. At the national level, the government collaborates with donors to provide supportive programs and policies that create a consistent framework, disseminate lessons learned, and provide targeted funding. The approach has been developed in phases since the late 1990s, largely through the Rural Enterprise Programme of the Ministry of Trade and Industry, with funding from the International Fund for Agricultural Development and the African Development Bank.

The local business advisory centers are the cornerstone of the system. Overseen on a technical basis by the NBSSI, they receive financial support from local governments (the municipal or district assemblies). The NBSSI funds up to two staff members, whose responsibilities include monitoring and liaising with the NBSSI. The business advisory centers match donor and government projects and programs to the needs of local clients and help to strengthen local associations of household, small, and medium enterprises. The associations have several important roles: expressing members' needs, organizing training, liaising with authorities, disseminating information, and in some cases assisting authorities in managing markets and collecting market fees.

One lesson learned as Ghana has sought to target youth self-employment more forcefully is that too many initiatives, with too little coordination, are under way in various ministries and nongovernmental programs. In response, the Ministry of Employment and Social Welfare, with support from the World Bank, has developed a National Strategy and Action Plan for Informal Enterprises. The plan establishes a national policy framework, identifies strategic areas for action by every ministry and agency from within their own resources and programs, and provides for coordination through a National Committee on the Informal Economy. Although the process of submitting the action plan to the cabinet was interrupted by the recent election, consultative validation with key stakeholders has disseminated some of its key messages and principles. The following areas are identified for concerted, coordinated action:

- Continue to work with local governments to improve the policy and business environment, especially the legal, regulatory, and fiscal environment and mechanisms for dialogue
- Reduce vulnerability, particularly through infrastructure and secure sites for business
- Improve access to finance and business development services
- Raise productivity and widen access to markets, especially by upgrading the apprenticeship system and standardizing the skills and qualifications system
- Use social protection to reduce household vulnerability

"The authorities are harassing us and confiscating our assets. I have decided to open my business at night. I do business when the government is asleep. I earn a living for my family by doing this." Tanzania

- Developing and enforcing rules on the use of private space (zoning regulations)
- Providing urban services to support local economic development, including local roads, street lighting, public transport, and security
- Vetting businesses in order to protect consumers (for example, ensuring that taxi drivers know how to drive, professionals have required training, and restaurant kitchens are hygienic)
- Setting and collecting fees and revenue to support local activities

Authorities have to balance many interests in executing these responsibilities, and HE

owners complain that their interests are not being adequately addressed.

For HEs, the lack of secure premises (a problem frequently exacerbated by outright legal or extralegal harassment from local authorities) delays start-ups, which especially handicaps youth. In a survey of tailors and dressmakers in capital cities in West Africa, 43 percent of enterprises in operation for less than one year reported the lack of an adequate locality for their business as a major problem (Grimm, Knorringa, and Lay 2012). This problem also prevents businesses from expanding. The most common and violent conflicts occur when police exert control over the space where hawkers and other traders attempt to reach potential customers. These conflicts usually erupt because local authorities fail to recognize the importance of these trading businesses to the local economy and do not provide adequate space for them to operate. Local authorities do not always consider how rapidly HEs can be expected to grow as urbanization increases. In some cases, authorities have attempted to develop markets or other work space for HEs, but without consulting them, so the space developed has been unsuitable. Different businesses have different needs. Traders and personal service providers need premises with foot traffic, not outside of town but in central business districts (on sidewalks, especially through the creation of pedestrian-only streets), at bus stops and terminals, near major road intersections, and other places that are convenient for people to shop and transact business. Repair shops and manufacturers such as metalworking operations need to cluster to realize agglomeration efficiencies and share technology, and urban areas need to provide suitable sites for them to do so. Industrial estates designed for large firms can include HEs in planning and space allocation, for the convenience of workers and the firms.

Cities that fail to anticipate the growth of HEs and proactively identify locations for their activity enter destructive cycles of "decongestion." The precipitating event is usually a forthcoming political or sporting event that will swell crowds and heighten security concerns. Authorities "decongest" the city by mobilizing police or other security forces to evict traders from the city center and other lucrative areas, sometimes confiscating their inventory and other assets, or demolishing their temporary business structures. Eviction is rarely permanent. HEs retreat, but many gradually amass the capital to return to their trading location until the next eviction.

Forceful eviction from the more lucrative areas where traders make spot sales presents a compelling case for the failure of local governments to support HEs (box 5.8 presents an example from Tanzania). Even though local authorities are simply enforcing the law, their operations are counterproductive: they increase rather than reduce poverty and heighten the

sense of insecurity and vulnerability among HEs (as borne out by Lyons and Msoka 2007; Liviga and Mekacha 1998; Sisya 2005).

Overlapping and insecure land rights complicate the problem of finding space. In Dar es Salaam, the local government is not allowed to develop its own rules on the use of land next to national roads because it does not own the land—the Ministry of Transportation owns it. The local government is therefore required to enforce rules set by the Ministry of Transportation and not allowed to develop and enforce rules that might support local enterprises in using the land. Land tenure systems based on a combination of customary and common law restrict the development of efficient land markets and can prevent HEs from obtaining land. In Nairobi, efforts to establish secure land tenancy for slum dwellers who run HEs are complicated by multiple land rights and land disputes (World Bank 2013).

Another problem limiting HEs' productivity is the poor quality of urban services they receive. The construction and maintenance of markets, where traders and service providers can congregate to sell and customers can gather to purchase, is one of the most important urban services needed by HEs, which pay a fee to locate in the market. In most urban areas, governments are simply not creating markets fast enough to keep up with population growth. In addition, although fees are paid, security and sanitation may not be provided as expected. As demand for valuable urban land goes up, developers pressure local governments to close markets rather than to develop higher-density, multiple-use solutions. In the end, HEs lose customers. Other key services that can affect their productivity are transport (taken by HE owners to reach markets and by customers to reach HEs) and water supply.

A common perception is that HEs do not pay their fees and taxes, so they do not deserve these services. Nothing could be further from the truth. Analysis suggests that although HEs may be exempt from national corporation taxes or value added tax registration, the majority of HEs pay local business taxes at a higher rate than large businesses (Fox and Sohnesen 2012). Taxes, fees, and local rules regarding land use are reported to be sources of petty corruption,

"I did well before the local authority moved the market. Now I have difficulty feeding my family and cannot afford to send my children to school." Rwanda

Weakening the local economy by perpetuating the *machinga* cycle in Dar es Salaam

Dar es Salaam has limited business premises in its high-rent, lucrative commercial areas. Owners of HEs take to the streets at the borders of these areas as mobile operators (*machingas*), crowding sidewalks and roads, even if zoning laws prohibit them from doing so. The proliferation of cars, foot traffic, and traders, especially during rush hours, is more than city authorities can manage. To curb the congestion that mobile vendors and service people bring to towns and cities, the authorities, especially in Dar es Salaam, Arusha, and Mwanza, regularly engage in "clean-up" operations, in which mobile traders are especially vulnerable targets. Faced with eviction, some HE operators abandon their business. Local authorities deploy disproportionate force to drive out those who remain. HE owners cite harassment by local government and law enforcement officers as their biggest problem. More than 60 percent of 622 operators interviewed for one study said that forceful eviction is their most vivid experience of government intervention. The same study catalogues *machingas'* losses from local eviction and relocation policies: physical capital (kiosks), operating capital (fines, confiscation of inventory), customers and supply lines (through increased distance), and trading time (through jail sentences or time spent rebuilding capital to return to business). Repeated cycles of loss and hardship resulting from these policies increase the poverty and deprivation of household members.

Local officials also subject HEs to inspections to check compliance with licensing, taxation, and other regulations,

even though most such regulations apply only to formal enterprises. HEs have little knowledge of the tax code or registration requirements and no place to complain. Many report paying large sums to unscrupulous officials to avoid having their merchandise confiscated.

In response to the lack of market space, the city of Dar es Salaam recently took out a loan and built a seven-story building for use by itinerant traders. Dubbed the "*machinga* complex," the project was estimated to cost T Sh 13 billion (approximately US$13 million), but it does not meet the needs of the *machingas*, who were not consulted in its design. Among other issues, the building has no elevators to move customers or merchandise. No parking is available. The building was designed to provide 10,000 work spaces (compartments or stalls), but in the end, only 6,500 rooms were built. Fewer rooms increased the average cost, requiring city authorities to raise rents to repay their loan. When the complex opened, only the bottom floor was filled by vendors, who then complained to authorities that the *machingas* selling on the sidewalk were undercutting them. Eventually, the upper floors were rented out to other tenants who prize the downtown location but do not need to locate goods on-site for sale. Meanwhile, the *machinga* problem has not been solved.

Source: Kweka and Fox 2011.

especially by police. Failure to pay the requested bribe can result in disproportionately negative consequences (such as confiscation of inventory). Often owners of HEs do not even know the current fee schedule or how much they should pay. Corrupt local officials can then take advantage of them.

Two overarching factors contribute to the poor business environment in urban areas for HEs: national policies and strategies exclude HEs, and local governments are not accountable to their citizens. In Rwanda, national policies that exclude HEs and strictly limit their locations in urban areas create indifference to HEs' needs among local authorities. The authorities see their job as enforcing national regulations to control HEs, not to support their development. In Ghana, the cooperation between HEs and local authorities is poor in Accra, where the

government is not elected by the citizens, but it is stronger outside the capital, where local authorities are elected and responsibility for local economic development has been decentralized. Outside Accra, local authorities focus more on creating space for HEs to operate and less on controlling space to exclude them (box 5.9). Improvements in the organization of HEs at the local level, facilitated by the locally recruited and managed business advisory officers, have reportedly enhanced communication between HEs and elected local officials.

Easing Access to Credit to Start and Sustain a Household Enterprise

HEs need capital to start a business and working capital to maintain it. Most HEs struggle to obtain capital. Over and over in surveys

Box 5.9

Clustering household enterprises for the benefit of all

In the city of Bechem, Ghana, national commitment and public-private-donor collaboration supported the establishment of a mini industrial site for metalworking, car repair, and carpentry workshops. Prior to the project, these workshops were scattered around the city, some occupying valuable downtown locations. The city endeavored to obtain a suitable parcel of land outside the most congested areas and to develop it for the HEs, allowing the workshops to form productivity-enhancing clusters and the city to assign use of the valuable city-center land to higher-density, higher-value projects.

The project, which required multiple consultations with HE associations, took nearly four years to develop, but it finally opened in 2012 with 37 masters and 68 apprentices. The rest of the space is being filled as new HEs move in. The site provides work space, electricity, and water. Once the site was open, seven spare parts dealers and some food vendors (also HEs) moved in behind the main tenants to supply support services. Organizations offering training in areas such as basic engineering skills and electronic engine servicing have also reached out to the HE owners, as they can easily reach a critical mass for their services.

When done with adequate prior consultation and preparation of facilities, such sites achieve mutually satisfactory objectives.

For the businesses:

- They gain a secure location.
- Through clustering, trades find it easier to obtain common services and participate in value chains (particularly if project-funded support services such as training or finance are located on-site).
- Access to business development services improves, because training providers easily reach clustered clients.
- Access to electricity, water, sewerage, and garbage removal improves.
- Business associations become stronger.

For local authorities:

- Activities that local governments prefer to locate outside the town center, such as metalworking, carpentry, and auto repair, are moved and clustered.
- Businesses are easier to tax and less prone to avoid taxes, because they see value for money in the public services they receive.

For clients:

- Suppliers concentrate in one location, giving easier access to regional as well as local markets.

Source: William Steel, personal communication.

---

asking about the major constraints to starting or expanding a business, HE owners list capital constraints at the top (see Fox and Sohnesen 2012; Grimm, Krüger, and Lay 2011). In Mozambique, in a survey of HE owners who had to close their business, 56 percent reported lack of capital or liquidity as the primary reason (Fox and Sohnesen 2013).

Unable to obtain credit through formal sources, they use their own savings and informal sources of credit to meet their needs (box 5.10). A complicating factor for HEs is that business and household finances are often linked, so efforts to smooth household consumption (to pay for lumpy expenditures such as school fees or home repairs) may compete with efforts to maintain business liquidity and potentially undermine the sustainability of the business. Access to credit would help to balance these competing needs. The gap between credit

needs and supply is widest for young people looking to start an HE.

At the root of this problem is the lack of financial inclusion for households in Africa (see focus note 3). Most households in Africa do not have access to a bank or microfinance institution (MFI), either for saving or for credit. Many households rely on informal savings groups to help them to save for business or household emergencies and to obtain short-term credit when savings are not enough. Young people have started to join these groups, and it is one of the reasons why more than 25 percent of youth in the low-income and lower-middle-income countries report having saved some funds in the last 12 months (FINDEX data).

Young people with access to a bank still have trouble getting a loan for start-up capital. Even MFIs in Africa, which target a lower-income population than banks, prefer to lend to indi-

Box 5.10

Sources of credit used by households to start a business in Tanzania

- I got my capital, amounting to T Sh 250, from my mother in 1986 and started by selling local brew known as *wanzuki*.[a]
- I started with a capital of T Sh 50,000, which I obtained from my father in April 2007.
- I started with a capital of T Sh 20,000 in 1994. I got the capital from selling maize which I had produced.
- I had accumulated a capital of T Sh 50,000 from my wages as I was formerly employed.
- I started with supplier's credit (*mali kauli*) to sell goods: 1 kilogram of sugar, 2 kilograms of rice, 1 liter of cooking oil, tea leaves, salt, and firewood that I collected from the bush.
- I started by hiring a sewing machine for T Sh 5,000 per month in 2007. I worked with that machine until I got enough money (T Sh 120,000), which I used to buy my own sewing machine.
- I obtained the initial capital amounting to T Sh 5 million from selling cashew nuts, and the profit from our shop. We then bought a milling machine.

- My initial capital of T Sh 5,000 was given by my husband, and I started selling vegetables.
- I started selling cooked food and local brew with locally borrowed money (T Sh 10,000). From this business I obtained a capital of T Sh 30,000. Then I decided to change business by opening a *genge* (fresh food stand).
- I am operating a grocery where I am selling beer and soft drinks and had started with an initial capital of T Sh 200,000, half of which was given by my mother and the other half was obtained from agricultural production.
- I borrowed materials for starting cooked food vending: 3 kilograms of rice, 2 kilograms of meat, cooking oil (a half liter), and salt. I obtained my initial capital amounting to T Sh 8,000 from my uncle, and I decided to do a business of keeping and selling guinea fowls.

Source: Kweka and Fox 2011.
a. Wanzuki is a local brew made of honey and yeast. Sometimes sugar, tea leaves, and yeast are used to make it when honey is not available.

viduals with a salary so that they have a better chance of repayment. Some MFIs will lend to households based on collateral (such as household assets) or the guarantee of a relative or friend who has a salary. In this case, an initial savings deposit is often required.

If young people are not creditworthy because they do not have enough savings or a track record with a formal savings institution, are grants an option to help them to start a business? Most of the NGO-led pilots in Africa that help people to start a business use grants instead of loans, and grants have been tried in South Asia and Latin America as well. In almost all cases, they facilitated entry into the sector. But in no cases did the experiment use only grants for start-up capital—either business training and support services or vocational training was supplied as well. Other experiments used matching grants plus financial education to encourage *saving* so that youths would have start-up capital. These approaches also produced positive results, but the target groups were quite well off by African standards. Grants provided

to existing businesses in Sri Lanka helped to improve sustainability, providing evidence of capital constraints both at start-up and during operation (De Mel, McKenzie, and Woodruff 2012b).

The main problem with the pilot grant programs for youths to start a business relates to the availability of funds: funds are not available to provide the 5 million or so youths who are expected to start a business every year in Africa over the next 10 years with a grant of US$100 (about the average size of grant used in the pilot programs). And even if youth grants on that scale were affordable, what about adults who want to start a business? Excluding them could be politically difficult. In Tanzania, government involvement in grant programs to support business creation led to poor targeting, suggesting that governments should tread carefully in this area (Kweka and Fox 2011). A more broad-based strategy would be to expand financial inclusion (especially savings) by reducing the costs of financial services and improving the range of products available to HE start-ups.

What Should Governments Do to Help Equip Youth with Skills for the HE Sector?

Training programs are the most common government and donor intervention to support HEs—both for facilitating entry and for improving incomes—whether targeted at youth or not.[3] Programs provide technical training in a specific sector (such as tailoring, metalworking, operating a bakery), business or financial literacy skills (such as basic accounting or money management), behavioral and life skills, or a mixture of skills. Programs targeted specifically to youth focus primarily on the skills needed to enter the sector and may include all four types of skills listed above. Programs targeted at existing HEs tend to focus on the business skills needed to strengthen or expand an enterprise, moving toward the goal of improving earnings and productivity. The good news for youth employment is that programs designed to facilitate entry appear to have had some success (more than those targeted at existing entrepreneurs), so there are some positive models.

Despite the large number of training programs, evidence of their effectiveness among HEs in Africa remains thin. Most training programs operate on a small scale, do not collect monitoring data on dropout or graduation rates, and are unable to track outcomes, let alone outcomes for a comparison group. Even the larger programs have not systematically documented success (or failure). Analysis of household survey data on HE earnings is not able to isolate specific returns to training, for several reasons:

- Participation in training programs is poorly captured in household survey data, particularly for the more prevalent types of apprenticeships or private training.
- The product itself is very heterogeneous, even in the same sector or skill.
- The majority of existing HE owners did not participate in any training, and training is not needed to start a business in, for example, trading. Training is needed to enter specific sectors, which often do provide higher

incomes (car repair, metalworking). But the effect of the training and the effect of other, unmeasured personal characteristics associated with choosing the sector are so comingled that the returns to the training are hard to identify.

- Many people who take training do not practice their skill for various reasons, including the inability to finance an enterprise.

As a result, more systematic and careful evaluations are needed, including impact evaluations that measure outcomes among program participants and a relevant comparison group (chapter 3, box 3.9). Only a few programs designed to foster self-employment were subjected to an impact evaluation in the past decade. More high-quality impact evaluations are needed, including studies that specifically evaluate the best ways to design youth employment programs (especially the best components to package together and the most effective agencies for delivering programs), the cost-effectiveness of those programs at scale, and their general equilibrium effects.

Despite the limited evidence, information from recent impact evaluations and other studies offers a starting point to guide policy and identify promising approaches to help youth to enter and stay in the HE sector. This section reviews evidence on the effectiveness of three major types of training—technical skills, business skills, and behavioral skills. It concludes that programs combining multiple interventions—different types of training or training plus capital—are more successful than programs offering one intervention. None of the combined interventions has been scaled up, however, and cost is an issue. Finally, we consider what the limited evidence suggests about the potential role for government and public policy in building skills for more productive and sustainable HEs.

Building Technical Skills

As discussed here and in chapter 3, technical training, through apprenticeships and other types of private training outside of the formal education system, is the most popular form of training for HEs. Informal training is very het-

"With some training the future will be better. Instead of simply resoling shoes, I would like to start manufacturing them." Uganda

"Our landlord had a wood workshop, and I passed in front of it every day when going to school. I started stopping there to play, and the owner introduced me, little by little, to "the profession." Madagascar

erogeneous. Training can be just a few months of on-the-job learning with a skilled HE owner, or it can last for years; it can combine classroom instruction with on-the-job learning. Many informal training programs or apprenticeships build narrow sets of technical skills (for example, in tailoring, carpentry, mechanics, or hairdressing). Little is known about which modalities are the most effective and about the best way of promoting them to ensure that they improve skills and productivity.

Household survey data show an association between private apprenticeships and increased employment and earnings—for example, in Nigeria, Rwanda, and Tanzania (Van Adams, Johansson de Silva, and Razmara 2013). Apprenticeships in Ghana offer a return in specific activities, such as construction, especially in rural areas, but not in other activities, such as tailoring (Fox and Sohnesen 2012). Apprenticeships also offer returns to workers who apprentice in a firm and then leave to found their own business. The former apprentice basically replicates both the technology and business practice of the firm, but as a self-employed individual (Frazer 2006). These former apprentices earn about 49 percent more a year than those who stay on as employees. Even though primary school completers are the group most likely to get an apprenticeship, returns to apprenticeships appear to be higher for individuals with lower levels of academic achievement, suggesting that apprenticeships can provide technical skills even to those without a basic education. Among currently employed people who have no formal education but who have had an apprenticeship, earnings are 50 percent higher (Monk, Sandefur, and Teal 2008).

The only impact evaluation of an apprenticeship program in Africa comes from a small-scale pilot that was part of a national apprenticeship program in Malawi. The pilot program targeted 1,900 low-income school dropouts. The great majority (84 percent) had completed primary school or less. Masters (with their own HE) selected through the Technical Education and Vocational Education and Training Authority (TEVETA) provided training to participants in occupations such as bricklaying,

vehicle repair, tailoring, and hairdressing. The apprenticeships lasted 3.3 months on average, including a week of life skills and business training; 63 percent completed their apprenticeships, and a small number received start-up capital. The estimated cost per participant was US$800. Participants were encouraged to start their own business upon completion of the apprenticeship. Results showed no improvements in labor market outcomes or returns in the short term, although the training did develop skills and improve business practices (Cho et al. 2012).[4]

Building Financial Literacy and Business Skills

Evidence suggests that financial literacy and general business skills are weak in the HE sector. According to a 2008 survey of micro, small, and medium businesses in Zambia, just 27 percent kept up-to-date financial accounts (FinMark Trust 2011). In a sample of tailors and dressmakers in Ghana, only 17 percent reported keeping any written financial records, only 7 percent said that they had spent money on marketing their services during the previous year, and only 30 percent rated their shop as very organized (Karlan, Knight, and Udry 2012). In a sample of microfinance clients in Tanzania (most of whom were SMEs, not HEs), two-thirds kept records, but only half engaged in marketing to attract customers (Berge, Bjorvatn, and Tungodden 2011).

The fact that many operate in the HE sector without strong financial literacy and business skills might suggest that young people do not need those skills to enter. Yet the lack of those skills could limit the sustainability and productivity of the enterprise, including those run by young people. Can business or financial literacy training boost the creation and productivity of HEs? The evidence on programs providing *only financial literacy* or *general business skills* is mixed. Very few studies have been done in Africa (see McKenzie and Woodruff 2012 for a review).[5]

Basic financial literacy is the most fundamental business skill for HEs (see the review in Xu and Zia 2012). Financial literacy can encompass many concepts, but among HEs in low-income countries it entails the most basic levels of financial awareness, the ability to understand the financial aspects of the business, and the ability to access financial services. Substantial inequalities in financial literacy prevail. Women and less educated people consistently measure lower (on average) on tests of financial literacy. Poor financial literacy could contribute to low access to the formal financial system—banking in particular.

There is very little evidence that interventions to build financial literacy in low-income countries affect the earnings of HEs or the capacity of youth to enter this sector. Evaluations are under way for generic programs (including some in Ghana, South Africa, and Uganda), but results are not available. One study from Indonesia found that financial literacy had no effect on promoting saving of trainees overall, although impacts were detected on trainees with the very lowest levels of initial financial literacy (Cole, Sampson, and Zia 2011; Xu and Zia 2012, 27).

General business skills training ranges from very basic "rule-of-thumb" programs to more advanced classroom programs designed to help small businesses to grow, which are often called business development services programs. One problem with such programs is that they are usually aimed at SMEs, not at the types of businesses found in the HE sector in Africa. Often the programs target microfinance clients, meaning that other constraints, such as start-up capital and access to work space, have already been surmounted. For these reasons, it is important to sift through the growing evidence on this training to determine if it is applicable to youth employment in African HEs.

Several programs piloted in other regions have facilitated entry into the HE sector for youth, but these programs were designed for more educated individuals, not for young people with only a primary education, which is the target group in Africa. Hands-on business training and coaching provided to university students in Tunisia increased their entry into self-employment, although the impact was small in absolute terms (Premand et al. 2012).[6] The training also improved business and behavioral skills. In contrast, comprehensive business training and financial literacy had no significant effects on business start-up in Bosnia and Herzegovina, in a sample where 85 percent of the participants had completed secondary school (Bruhn and Zia 2011). In a lower-income context, a "Start and Improve Your Business" Program in Sri Lanka for urban women ages 25–45 with a secondary education increased their likelihood of launching a business (De Mel, McKenzie, and Woodruff 2012a). An eight-day business training course in Pakistan, targeted to new microfinance clients with much less education, yielded no impacts on business creation among households that did not operate an enterprise at baseline (Giné and Mansuri 2011). Efforts to evaluate the integration of entrepreneurship training in secondary school are under way in Uganda.

The record on general business training for existing HEs is even weaker. While evaluations show that business training has changed business practices, it has rarely improved productivity or survivorship of the typical small businesses in the HE sector. Studies show that some programs have changed business practices and knowledge, such as recording sales and recording money taken for household needs (HEs in Pakistan); keeping records of withdrawals from the business, reinvesting profits into the business, and innovating in business (HEs and SMEs in Peru); improving business practices among the "Start and Improve Your Business" Program participants (HEs in Sri Lanka); and separating personal and business expenses, keeping accounting records, and formally calculating revenues (both HEs and SMEs in the Dominican Republic).[7]

More "intensive" programs have somewhat larger impacts. In Peru, intensive personalized business training for microfinance clients (most of whom had businesses larger than an HE) improved business practices and outcomes, whereas simple classroom-based instruction yielded no impacts (Valdivia 2011). The evidence that "more is better" does not always hold, however. In the Dominican Republic, a rule-of-thumb approach that taught simple rules for financial decision making was compared to a more formal approach that focused on the fundamentals of financial accounting.

All of the program's impacts came from the rule-of-thumb training. In both the Dominican Republic and Pakistan, follow-up visits yielded no additional impacts (Drexler, Fischer, and Schoar 2010 for the Dominican Republic; Giné and Mansuri 2011 for Pakistan).

But changes in business practices do not always translate into improvements in productivity or business survivorship. In none, of the studies just mentioned (the Dominican Republic, Pakistan, Peru, Sri Lanka) did changes in business practices measurably increase sales, revenues, profits, or employment. In Pakistan, some impacts were measured among men, and in Peru some impacts were measured in particularly bad months, but overall the evidence is weak that training improved business performance. In Ghana, a program delivering business skills training and support to existing tailoring businesses did not lead to higher profits, despite short-term improvements in business practices (Karlan, Knight, and Udry 2012).

One exception to this pattern comes from Sub-Saharan Africa, but not from HEs. An evaluation of a high-quality intensive business training program in Tanzania targeted to SME microfinance clients (who already had employees) yielded profits that were 29 percent higher among males but had no effect on profits for females. The effect came mainly through business expansion but also through better management of employees. In this case, simply graduating clients to a larger loan did not improve outcomes (Berge, Bjorvatn, and Tungodden 2011).[8] Still, it is not clear that this type of intensive training would pay off even for male HE owners (or that they would have the time to attend such a program).

Clearly the heterogeneity in results across settings suggests that much remains to be learned about building business capacity— both how to do so and for whom. Positive impacts suggest that the lack of business skills may be a constraint in some settings and that interventions may improve practices—and sometimes business outcomes. At the same time, the results confirm that growth-oriented businesses are rare in the HE sector, so perhaps sustainability, not growth, is the better outcome to target. The studies also suggest that skills may not be the only constraint or even

the binding constraint. Given the expense of these programs for both the providers and the beneficiaries, it may not be justified or feasible to expand this kind of program to HEs. At least, more careful cost-effectiveness is required.

Building Life Skills for Work

Limited socioemotional, or limited behavioral skills, or even low aspirations can prevent potential entrants from finding and seizing opportunities in the HE sector. Among other hurdles, the lack of these skills or aspirations may make it hard for youth to attempt to enter the sector or take up interventions designed to overcome barriers to entry, such as skills training or capital. Because behavioral skills are still malleable among young people, various programs have been shown to affect them. Changing the mind-set and attitudes of young people (especially young women) seems to help them to transition into the HE sector. Changes in behavioral skills may be part of the benefits of apprenticeship or other on-the-job training.

Young females face specific challenges in entering the HE sector (see chapter 2), and there is some evidence that behavioral skills training, combined with social support, can help them to overcome those challenges by teaching skills, influencing attitudes toward the future, or unlocking aspirations. These particular components, included in a broader program, may reduce risky behavior or early pregnancy in females and allow them to develop a plan to enter the HE sector while they are young.

Partly because behavioral skills training is often one part of a comprehensive program, there is little evidence that programs focused *only on building behavioral skills* can improve labor market outcomes. However, programs that aim to shape *behavioral skills together with other skills* have shown promise.

Building a Range of Complementary Skills

Youth often face multiple skill constraints in entering the HE sector. Programs attempting to build one skill at a time may have limited impact, but evidence from pilots that *build a range of complementary skills together* is more promising. These programs include "bundled interventions" that deliver behavioral, business, and technical skills training as part of a comprehensive package of support.

For example, in Uganda, BRAC delivered training in *behavioral skills and technical skills* targeted to adolescent girls ages 14–20.[9] The program increased employment 32 percent, mainly through entry into self-employment, and it shaped life skills and reduced risky behavior (Bandiera et al. 2012). The direct cost per participant was US$18 per eligible girl, or approximately US$85 per participating adolescent girl.

In Liberia, a program for adolescent girls and young women combined either *technical and behavioral skills* or *business and behavioral skills*. The program was highly effective in increasing employment and income among adolescent girls, most of whom had some secondary education (World Bank 2012). The training package combining business and behavioral skills was more effective at facilitating entry into self-employment than the training package combining technical and behavioral skills.[10] Direct cost per participant was US$1,221 for the business and behavioral skills training, leading to an increase in monthly income of US$75 on average (a 115 percent increase).

The rural enterprise projects of the International Fund for Agricultural Development (IFAD), operating in several African countries, finance demand-driven, privately provided technical training to improve the productivity and sustainability of existing enterprises and to help new entrants to start an enterprise (box 5.11). While no impact evaluation is available, tracer studies on beneficiaries in Ghana suggest that both objectives can be achieved at very low cost. Although the project specifically targeted employment growth through business expansion, most of the employment created was through start-up self-employment.

Combining Skills and Capital

Consistent with the evidence that multiple constraints hinder entry into the HE sector, bundled interventions combining skills training with capital are also promising.

To stimulate economic development and employment in northern Uganda following the cessation of hostilities, a program delivered cash grants to youth groups for *investment capital and vocational training*. The program had large, sustainable impacts on employment and earnings, especially for male participants.[11] Monthly real earnings increased by U Sh 17,785 (about US$9.88) after two years and U Sh 19,878 (US$11) after four years, corresponding to increases in income of 49 and 41 percent, respectively, relative to the control group. The average grant was US$374 (U Sh 673,026) per group member, so the estimated return to the average grant was 35–39 percent.

Another pilot program in northern Uganda targeted to very poor women provided four days of *business skills training*, an individual *start-up grant* of US$150, and *regular follow-up* by trained community workers. The program led to a large increase in income of 98 percent, or US$6.50 a month. The program was particularly effective for the poorest women. Additional technical assistance through follow-up had little additional impact (Blattman et al. 2013). The program cost US$688 per beneficiary.

These results have two main implications for designing programs to facilitate productive employment for youth in the HE sector. First, to facilitate entry, integrated strategies tackling multiple constraints—such as building a range of skills or combining skills with increased access to capital and urban space—are more promising.[12] Both behavioral skills and business skills are best included in these integrated packages. Second, it is not clear that current HE owners need more training to raise their productivity or sustainability. Most operators do not list skills—business or technical—as their main problem. They are much more likely to mention the need for finance or customers (access to markets, market information, or work space). But when technical or business training is offered at little or no cost, participation is substantial. For privately provided, demand-driven technical training, the tracer studies on the Jua Kali Program in Kenya (chapter 3, box 3.7) and the IFAD program in Ghana (box 5.11) suggest that benefits can accrue to trainees. For business training, the outcomes on productivity are elusive, especially for owners of HEs.

Box 5.11

Rural enterprise projects bolster skills and business development in Ghana and Senegal

The International Fund for Agricultural Development (IFAD) supports rural enterprise projects to provide the skills and other resources that help rural people, especially women and young people, to create and develop local businesses that provide income and employment off the farm. Projects may include the following components:

- *Business advisory centers* provide a range of business development services, including business orientation seminars, community-based skills training, small business management training, literacy and numeracy training, and information and referral services.
- *Rural technology facilities* support master craftspersons, traditional apprenticeships, and the promotion, dissemination, production, and repair of technology for rural HEs and microenterprises.
- *Rural financial services,* offered in conjunction with financial institutions, include credit for on-lending to small rural businesses and training for financial institutions to provide financial services to vulnerable groups.
- *Support for rural household and microenterprise organizations* includes support for local trade associations to build partnerships with stakeholders and support for formulating and strengthening polices through a working group on enterprise development.

In Africa, IFAD has implemented rural enterprise projects in Ghana, Madagascar, Rwanda, and Senegal. Impacts and challenges of projects in Ghana (the longest-running project) and Senegal are highlighted here.

The *Rural Enterprise Project* in Ghana was implemented in two phases between 1993 and 2012. During the second phase (2003–12), the project collaborated with Ghana's NBSSI and the Ghana Regional Appropriate Technology Industrial Service to develop 53 business advisory centers and 13 rural technology facilities in 24 districts at a cost of US$30 million, financed by IFAD, the African Development Bank, the Government of Ghana, and contributions from project beneficiaries (62 percent of whom were women). Almost half (47 percent) of participants reported that they had increased their profits as a result of better record and bookkeeping practices, and 37 percent reported that they had improved their management and marketing skills. Following technical training in skilled occupations such as processing palm oil, producing tie-dyed and batik cloth, and making leather goods and soap, 22,000 new enterprises were established, 63 percent headed by women. About 15 percent of the start-ups later became inactive because they lacked a market, working capital, or raw materials; their processing equipment failed; or they had personal reasons for closing the business, such as moving to another area. About 4,300 loans were disbursed through participating rural banks and MFIs; 87 percent were

repaid. But the participation of banks and MFIs in the credit component was low owing to creditworthiness issues with the start-ups. (Typical reasons for such low participation are discussed in focus note 3.) Microenterprise subcommittees established within local governments help to sustain project gains (see box 5.7). Although the second phase specifically targeted employment growth through business expansion, most of the employment created was through self-employment in a start-up (sometimes following a paid apprenticeship). This result reinforces the point that targeting start-ups is the most promising avenue for creating employment.

The *Promotion of Rural Entrepreneurship* (PROMER) Project in Senegal, implemented by IFAD in 2006, sought to reduce rural poverty by fostering and consolidating profitable rural HEs and microenterprises capable of offering stable jobs. PROMER focused on strengthening and professionalizing rural entrepreneurship and improving the overall political, legal, and institutional environment for such enterprises. For its target population—rural youths and women ages 18–35 who were poor, unemployed, and out of school and who either operated or wanted to start an enterprise—PROMER provided a combination of technical and management training and funding. Technical skills training primarily involved agribusiness, including food processing, and provided skills to 700 entrepreneurs in metalworking, equipment manufacturing, textile and clothing production, and hygiene and quality monitoring. Management training was provided to about 500 entrepreneurs. The project cost CFAF 10 billion from 2006 to 2013.

PROMER helped to create 240 enterprises, consolidate 665 enterprises, create 3,750 jobs, and teach 458 people to read. It usually takes enterprises three to five years to reach their full potential, and finding a niche in the economy can be critical for success. Through the project, for example, a baker started to make traditional bread, which was in high demand in periurban areas but not supplied by modern bakeries. Apprentices trained informally by the baker opened 20 enterprises of their own and created about 84 jobs.

Other rural enterprises were not as successful. Some developed products that succeeded in rural markets but not in urban markets because of high transport costs, poor marketing, or poor quality. Most entrepreneurs reported challenges in maintaining quality and continuous production. Rural enterprises had trouble finding an urban location in which to present their products, a result that highlights the problem of multiple constraints. Exhibitions have played a major role in bringing some rural products to a wider market, especially furniture, and have attracted better contracts that have led to modest job creation.

Sources: IFAD 2011; Senegal Ministry of Agriculture 2011.

Government's Role in Building Skills

The role of public policy in building young people's skills for productive employment in the HE sector needs to be considered carefully. The accumulating evidence that building skills can help to facilitate entry and raise earnings in HEs, along with the fact that a range of skills matters for productivity, does not constitute a case for public financing or provision of skills training. Not every type of training is cost-effective, and the private sector routinely provides many types of training. For all of these reasons, governments must carefully assess and justify whether there is scope for directly financing or providing specific training opportunities. The rationale for public intervention needs to be informed by well-identified market failures and assessed against risks of "government failures" in providing or financing training.

If young people cannot afford to finance their training, governments may need to help. Youths from the poorest households have the least access to training. For example, young people from the richest quintile of the welfare distribution are three times more likely to apprentice than those from the poorest quintile (chapter 3). Gender patterns in participation in training and the types of training selected are also strong. Females are less likely to pursue training; when they do, they often choose training that builds a narrow set of skills, such as tailoring or weaving. In this context, public policies to facilitate inclusion can be put in place. Government interventions have shown that financial barriers to training opportunities can be overcome through interventions such as vouchers (see box 3.7 on the Jua Kali Program in Kenya) or cash grants targeted to youth groups (the Youth Opportunities Program in northern Uganda; Blattman et al. 2013).

Information failures lead not only to underinvestment in training but also to investment in suboptimal types of training. Poor information can also contribute to a misalignment of aspirations, expectations, and attitudes toward self-employment among young people. In this context, government involvement in providing better information on existing training options and employment opportunities is warranted. For instance, information on training opportunities or on earnings in different occupations can influence women's choice of training. As

mentioned in box 5.2, young people in Kenya had misperceptions about the returns to vocational training.

There is limited justification for governments to provide directly the type of training in basic technical skills that is delivered routinely by private providers active in countries today. Governments should not create additional distortions in training markets. Attempts to limit or overly regulate the many small training providers have proven ineffective and should be avoided. However, private providers rarely provide other relevant skills such as behavioral or business skills. There may be scope for public policy to encourage the provision of these complementary skills, which are particularly relevant for the HE sector (curriculum development is one option for doing so).

Overall, the appropriate role for government is likely to be greater for financing than for providing training. Governments can leverage the private sector, including NGOs, to deliver the most promising models. The range of training delivered by private providers is very diverse, and so are the content, duration, and quality of that training. Given the lack of data on the full range of privately provided training, the degree to which training prices accurately signal the quality of training opportunities remains unclear. When governments finance training, they should strongly consider performance-based contracting of private providers based on outcomes or at least key indicators of quality. For instance, Liberia's Economic Empowerment of Adolescent Girls and Young Women Project (EPAG) Program for adolescent girls achieved a dropout rate of less than 5 percent through innovative design elements that ensured high participation and training quality (see World Bank 2012; and box 3.7 in chapter 3). Training providers were incentivized through performance bonuses, and the program included frequent and unannounced monitoring visits to check on the quality of provision.

National Skills Strategies

Many governments develop national skills strategies, but too often they focus exclusively on the formal labor and training markets. Often these strategies fail to recognize the importance of the nonfarm HE sector and fail to acknowledge the prevalence of private providers and the existence of training markets.

The strategies could identify areas where failures exist in the HE training market, such as failures in information provision, and consider the role that government programs and policies could play in addressing them, mindful of the cautions noted earlier. Governments could also use these strategies to provide information about market needs and successful approaches to the multitude of donors and NGOs active in this area. In developing these strategies, governments could consider the following options:

- *Focus programs for youth on the transition into the nonfarm HE sector.* Programs appear most effective at facilitating entry into the nonfarm HE sector, including programs that enable young people to transition out of agriculture. Evidence is weaker on how to raise the earnings of those who already operate HEs. Policies aimed at facilitating entry are more likely to yield the highest earnings and productivity gains.

- *Adopt an evidence-based and learning-based approach.* At the very minimum, encourage all programs to track and report outcomes. This monitoring should be done through provider organizations, not through expensive and bureaucratic registration and certification processes. Overall, the government's role in building skills in the HE sector needs to be selective, performance driven, and evidence based. As discussed, packages or integrated interventions show the most promise, although many design questions remain, especially with respect to scalability, cost, and cost-effectiveness. Therefore, governments should use a learning-based approach to design, pilot, and evaluate models to find cost-effective and scalable interventions. The evidence discussed in this chapter can guide the initial choice of models.

- *Encourage the delivery of "bundled" interventions that tackle multiple constraints.* Specifically, these interventions include programs that deliver behavioral, business, or technical skills training as part of a comprehensive package or programs that combine skills training with increased access to capital.

- *Experiment with demand-driven financing for training.* Such experiments would include using techniques that have shown some results in other programs, such as vouchers.

- *Prioritize financial assistance and programs targeting the poor and women.* Targeting the poor and women should be a priority for reasons of efficiency and equity. Recent impact evaluations found that programs for the poor and for women may have high returns (Macours, Premand, and Vakis 2013). Programs that are simply offered "on demand," however, may not reach the poor or women. Indeed, those groups might not aspire to participate in such programs, and they are more likely to lack the social networks that facilitate access to them. To design inclusive programs that reach the poor and women, explicit efforts are required, as well as close attention to the barriers that females face in entering the HE sector and earning an adequate return. Pilot programs such as BRAC's program in Uganda (targeting females) should be encouraged as a means of identifying the most effective and scalable approaches.

- *Finance the development of a curriculum and learning materials to teach very basic business skills in local languages and incorporate training in those skills into education and training programs.* As part of this effort, the use of existing modules—tested and evaluated in the local context—should be encouraged.[13]

- *Consider providing information to primary school students and their parents on economic opportunities in the HE sector and on the types of training that have had the best outcomes.*

Market Access and Voice

Current and prospective HE owners report that poor access to input and product markets is a serious constraint. Although traditional private sector development approaches assume that HEs' exclusion from defined markets and large value chains cannot be remedied, new research is challenging that assumption. HEs can participate in international value chains if producer associations can be created and markets structured to include them. Recent analysis by the Monitor Group highlights how imaginative new "bottom of the pyramid" business models in low-income Sub-Saharan Africa can include HEs (Kubzansky, Cooper, and Barbary 2011). Three distinct business models are identified:

- *Distribution and sales through informal shops.* In this model, enterprises develop a route to market that leverages (and sometimes upgrades) informal distribution and sales channels to sell products through multiple fragmented or unorganized shops.

- *Contract production.* This system sources produce directly from a large number of small-scale producers in (often rural) supply chains. The contractor organizes the supply chain from the top and provides critical inputs, specifications, training, and credit to suppliers. The suppliers provide assured quantities of specialty produce at fair and guaranteed prices.

- *Direct procurement.* Direct procurement setups bypass traditional intermediaries and purchase directly from large networks of low-income producers, often providing training to meet quality and other specifications.

The first model, the *producer-led* model, is probably the best known. It has been used by Coca-Cola, Bayer, mobile phone companies, and the M-PESA mobile money system, for example. These companies have been able to forge links with HE traders, using simple methods of distribution to benefit from access to the wide marketing channels that petty trading provides for their products or services. Kottoh (2008) found that the proliferation of trading in mobile phone credits by hawkers for MTN, Vodafone, and other telecommunication giants in Ghana is providing above-average income to the HEs while benefiting the companies. By training small-scale traders to be its agents in rural and periurban areas, M-PESA quickly gained a dominant market share of Kenya's money transfer and e-money market.

The second and third are *buyer-led* models, because the buyer helps to organize the value chain so that producers can access a bigger or more secure market. These models require HE producers to organize in associations or cooperatives, with which the buyer works to obtain a product for a market defined by the buyer. For example, the buyer provides output specifications and the necessary training to the association or cooperative and manages and monitors the quality of the output. The contract production model has been successful in the handicraft sector (box 5.12). It relies on a dedicated entrepreneur at the top of the value chain to organize both production and export into existing distribution channels. The deep procurement model relies on existing large contractors to reach out to HEs as subcontractors to supply their value chains.

Young people are well placed to participate in these initiatives. They more easily adopt new technology and methods brought to the HE sector by the large companies; this was especially true for the mobile phone and mobile money value chains, where many youths got their first job as sellers of air time or pay-per-use phones. Governments have usually not played a direct role in facilitating these efforts, as private sector expertise is required. However, by encouraging partnerships and donor financing of technical assistance and initial risk capital as well as providing the enabling environment, governments can support these efforts. For example, the Rwanda government was a key partner in scaling up the Rwanda basket initiative. Challenge grant funds from the Department for International Development in the United Kingdom helped to develop M-PESA in Kenya, with the support of Kenya's central bank.

Associations

HE associations are critical to successful development of the sector. As millions of individuals operating millions of very small, scattered businesses, HE owners lack a unified voice and struggle to be heard alongside the multiple players in the development process. Individually, HEs are an easy target for predatory

"My main challenge is stiff competition, made worse by customers who take long to pay or don't pay, including the subcounty government, whose failure to pay compelled me to lay off workers." Uganda

Box 5.12

Taking a household business to the international market: Gahaya Links and Rwanda's peace baskets

A basket-weaving tradition made its way from the villages of Rwanda to American households, changing the lives of thousands of Rwandan women basket weavers. For decades, women in Rwanda have produced distinctive, cone-shaped baskets that are traditionally used to carry wedding gifts. The baskets are handcrafted from enzyme-washed papyrus and banana leaf. The traditional zigzag design tells an ancient story of friends walking together, visiting neighboring villages along the way. The women who weave the baskets at home used to hawk them on the streets in tourist locations. In 1995, Janet Nkubana, who was managing a hotel in Kigali, decided to set up a shop on the hotel premises to market the baskets to hotel guests. She also took some baskets to sell in the United States when she visited her sister. Their popularity there encouraged the two sisters to set up a factory with the women weavers and market the baskets worldwide. The baskets were renamed "peace baskets," because the weaving groups include Hutu and Tutsi women, who find that working together is a healing process.

Gahaya Links initially started with 27 weavers as employees. It gained international exposure after a *Marie Claire* feature on reconciliation through peace baskets brought orders for 1,000 baskets. This order was a huge challenge for Gahaya Links, but it provided an opportunity to identify and remedy flaws in their products and to develop a new business model. The sisters worked with the weavers to develop uniform designs and use stronger materials. To expand rapidly, the company recruited women through churches, villages, and word of mouth to serve as contract weavers. They established a rigorous training program starting with master weavers, who could then train others in the area to meet high standards of quality. The Government of Rwanda helped by organizing the self-employed women weavers into cooperatives and building local training centers. Rwanda also joined the African Growth Opportunity Act, which allowed Rwandan crafts to enter the United States market duty free. Participation in a New York trade show in 2005, sponsored by the U.S. Agency for International Development, facilitated connections with international retail stores.

Gahaya Links reported annual sales of US$300,000 in 2007; that same year, it contracted with approximately 3,200 women in household basket-weaving enterprises across Rwanda to make their product. Gahaya Links issues purchase orders based on standard designs, and the weavers receive one-third of the proceeds from basket sales. The company thrives because it focuses on quality, training weavers to supply a product consistently valued by international consumers.

Source: World Bank 2008.

---

officials or economic agents (box 5.13). Their contribution to the local economy may not be recognized. Because policies and regulations are developed without their input, these businesses are often over- and underregulated (Roever 2006). HE associations make it possible to manage the consultation required to develop and implement successful projects to supply public goods that benefit HEs and the local economy (such as development of the workshop cluster in Ghana, described in box 5.9). Economic agents seeking to work with HEs to strengthen value chains also need effective producer organizations as partners. HE associations can provide the necessary channels to transmit information about support programs and can be used by private sector operators seeking to integrate HEs into their value chains. For example, Procter and Gamble works through the hairdressers' association in Ghana to distribute information about new products being brought to the market.

Effective participatory organizations are rarely created by governments, but governments can easily undermine them. National strategies should recognize the need for effective associations. Local government policies and regulations covering the use and disposition of public space should recognize the need to consult with HEs and encourage the formation of local associations to facilitate this process. Donors and other international actors can be helpful in encouraging and supporting associations. Donor financing for associations of HEs through the Trade Union Congress in Ghana was helpful in building the capacity of these groups, and support for creating local HE associations was included in the terms of reference for the business advisory centers supported by IFAD's Rural Enterprise Project in Ghana.

Reducing isolation and exploitation through self-help associations

Gaining a voice in the national policy dialogue is especially challenging for Africa's youth, whose livelihoods depend overwhelmingly on activities outside traditional wage employment (and will do so for the foreseeable future). These activities are inherently vulnerable to high volatility in earnings, lack of legal recourse in case of expropriation or theft, and limited access to safety net programs. These vulnerabilities are compounded by an inability to influence the policies that affect their working conditions. For women and youths, who are overrepresented in most forms of "vulnerable employment"[a] in Africa, the need for formalized channels that allow access to policy makers and afford a measure of visibility in the public sphere is especially pressing.

These conditions are not inevitable. Over the past few decades, new models for collective action have emerged, enabling workers to advocate for their interests directly with buyers, sellers, and the state (often at multiple levels—local, national, and international). These "worker associations" occupy a unique space somewhere between an NGO, which provides services to its members, and a labor union, which represents workers in negotiations with employers. Associations in Africa and other regions are growing in number and establishing this form of organizing as a viable means of improving conditions in nonwage work.

The world's largest and probably best-known worker association is in India. The Self-Employed Women's Association (SEWA), established in 1972, broke traditional barriers to form organizations representing cigarette rollers, head porters, and others who did not have "employers" to bargain with and hence were excluded from the trade union movement. After decades of developing innovative organizing modalities to negotiate with municipalities, buyers (such as cigarette and garment factories), and other actors (such as forest management councils), SEWA has established itself as a leading force in India's trade union movement. SEWA's activities include obtaining official identification cards for workers to allow them to access state social protection programs, programs to develop and upgrade members' skills, bargaining over piece rates paid to contract workers, provision of space and licenses for vendors in marketplaces, and lobbying for better access to forests and markets for gum collectors. SEWA representatives participated in crafting national legislation on sexual harassment in the workplace in 2010, a law that explicitly covers domestic workers, and in developing a national policy on vendors and hawkers in 2004.

Given that nonwage work is likely to persist in Africa and given its strong gender and youth dimensions, finding ways to support active engagement offers a better way forward than ignoring them, "formalizing" them, or suppressing their activities. With rare exceptions (Ghana's Trade Union Congress is one), including trade unions in the policy dialogue is unlikely to suffice, because traditional trade unions usually exclude nonwage-earning participants in the labor force. Policies on issues as diverse as natural resource management, urban zoning, sexual harassment and discrimination, the minimum wage, and social safety nets affect all workers, not just the minority with a formal contract or registered business. Without associations that legitimately represent their interests, the voices of informal workers are unlikely to be heard or taken seriously.

Although an organization of SEWA's breadth and experience has yet to develop in Africa, several organizations are applying similar models. The results of these efforts can be as straightforward as improving the visibility of HE owners and casual workers in national statistics and as far-reaching as including HE owners and casual workers under public health insurance programs. Associations of street vendors have been among the most successful to date. For example, they have enabled street vendors in Ghana, Kenya, Liberia, and South Africa to receive literacy and skills training, organize child care and informal schooling, rehabilitate markets, finance their operations, and arrange to source, transport, and store merchandise.

a. The ILO defines "vulnerable employment" as self-employed and contributing family workers. Those pursuing such activities "are less likely to have formal work arrangements and are therefore more likely to lack elements associated with decent employment such as adequate social security and recourse to effective mechanisms of social dialogue. Vulnerable employment is often characterized by inadequate earnings, low productivity, and difficult conditions of work that undermine workers' fundamental rights" (ILO 2010).

Conclusion

Governments need to give serious consideration to the HE sector's potential to create jobs for youth. Even exceptionally high economic growth in nonfarm sectors has not and will not generate enough new nonfarm wage employment to absorb both the new entrants and those who seek to leave agriculture. HEs are growing as a share of the labor force not because of failures in regulation and economic growth, but because households that manage to stay in the sector make money—more than those working only in agriculture or as casual laborers.

Young people see these opportunities and are trying to enter the sector, but they are frustrated by the lack of capital, information on markets and opportunities, productivity-enhancing skills, and locations to work. Because the HE sector grows when new businesses arise, the strategy for increasing employment in this sector is to encourage business creation, support higher earnings, and increase sustainability. Initiatives that address the most important constraints on creating a business—lack of finance and space to work—will be the most effective.

Most countries have no such strategy for the HE sector. Instead, they have a fragmented youth employment strategy focused primarily on the wage sector and a strategy for SMEs. This set of strategies is not working. Initiatives for SMEs rarely reach HEs. Boutique NGO projects cannot reach enough prospective HE owners to make a difference.

A comprehensive national HE strategy should focus on approaches that are demand driven and address the main constraints to start-up and sustainability. Elements of a comprehensive national strategy for the HE sector, based on a shared vision of the sector's potential to generate productive employment, include the following:

- *National strategies.* Growth and employment strategies need to recognize the sector's potential and propose a supportive policy framework. The strategy should endorse the creation of independent HE associations to reduce the costs of reaching individual enterprises and to give this sector a voice in government decision making. The specific outcomes to be attained in the sector should be to expand the number of businesses and increase their productivity.
- *Urban policies.* HEs also need to be recognized as an important element in local economic development. Local governments must be accountable to HEs and include them in decisions related to planning, zoning, and land use, land markets and land tenure, and infrastructure. HE associations should be encouraged at the local level so that HEs can have a voice.

- *Better financial access for households.* Regulatory reform is needed to reduce the costs of retail banking, encourage savings, and develop youth-focused products. NGOs should be encouraged to expand low-cost strategies to help youth to save start-up capital, such as village savings groups.
- *More effective skills strategies.* Governments should focus their efforts on market-enhancing programs, such as programs to disseminate information about opportunities and facilitate access to existing training for disadvantaged youth and not attempt to deliver training directly. They should also invest selectively in good-quality training programs that tackle multiple constraints, either by building a range of skills such as technical, business, and behavioral skills or by combining skills with capital.
- *Development of value chains.* This activity resides primarily with the private sector. Governments should encourage social entrepreneurs to include HEs in value chain development.
- *Associations.* Associations are especially important at the local level. Regulations on consultation prior to land use planning or implementation should encourage local governments to work through independent HE associations. Donors and NGOs should extend support to these associations, helping to develop their capacity.

Notes

1. In many countries, rural households include households in market towns or periurban areas. They are often designated rural because agriculture is still the predominant economic activity.
2. This section draws from World Bank studies of HEs in the Republic of Congo, Ghana, Kenya, Rwanda, Tanzania, and Uganda as well as broader reviews of the literature and evidence.
3. At the time of writing, the youth employment inventory included 86 youth employment projects in Africa, of which 79 provide skills training. In a review of interventions to support young workers in Sub-Saharan Africa, Rother (2006) found, "In most cases, these programs

include elements targeted at helping young people to start their own businesses, combined with elements of skills development and training."

4. Outside Africa, few studies offer evidence that technical training by itself can facilitate entry into self-employment. For instance, skills training had no significant impact among a sample of workfare participants in a welfare-dependent region of Argentina (Galasso, Ravallion, and Salvia 2004).

5. While the number of programs providing business skills or financial literacy training has been increasing in Africa (see Messy and Monticone 2012; Xu and Zia 2012), only a handful of recent impact evaluations analyze the effect of such programs on entry into self-employment. For instance, most evaluations quoted by Messy and Monticone (2012) analyze the effect on intermediary outcomes (such as knowledge of financial literacy or savings behavior), but not on employment outcomes (such as entry into self-employment) or earnings.

6. In developed countries, Oosterbeek, van Praag, and Ijsselstein (2008) studied the impact of entrepreneurship education on students' competencies and intentions. They found that the program did not have the intended effects: the effect on students' self-assessed entrepreneurial skills was insignificant, and the effect on the intention to become an entrepreneur was significantly negative.

7. For Pakistan, see Giné and Mansuri (2011). For Peru, see Karlan and Validivia (2011). For Sri Lanka, see De Mel, McKenzie, and Woodruff (2012a). For the Dominican Republic, see Drexler, Fischer, and Schoar (2010).

8. The business training course consisted of 21 sessions, each lasting 45 minutes, and covered topics such as Entrepreneurship and Entrepreneurial Character, Improving Customer Service, Managing People in Your Business, and Marketing Strategies. Overall, these results suggest that insufficient human capital among poor micro and small business owners may be the more important constraint to increasing productivity. The results also highlight the need for more comprehensive measures to promote development among female entrepreneurs.

9. The program was implemented in urban and rural areas through local "adolescent development clubs" in which a female mentor led the activities. The program targeted girls ages 14–20 who were still in school or had dropped out. Of the girls in the target communities, 21 percent participated in the training; of those who participated, 85 percent took part in the life skills training and 53 percent took part in the vocational skills training (primarily in dressmaking or tailoring).

10. The latter package was designed primarily to help females to attain a wage job. The main reason for the low impact is that there was little demand in the wage employment sector for the graduates.

11. Cash grants targeted to youth groups can affect occupational choice and improve income. Blattman, Fiala, and Martinez (2013) evaluate the impact of a Youth Opportunities Program implemented by the Ugandan government in the context of the northern Uganda Social Action Fund. The program targeted youth groups of 10–30 persons, who received grants averaging US$374 per group member. (Participants were poor by most measures, but the average applicant was slightly above the average wealth and education level in the region. For instance, 93 percent had completed some primary school, 45 percent had completed some secondary, and only 7 percent had no education.) Of those who received the cash transfer, 80 percent enrolled in vocational training, and most invested heavily in business assets. The program was effective in changing the type of work that youth perform in an environment where most employment is outside the modern wage sector: 68 percent of grant recipients were working in a skilled trade, compared with 34 percent of the control group. Income was also higher for grant beneficiaries. On average, grant recipients had net income 50 percent higher than the control group, a return on the initial transfer amounting to 35 percent a year.

12. Another example of integrated intervention can be found in rural Nicaragua, where beneficiaries from a cash transfer program also received either technical training or a business grant. The business grant packages led to entry into self-employment as well as higher average income and consumption. The vocational training package led to entry into self-employment for the poor and higher wage income for the nonpoor, but had no impacts on income or consumption on average (Macours, Premand, and Vakis 2013). Both the training package and the business grant package also helped households to protect themselves against shocks by allowing them to smooth income through diversification (Macours, Premand, and Vakis 2012).

13. Examples of modules in wide use include ILO's Start and Improve Your Business Program (see http://www.ilo.org/empent/areas/start-and-improve-your-business/lang--en/index.htm) and various materials produced by the Peace Corps (http://www.peacecorps.gov/library/pubindex/); for example, see the Microenterprise Training Guide (http://files.peacecorps.gov/multimedia/pdf/library/M0068_microent.pdf).

References

Ayyagari, Meghana, Asli Demirgüç-Kunt, and Vojislav Maksimovic. 2011. "Small vs. Young Firms across the World: Contribution to Employment, Job Creation, and Growth." Policy Research Working Paper 5631, World Bank, Washington, DC.

Bandiera, Oriana, Robin Burgess, Selim Gulesci, Imran Rasul, and Munshi Sulaiman. 2012. "Can Entry-Level Entrepreneurship Transform the Economic Lives of the Poor?" London School of Economics.

Berge, Lars, Kjetil Bjorvatn, and Bertil Tungodden. 2011. "Human and Financial Capital for Microenterprise Development: Evidence from a Field and Lab Experiment." NHH Department of Economics Discussion Paper 1/2011, Chr. Michelsen Institute, Bergen.

Blattman, Christopher, Nathan Fiala, and Sebastian Martinez. 2013. "Credit Constraints, Occupational Choice, and the Process of Development: Long-Run Evidence from Cash Transfers in Uganda." Columbia University, New York.

Blattman, Chris, Eric Green, Jeannie Annan, and Julian Jamison, with F. Aryemo, N. Carlson, M. Emeriau, and A. Segura. 2013. "Building Women's Economic and Social Empowerment through Enterprise: An Experimental Assessment of the Women's Income Generating Support (WINGS) Program in Uganda." Innovations for Poverty Action, New Haven, CT. http://www.poverty-action.org/sites/default/files/wings_full_policy_report_0.pdf.

Bridges, Sarah, Louise Fox, Alessio Gaggero, and Trudy Owens. 2013. "Labour Market Entry and Earnings: Evidence from Tanzanian Retrospective Data." Paper prepared for the CSAE conference "Economic Development in Africa," Oxford University, Oxford, March.

Bruhn, Miriam, and Bilal Zia. 2011. "Stimulating Managerial Capital in Emerging Markets: The Impact of Business and Financial Literacy for Young Entrepreneurs." Policy Research Paper 5642, World Bank, Washington, DC.

Campos, Francisco, Markus Goldstein, Laura McGorman, Ana Maria Munoz Boudet, and Obert Pimhidzai. 2013. "Breaking the Metal Ceiling: Female Entrepreneurs Who Succeed in Male-Dominated Sectors in Uganda." United Nations Foundation; ExxonMobile Foundation.

Cho, Yoonyoung, Davie Kalomba, Mushfiq Mobarak, and Victor Orozco. 2012. "The Effects of Apprenticeship Training for Vulnerable Youth in Malawi." Working Paper, World Bank, Washington, DC.

Cole, Shawn, Thomas Sampson, and Bilal Zia. 2011. "Prices or Knowledge: What Drives Demand for Financial Services in Emerging Markets?" Journal of Finance 66 (6): 1933–67.

De Mel, Suresh, David McKenzie, and Christopher Woodruff. 2012a. "Business Training and Female Enterprise Start-up, Growth, and Dynamics: Experimental Evidence from Sri Lanka." Policy Research Working Paper 6145, World Bank, Washington, DC.

———. 2012b. "One-Time Transfers of Cash or Capital Have Long-Lasting Effects on Microenterprises in Sri Lanka." Science 335 (6071): 962–66. doi: 10.1126/science.1212973.

De Wolf, Stefan, Yves Rolland Rakotoarisoa, Laurence Vanpaeschen, and Honoré Rabekoto. 2008. Madagascar: Le Grand Livre des Petits Métiers: Portraits of Daily Life Professions. Heule, Belgium: Snoek Publishers.

Drexler, Alejandro, Greg Fischer, and Antoinette S. Schoar. 2010. "Keeping It Simple: Financial Literacy and Rules of Thumb." CEPR Discussion Paper, Centre for Economic Policy Research, London. http://dev3.cepr.org/meets/wkcn/7/784/papers/FischerFinal.pdf.

Fafchamps, Marcel, David McKenzie, Simon Quinn, and Christopher Woodruff. 2011. "When Is Capital Enough to Get Female Microenterprises Growing? Evidence from a Randomized Experiment in Ghana." CSAE Working Paper 2011-11, Centre for the Study of African Economies, Oxford.

Falco, Paolo, William F. Maloney, Bob Rijkers, and Mauricio Sarrias. 2012. "Heterogeneity in Subjective Well-Being: An Application to Occupational Allocation in Africa." Policy Research Working Paper 6244, World Bank, Washington, DC.

FinMark Trust. 2011. "Financial Education in Zambia: What Does FinScope Tell Us?" Financial Access Matters 6, Marshalltown, South Africa. http://www.finmark.org.za/publication/financial-education-in-zambia-what-does-finscope-tell-us/.

Fox, Louise, and Obert Pimhidzai. 2012. "Is Informality Welfare-Enhancing Structural Transformation? Evidence from Uganda." Policy Research Working Paper 5866, World Bank, Washington, DC.

———. 2013. "Different Dreams, Same Bed: Collecting, Using, and Interpreting Employment Statistics in Sub-Saharan Africa: The Case of Uganda." Policy Research Working Paper 6436, World Bank, Washington, DC.

Fox, Louise, and Thomas Pave Sohnesen. 2012. "Household Enterprises in Sub-Saharan Africa: Why They Matter for Growth, Jobs, and Livelihoods." Policy Research Working Paper 6184, World Bank, Washington, DC.

———. 2013. "Household Enterprises in Mozambique: Key to Poverty Reduction but Not on the Development Agenda?" Policy Research Working Paper 6570, World Bank, Washington, DC.

Frazer, Garth. 2006. "Learning the Master's Trade: Apprenticeship and Human Capital in Ghana." *Journal of Development Economics* 81 (2): 259–98.

Galasso, Emanuela, Martin Ravallion, and Augustin Salvia. 2004. "Assisting the Transition from Workfare to Work: Argentina's Proempleo Program." *Industrial and Labor Relations Review* 57 (5): 128–42.

Gelb, Alan, Taye Mengistae, Vijaya Ramachandran, and Manju Kedia Shah. 2009. "To Formalize or Not to Formalize? Comparisons of Microenterprises from Southern and East Africa." CGD Working Paper 175, Center for Global Development, London.

Ghana, Republic of. 2006. "Poverty Reduction Strategy Paper." National Development Planning Commission. IMF Country Report 06/225, IMF, Washington, DC, June.

Giné, Xavier, and Ghazala Mansuri. 2011. "Money or Ideas? A Field Experiment on Constraints to Entrepreneurship in Rural Pakistan." World Bank, Washington DC. http://siteresources. worldbank.org/DEC/Resources/Money_or_Ideas.pdf.

Grimm, Michael, Peter Knorringa, and Jann Lay. 2012. "Constrained Gazelles: High Potentials in West Africa's Informal Economy." *World Development* 40 (7): 1352–68.

Grimm, Michael, Jens Krüger, and Jann Lay. 2011. "Barriers to Entry and Returns to Capital in Informal Activities: Evidence from Sub-Saharan Africa." *Review of Income and Wealth* 57 (5): s27–53. doi: 10.1111/j.1475-4991.2011.00453.x.

Gulyani, Sumila, Debabrata Talukdar, and Darby Jack. 2010. "Poverty, Living Conditions, and Infrastructure Access: A Comparison of Slums in Dakar, Johannesburg, and Nairobi." Policy Research Working Paper 5388, World Bank, Washington, DC.

Haggblade, Steven, Peter Hazell, and Thomas Reardon. 2010. "The Rural Non-Farm Economy: Prospects and Poverty Reduction." *World Development* 38 (10) 1429–41.

Hicks, Joan Hamory, Michael Kremer, Isaac Mbit, and Edward Miguel. 2011. "Vocational Education Voucher Delivery and Labor Market Returns: A Randomized Evaluation among Kenyan Youth." Report for the Spanish Impact Evaluation Fund (SIEF) Phase II, World Bank, Washington, DC.

IFAD (International Fund for Agricultural Development). 2011. "Promoting Rural Enterprise Growth and Development: Lessons from Four Projects in Sub-Saharan Africa." Field Experiences 2, IFAD, Rome.

ILO (International Labour Organization). 1993. "Resolution Concerning the International Classification of Status in Employment (ICSE), Adopted by the Fifteenth International Conference of Labour Statisticians." ILO, Geneva. http://www.ilo.org/public/english/bureau/stat/download/res/icse.pdf.

———. 2010. "Global Trends in Employment: January 2010." ILO, Geneva.

Inchauste, Gabriela, and Sergio Olivieri. 2012. "Understanding Poverty Reduction in Bangladesh: A Microdecomposition Approach." Background Paper prepared for the 2012 Poverty Assessment, World Bank, Washington, DC.

Karlan, Dean, Ryan Knight, and Christopher Udry. 2012. "Hoping to Win, Expected to Lose: Theory and Lessons on Micro Enterprise Development." NBER Working Paper 18325, National Bureau of Economic Research, Cambridge, MA.

Karlan, Dean, and Martin Valdivia. 2011. "Teaching Entrepreneurship: Impact of Business Training on Microfinance Clients and Institutions." *Review of Economics and Statistics* 93 (2): 510–27.

Kottoh, M. 2008. "Linking Corporations to Household Enterprises: Ghana Telecom (Vodafone Ghana) Value Chain." New Legon Observer, Institute of Statistical, Social, and Economic Research, University of Ghana.

Kubzansky, Michael, Ansulie Cooper, and Victoria Barbary. 2011. "Promise and Progress: Market-Based Solutions to Poverty in Africa." Monitor Group. http://web.mit.edu/idi/idi/Africa-%20PromiseAndProgress-MIM.pdf.

Kweka, Josaphat, and Louise Fox. 2011. "The Household Enterprise Sector in Tanzania: Why It Matters and Who Cares." Policy Working Paper 5882, World Bank, Washington, DC.

Lanjouw, Peter, Jaime Quizon, and Robert Sparrow. 2001. "Non-Agricultural Earnings in Periurban Areas of Tanzania: Evidence from Household Survey Data." *Food Policy* 26 (4): 385–403.

Liviga, Athumani, and Rugatiri Mekacha. 1998. "Youth Migration and Poverty Alleviation: A Case Study of Petty Traders (*Wamachinga*) in Dar es Salaam." Research Report 98.5, Research on Poverty Alleviation, Dar es Salaam.

Lyons, Michal, with Colman Msoka. 2007. "Microtrading in Urban Mainland Tanzania: The Way Forward." Report for HTSPE Development Consulting Services for the Development Partner Group, Tanzania.

Macours, Karen, Patrick Premand, and Renos Vakis. 2012. "Transfers, Diversification, and Household Risk Strategies: Experimental Evidence with Implications for Climate Change Adaptation." Policy Research Working Paper 5137, World Bank, Washington, DC.

————. 2013. "Demand versus Returns? Pro-Poor Targeting of Business Grants and Vocational Skills Training." Policy Research Working Paper 6389, World Bank, Washington, DC.

McKenzie, David, and Christopher Woodruff. 2012. "What Are We Learning from Business Training and Entrepreneurship Evaluations around the Developing World?" Policy Research Working Paper 6202, World Bank, Washington, DC.

Messy, Flore-Anne, and Chiara Monticone. 2012. "The Status of Financial Education in Africa." OECD Working Paper on Finance, Insurance, and Private Pensions 25, OECD Publishing, Paris. doi: 10.1787/5k94cqqx90wl-en.

Ministry of Agriculture, Senegal. 2011. "La promotion des micro et petites entreprises rurales: Un moyen efficace pour lutter contre la pauvreté en milieu rural; livret de capitalisation (PROME-RII)." Dakar.

Monk, Courtney, Justin Sandefur, and Francis Teal. 2008. "Does Doing an Apprenticeship Pay Off? Evidence from Ghana." CSAE Working Paper 2008-08, Centre for the Study of African Economies, Oxford.

Oosterbeek, Hessel, Mirjam van Praag, and Auke Ijsselstein. 2008. "The Impact of Entrepreneurship Education on Entrepreneurship Competencies and Intentions: An Evaluation of the Junior Achievement Student Mini-Company Program." IZA Discussion Paper 3641, Institute for the Study of Labor, Bonn.

Pasquier-Doumer, Laure. 2013. "Intergenerational Transmission of Self-Employed Status in the Informal Sector: A Constrained Choice or Better Income Prospects? Evidence from Seven West-African Countries." *Journal of African Economies* 22 (1): 73–111. doi: 10.1093/jae/ejs017.

Premand, Patrick, Stefanie Brodmann, Rita Almeida, Rebekka Grun, and Mahdi Barouni. 2012. "Entrepreneurship Training and Self-Employment among University Graduates: Evidence from a Randomized Trial in Tunisia."

Policy Research Working Paper 6285, World Bank, Washington, DC.

Roever, Sally. 2006." Enforcement and Compliance in Lima's Street Markets: The Origins and Consequences of Policy Incoherence toward Informal Traders." In *Linking the Formal and Informal Economy: Concepts and Policies*, edited by Basudep Guha-Khasnobis, Ravi Kanbure, and Elinor Ostrom, 246–62. Oxford: Oxford University Press.

Rother, Friederike. 2006. "Interventions to Support Young Workers in Sub Saharan Africa: Regional Report for the Youth Employment Inventory." World Bank, Washington, DC.

Sisya, Marietta R. 2005. "The Impact of Relocation of Petty Traders on Income Generation for Local Authorities to Finance Social Services: The Case of Ilala Municipal Council." MPA thesis, Mzumbe University, Morogoro.

Tokman, Victor E. 2007. "Modernizing the Informal Sector." DESA Working Paper 42, United Nations Department of Economic and Social Affairs, New York.

Uteng, Tanu Priya. 2011. "Gender and Mobility in the Developing World." Background paper for the *World Development Report 2012: Gender Equality and Development*, World Bank, Washington, DC.

Valdivia, Martin. 2011. "Training or Technical Assistance? A Field Experiment to Learn What Works to Increase Managerial Capital for Female Microentrepreneurs." Grupo de Análisis para el Desarrollo (GRADE), Lima.

Van Adams, Arvil, Sara Johansson de Silva, and Setareh Razmara. 2013. *Improving Skills Development in the Informal Sector: Strategies for Sub-Saharan Africa*. Washington, DC: World Bank.

World Bank. 2008. "Weaving Peace in Rwanda." In *Doing Business: Women in Africa*, 17–21. Washington, DC: World Bank.

————. 2012. "Preliminary EPAG Midline Report: Economic Empowerment of Adolescent Girls and Young Women (EPAG) Project in Liberia." World Bank, Washington, DC.

————. 2013. "Time to Shift Gears: Accelerating Growth and Poverty Reduction in the New Kenya." Kenya Economic Update, World Bank, Washington, DC.

World Bank and IPAR (Institute of Policy Analysis and Research Rwanda). 2012. "Raising Productivity and Reducing Risks of Household Enterprises in Rwanda." World Bank, Washington, DC.

Xu, Lisa, and Bilal Zia. 2012. "Financial Literacy around the World: An Overview of the Evidence with Practical Suggestions for the Way Forward." Policy Research Working Paper 6107, World Bank, Washington, DC.

Financial Inclusion and the Transition to Sustainable Livelihoods for Young People

"Financial inclusion" means that individuals can obtain a range of financial products—savings, credit, insurance, and payment systems, including systems to send remittances—at a reasonable cost and on a sustained basis (Gardeva and Rhyne 2011). Financial inclusion remains elusive for many African households, which generally develop their own strategies for saving and rely on loans from family, friends, and informal lenders to meet their need for credit. The gap in access to savings vehicles is at least as important as the gap in access to credit. Closing these gaps is challenging for most households, especially for young people, whose access to formal financial services is often limited by banking regulations, the lack of products designed to meet their particular needs, and the difficulty of establishing their creditworthiness. Across Africa, technology is reducing the cost and increasing the accessibility of formal financial services; at the same time, informal savings and credit groups are expanding. These informal groups may offer a promising venue for integrating the delivery of youth programs in communities, including programs to foster savings behavior, build business and soft skills, empower females, and expand financial inclusion, with the goal of enabling young people to pursue sustainable livelihoods.

Gaps in Access to Savings and Credit

The ability to save is intricately linked with the ability to obtain credit. Without the habit of regularly setting money aside, individuals have difficulty repaying loans. In addition, lenders will always require borrowers to use a portion of their savings to pay for part of a proposed investment (the down payment). Savings can also serve as a form of self-insurance when households take out a loan to make potentially high-yielding but risky investments.

Agricultural households need to save and borrow for a range of reasons—to obtain and sustain land to farm, to buy or rent equipment, and to acquire other inputs that make their efforts more productive. Households that operate a nonfarm enterprise also need to save and borrow to start and maintain their business.

A complicating factor for farm households and households operating nonfarm enterprises is that the finances of the farm, household enterprise (HE), and household itself are often linked, so household income smoothing and credit needs (for example, funds to pay for lumpy expenditures such as school fees or home repairs) may compete with farm or business liquidity needs, potentially reducing the sustainability of the business. For this reason, the gap in access to credit occurs at both the household and the enterprise level.

Young or aspiring farmers and HE owners can have the most difficulty mobilizing capital, because their capacity to save and borrow is often so constrained. In many countries, young people cannot access the formal banking system even if they want to, because laws prohibit opening a bank account before age 18.[1] Even where no legal obstacles stand in their way, young people can be frustrated by the lack of products designed to meet their particular needs as savers and borrowers of small amounts.

Despite these limitations, low-income youths in various situations (at home with parents, living away from home, or living on the street) persist in saving for school, emergencies, and less often, to start a business (USAID 2009). Saving not only is important for meeting those needs, but having financial assets by itself has positive behavioral effects for young people, "increasing future orientation, long-term thinking, planning, and self-efficacy" (Kilara and Latortue 2012). Research shows

"It is not easy for us to access credit like the adults." Uganda

that behaviors such as saving and exercising financial discipline are best developed at a young age. If young people do not develop the habit of saving, they will have trouble starting and sustaining farm and nonfarm enterprises later on.

Formal Savings Services: Issues and Options

A secure place for savings allows people to improve their planning, financial decisions, and risk management by keeping their money out of temptation's way (Mullainathan and Shafir 2011; Collins et al. 2009). Although low-income households and individuals may have very little cash on a given day, a savings habit can transform that cash over time into a larger sum, which can then be used for lumpy expenditures such as school fees or investment in inventory or tools for an HE. But when people lack a secure place to put their money, they are much less likely to save, as the difficulties of daily life for the household and the extended family demand a short-term financial focus, and multiple requests for cash reduce self-control. Access to a secure place for savings is particularly important for women's ability to build up capital for a business, because women are especially subject to pressure for funds from other members of the family (Dupas and Rob-

inson 2009). Women sometimes go to extraordinary lengths to set money aside. For example, in the absence of other mechanisms to save, market women in India with more established businesses report taking loans from informal moneylenders at very high interest rates just so they will be required to put funds aside every day. They resort to this strategy even though they could accumulate much more capital and profits if they were to save a part of their profits every day to self-finance the next replacement of inventory (Karlan and Appel 2011).

African Households Save, but Rarely at the Bank

African households are no different from households elsewhere—they know the value of savings. Controlling for national income, African adults are actually more likely to save than non-African adults, especially in low-income countries (figure F3.1). African youths in lower-income countries also report saving more than their counterparts in countries with similar income levels. In some countries, more than 20 percent of individuals ages 15–25 reported that they had been able to save some funds in the last year.

Although youths and older adults say that they save, they do not use a bank account for that purpose. Some use informal savings groups in the village or neighborhood, but many simply keep their cash at home, the least

Figure F3.1 Percentage of population ages 15 and older who reported saving any amount in the last 12 months, by savings mechanism

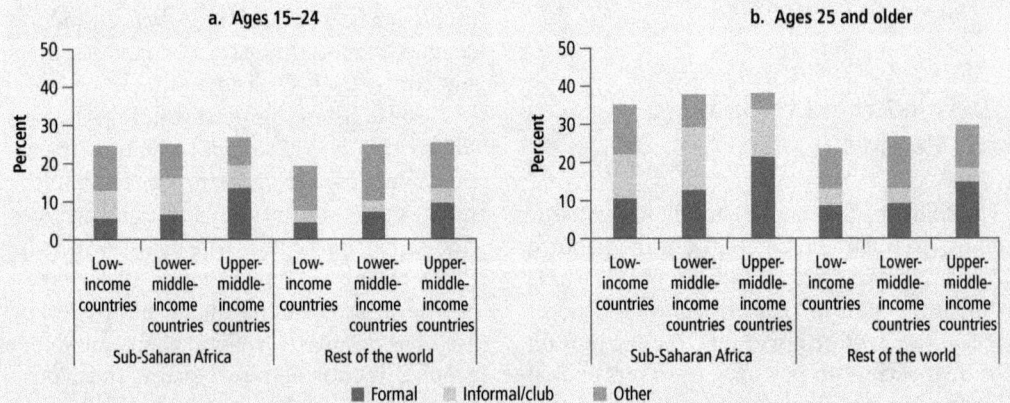

Source: Based on FINDEX data.

safe place. In surveys, young people and adults express a desire for an affordable, convenient, safe place to keep their money—a service usually provided by a bank.

Access to banking services rises with income and urbanization. Banking is an industry with economies of scale, so banks go where the money and the customers are (unless special provisions are made; see box F3.1 for an example of rural banking from Ghana). Given the low incomes and low population density prevalent in Africa, it is not surprising that few households use formal banking services: only 24 percent of households in Africa have access to a bank account.[2]

But the lack of a bank account is far from the whole story in Africa. As in the rest of the world, in Africa's banking industry, technological innovation and regulation interact in complex ways to influence how much it costs to provide financial services and who can obtain them.

Options for Lowering Costs and Expanding Outreach

At the firm level, the high fixed costs of operating a bank office (building, machinery, banking staff, security), the need for reliable infrastructure and services (electricity and communications), and customers' unwillingness to use a bank that is far from their work or home mean that high population density is a prerequisite for traditional banking services to spread.[3] Given the fixed costs associated with maintaining customer accounts (recording transactions, processing fees and interest), small account balances can be a losing proposition for the bank and for the customer, to whom those costs are passed in the form of account and transaction service charges. Regulations can compound the cost problem when they require proof of identification (birth certificates and similar documents), which many low- and moderate-income individuals lack and which are difficult to acquire. In Kenya and India, to cite just two examples, technology is helping consumers to bypass these problems (box F3.2).

Recent technological applications such as mobile banking have sharply reduced the costs of retail banking, offering a major new opportunity to increase household access to secure savings and payment mechanisms. Low

Box F3.1

Rural banks in Ghana: Reaching clients who are underserved by other banks

Ghana's rural and community banks (RCBs) were established by the government in the late 1970s to facilitate Cocoa Board payments to farmers. The banks were privatized and became microfinance institutions in the 1990s, and today they provide various affordable savings products (savings accounts, current accounts, daily deposits collected by agents who go door to door, and fixed or time deposits), credit products (microfinance loans, personal loans, salary loans, and overdraft facilities, for example), and money transfer and payment services. Ghana's RCBs reach 2.8 million depositors and 680,000 borrowers, consisting mainly of farmers, government employees, and small and microentrepreneurs—clients often underserved by formal financial institutions. They are now the largest providers of formal financial services in rural Ghana. With some additional outreach, they could benefit young people—another underserved population.

Source: IFPRI and World Bank 2010, brief 5.

population density makes brick-and-mortar branch banking unprofitable, but the construction of cell phone towers and networks has opened opportunities to bank through a mobile phone, ATM, or point-of-sale device. In branchless banking, the costs of savings account and bill payment services are as much as 50 percent lower, and the costs of money transfers are about 20 percent lower, than they are in traditional banking by microfinance institutions (MFIs) and other banks oriented toward the poor (McKay and Pickens 2010).[4] The rapid spread of M-PESA in Kenya, which increased household access to formal finance by 10 percentage points in three years, shows the potential (King 2012). The use of mobile phones and other new technology to expand access to formal banking is particularly attractive for young people, who are always early adopters.[5]

At the same time, banks need to use these new channels for connecting with young people—to offer products attractive to youths and bring them in as customers early—even if the benefits are more likely to materialize over the long term. This effort may require support as part of financial sector development.

"Even if you have 100 shillings, you can save your little money." Uganda

Use of technology: Bringing secure financial services to new markets in Kenya and India

Just as the cellular telephone revolution has lowered the cost of communication and allowed poor countries in Africa and elsewhere to leapfrog over the problem of building a landline phone network, branchless banking using mobile phones and "micro automated teller machines (ATMs)" that read unique bioidentifiers could be used to extend financial access to the vast "unbanked" population. Already, Africa is the second-largest mobile money market, in part because remittances are so important in this region. But as with the rollout of mobile phones, regulatory policy will be as important as innovation in determining the outcome.

Kenya's Venture into Mobile Money

Since its launch in Kenya in 2007, M-PESA, a mobile phone–based banking system run by Safaricom, has dramatically changed the financial services landscape. M-PESA allows registered users to store money in their account by buying phone credits, to transfer money to or receive money from other registered users through their mobile phone, as well as to transform their credit balance into cash at any authorized dealer. By building on its existing cell phone record-keeping infrastructure and agent network, Safaricom has been able to offer basic banking services at much cheaper prices than a branch bank (about 50 percent cheaper, depending on the service and size of transaction). It has doubled the share of the population with access to a secure place to store cash, and, by operating as a debit card (or electronic wallet), it has reduced users' vulnerability to robbery.

M-PESA differs from a bank in two important ways. It does not offer loans (although M-PESA customers can use the system to link with banks, receive loaned funds, and make the required loan payments), and it does not pay interest on its accounts. Given that the interest earned on small savings accounts in commercial banks is usually eaten up by account fees, small savers are better off using M-PESA, even without the interest. In 2012, an analysis concluded that M-PESA's branchless banking system had brought banking to previously unserved low-income populations and had "flattened the geographical constraints to access" across Kenya (King 2012, 28). Despite being a low-income country, Kenya has one of the highest levels of financial access in Africa, with mobile money transactions equivalent to 60 percent of Kenya's gross domestic product (GDP) in 2012 (Blycroft Ltd. 2012).

At least as important as Safaricom's product innovation and successful implementation was the stance of the bank regulator, the central bank of Kenya. When M-PESA was launched, Kenya had no law regulating nonbank e-money issuers and e-money transactions. Rather than simply blocking Safaricom from operating the system, the central bank negotiated an agreement under which Safaricom would operate the system. The agreement stipulated that the e-money on deposit with Safaricom through M-PESA would be separated from the company's accounts and cash flow (in the same way that other nonbank financial institutions, such as stock brokerages, are required to isolate customers' assets from the assets and accounts of the company). The central bank kept a close watch on the system's operations, including sporadic checks to see that at the close of the day the amount of funds that e-money customers had stored with Safaricom in their phone accounts was equal to the amount of funds that Safaricom had placed in its trust account at its partner bank. After three years of this "test-and-learn" supervision, the central bank began work on a set of e-money and e-payment regulations.

India's Solution to the High Cost of Verifying Bank Clients

For low-income populations, a major obstacle to interacting with the formal banking system is the lack of verifiable identification. Banking systems need to be able to identify their customers to ensure that financial transactions are secure; in addition, they have to comply with supervisory reporting requirements on transactions, some of which are set internationally as part of global anticorruption and antiterrorism regulations. Low-income countries are less likely to have reliable national identification systems, and these databases are unlikely to cover lower-income populations and people in rural areas. Faced with the high cost of verifying the identity of such clients, banks often choose not to serve them at all.

The Government of India is finding a way around this problem through the Unique National Identification project, in which identification is based on biometrics rather than standard approaches such as birth certificates and postal addresses. At a very small cost per participant, more than 300 million people registered in the first two years. Banks have responded enthusiastically to this system, investing in basic biometric readers, which are linked to the database and can instantly identify and verify account holders. Agents in rural areas have been equipped with "micro ATMs"— point-of-sale devices—that read the client's biometrics (usually fingerprints) and record the transactions in the bank database, reducing the need for customers to travel to bank branches. Government agencies are using this system to disburse cash transfers to households through low-cost bank accounts, and citizens can also pay school fees and

(continued)

(continued)

utility bills through this system. Initially envisaged as a way to simplify administrative procedures and reduce the costs of service delivery (including leakages), the system is set to transform the financial services landscape in India, pav-ing the way for dramatically increased access by providing financial services at a much lower cost.

Sources: King 2012; Lauer and Tarazi 2012.

Regulation to Increase Financial Inclusion and Encourage the Use of New Technology

As figure F3.2 shows, even at the same income level, national policies for the financial sector can produce very different results. Countries such as Kenya, Mauritius, and Rwanda in Africa and China, India, Mongolia, and Thailand in Asia have achieved much higher financial access than other countries at similar levels of income. And given income levels, Africa is not doing badly. Among poor countries (with GDP per capita under US$1,000), the majority of African countries for which we have data are actually above the trend line of the rest of the world. The exception is countries in the CFA (Communauté Financière d'Afrique) zone, which tend to lag the rest of the world in extending bank accounts to households.

Countries with high household access to finance tend to have one or more of the following features: (1) a competitive banking sector, which encourages banks to look for customers; (2) a vibrant microfinance sector, which tends to specialize in products tailored to the needs of lower-income households; (3) proportionate supervision, including a "test-and-learn" approach, which encourages innovation; and (4) a national strategy. The national strategy encompasses the first three characteristics. It can also include policies to encourage banks to offer products that are appropriately designed and priced for low-income people, along with policies that require all government payments to individuals (G2P payments) to be electronic, which encourages financial inclusion. For example, Kenya has both a vibrant microfinance sector and a policy environment that encourages innovation (box F3.2). Rwanda's national strategy to encourage financial inclusion is reflected in policies to encourage micro-

finance expansion and mobile banking as well as programs to support the growth of affordable credit to nonfarm businesses in rural areas. Mongolia has used a dynamic mobile network system and a G2P payment system to broaden access. Given the rapid evolution of banking technology and its potential to change the financial landscape, countries need to develop a regulatory structure that encourages the spread of the technology, while protecting consumers through interoperability and other regulations (see Dias and McKee 2010; Lauer and Tarazi 2012; World Bank 2013).

In the CFA system in Western and Central Africa, regulation has restrained innovation in the financial sector. Regional central banks are involved in financial regulation, and changes to the system require the agreement of all participants. This arrangement has kept competition in the formal banking sector low, and household financial inclusion well below the trend for the rest of Africa and the world. It has benefited insiders at the expense of new entrants (World Bank 2013). The penetration of MFIs is low, and regulations to facilitate their growth were not adopted by all countries of the West African Economic and Monetary Union until 2012 (Riquet and Mbenge 2013). Mobile carriers such as Safaricom (Kenya) cannot start mobile banking initiatives—only banks have the right to do so, and they have no incentives to serve low-income customers. Ideally, a regional regulator could spur the development of a large market for mobile banking by developing harmonized cross-border payment systems, but that has yet to happen. There are signs that the regulatory environment is adapting, however. It is hoped that the new MFI regulations will help to create a trustworthy system interested in serving the currently unbanked population. A new financial inclusion strategy, which will

Figure F3.2 Percentage of individuals with an account at a formal financial institution

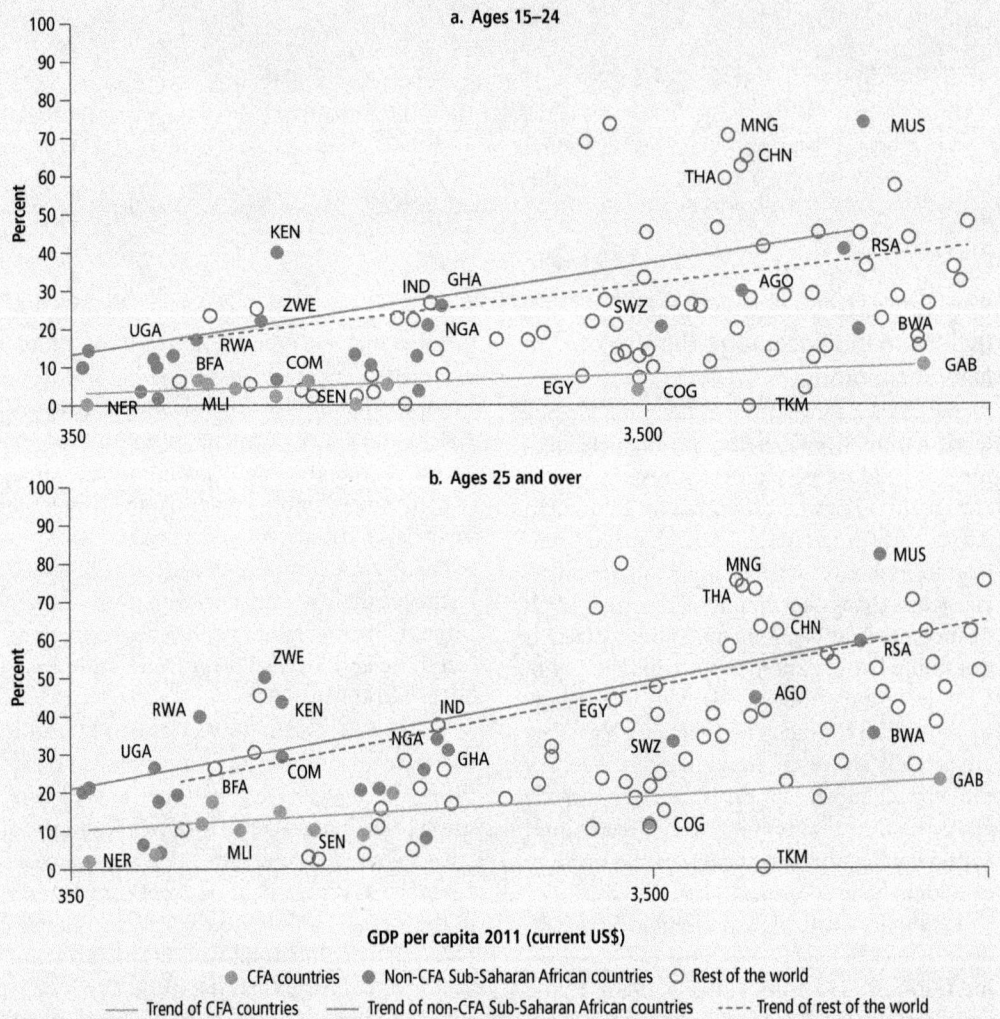

a. Ages 15–24

b. Ages 25 and over

GDP per capita 2011 (current US$)

● CFA countries ● Non-CFA Sub-Saharan African countries ○ Rest of the world

—— Trend of CFA countries —— Trend of non-CFA Sub-Saharan African countries ---- Trend of rest of the world

Source: Based on FINDEX data.
Note: The x axis of this figure is on a log scale.

require all financial service providers to offer a basic bank account with a package of free services, is scheduled to be adopted in 2013. Thus the prospects for improved household financial access are high in this region.

Formal Credit Services: Challenges in Expanding Options for Smallholders, Household Enterprises, and Young People

Even if retail banking costs fall and savings accounts become cheaper, the costs of lending to smallholders, HE owners, and young people will remain high. There are fixed staff costs in loan appraisal. Because most loans are for such small amounts, even the best MFIs report that they must earn an average of 19 percent a year on their loan portfolios just to cover operating costs of US$114 per loan (see MIX 2008). Large nonprofit MFIs such as BRAC and Grameen Bank in South Asia cover part of these costs through donations, but the commercially oriented MFIs that are more common in Africa, such as Ecobank and Equity Bank, have to charge high interest rates to cover these costs.

For banks, lending to smallholders is risky. Agricultural cycles are unpredictable. The clients are in remote locations, are often unfamiliar with financial services, and have few assets to use as collateral. Young smallholders can offer few assurances to formal lenders, but they are likely to need capital to acquire the agricultural technologies, land, and equipment that will allow them to pursue more productive and often more commercial agricultural livelihoods. Chapter 4 discusses constraints on financial services in agriculture and details several ways in which banks and nongovernmental organizations (NGOs) are innovating to provide them. Financial services alone may not be a strong springboard for smallholders to improve agricultural productivity and commercial activity. Some approaches combine the provision of financial services with the provision of agricultural information (planting and marketing advice, for example; see the discussion of BASIX in chapter 4). Other approaches recognize that integrating smallholders with agribusiness—domestic supermarkets, agroprocessors, or (further along the supply chain) exporters—may reduce some of the risk in providing financial services to smallholders. Kenya's DrumNet Project is one example of a supply-chain approach to agricultural lending (box F3.3).

Lending to HEs has similar problems. HEs face high risks of doing business (ranging from fluctuating demand to seizure of goods by authorities), and they are vulnerable to shocks and demands for cash within the household (sickness, for example) and community (funerals). HEs may be unable to generate the rates of return required to pay back a loan. Lenders have to assess these risks and price loans accordingly. HEs that can generate the returns to pay the loan back may not maintain a business account, however, and thus may not be able to present themselves as creditworthy, even to financial institutions oriented toward serving low-income households.

Microfinance programs use group liability lending to ameliorate some of the risk and high cost of lending to people with very limited assets. Because the group guarantees the credit of the individual members, it acts as a support mechanism for the farmer or enterprise owner and as a risk reduction mechanism for the lender. The lending methodologies applied by leading MFIs have succeeded in holding their portfolio at risk (more than 30 days) below an average of 3 percent (MIX 2008).

"We form groups to borrow money to engage in petty trade, pay school fees, and to build or improve on our houses."
Uganda

Box F3.3

Linking smallholders to supply chains to improve their access to financial services

DrumNet (a project of PRIDE AFRICA, a microfinance nonprofit) sought to improve Kenyan smallholders' access to financial services through a pilot program that integrated them into the supply chain for oilseeds. The pilot, which lasted from 2007 to 2009, involved Equity Bank and Bidco, a large manufacturer of vegetable oils, fats, margarines, and protein concentrates in East Africa. Bidco required an assured supply of sunflower seed. Farmers were recruited to grow sunflowers instead of their typical crop. The other partners were input suppliers and AgriTrade (which recruited farmers and managed sunflower production, harvest, and collection). DrumNet brought the parties together, negotiated the contracts on which their collaboration was based, and managed the flow of information and financial transactions among them, earning revenue for those services.

Farmer groups (usually about 20–100 farmers in the same area) opened an account with Equity Bank, through which all payments were made. Each farmer contributed to a Transaction Insurance Fund, which was 25 percent of the value of the input credit and served as security for the loans. After signing a fixed-price contract to supply sunflower seed to Bidco, farmers received credit for inputs from Equity Bank. Farmers obtained no cash from Equity Bank; instead, the bank paid input suppliers directly for inputs that farmers purchased with the credit. When farmers delivered their produce to Bidco, Bidco paid them through DrumNet, which deducted the cost of the loan and transferred it to Equity Bank. The remainder was deposited in the farmer's account with Equity Bank. DrumNet facilitated the financial transactions and communication via mobile phones, text messages, and e-mail.

More than 2,000 smallholders participated in the sunflower pilot. The arrangement between farmers, buyers, banks, and retailers, although complex, brought smallholders into the formal financial system, integrated them into a supply chain for a commercial crop, and improved efficiency throughout the oilseed supply chain.

Source: World Bank 2011.

Shifting from group to individual liability lending as a positive microfinance innovation: Evidence from the Philippines

A central decision in designing credit programs for poor people is whether to rely on group or individual liability. Individual liability places more responsibility on the lending institution, so borrowers prefer it (Karlan and Appel 2011). Although individual liability lending is becoming more common in microfinance, little empirical research has compared the two approaches. Between 2004 and 2007, two randomized controlled trials with Rural Green Bank of Caraga, an MFI in the Philippines, examined how loan monitoring and repayment differed under group liability and individual liability lending. All of the loans (roughly US$18–US$90) went to female owners of HEs to expand their businesses.

The first trial converted group liability lending programs to individual liability, while retaining the group structure. No increase in defaults or loss of profits was found for centers that switched. Individual liability centers gained more clients (new clients were more likely to remain in the program), but because clients' loans were smaller, the individual liability centers disbursed about the same amount as the group liability centers. Groups that switched to individual liability spent less time monitoring repayment by other group mem-

bers. The finding that monitoring decreased but repayment was stable suggests that the screening process changed without worsening repayment. One possibility is that the removal of group liability may have induced credit officers to increase screening and monitoring, although their workload did not increase.

The second trial offered new borrowers group liability in some areas and individual liability in others. No statistically or economically significant difference was found in repayment rates. The move toward individual liability lending appears to have distributed the burden for screening, monitoring, and enforcement more equitably between clients and credit officers. The level of institutional enforcement seen in the two trials was sufficient for the lender to recover loans without group liability and, in some cases, to attract and retain more clients. Although the experiment was limited to one MFI in one setting, the results imply that other microfinance innovators that are pursuing strategies for individual (and more flexible) lending to the poor may be moving in the right direction.

Source: Giné and Karlan 2013.

Yet microfinance groups can require substantial time and financial guarantees from participants. The time required to participate in the group may deter smallholders or owner-managers of an informal enterprise from using MFI services. If the group is not formed properly and someone defaults, the downside shock to smallholders and HE owners, whose margins are already low and who have their own loans to pay off, is high (box F3.4). The combination of group liability with low flexibility on the part of the lender excludes borrowers who want to finance risky projects or investments that will take some time to pay off, creating a bias toward small, safe projects. In short, microfinance group lending methodologies that help to solve the problems of high cost and risk to the financial institutions effectively impose part of these costs on the clients; therefore, they are suited only for particular types of customers.

Alternative strategies, such as lending to individuals on more flexible terms but requiring them to pledge key assets such as land

(especially for farmers) or business equipment as collateral, also have downsides. Smallholders and HE owners could lose critical assets just when they need them most. MFIs using these strategies in Africa are more selective; they prefer to lend to households where a wage earner can act as a cosigner for the loan. These requirements help to explain why HE owners and farmers, who constantly face liquidity problems because of low and uncertain cash flow, rarely borrow from banks or MFIs and remain within their informal financial networks.

Informal Services to Fill the Savings and Credit Gaps

Although their scope is almost always small, informal financial services have sprung up in Africa to fill the gap in savings and credit services for households. These various savings and credit services have a long history and have developed rules for participation that ensure success (box F3.5). They meet a need that cannot be met through more formal financing arrangements, owing to the small amounts and numerous small transactions involved, as well as the lack of information on the participants' creditworthiness. Informal services are a valuable bridge to financial literacy, a widespread savings culture, and, eventually, formal financial inclusion and more productive enterprises, as African countries continue to develop their formal financial sectors.

As seen in figure F3.1, savers in Africa use formal financial services more than savers anywhere else in the world, especially in Africa's lower-middle-income countries, where the overwhelming majority of households no longer suffer from extreme poverty. The use of informal savings mechanisms is more common among adults over 25; almost half of adults in lower-middle-income countries who save use these groups. These groups also help young people to save, and they may explain why the youth savings rate in Africa is the highest in the world.

A key tenet of savings groups that also provide credit is that members must save before they can obtain other services. This practice screens out borrowers who are less likely to repay loans. Members in effect pledge their savings deposit as partial collateral against the loan. To ensure that members save, some groups employ a member or other person to collect funds daily or weekly from members at their homes (a *susu* collector). Informal

Box F3.5

ROSCAs, VSLAs, SHGs, and SACCOs: Examples of informal savings and credit systems

Rotating savings and credit associations (ROSCAs) form when individuals agree to save together. They have evolved throughout the world—witness West Africa's *tontines,* Nepal's *dhikuti,* and Indonesia's *arisan.* Members meet regularly, and all deposit the same amount of money into a common pot at every meeting. At each meeting, on a rotating basis, one member gets the whole pot. ROSCAs have advantages. They require no bookkeeping (an asset where literacy is limited), everyone witnesses the transactions at every meeting, and the sums involved are small. Their accessibility and simplicity make ROSCAs an important source of financial services even where specialized MFIs operate. ROSCAs empower their members (the majority of whom are women) and help to build social capital in communities. The structure can be useful in operating informal social protection schemes as well, such as burial societies. Yet these associations also have drawbacks. Members cannot always access savings when they want them, and the timing of required contributions and payouts may not match their cash flow needs. The approach favors people with steady incomes who can contribute consistently.

Village savings and loan associations (VSLAs), also called *accumulating savings and credit associations (ASCAs),* were pioneered in the early 1990s by CARE International, which developed a standard model for VSLAs based on Niger's *tontines.* Generally 15–25 individuals agree to join forces for saving and borrowing during a fixed period (usually one year). The group elects a management committee and money counters. No one else handles the money, which is stored in a cash box with multiple locks. The key holders are not part of the management committee. The group determines the services offered (savings, lending) and corresponding terms and conditions. At regular meetings, members purchase one to five savings shares; the share price is determined by the group and remains unchanged throughout the year. These savings capitalize a loan fund for members, who can borrow amounts not exceeding three times their savings. Loans are given to individuals or groups, for a term not exceeding the groups' end point, at a monthly interest rate of 5–10 percent (though rates as low as 1 percent or as high as 20 percent are reported). Record keeping takes three forms: memorization, passbooks that record only the ending fund balance, or central ledgers that track financial activity. When a cycle ends, group members share the savings and corresponding interest. Returns can range from 35 to 50 percent; after only a few years, a group might manage US$2,000–US$10,000. Through small periodic contributions, groups may also maintain a social fund available to the entire community. Members may leave the group at any time, under terms decided by the group. As a result, unlike ROSCAs, VSLAs intermediate funds between savers and investors within a group over a short period of time.

Aside from CARE, numerous organizations have promoted VSLAs, including Aga Khan Foundation, Catholic Relief Services, Oxfam/Freedom from Hunger, Pact-WORTH, PLAN, the United States Peace Corps, World Relief, and World Vision. VSLAs have reached at least 61 countries in Africa, Asia, and Latin America and have more than

(continued)

savings and credit groups limit banking costs through their own outreach, governance, and accounting, and they can recruit staff locally at relatively low salaries. For this reason, they can charge lower interest rates than MFIs. Larger groups with access to a local bank may opt to protect funds there at an affordable cost (account charges are shared across members, along with any interest earned on the deposit).

These informal services have some disadvantages. Their local nature and structure limit intermediation. They depend on members for funds and can lend only the money that is available in the group. The lending terms are short, rarely exceeding one year and usually lasting only a few months. This brief time horizon has the benefit of allowing close supervision and limiting losses (little time passes before it is clear whether a member can honor an obligation). The loans are useful for covering lumpy household expenditures such as school fees or the expenses related to a festival, but they are not suited to an investment in a farm or in HE equipment, which may require a longer repayment period. Everyone in the group pays the same interest on loans—even risky loans—which appropriately biases risk downward. Even the larger and more sophisticated savings and credit cooperatives (SACCOs) may struggle with profitability, as their membership base may never be large enough for them to spread out the basic overhead costs of facilities, management, and security and achieve lower unit costs than other financial institutions, espe-

---

Box F3.5

(continued)

6 million active participants. The organizations promoting the savings groups train the members in group operation and governance, but because these groups are essentially self-managed, the risk that funds may be lost through fraud, theft, or borrower default remains. Larger groups in or near urban areas may safeguard their funds in a bank, and CARE is testing the use of mobile banking technology to store and withdraw group funds in VSLAs in East Africa.

Self-help groups (SHGs) are small village groups of 10–20 women who pool their savings over a few months until they have sufficient capital to lend to group members or to others in their village. SHGs link with banks and form federations with other villages, allowing them to accumulate more capital for lending. The interest is not distributed back to members; it is left to grow. Used widely in India, SHGs have potential in Africa, but efforts to establish them have had mixed success. In India they rely on strong social dynamics among women within villages and social connections between villages to catalyze federations. The social structures in African villages are not as conducive to developing strong women's groups, and women in Africa are less able than women in India to devote the time required to attend meetings, in part because the lower density of settlement requires them to travel longer distances.

Savings and credit cooperatives (SACCOs), or credit unions, are member owned, not-for-profit financial cooperatives providing savings, credit, remittances, and other services to members connected in some way (for example, they may belong to the same workplace, community, or religious group). A volunteer board of directors is elected from among the membership; each member has one vote. SACCOs finance their loan portfolios by pooling members' voluntary savings rather than seeking outside capital. Ideally, members earn higher returns on savings, pay lower interest on loans, and generally pay fewer fees. SACCOs' local nature can prevent them from expanding and reducing their unit costs, especially in rural areas. Their democratic nature requires members to balance borrowers' preference for low interest rates against the high returns sought by shareholders, who mainly save. Finally, because SACCOs operate far more like banks than cooperatives, their governance and regulation urgently demand attention. Although their assets form a very small share of the banking system's assets, SACCOs serve a very large (and relatively poor) population. A system to guarantee SACCOs' probity, stability, and accountability may not necessarily be costly. It may suffice to institute sound governance and internal controls to protect members' deposits and limit SACCOs' exposure to risk, but much more research is needed to determine what works best.

Sources: Allen and Panetta 2010; Bakiene et al. 2012; Collins et al. 2009; IFPRI and World Bank 2010, brief 3; VSL Associates, "About Us: VSL Model," http://www.vsla.net/aboutus/vslmodel; "Rotating Savings and Credit Association," http://en.wikipedia.org/wiki/Rotating_Savings_and_Credit_Association; "What Is a Credit Union?" http://www.woccu.org/about/creditunion.

cially in sparsely populated rural areas (5,000 clients is often considered a minimum efficient size for MFIs). The agreed rates on loans are typically 3.0–3.5 percent a month for SAC-COs in Uganda, which may still exceed what many smallholders and HE owners can afford while still being able to profit from a loan for an enterprise (Bakiene et al. 2012; Collins et al. 2009).

The Role of Government: Increasing Access and Protecting Consumers

Normally, informal finance exists outside the scope of government regulation and support, but government, NGO, and donor programs have supported the spread of SACCOs and VSLAs through outreach, training, and the formation of national SACCO member associations. Program staff train group members on procedures to keep the funds safe and limit the loss of funds through theft, fraud, or bad loans, but according to all accounts, reliability remains a problem.[6]

To protect consumers, governments are looking for ways to supervise the larger groups, such as SACCOs, but supervising a large number of small groups is rarely feasible.[7] Government involvement in SACCOs and VSLAs can also backfire. Informal groups operate on trust, supported by a set of procedures to ensure transparency. They keep costs down for their members because they operate efficiently and do not have to spend time complying with regulators' requests for information. For larger SACCOs, in which members find it more challenging to exert proper supervision themselves and the sums involved are substantial enough to undermine the SACCO program, some sort of public supervision may be justified.

In general, however, governments should keep their involvement in informal savings groups to a minimum. The public tends to interpret government involvement in such programs as a signal that participants can exert less financial discipline, which undermines the approach. In Tanzania, a qualitative study documented numerous cases in poor districts where public funds intended to provide grants or bring cheap credit to owners of HEs never materialized. Instead, the funds stayed in the district capitals, presumably in the hands of the officials there. Only the NGO-organized VSLAs effectively provided capital to HE owners (Kweka and Fox 2011).

An especially damaging practice is for governments or NGOs to use an informal savings group to inject capital into the community. Studies show that this practice reduces the groups' incentives to build up their own savings pool and places the sustainability of the initiative at risk. For this reason, NGOs seem better suited than governments to the task of developing and supporting informal savings groups.

The Role of Informal Financial Institutions: Expanding Financial Inclusion

VSLAs and SHGs both hold potential for including young people and addressing their capital constraints, particularly if the group offers mentoring and access to information as well as finance. In Uganda, an innovative strategy is being developed to work through NGOs to establish VSLAs and promote the inclusion of young people. A donor (the International Fund for Agricultural Development) will provide funds for the Ministry of Finance and Economic Development to contract with NGOs to develop and nurture VSLAs. The proposed target is to establish 15,000 new VSLAs over five years. At least 15 percent of the new members are expected to be young people, either through the formation of youth savings groups or the incorporation of young people into VSLAs. Project funds will support the staff and materials to train local groups; no funds will be provided as paid-in capital to the groups.[8]

In addition to providing informal financial services, savings groups support their members in the same way as lending circles in MFIs—they provide encouragement and a forum for members to share experiences. Numerous descriptions of savings groups attest to the importance of this feature (see box F3.6 for an example from Mali), which could be a valuable means for young people to learn from others and build social capital (Banerjee and Duflo 2011; Nimusiima et al. 2012). As savings groups spread to young people, group members are approaching their NGO partners for additional

"Group management of loans is very bad. One lady in our group borrowed T Sh 500,000 and then ran away. I had borrowed only T Sh 100,000. How come the one who had borrowed T Sh 100,000 had to pay for someone who had borrowed T Sh 500,000?" Tanzania (US$1 = T Sh 2,500)

Village women in Mali: Achieving food and financial security through savings and credit groups

Saving for Change (SfC), a village savings and loan program initiated in rural Mali in 2005, places women firmly in charge of their own financial inclusion. The women served by the program are largely illiterate, poor (mostly living on less than US$1 a day), and living in very isolated areas. By regularly saving small amounts and lending group funds short term to members with interest, each group of about 15–25 women accumulates and mobilizes capital without relying on matching or external funds. By July 2008, SfC had 95,000 members; later that year, the program expanded into four of Mali's five nondesert regions. By April 2013, SfC served 18,804 groups (423,654 members). A rigorous evaluation of SfC's impact was conducted between 2009 and 2012 to document the program's contribution to household livelihood strategies and savings and credit provision.

A randomized controlled trial (RCT)—the gold standard for impact assessment—used detailed socioeconomic surveys of 6,000 households in 500 villages in 2009 and 2012 to gather information from SfC participants and nonparticipants in treatment and control villages. In the interim, researchers repeatedly surveyed a subset of 600 households from treatment and control villages on their financial transactions, assets, income generating activities, consumption, and health. The resulting information provided insights into how households were evolving over the course of the study.

To interpret and contextualize the RCT data, qualitative research elicited detailed information from a small sample of 19 villages chosen to reflect some of the variation—in geographic location, ethnicity, livelihood strategies, and other variables—across SfC sites. Fifteen of the villages were located within the RCT zone in Ségou; four were outside the RCT zone and had participated in SfC since 2005. In each village in 2009 and 2012, researchers spent two to three days conducting focus group discussions, community interviews, and key informant interviews. In the villages familiar with SfC since 2005, these activities provided details on how community members had adapted the SfC model to meet local conditions, needs, and livelihood strategies over time.

The RCT found an overall increase in savings (by 31 percent), a greater flow of credit to women in SfC villages (12 percent more women reported borrowing from the savings groups), the accumulation of assets (livestock holdings grew in value by 13 percent in SfC villages), and a reduction in hunger during periods of food insecurity. Most women cited a less tangible impact—the social capital generated through participation in a savings group—as one of the program's most highly valued benefits. The groups included younger, less socially integrated women, although they joined slightly later than the initial participants. Finally, the savings groups had no measurable impact on business development or expansion, perhaps because many groups are located in such remote areas.

SfC seems to have improved food and financial security in these isolated, food-insecure, and impoverished areas. The fact that some women surveyed in the control villages formed savings and credit groups on their own, without external advice from SfC, indicates that these groups offer perceived advantages and are well adapted to local needs.

Source: BARA and IPA 2013.

services, including business education and life skills training. Plan International, an NGO active in supporting youth savings groups in West Africa, has been meeting these requests by contracting with local trainers to provide short courses on demand. Based on this experience, they are developing a holistic training syllabus for their youth savings groups. The content, which is adapted to the needs and learning preferences of young people, is designed to support disadvantaged youths in the transition to adulthood and a sustainable livelihood.[9]

Savings groups may be an effective venue to integrate the delivery of youth programs in communities. Through such groups, national strategies for youth could combine programs to foster savings behavior, build business and soft skills, support female empowerment, and expand financial inclusion, with the goal of enabling young people to pursue sustainable livelihoods.

Notes

1. In these countries, a bank account is considered a contract; the minimum age to sign a contract is 18, and no provision is made for an adult cosigner.

2. See the FINDEX website, http://go.worldbank. org/1F2V9ZK8C0.

3. Postal savings account systems were developed to get around this problem by making use of underused rural postal service staff, offices, and security systems to bring savings accounts to populations not served by traditional banking systems.

4. Gains are even higher when compared with account charges at up-market commercial banks.

5. CGAP blog, January 2012 (http://www.cgap.org/ blog/looking-back-trends-branchless-banking-2012).

6. See Collins et al. (2009), Karlan and Appel (2011), and Banerjee and Duflo (2011) for discussions on how and why this occurs.

7. This section draws on Glisovic and El-Zoghbi (2011).

8. Based on draft project document, November 2012 (see IFAD 2012).

9. See http://plan-international.org/what-we-do/ economic-security.

References

Allen, Hugh, and David Panetta. 2010. "Savings Groups: What Are They?" SEEP Network, Washington, DC.

Bakiene, Amor, Louise Fox, Obert Pimhidzai, and Elizabeth Mehta. 2012. "How Non-Farm Enterprises Create Jobs for the Middle Class in Uganda and How Policies Can Raise Productivity and Reduce Risk." Policy Research Working Paper, World Bank, Washington, DC.

Banerjee, Abhijit V., and Esther Duflo. 2011. *Poor Economics: A Radical Rethinking of the Way to Fight Global Poverty*. New York: Public Affairs.

BARA (Bureau of Applied Research in Anthropology) and IPA (Innovations for Poverty Action). 2013. "Final Impact Evaluation of the Saving for Change Program in Mali, 2009–2012." Oxfam America. http://www.oxfam america.org/issues/community-finance/files/ final-impact-evaluation-saving-for-change.

Blycroft Ltd. 2012. "African Mobile Factbook." Africa and Middle East Telecom-Week. http:// blog.bearing-consulting.com/wp-content/ uploads/2012/10/Africa.Mobile.Fact_.Book_ .2012.pdf.

Collins, Daryl, Jonathan Morduch, Stuart Rutherford, and Orlanda Ruthven. 2009. *Portfolios of the Poor: How the World's Poor Live on $2 a Day*. Princeton, NJ: Princeton University Press.

Dias, Denis, and Katherine McKee. 2010. "Protecting Branchless Banking Consumers: Policy Objectives and Regulatory Options." CGAP Focus Note 64, Consulting Group to Assist the Poor, Washington, DC.

Dupas, Pascaline, and Jonathan Robinson. 2009. "Savings Constraints and Microenterprise Development: Evidence from a Field Experiment in Kenya." *American Economic Journal: Applied Economics* 5 (1): 163–92.

Gardeva, Anita, and Elisabeth Rhyne. 2011. "Opportunities and Obstacles to Financial Inclusion: Survey Report." Publication 12, Center for Financial Inclusion, Accion International, Washington, DC.

Glisovic, Jasmina, and Mayada El-Zoghbi, with Sarah Forster. 2011. "Advancing Savings Services: Resource Guide for Funders." Technical Guide, Consultative Group to Assist the Poor, Washington, DC.

Giné, Xavier, and Dean Karlan. 2013. "Group Versus Individual Liability: Short- and Long-Term Evidence from Philippine Microcredit Lending Groups." World Bank, Washington, DC, June.

IFAD (International Fund for Agricultural Development). 2012. "Republic of Uganda: Project for Financial Inclusion in Rural Areas Detailed Design Report." Report 2772-UG, IFAD, Rome.

IFPRI (International Food Policy Research Institute) and World Bank. 2010. "Innovations in Rural and Agriculture Finance: Focus 18." IFPRI and World Bank, Washington, DC.

Karlan, Dean, and Jacob Appel. 2011. *More Than Good Intentions: How a New Economics Is Helping to Solve Global Poverty*. New York: Dutton.

Kilara, Tanaya, and Alexia Latortue. 2012. "Emerging Perspectives on Youth Savings." CGAP Focus Note 82, Consultative Group to Assist the Poor, Washington, DC.

King, Michael. 2012. "Is Mobile Banking Breaking the Tyranny of Distance to Bank Infrastructure? Evidence from Kenya." IIIS Discussion Paper 412, Institute of International Integration Studies, Trinity College, Dublin.

Kweka Josephat, and Louise Fox. 2011. "The Household Enterprise Sector in Tanzania: Why It Matters and Who Cares." Policy Research Working Paper 5882, World Bank, Washington, DC.

Lauer, Kate, and Michael Tarazi. 2012. "Supervising Nonbank E-Money Issuers." CGAP Brief (July), Consultative Group to Assist the Poor, Washington, DC.

McKay, Claudia, and Mark Pickens. 2010. "Branchless Banking 2010: Who's Served? At What Price? What's Next?" CGAP Focus Note 66, Consultative Group to Assist the Poor, Washington, DC.

MIX (Microfinance Information Exchange). 2008. *MFI Benchmark Data | Microbanking Bulletin* 17 (August). http://www.themix.org/publications/microbanking-bulletin/2008/08/mfi-benchmark-data-microbanking-bulletin-august-2008-issu.

Mullainathan, Sendhil, and Eldar Shafir. 2011. "Savings Policy and Decision-Making in Low-Income Households." In *Insufficient Funds: Savings, Assets, Credit, and Banking among Low-Income Households*, edited by Michael Barr and Rebecca Blank, 121–46. New York: Russell Sage Foundation Press.

Nimusiima, Catherine, Fiona Nshemerirwe, Helen Nyamweu, and Skye Dobson, eds. 2012. *10 Years of Owegatta: A History of the National Slum Dwellers Federation of Uganda (NSDFU) Narrated by Members*. Kampala: Act Together Uganda.

Riquet, Corinne, and Djibril Maguette Mbenge. 2013. "Deepening Financial Inclusion in West Africa." CGAP blog post, Consultative Group to Assist the Poor, January 25, http://www.cgap.org/blog/deepening-financial-inclusion-west-africa.

USAID (United States Agency for International Development). 2009. "Youth Savings Account: A Financial Service Perspective; a Literature and Program Review." MicroREPORT 163, USAID, Washington, DC.

World Bank. 2011. "Module 7: Broadening Smallholders' Access to Financial Services through ICTs." In *ICT in Agriculture: Connecting Smallholders to Knowledge, Networks, and Institutions*. Washington, DC: World Bank.

———. 2013. *Global Financial Development Report 2014: Financial Inclusion*. Washington, DC: World Bank.

Chapter 6

Raising Productivity in Africa's Modern Wage Enterprises to Foster Job Growth for Youth

Although small (around 16 percent of the labor force), the wage employment sector represents Africa's engine for employment and growth in the medium to long term, especially given the sector's potential to exploit economies of scale and produce for export. Yet wage employment is growing unevenly across Africa. Modern manufacturing firms, in particular, account for only 3 percent of employment and export very little. This limited competitiveness in export markets is mainly the result of low productivity in the modern wage sector. It signals the presence of government and market failures, which vary across the subcontinent but have similar effects. Complementary inputs to labor (electricity, overland transport, and so on) are costly, regulations strangle business processes and the movement of goods, the high costs of financial intermediation starve investors of capital, and the small domestic markets and trade barriers suppress competition and reduce pressure to innovate and improve productivity.

Governments in Africa can do much to remedy this situation. The most important step is to improve the business climate through key reforms to improve access to finance and infrastructure services, improve trade logistics, and ease regulatory constraints to entrepreneurship. Many reforms are not so expensive in monetary terms and can deliver huge impacts in the short run by reducing distortions and increasing efficiency. Selective and spatially targeted support to emerging clusters can promote agglomeration economies. For young people to be truly productive in modern firms, governments should foster a strong foundation in basic skills by improving the quality of general education. In the training sector, governments should focus on "public goods" such as quality assurance and information to foster a sector that is efficient and relevant to the market for skills. Programs for disadvantaged youth that integrate training with internships show promise, as do programs offering managerial training.

Alongside employment in household farms and firms, discussed in the previous two chapters, employment in modern enterprises is becoming increasingly important to African youth. If history is any guide, this trend will only continue. As European and North American countries developed, jobs in modern enterprises gradually replaced other kinds of jobs, even in agriculture. In developed countries today, the modern wage sector dominates employment. In East Asia and China, the growth of jobs in modern firms is following a similar pattern.

The modern wage sector, as defined in this report, includes small, medium, and large firms that continuously employ five or more workers. It also includes the public sector. Historically wage employment grew as jobs in public services and public manufacturing enterprises expanded, but no more. As governments have sought to curb inefficiency and improve competitiveness, they have rolled back employment in the public sector—in some cases drastically, as in Ethiopia and Ghana in the 1990s—which has reduced the share of public sector employees among wage and salary earners. For young people seeking wage employment, a public sector job may be more elusive than ever. Instead, the primary challenge is to sustain high rates of investment and job creation in the private sector, where productivity and competitiveness really matter.

This chapter closely examines employment in modern enterprises in manufacturing, services, and other nonfarm sectors such as construction because they have the greatest potential to drive productivity and employment in the medium to long term, as Africa's young workforce grows. Unlike household farms and firms, modern enterprises in these sectors are not limited by family size, so they can expand to exploit economies of scale, and they are far more likely to adopt the new technologies that permit them to do so. Because modern firms can impel higher productivity and create jobs, policy makers are understandably concerned with their development. But as shown in the discussion that follows, the circumstances must be right for entrepreneurship and productive firms to grow.

Africa's Modern Enterprise Sector: An Overview

Modern nonfarm wage employment is growing across Africa, but inconsistently. With the exception of some countries—notably Mauritius and South Africa—nonfarm enterprises account for under 20 percent of the wage employment in Africa (figure 6.1, panel a). Despite reductions in public sector employment, the private modern wage sector still provides less than 10 percent of employment in most African countries (figure 6.1, panel b). Even by the standards of Asian and Latin American countries with comparable levels of per capita income, employment in Africa's modern nonfarm enterprises is low, and it is extremely low in comparison with larger emerging economies such as Brazil, China, and Indonesia.

The expansion of employment in modern wage enterprises has been quite inconsistent across Africa. Labor force surveys reveal that while the modern wage sector has absorbed a growing share of the labor force in Madagascar, Mali, Tanzania, and Uganda, its share in total employment has changed little in Ethiopia, Kenya, and Zambia and has declined in other countries, such as Malawi and Senegal (figure 6.2).

Africa's young people seem to have no special advantage when it comes to modern wage employment (box 6.1). Although the current generation has more education than its predecessors, employers seem to value the experience brought by older workers.

Service jobs, both with and without a formal contract, dominate wage employment in Africa.[1] The single largest share of formal wage employment in services consists of jobs in education, health, and other social services (largely in the public sector). The next largest share consists of jobs in commerce (retail and wholesale) and transportation (figure 6.3, panel a).

Outside the service sector, manufacturing and construction each account for about 10 percent of wage jobs. Almost half of all manufacturing employment in modern firms is found within industries broadly classified as food and textiles (including leather and leather goods) (figure 6.3, panel b). Some countries, such as Cameroon and Rwanda, have significant employment in the wood-processing industry. Employment in high-tech industries, such as machinery and electronics, is quite limited, although employment in the chemicals, plastic, glass, and paper industries is important in some countries.

Modern Manufacturing Delivers Little Employment, Few Exports

Despite their considerable untapped potential for employment growth, modern manufacturing enterprises currently account for less than 3 percent of total employment in Africa, which is a good deal lower than in other regions of the world (figure 6.4). The ratio of manufacturing wage employment to total employment varies significantly from one country in Africa to the next (and it is declining in some countries), but there is no indication that Africa as a whole is catching up with its comparators.

The concern is not just that the manufacturing sector is so small, but that manufacturing firms export so little of what they produce. The percentage of African manufacturing firms exporting is among the lowest in the world; the share of African manufacturing output sold domestically is among the highest (figure 6.5). The poor performance of Africa's manufacturing sector is especially worrying because trade-oriented manufacturing may offer the best chance of quickly creating modern wage jobs. African economies are small, so developing an export-oriented sector is more important to them than to developing countries in other regions like South Asia, where domestic markets are generally much larger (Dinh et al. 2012). Small markets curb productivity and growth in employment by limiting the potential scale economies that industries can achieve. Because a small domestic market can support only a limited number of firms, the resulting lack of competitive pressure puts a brake on investment and growth.[2] In the absence of trade, small economies are also less likely to benefit from agglomeration economies, simply because manufacturing clusters are much less likely to emerge (Collier and Venables 2008).

Figure 6.1 Africa has less nonfarm wage employment than other regions

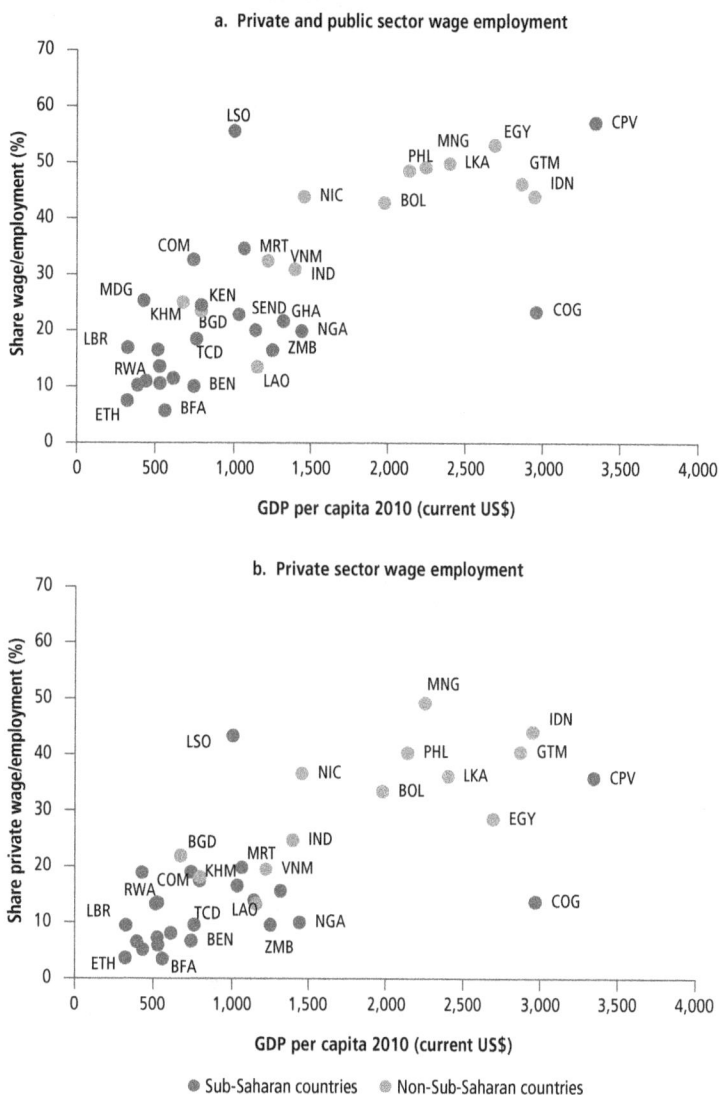

a. Private and public sector wage employment

b. Private sector wage employment

● Sub-Saharan countries   ● Non-Sub-Saharan countries

Source: Based on household and labor force surveys.

Given the potential significance of trade to Africa and the fact that manufactured goods are inherently more tradable than most services, the analysis in this chapter focuses more on manufacturing than on services. The reason for this approach is not that manufacturing is the only alternative for creating productive modern wage jobs in Africa. It is not. Services represent an increasingly important share of global trade, and Africa can certainly pursue this means of expanding wage employment.

Figure 6.2 Wage employment is growing inconsistently across Africa

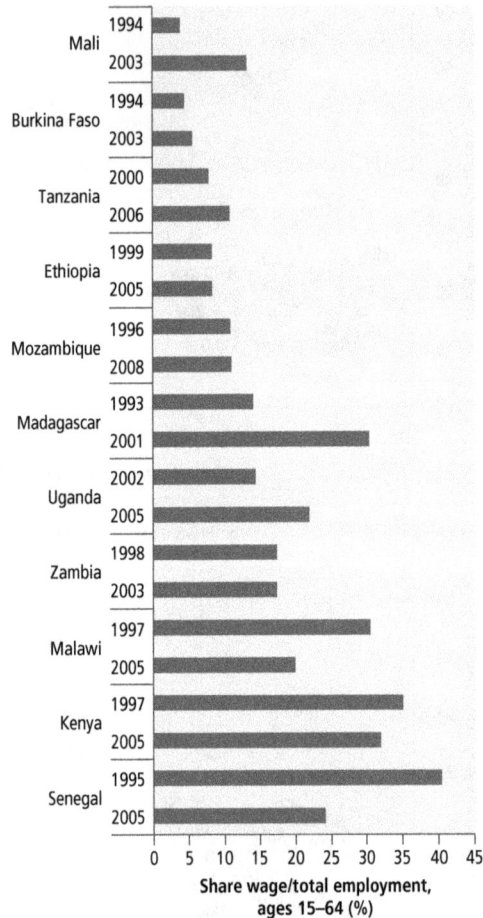

Share wage/total employment, ages 15–64 (%)

Source: Based on household and labor force surveys.

Productivity growth in nontraded sectors can also create wage jobs, as demonstrated by recent growth in Africa's construction sector. But as East Asia's rapidly growing economies suggest, trade-oriented manufacturing may offer the greatest potential to create wage jobs. Equally important is the positive feedback from manufacturing to other domestic sectors. A growing manufacturing sector that is driven by trade—and hence not limited by the size of the domestic economy—will expand domestic demand for other industries (including services and construction) by raising incomes. Manufacturing firms will also demand a range of intermediate goods and services as inputs from domestic suppliers.

A final consideration is that manufacturing has been the subject of more research than other sources of wage employment in Africa. More and better data are available for the analysis, and the resulting policy lessons can be applied to firms in other sectors.

How Competitive Is Modern Manufacturing in Africa?

Traditional thinking on international trade contends that the relative abundance of production factors like labor, capital, and natural resources in a given country strongly determines which of its economic activities are internationally competitive. Given that Africa has rich natural resources but relatively poor human capital, Africa is thought to have a comparative advantage in producing primary commodities for export rather than manufactured goods for export (Wood and Berge 1997; Wood and Mayer 2001). More recent thinking suggests that factor endowments alone do not determine trade and that Africa could potentially become competitive in manufacturing.

First, aside from labor, capital, and natural resources, good infrastructure and public services also contribute to competitiveness. Utilities like electricity and water affect how much a firm can produce from a given amount of labor, capital, and raw materials. Transport costs influence the competitiveness of a country's exports by affecting the cost of sending the output to export markets and the cost of importing inputs. Manufacturing, with its relatively complex supply chains, relies more heavily on infrastructure services than agriculture and extractive industries. Conceivably, investment in infrastructure could give rise to an internationally competitive manufacturing sector regardless of factor endowments.

Second, newer trade theories suggest that comparative advantage can be acquired over time, though not necessarily in a predictable way. For instance, an industrial cluster can sometimes become internationally competitive over time because of agglomeration econ-

Box 6.1

Where do young people figure in Africa's wage employment picture?

At present, in a cross-section of African countries, the ratio of wage employment to total employment among youth is remarkably similar to the ratio in the general population (see figure B6.1.1). The implication is that firms have no special proclivity to hire youth. Youth employment in modern enterprises simply grows in proportion to the growth of modern enterprises—no more, no less.

At the same time, this figure may not tell the whole story. It may be possible to enhance the impact of growth in wage enterprises on youth employment. Evidence presented in chapter 1 indicates that many individuals move into wage employment only when they are 30 years and older, which could reflect a preference for experienced workers. Policies that facilitate young people's transition to wage employment, such as programs to support on-the-job training through internships or informational interventions to connect youths to firms needing their skills, might enable more young people to fulfill their aspirations for wage employment sooner rather than later. The scope for pursuing such policies and evidence of their effectiveness are discussed toward the end of this chapter.

Figure B6.1.1 The share of youth in wage employment tracks the share in the general population

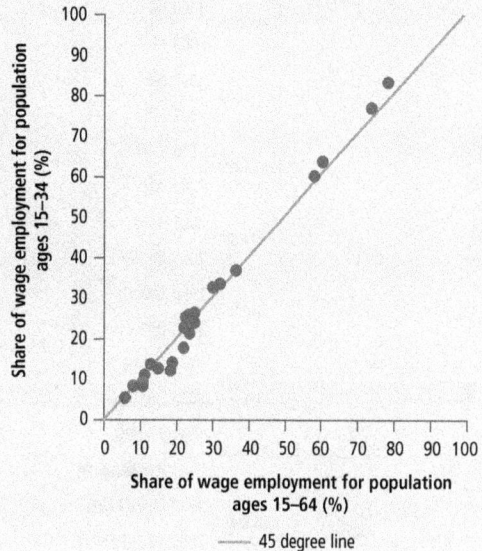

Source: Based on household and labor force surveys.

Figure 6.3 Services form the largest share of nonfarm wage employment; within manufacturing, the food and textile industries dominate

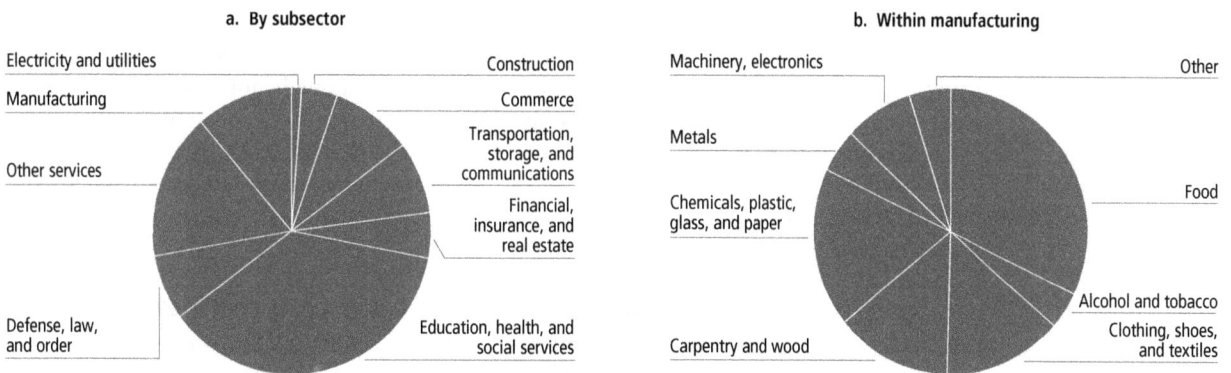

a. By subsector

b. Within manufacturing

Source: Based on standardized and harmonized household and labor force surveys (see appendix).

omies. An agglomeration economy can arise when many input suppliers locate in industrial clusters, and the resulting competition between suppliers reduces input costs for the exporting industry. Knowledge spillovers across firms located near each other constitute another

Figure 6.4 Africa's modern wage manufacturing sector continues to have a small share in employment

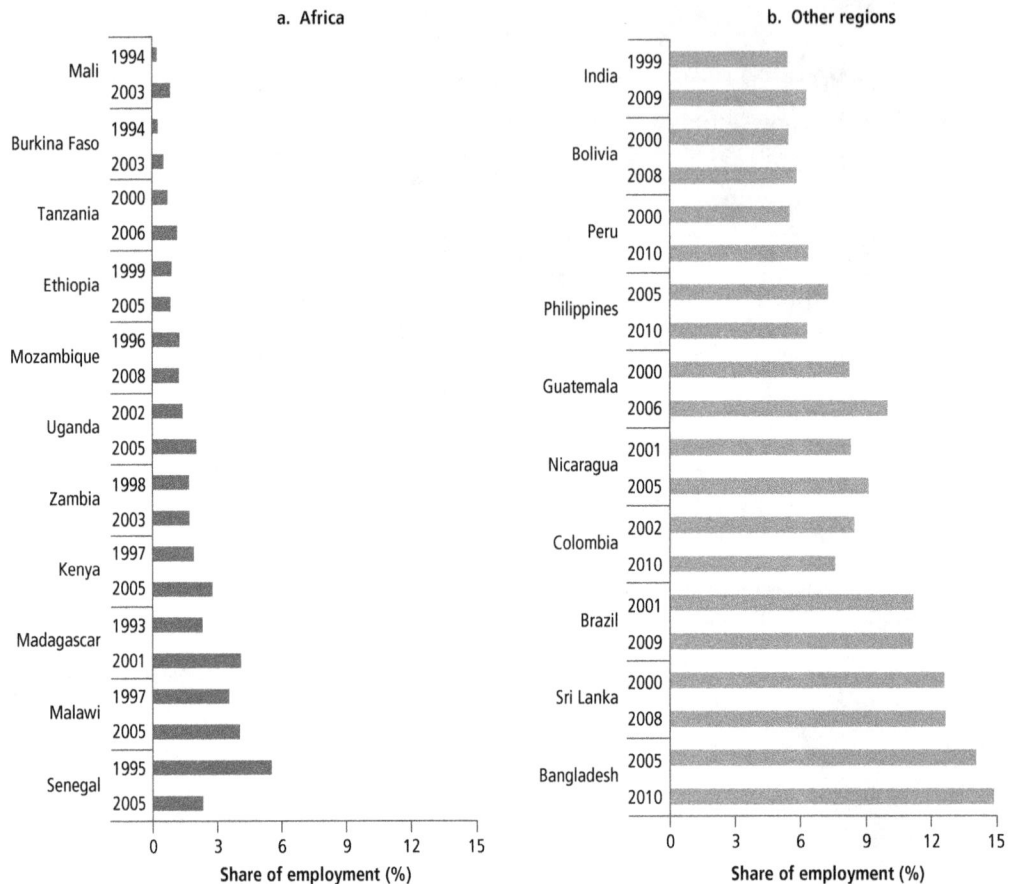

Source: Based on household and labor force surveys.

potential agglomeration economy (Fujita, Krugman, and Venables 1999). The development of India's high-tech information technology clusters is a case in point.

Third, productivity at the firm level is now seen as a key determinant of international trade patterns. Firms in the same industry but located in different countries can both export, provided they are productive by international standards and can profitably charge competitive prices.[3] Firms within the same industry can also vary significantly in their level of productivity. The implication is that, aside from resource endowments and factors that broadly influence comparative advantage across sectors, there are other factors, perhaps equally important, that determine competitiveness at the firm level.

Thus comparative advantage in extractive industries alone is not an inevitable outcome of Africa's resource endowments. The question then becomes whether other sectors, particularly manufacturing, can become internationally competitive.

Unit Labor Costs as a Measure of Manufacturing Competitiveness

One measure of Africa's manufacturing competitiveness is how much an industry has to pay workers for producing each unit of output. The specific measure used here is unit labor costs—wages divided by labor productivity (output per worker)—which are a more comprehensive measure of competitiveness than labor productivity or wages alone. Lower unit labor

Figure 6.5 **African firms export relatively little**

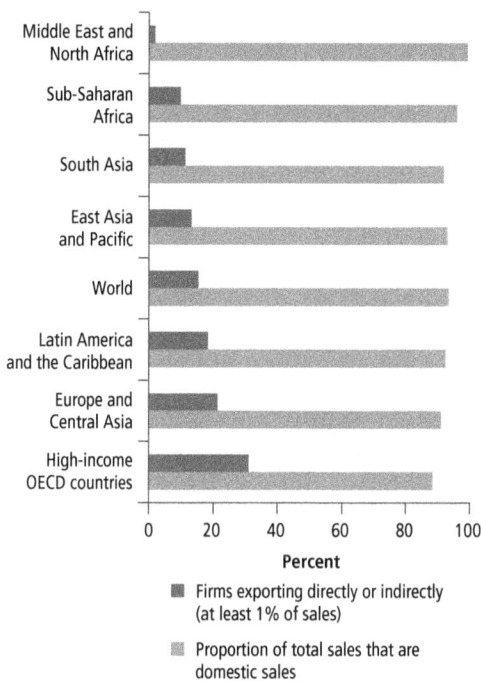

- ■ Firms exporting directly or indirectly (at least 1% of sales)
- ▨ Proportion of total sales that are domestic sales

Source: Based on World Bank enterprise surveys.

costs indicate a higher degree of competitiveness (although unit labor costs have potential limitations as a single indicator of competitiveness; see box 6.2).

China's experience illustrates how growth in manufacturing depends on maintaining international competitiveness. Between 1980 and 2007, China's manufacturing workforce grew threefold, from 24 million to 72 million (figure 6.6, panel b). For a long time, the exceptional performance of China's manufacturing industries benefited from China's low wages relative to the rest of the world—including Africa. As employment started to expand, so did wage rates, which quadrupled between the early 1980s and 2007. But even as China was losing its labor cost advantage, its labor productivity grew at a rate that compensated for this cost increase, leaving unit labor costs virtually unchanged. As shown in figure 6.6 (panel b), China's unit labor costs remained below those of other emerging economies throughout that period.

Box 6.2

Measurement issues and other limitations of unit labor costs

Unit labor costs—labor costs per worker divided by labor productivity or *real* (physical) output per worker—have some limitations as a measure of competitiveness. For instance, the unit labor costs in a shirt-making firm are its wages divided by the number of shirts produced per worker. However, the analysis in this chapter approximates labor productivity by value added per worker, where value added is revenue minus the cost of raw materials. This is standard practice when measuring labor productivity, and it is largely unavoidable, given that physical output is difficult to measure and to compare or aggregate across firms producing different goods.

Revenue and value added depend on both physical output and prices. Using revenue and value added instead of physical output can artificially inflate the measurement of productivity when firms charge higher prices than they would be able to charge in perfectly competitive markets (that is, a *price mark-up*). To the extent that high value added reflects a firm's ability to charge high prices because of low market competition, it will overstate that firm's competitiveness in international markets. If domestic market competition is rel-

atively weak in Africa, then its competitiveness will be overestimated by revenue-based measures of labor productivity.

To account for price effects, revenue or value added per worker is deflated by an aggregate industry-level price index. Although this practice adjusts for changes in prices over time, it does not adjust for differences in price mark-ups across firms in the same industry. Nor does it adjust for differences in mark-ups across countries.

Another limitation of unit labor costs is that a firm's competitiveness depends on total costs per unit of output, not just on labor costs. If the costs of other "indirect" inputs (such as water and electricity) are similar across the countries being compared, then labor costs per unit of output are what really matter. Evidence that African firms pay relatively more for indirect inputs than firms in other developing countries suggests, however, that unit labor costs overstate the competitiveness of African firms compared to firms in other developing countries.

Sources: Clarke 2011; Eifert, Gelb, and Ramachandran 2008.

Figure 6.6 China's unit labor costs have remained below those of other emerging economies

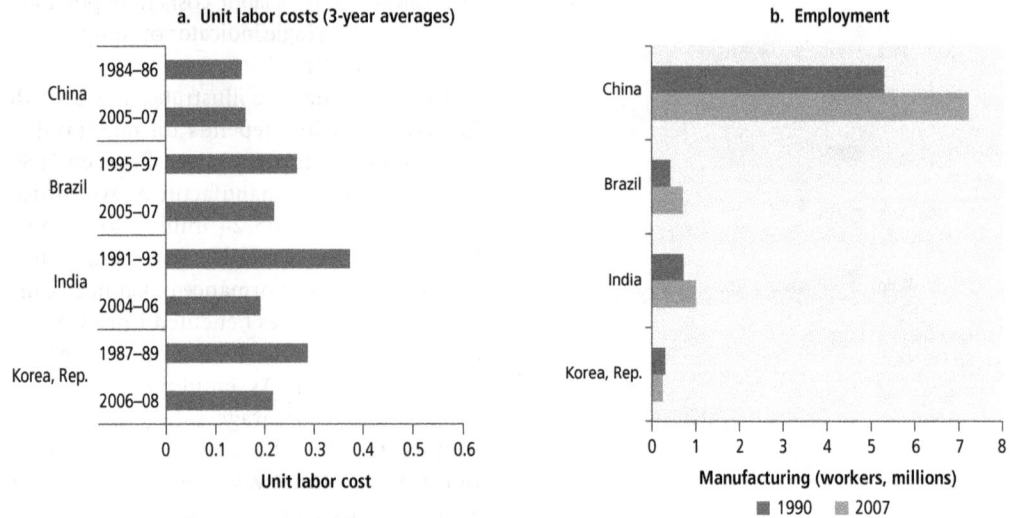

a. Unit labor costs (3-year averages)

b. Employment

Source: UNIDO statistics.

Manufacturing Is Not Competitive in Most African Countries

Comparing trends in manufacturing employment and unit labor costs across Africa and emerging economies can help to determine whether African countries are competitive or on their way to becoming competitive. The comparison with China is especially important, because China maintains the lowest unit labor costs among large emerging economies and has a large export presence in most industries. Potential large competitors such as India seem to be reaching for similarly low unit labor costs. Because China's market penetration is so widespread, even African firms considering exporting to nearby markets must maintain competitiveness with China. Seen through this lens, the manufacturing sector in most African countries is not competitive, although some countries may have reached competitive levels of unit labor costs. As labor costs rise elsewhere in the world—especially in China—they may create an opening for African manufacturing.

The countries selected for review are reasonably representative of Sub-Saharan Africa. They include low-income (Ethiopia, Kenya, Malawi, and Tanzania) and middle-income (Cameroon, Ghana, and Senegal) countries; resource-rich (Cameroon and Ghana) countries; countries

from West and East Africa; and countries with large and small populations. Data for this sample are compared to data for emerging economies, particularly China.

Growth in manufacturing employment since 1990 has been inconsistent in these African countries (figure 6.7). Ethiopia and Kenya saw significant growth. Although small relative to total employment, manufacturing employment in Ethiopia increased from 82,000 in 1990 to 135,000 in 2007; over the same period, manufacturing employment in Kenya grew from 188,000 to 256,000. Cameroon, Ghana, and Malawi also experienced growth, though to a lesser extent. In contrast, Malawi, Senegal, and Tanzania saw relatively little change in the size of the manufacturing workforce.

Figure 6.8 depicts unit labor costs across the sample of African countries and three important emerging economies (Brazil, China, and India). As with manufacturing employment, trends in unit labor costs are mixed in Africa, suggesting that some countries could become competitive.

Based on the limited data available, Ghana appears to have unit labor costs that are comparable to those in Brazil, China, and India. Ghana's level of unit labor costs is consistent with its growing level of manufacturing employment. Ethiopia too has low unit labor

Figure 6.7 Growth in manufacturing wage employment has been inconsistent across African countries

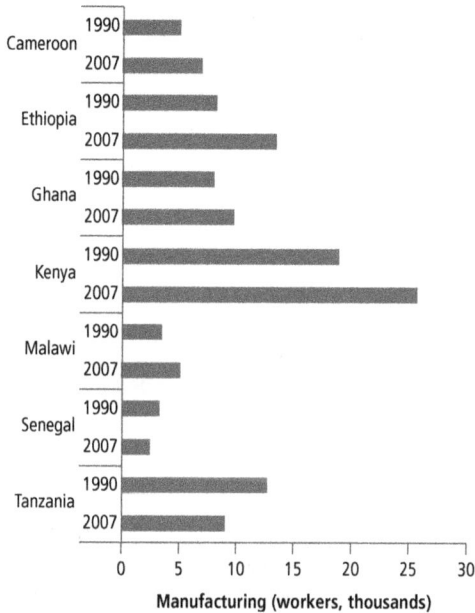

Source: UNIDO statistics.

Figure 6.8 Based on unit labor costs, some African countries could become competitive with other emerging economies

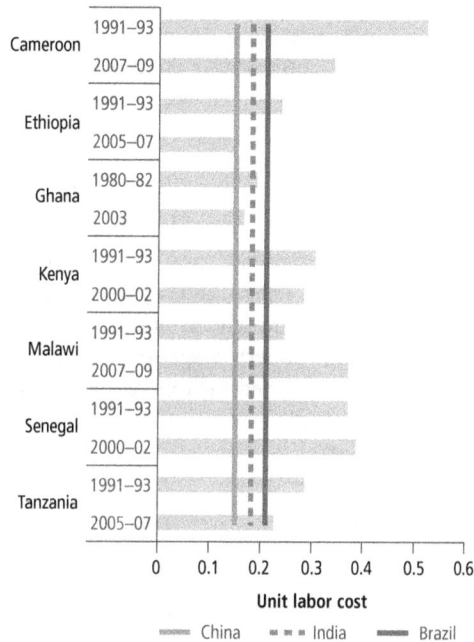

Source: UNIDO statistics.
Note: The vertical lines show current unit labor costs in China, India, and Brazil.

costs, and the years in which manufacturing rapidly created jobs in Ethiopia coincided with a sharp decline in unit labor costs. In recent years, Ethiopia and Ghana have maintained unit labor costs almost on par with historical levels in China and well below levels in other major emerging-market economies, including Brazil and India.

Consistent with their disappointing growth in manufacturing employment, Senegal and Tanzania have higher unit labor costs compared to the large emerging economies. Tanzanian unit labor costs have declined in recent years, but they are not yet lower than those in Brazil, China, or India. Senegal's unit labor costs have remained high for a long time.

The association between unit labor costs and employment trends has some exceptions. Unlike Ethiopia and Ghana, Kenya has seen significant growth in manufacturing employment despite having higher unit labor costs than the large emerging economies. Similarly, manufacturing employment has grown in Cameroon and Malawi, even though their unit labor costs have been relatively high in recent years.

Other approaches to measuring competitiveness consistently suggest that Africa is less competitive than other developing regions. For example, in the World Economic Forum's Global Competitiveness Index, which defines competitiveness as "the set of institutions, policies, and factors that determine the level of productivity of a country," African countries clearly rank the lowest among developing countries (World Economic Forum 2012). In the World Bank's Doing Business index, which focuses largely on the regulatory environment, Sub-Saharan Africa ranks the lowest as well (World Bank 2012b).

Is manufacturing creating jobs in some countries?

Growth in total manufacturing employment has been disappointing in Malawi, Senegal, and Tanzania, but their wood-processing industries (excluding furniture) have created jobs. In Malawi, the furniture industry and the rubber and plastics industry have also created jobs. This information suggests that industry-specific factors, and not just national determinants, also matter for manufacturing growth.

Some industries have done well in several countries, while others have fared poorly. The number of jobs in the food, beverage, and wood-processing industries (and to a lesser extent the rubber and plastics industry) has grown substantially in Cameroon, Ethiopia, Ghana, and Kenya. The rubber and plastics industry has generated jobs in Cameroon, Ethiopia, Ghana, Kenya, and Malawi. In contrast, the textile and leather industries have been shedding modern wage jobs in almost every country analyzed for this report, except for Ethiopia (leather and leather goods) and Kenya (textiles).

These findings do not imply that certain industries are destined to do well regardless of the country context. For instance, although the furniture industry has recently created thousands of new jobs in Ethiopia, Ghana, Kenya, and Malawi, it has contracted steadily over the past two decades in Cameroon, Senegal, and Tanzania.

Instead, these findings indicate that industries do well when they are competitive. With some exceptions, employment trends in a given industry tend to mirror trends in its unit labor costs. For instance, the textile industry in Africa has higher unit labor costs than its counterparts in China and India, and it is losing jobs. Similarly, the leather industry has high unit labor costs in most African countries examined here, except for Ethiopia. In contrast, unit labor costs in the food-processing industry, which has created thousands of jobs in several African countries in recent years, compare favorably with those in emerging economies like China and India.

Low Wages Are Not Enough: Productivity Is the Linchpin of Competitiveness for Africa

Can African countries become competitive on the basis of low labor costs alone? It seems unlikely. African countries do not have a uniform wage advantage over other developing regions (figure 6.9). Although median labor

Figure 6.9 Africa does not have a uniform wage advantage over other developing regions

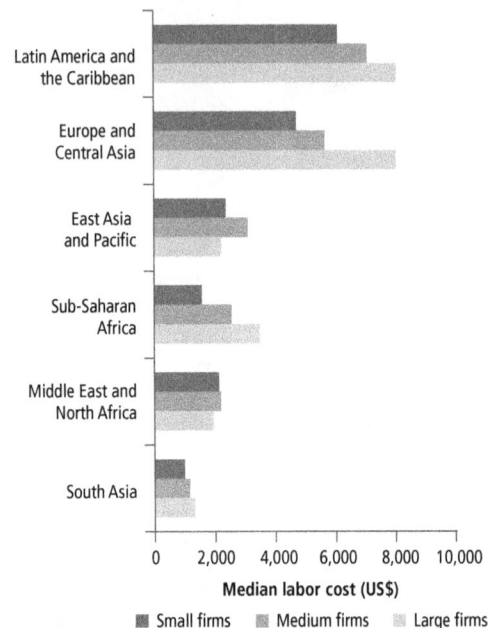

Source: Based on World Bank enterprise surveys.
Note: The figure shows median labor costs (per full-time employee per year in constant U.S. dollars) across firms. Costs are based on surveys conducted in selected countries during 2008–10.

costs in small and medium-size firms are slightly lower than in East Asia and the Pacific, they are similar to those in South Asia. Median labor costs in large firms in Africa are higher even than those in East Asia and the Pacific, which is significant because large firms tend to be the leading exporters in export-oriented industries.

Some African countries have a wage advantage over China and India, but it is more than offset by low labor productivity. Even though wages have been rising faster in China and India than anywhere in Africa over the past two decades, Africa is not closing the unit labor cost gap with them, because labor productivity has not been rising as fast in Africa as in China and India.

If Africa cannot compete with large emerging economies like China or India, could it compete with smaller developing countries on the strength of low wages? Again, it seems unlikely. Wages are not lower in African coun-

Box 6.3

Does Africa really have a labor cost advantage?

As labor costs in manufacturing continue to rise in China, a common observation is that other developing countries with lower labor costs will be poised to compete with China (Lin and Monga 2011). Wages are expected to be lower in countries with significantly lower per capita incomes than China, including African countries. Recent research using firm-level data seems to contradict that view, however, suggesting that industrial labor costs in Africa are far higher than might be expected solely on the basis of gross domestic product (GDP) per capita (Gelb, Meyer, and Ramachandran 2013). Labor costs per worker are nearly 80 percent higher in firms in African countries than in firms in other countries at the same level of GDP per capita.

These findings are partly explained by an "enclave effect": compared with countries at the same income levels in other regions, African countries have an enclave of manufacturing firms that have high labor productivity and pay high wages. But even after adjusting for this effect, African firms face nearly 50 percent higher labor costs.

Higher labor costs could be explained by labor market factors such as regulation and unionization, but on average indicators of labor market regulation do not differ significantly between African countries and the comparators. Another explanation is that prices are generally higher in African countries. This explanation is supported by a comparison of price levels, so it is possible that firms in Africa have to pay relatively high wages to compensate workers for the relatively high cost of living.

In turn, the high cost of living could result from the dominance of resource-based industries in Africa. High prices are a typical feature of resource-abundant countries, because the high income from resources raises the price of nontraded goods, including labor. These interactions are often cited to explain why resource-rich countries tend to perform so poorly when they rely on export-led growth alone (Sachs and Warner 2001).

Larger firms, in particular, pay higher wages in African countries. Research based on matched employer-employee data from 10 African countries suggests that larger firms pay higher wages partly because labor management is especially problematic in Africa, which has a much higher supervisor to worker ratio than elsewhere (Fafchamps and Soderbom 2006).

tries than in other developing countries with similar levels of per capita income. The exact reasons for this difference are unknown, although some plausible hypotheses have been put forward (box 6.3). Given the difficulty of lowering wages in dollar terms, the inescapable conclusion is that labor productivity is the linchpin of competitiveness in Africa. This conclusion is particularly relevant for resource-rich countries, where wages are driven up by the high cost of living.

Sources of Productivity Gaps in African Manufacturing

To understand how African manufacturing can become internationally competitive, it is necessary to pry labor productivity open and examine its component parts. This section examines components of labor productivity in a group of developing countries, including many from Africa, using firm-level data collected by the World Bank's enterprise surveys.[4] To avoid complications arising from technological differences across industries, the analysis focuses on the textile industry, which is generally oriented toward exports and therefore more comparable across countries than domestically oriented industries.

The firm-level data show that labor productivity is particularly low in Africa, especially in the region's low-income countries.[5] Figure 6.10 illustrates this point by showing sales per worker, a measure of labor productivity, in the textile industry. For example, the annual turnover per employee in Tanzania's textile industry is just US$9,000, compared to US$25,000 in Malaysia's garment industry.

Labor productivity is low in Africa's low-income countries partly because workers are not as well equipped with fixed capital (that is, plant and machinery) as their counterparts elsewhere in the world, such as China, Malaysia, Mexico, and Thailand (figure 6.11). The typical textile manufacturer in China, for

Figure 6.10 Labor productivity is particularly low in low-income African countries

Sales per worker in the textile industry

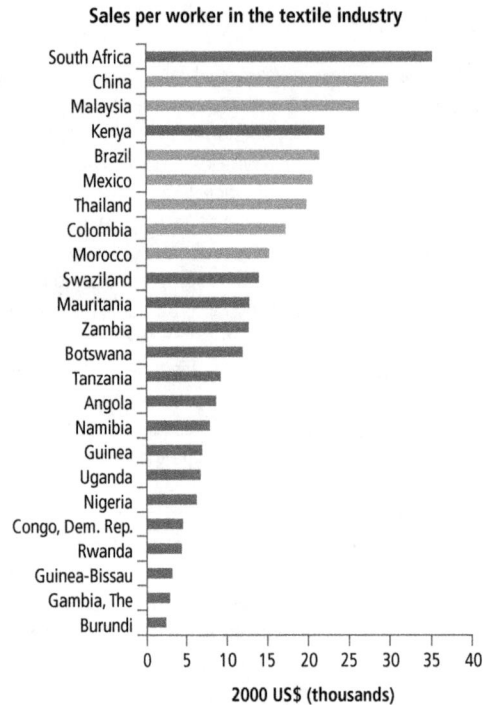

2000 US$ (thousands)

Source: World Bank enterprise surveys, 2002–08.

Figure 6.11 African workers are not as well equipped with fixed capital as their counterparts elsewhere in the world

Fixed assets per worker in the textile industry

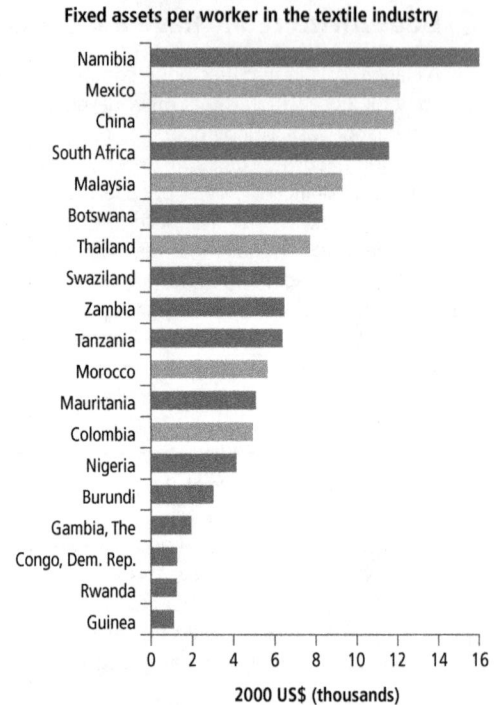

2000 US$ (thousands)

Source: World Bank enterprise surveys, 2002–08.

example, equips every worker with twice as much plant and equipment as a manufacturer in Tanzania.

Why does African manufacturing use so little capital per worker? A major reason for low capital intensity in Africa is that African firms do not have access to the same supply of capital as their counterparts in China.[6] Although access to international capital is particularly important to African manufacturing (given low per capita incomes), studies of international capital flows suggest that Africa and other developing regions have limited access to international capital markets (see, for example, Kalemli-Ozcan, Alfaro, and Volosovych 2008).[7] Imperfections in Africa's domestic credit markets, discussed later, are also likely to be worsening their access to capital.

A low level of fixed capital can only partly explain why output per worker is so much lower in most African countries than else-

where. The difference in fixed capital between firms from Africa and those from other parts of the world is not as great as the difference in output (figure 6.11). For instance, the difference in fixed assets between Tanzanian and Chinese textile firms is significantly lower than the difference in output. Namibian textile firms produce significantly lower output per worker than their Chinese counterparts but have similar levels of fixed assets.

Even with the same level of plant and machinery, it is possible that workers in one country cannot produce as much as those in another. A range of factors other than plant and machinery affect labor productivity. Some of these factors are internal to a given firm, such as the quality of management. Others are external, such as the quality of infrastructure. In general, these other factors are less concrete than plant and machinery and difficult to quantify. To distinguish them from machinery and other

Figure 6.12 African countries have lower productivity than other regions

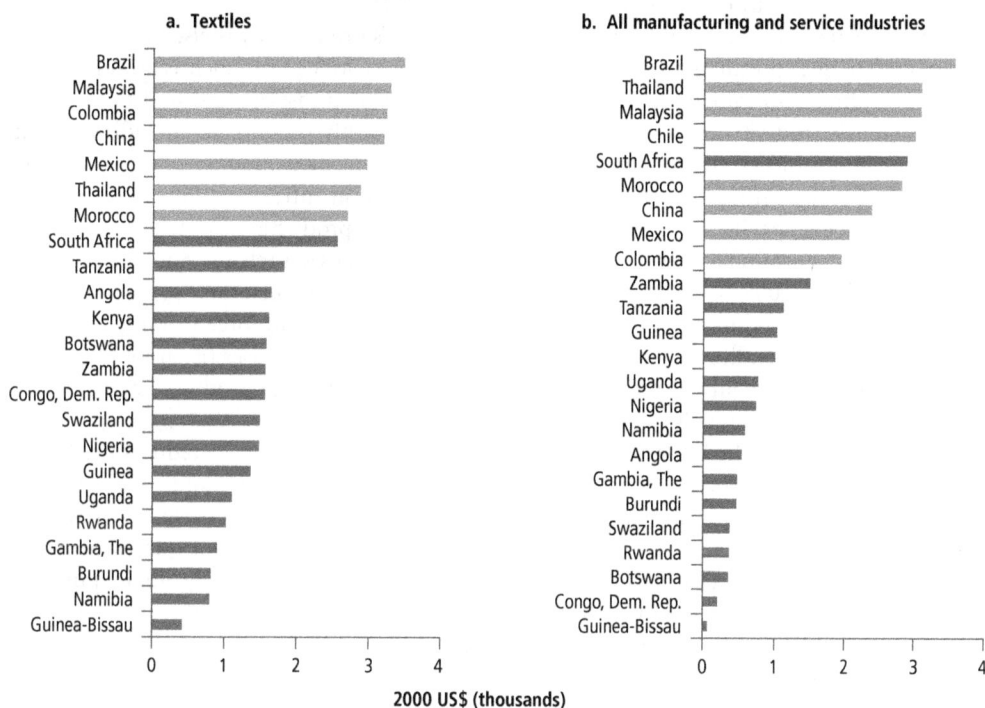

a. Textiles

b. All manufacturing and service industries

2000 US$ (thousands)

Source: Based on World Bank enterprise surveys, 2002–08.

concrete inputs, these factors are often lumped together under the term "productivity" (as opposed to labor productivity).[8]

Since the individual components of productivity cannot be measured directly, their net effect is simply inferred as that part of total output which cannot be explained by the level of measured inputs such as labor, plant, and machinery. Estimated as this residual, productivity is known to account for a large part of the difference in output per worker across countries (Hall and Jones 1999).

When accounting for the difference in labor productivity between African and Chinese firms, productivity is found to be responsible for a larger share of the gap than fixed assets. As figure 6.12 shows, the shortfall in productivity in Tanzania's textile industry relative to China's is slightly larger than its shortfall in fixed assets. This productivity gap between African and Chinese firms persists throughout a range of manufacturing industries and services (figure 6.12, panel b).

What Determines Productivity at the Firm Level?

Although productivity is often equated with production technology, it should be interpreted more broadly. The quality of a firm's management and its organizational efficiency (which includes elements such as the quality of factory floor and workplace organization, workforce incentive and supervision structures, and supply chain management) also contribute to productivity. Productivity is influenced by elements of a firm's human and knowledge capital, which cannot be captured in data on the formal qualifications of its workforce. For example, firm-specific skills generated by on-the-job learning and training for the workforce can make employees more productive. Knowledge and tacit technology, such as a more efficient production process developed through internal research and development (R&D), are other firm-level components of productivity, as are computerized processes and databases tailored to a firm's needs. Firms often become more productive by adapting a technology to their context—whether through trial and error or a more formal R&D process—and such adaptation also raises productivity.

Understanding how much these specific factors matter to productivity is very relevant for policy.[9] Some studies attempt to unpack productivity by examining how much firms *spend* on acquiring specific types of human, knowledge, or organizational capital (Corrado, Hulten, and Sichel 2005; OECD 2010). For instance, a new production process could be the result of R&D expenditures incurred over many years. While the quality of the new production process itself is difficult to quantify, it is likely to be reflected in the R&D expenditure incurred to develop the process. In developed countries, such spending on human, knowledge, or organizational capital is at least as high as spending on plant and machinery. It is not as high in the two emerging economies where attempts have been made to measure it (Brazil and China), but it is still quite sizable and rising. These differences suggest that variation in firms' human, knowledge, and organizational capital could account for a large part of the productivity gap between Africa and other

parts of the world (Hao and Hulten 2011; Dutz et al. 2012).

A firm's productivity is also affected by factors external to the firm, such as the quality and reliability of transport and logistics systems and the supply of utilities, including power, telecommunications, and water services.[10] Poor transportation infrastructure can reduce the efficiency of production by making the supply of raw materials less reliable. Similarly, an inadequate and unreliable utility supply can interrupt production and force workers to remain idle. In effect, it increases the amount of labor and capital needed to produce a given level of output.

Poor infrastructure also reduces productivity by forcing firms to adopt inefficient and costly coping mechanisms. Firms may have to compensate for the poor quality of public services on their own; they might purchase generators as back-ups for the public electricity supply, for example. A recent study shows that costs related to infrastructure services account for a relatively high share of firms' costs in poor African countries, thus imposing an extra burden on the competitiveness of African firms (Eifert, Gelb, and Ramachandran 2008). Figure 6.13 shows firm-level indicators of the quality of transport, water, and electricity supply in different parts of the world. Along with South Asia, the Middle East, and North Africa, Sub-Saharan Africa is generally near the bottom of the rankings.

Figure 6.13 Africa fares poorly in firm-reported indicators of transport, water, and electricity supply

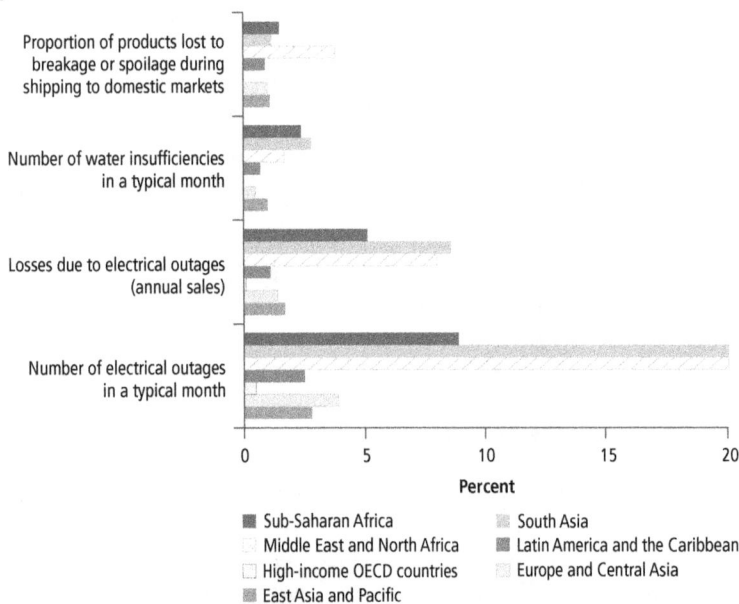

Source: Based on World Bank enterprise surveys.

How Unproductive Firms Survive and Hurt Industry-Level Competitiveness

One way to raise an industry's competitiveness is to make all of its firms more productive. Another way is to let competition between firms run its course and ensure that only the most productive firms thrive. The latter is signifigant because differences in productivity across firms in the same industry can be surprisingly large, especially in developing countries (Syverson 2011; Banerjee and Duflo 2005). According to one study on China and India, if manufacturing plants are ranked according to their productivity, those near the top of the rankings produce about five times more with the same amount of labor and capital as those

Figure 6.14 Decomposing textile industry productivity

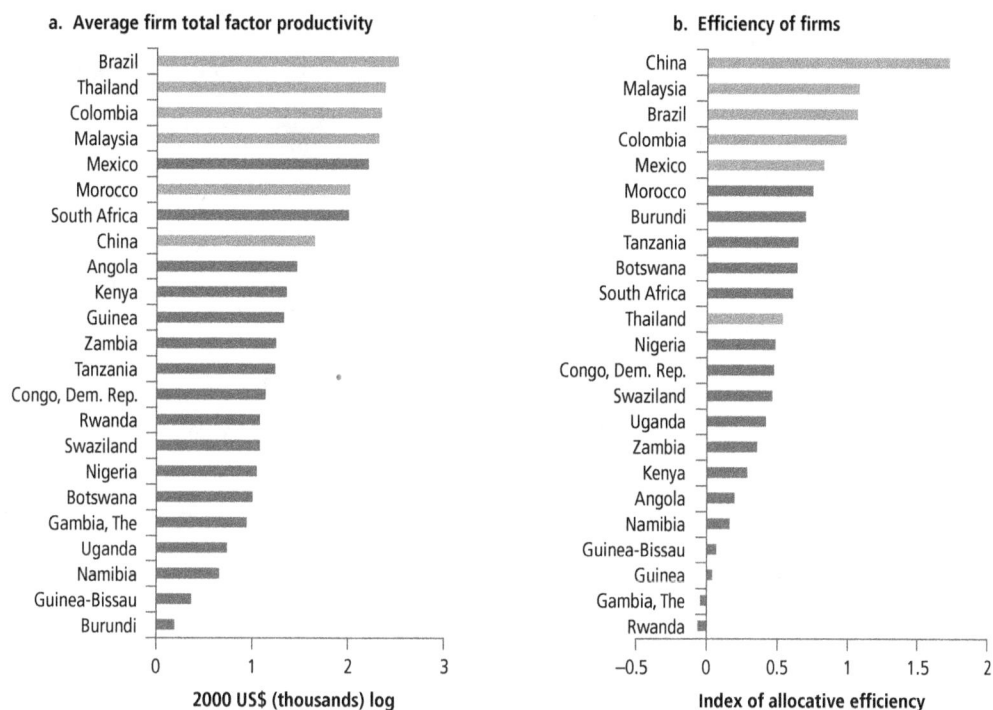

a. Average firm total factor productivity

b. Efficiency of firms

Source: Based on World Bank enterprise surveys, 2002–08.

near the bottom (see, for example, Hsieh and Klenow 2009). A reallocation of workers from the least to the most productive firm in an industry would thus raise the productivity of the industry fivefold.

Indeed, an increase in competition in an industry is often seen to result in such reallocation, or shifting, of labor and other inputs from less to more productive firms. Conversely, market distortions that reduce competition tend to protect the market share of less productive firms, which in turn reduces the (aggregate) productivity of the industry.

The productivity of an industry is the sum total of the productivity of firms in it. Thus an industry could be more productive in Country A than in Country B for two reasons. The first is that, relative to Country A, the typical firm in Country B may be less productive.[11] The second is that, compared to Country A, less productive firms may control a larger share of the market in Country B. The net productivity dif-

ference between countries can be decomposed into these two components.[12]

How much of Africa's lower productivity is due to the lower productivity of the typical firm, and how much is due to the fact that less productive firms are more likely to survive and maintain outsized market shares? Figure 6.14 illustrates these components of productivity for the textile industry in a sample of countries, including some in Africa. This case is typical of most manufacturing and service sectors, and it shows that the greater survival and abnormally large share of unproductive firms ("allocative inefficiency") in Africa explain a large part of the productivity gap between African economies and emerging economies such as Brazil and China.

For example, about one-third of the productivity gap between the textile industries in Tanzania and China is explained by the fact that the average Chinese textile firm is more productive than its Tanzanian counterpart. The other two-thirds of the gap is explained by the fact that in Tanzania, unlike China, unproductive firms have captured too much market share. A comparison of South Africa and China illustrates the significance of this allocative efficiency even more strongly. The average productivity of South African textile firms is actually higher than that of their Chinese counterparts, but this advantage is completely overturned by the dominance of unproductive firms within South Africa.

Potentially, several market distortions could explain why unproductive firms are more likely to survive and maintain inefficiently large market shares in Africa. Credit market inefficiency is a case in point. In the short run, a working capital constraint can prevent a relatively productive firm from producing as much as it profitably could.[13] Credit constraints can also prevent a productive young firm from investing in fixed capital and growing to its optimal size. Larger, older incumbents may have easier access to credit, even if they are less productive. Similarly, political favoritism—such as preferential access to land or other inputs granted to politically connected firms—can enable unproductive firms to capture a large market share.

Regulations can also affect allocative efficiency. For example, labor market regulations can prevent the allocation of labor to its most productive uses by hampering the movement of labor across firms.[14]

Entry barriers (such as high costs or onerous procedures for establishing a new enterprise) can also enable unproductive firms to sustain large market shares by preventing competition from entrants who could be more productive. A reduction in entry barriers can reallocate resources away from unproductive incumbents and toward more productive entrants (Chari 2011).

From the Factory to the Market: How Poor Trade Logistics Hurt Africa's Competitiveness

When it is costly to transport goods from the factory to international markets, an otherwise productive industry can become uncompetitive in those markets. Africa does poorly on this dimension of competitiveness (figure 6.15).

Figure 6.15 Trading across borders is expensive and slow in Africa

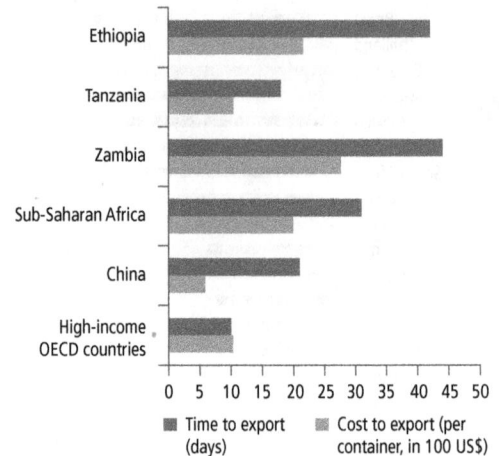

Source: World Bank Doing Business indicators, 2012.

It costs 60 percent more to ship to the United States from Djibouti than from China and about the same to ship to Europe, despite the much greater distance from China. The costs of inland transportation from the factory to ports are also high. A World Bank study estimates that higher shipping and inland transportation costs add a 2.5 percent production cost penalty for textiles in Ethiopia and Zambia (Dinh et al. 2012).

Export competitiveness is also affected by port and terminal handling fees, customs clearance and technical control fees, costs of document preparation and letters of credit, and the cost of foreign exchange. These additional trade costs are exceptionally high in Africa, adding a 5.5 percent production cost penalty for textiles in Ethiopia and Zambia, for example.

Making African Firms Competitive: Priorities for Improving the Business Climate and Workforce Skills

Making modern enterprises more competitive by increasing their productivity is critical for creating more modern wage jobs that are accessible to Africa's youth. Increasing productivity involves a complex set of reforms and interventions. The most important measures include broad interventions that foster improvement in the business environment by ensuring macroeconomic and political stability, strengthening infrastructure services, reducing trade barriers, and improving access to finance and more localized interventions that promote competitive industrial clusters. Such measures must be complemented by steps to improve the human capital of young people, making them more employable and productive.

Because the range of potential reforms and interventions is so large, this section identifies the priority areas. Actions within each area are classified according to whether they are easier to implement but have a lower impact (typically those that seek to correct a market failure) or are much harder to implement but have a higher impact (typically those that correct a government failure).

Providing a Stable Macroeconomic Framework

Macroeconomic uncertainty and volatility, such as fluctuations in the cost of borrowing abroad and changes in inflation and exchange rates, disrupt lending and investment. The volatility of key macroeconomic indicators is quite pronounced in Africa, because primary commodities constitute such a large share of exports and because government finances depend so greatly on trade in those commodities. Macroeconomic shocks appear to disrupt credit flows more frequently, with greater force, in African countries than in countries where production is more diversified.

When the World Bank assessed Zambia's business environment in 2003, it found that firms faced an extremely high cost of borrowing, which appeared to be strongly related to high rates of inflation and currency volatility at that time (World Bank 2004). When the Bank revisited the country with a second assessment in 2007, the situation was radically different. A large debt relief program and a copper price boom had dramatically reduced government borrowing and helped to stabilize the currency. Real interest rates had dropped sharply, and as the inflation rate fell to single digits, business lending expanded. In 2007, less than 15 percent

of survey respondents regarded macroeconomic instability as a major obstacle to business growth, compared to 80 percent of respondents surveyed in 2003 (World Bank 2009). These encouraging conditions deteriorated in the wake of the 2008 global recession, demonstrating that the structure of the Zambian economy (like the economies of other resource-rich countries in the region) is especially vulnerable to the forces of macroeconomic instability. Maintaining price and exchange stability and bringing government borrowing under control over the long term are critical to the smooth functioning of finance and business investment in such countries.

Strengthening Infrastructure Services

The poor quality and inadequacy of physical infrastructure in Africa is the most visible aspect of a deep, pervasive infrastructure problem that inhibits the competitiveness of African firms. The more reassuring aspect of this problem is that governments can begin to address it without building new infrastructure. Evidence points to government failure as the main source of Africa's infrastructure problem, reflected, for example, in the underpricing of electricity and water or the monopoly power of trucking companies. There is also evidence that infrastructure policies and regulations block firms' access to infrastructure services and undermine the incentives for further investment (Briceño-Garmendia and Foster 2010).

Dealing with electricity and other public utility shortages. In countries with chronic shortages in infrastructure services, established businesses report that frequent outages cause significant losses of revenue. Such shortages particularly affect smaller, younger firms and manufacturing firms. Start-ups can wait months to be connected to the public utility grid, a delay that is likely to reduce firm formation and business entry rates.

As electricity shortages have become increasingly common, governments have sought to promote long-term solutions in the form of large investments in maintenance and in additional generating and transmission capacity. Such solutions ignore opportunities for quicker wins through steps to address the causes of underinvestment and inefficiency in the power sector. These include the deliberate underpricing of electricity to subsidize household consumption, the failure of poorly managed state-owned operators to collect payments, and the absence of a workable legal and regulatory framework for private investment.

The specific measures needed to resolve the problem depend on which of these causes is most prevalent in a given country. Regulatory agencies could revise power tariffs. State-owned power companies could be privatized or reorganized on a more commercial footing to improve payment collection and minimize transmission and distribution losses. Countries are often advised to reorganize the industry by separating power generation, transmission, and distribution into independent operations conducted by independent enterprises. Cross-border and regional initiatives to supply power are often encouraged because they entail economies of scale. Initiatives could range from cross-border pooling of power based on existing power grid connectivity among neighboring countries to establishing a regional market in electricity as a component of an integrated regional energy market, as planned in Southern Africa.

Improving transport infrastructure. Inadequate and costly transport infrastructure is by far the most important factor in Africa's exceptionally high trade costs, the fragmentation of the domestic market for manufacturing and service industries, and the region's isolation from other regional and global markets. Inadequate transport infrastructure is a powerful drag on productivity and economic growth, manifested in many ways (the port of Dar es Salaam is one manifestation; see box 6.4). Problems with transport infrastructure not only limit scale economies but also bestow market power on firms already in the trade by removing the threat of foreign competition and preventing potentially more productive firms from entering local markets.

Ultimately, the solution to high transport costs is large-scale investment in road and rail-way networks. But immediate measures to promote more efficient use of the infrastructure that already exists can also help. Nor is government investment the only option for building new networks. Private participation can be expanded if policy reforms create the right conditions. Mozambique, where high transport costs originate with inefficient railway and port services, is both rehabilitating and expanding the network as a long-term solution. At the same time, it is enacting a series of structural reforms to improve operations and encourage private participation in the management of state-owned transport operators. Improving rail services is the key to cutting transport costs in Lesotho, where the chronically dysfunctional rail sector has caused exporters to rely exclusively on road transport, which costs three times as much as rail.

Reducing Barriers to Trade: Trade Liberalization, Costs, and Logistics

When the domestic market for manufacturing and service industries is fragmented or isolated from regional and global markets, it is hard for productivity to grow in those industries.[15] Such conditions insulate incumbent firms from competition (domestic or foreign), reduce the entry of potentially more productive firms, and limit incumbents' incentives to innovate.

A central argument for trade liberalization is that it increases the competitive pressure on domestic firms and encourages them to become more productive. The liberalization of import tariffs by most African countries in the 1990s and early 2000s may have constituted one of the most significant policy developments in Africa's recent economic history. Although there are no systematic assessments of their impact in the region, anecdotes and studies of the effects of similar reforms in other regions suggest that in Africa they could have led to substantial and widespread productivity gains by exposing local producers to greater competitive pressure and reshaping the structure of domestic production.

Recent studies of other developing regions and developed economies report that trade liberalization reforms of the kind that took place in Africa lowered domestic prices and mark-up rates, increasing competitive pressures on the large players in the domestic economy. Those studies also provide evidence that increased openness to trade generates productivity gains in three distinct but complementary ways: by allowing more productive firms to take fuller advantage of their superior productivity and gain market share from unproductive firms, by encouraging innovation and the adoption of better techniques of production, and by facilitating economies of scale (see, for instance, Melitz and Trefler 2012; Krishna and Mitra 1998).

Another, newer argument for import liberalization originates in the increasing frag-

---

Box 6.4

The high price of inefficiency at the port of Dar es Salaam

The Dar es Salaam Port—East Africa's second-largest port after Mombasa—is the conduit for about 90 percent of Tanzanian trade, and it is also a gateway for Tanzania's landlocked neighbors, including Burundi, the Democratic Republic of Congo, Rwanda, Uganda, and Zambia. For Tanzania especially, manufacturing, trade, and economic expansion depend on the efficient movement of goods through the port.

The main agencies involved in the port's operations are the Tanzania Port Authority (TPA), the landlord and service provider; Tanzania International Container Services (TICTS), a private container stevedoring contractor; and the Surface and Marine Transport Authority (SUMATRA), the multisectoral regulatory agency.

The port is not efficient by international or East African standards. In mid-2012, container vessels waited an average of ten days for a berth in Dar es Salaam, compared to less than one day in Mombasa. Merchandise took ten days on average to clear and exit the port, compared to three to four days in Mombasa (and 48 hours in many East Asian ports). Official and unofficial fees are numerous, high, and inconsistently applied. The additional costs incurred by shippers and shipping companies in Dar es Salaam compared to Mombasa are equivalent to an additional tariff of 22 percent on container imports and 5 percent on bulk imports. Compared to the port of Mombasa, inefficiencies at the port of Dar es Salaam cost Tanzania and its neighbors an estimated US$2.5 billion a year. Reforms have been initiated but have progressed very slowly.

Merchandise fails to clear the port rapidly because processes (especially customs clearance) are slow and storage periods are quite long. The rules are not transparent and oversight is poor, creating opportunities for corruption. In Dar es Salaam, where the port charges fees in proportion to the value of the merchandise, official port fees are 74 percent higher than those in Mombasa, where the port charges flat fees. Customs valuations of goods imported via Dar es Salaam also vary more widely than can be explained by normal variations in quality and price. For example, the stated customs values for 1 kilogram of fertilizer ranges from US$0.39 to US$5.00 (the global price is US$0.60–US$0.80), and the ratio between the highest and lowest reported customs values is 152 for rice and 33 for palm oil.

Storage tariffs are structured in ways that discourage rapid clearance of merchandise from inland container depots. After the free storage period of seven days expires, each additional day represents a direct additional profit for TPA, TICTS, and the container depots. TPA's revenues are higher when TICTS is less efficient. When berths managed by TICTS are full, some of the container traffic is redirected to TPA berths, creating a situation in which the landlord of the port (TPA) competes against its own service provider (TICTS). TPA obtained an estimated US$36.5 million in this manner in 2011.

Such arrangements reduce incentives among port operators to invest in increased capacity. While a small, well-connected coterie benefits from the status quo, Tanzanian workers, firms, consumers, and the government bear the costs. An uncompetitive manufacturing sector creates fewer jobs for workers and produces more expensive goods for consumers. Tanzanian agriculture suffers because port inefficiency adds an estimated 5.2 percent to the cost of imported fertilizer. Policy makers may well ask whether making a single large investment to improve efficiency at the port would be better than continuing to subsidize fertilizer year after year.

The cost of inaction is mounting. The port of Dar es Salaam will decline in importance as ports and railways in neighboring countries become operational and prove more efficient. The authorities have been moving to improve port operations, yet more pointed reform is needed, beyond actions to improve infrastructure (such as building new berths). Efficiency-enhancing reforms would ensure that end users are aware of the costs related to the port's inefficiency and participate in decisions related to port reform, strengthen competition among port operators, and reduce corruption through streamlined and transparent procedures and improved oversight.

Source: World Bank 2013b.

mentation of export value chains. The different stages involved in producing a particular final good are now often performed in many different countries, and a country can specialize in specific "tasks" in this value chain. For an African firm to succeed in exporting a manufacturing task, it must be able to import all the complementary upstream tasks as easily as any international competitor that specialize in the same task (Collier and Venables 2007). Import liberalization and other measures to improve access to imported inputs can help African firms to insert themselves in international value chains.

Has Africa experienced benefits similar to those attributed to tariff reductions in other regions? Lower tariff barriers should have made African firms more productive by opening them up to competition and enabling their integration within global value chains. Africa's experience with the Multifiber Agreement suggests that such outcomes did not occur. During the final years of the Multifiber Agreement, the United States imposed strict import quotas on Chinese apparel and awarded duty- and quota-free access to African apparel. If African firms were truly competitive, they should have taken advantage of such preferential access to the U.S. market. African apparel exports did rise, but the rise was temporary and has been attributed to Chinese firms that shifted their final assembly steps to Africa to avoid the quota (Rotunno, Vézina, and Wang 2012).

The productivity benefits of tariff liberalization may have failed to materialize in Africa because the costs of trade remain extremely high for reasons unrelated to tariffs, such as the region's onerous transport costs. Reducing such costs could enable African firms to realize the gains of trade liberalization (Djankov, Freund, and Pham 2010).

Freight costs are often the largest component of trade costs in most countries, implying that investment in transport infrastructure and ports could significantly ease constraints to regional and global trade. Such investment is expensive and will take time. In the short run, tackling nontariff barriers such as inefficient customs administration and high regulatory costs of cross-border transactions would also

significantly reduce trade costs. Many countries could considerably reduce trade costs by simplifying customs clearance and import procedures and increasing the use of inland clearance facilities to shorten processing times.

Land border crossings remain a major obstacle to regional integration in Africa. These obstacles are common along the gateway corridors serving the landlocked countries, and they also hinder regional trade and international transit. Aside from improvements in transport infrastructure, improved management of border crossing through institutional reform and increasing border coordination could also have a major impact on border-crossing times. East Africa's one-stop border post (OSBP) initiative is a step in this direction. A pilot OSBP between Kenya and Uganda seems to have produced dramatic results even in the absence of infrastructure refurbishment (see box 6.5; Fitzmaurice and Hartmann 2013).

Improving Access to Finance

The lack of finance is another serious constraint on the growth of manufacturing and tradable services in Africa (World Bank 2008, 2012c; IFC 2013; see also Dinh, Mavridis, and Nguyen 2012; Harrison, Lin, and Xu 2013; Li, Mengistae, and Xu 2011). Firm surveys suggest that the cause is poor access to formal bank financing (figure 6.16). A survey comparing firms in China to firms in Ethiopia, Tanzania, and Zambia found that the most visible advantage enjoyed by Chinese firms was access to bank finance at favorable conditions, such as low interest rates and low collateral requirements (Fafchamps and Quinn 2012). Expensive or limited financing suppresses growth in productivity by forcing firms to operate at a suboptimal size or to use substandard technologies. Research suggests that many firms cannot take advantage of profitable opportunities for expansion because they cannot obtain financing.[16]

Access to finance varies by type of economic activity and is generally more constrained for smaller and younger firms. In Namibia, for example, banks require small firms (employing fewer than 30 workers) to provide twice the amount of collateral on average as mid-size

Box 6.5

Improving land transportation through increased international cooperation and comprehensive procedural reforms: The Malaba border-crossing pilot

The long-standing response to the chronically slow movement of goods within Africa has been to build better roads and border facilities, but better physical infrastructure alone has not solved the problem. Twenty-five years ago, only 20 percent of Africa's main road network was considered to be in "good" condition. Today, almost half of it is considered good. Border facilities have been remodeled. But a lot of time is still lost at the border, largely due to procedural delays at border crossings.

A more recent approach to resolving border delays is the development of one-stop border posts. OSBPs include more than refurbished facilities; they involve improved coordination between border agencies from neighboring countries and better coordination among the domestic agencies managing aspects of transport and border crossings in each country. Interagency coordination is challenging to achieve, however, and many OSBPs have not met expectations.

The Transit and Transport Coordination Authority of the Northern Corridor has been trying to improve OSBPs in East Africa by gathering better data on their performance. The authority is supported by the Sub-Saharan Africa Transport Policy Program (SSATP), an international partnership for policy reform and capacity building in Africa's transport sectors. Their efforts include border-crossing surveys to gain insight into the reasons for slow border processing and to document the impact of reforms.

During 2011–12, customs authorities in Kenya and Uganda modified selected business procedures related to border crossings. They had a unique opportunity to observe the impact of those reforms, because the Malaba border post between Kenya and Uganda (one of the pilot OSBPs)

was included in a border-crossing survey commissioned by the northern corridor authority.

The survey found that the border crossing at Malaba improved dramatically after the reforms. The average time to cross the border dropped from 24 to 4 hours. The SSATP study estimated that the reforms may have saved up to US$70 million a year. Notably, these results occurred in the absence of infrastructure refurbishment, which is expected to take place at a later stage. What was so special about the Malaba border-crossing reforms?

The primary insight from this case is that simply changing the procedures is probably not sufficient to improve border crossings. Before launching the reforms, the authorities undertook significant preparatory work to build a culture of cooperation across border agencies (within and between the two countries), develop a legal framework enabling that cooperation to take place, and install the information technology infrastructure making it possible to start the documentation process even before trucks arrive at the crossing.

Unlike many other OSBPs, at the Malaba OSBP the reforms targeted all of the key parties involved in border crossings:

- *Border management agencies,* through advance preparation with prearrival lodgment of the customs declaration and better coordination between agencies at the crossing
- *Clearing agents,* through mandatory prearrival lodgment of declarations (which used to be optional and rarely used)
- *Truck drivers,* through traffic and parking rules to ease congestion in the customs zone

Source: Fitzmaurice and Hartmann 2013.

---

firms (World Bank 2010; Barker and Mengistae 2013). This differential access implies that smaller and younger firms are less likely to exploit potentially profitable opportunities than larger and older firms. To the extent that younger firms are a source of innovation and productivity growth, such restrictions pose a particular threat to competitiveness.

To some degree, however, the problems that smaller and less established firms encounter in obtaining credit may reflect the higher costs and risks involved in lending to them. For

banks, the high fixed costs per transaction and difficulty in attaining scale economies make it costlier to lend to smaller firms. As bank managers observed in a survey in Rwanda, the poor quality of financial statements and business plans, lack of business skills, inability to manage risks, and informality of smaller enterprises constitute a big challenge for lenders (World Bank 2012c). These observations suggest that the problem could be remedied partly by improving the management and transparency of firms.

Figure 6.16 African firms use relatively little bank financing

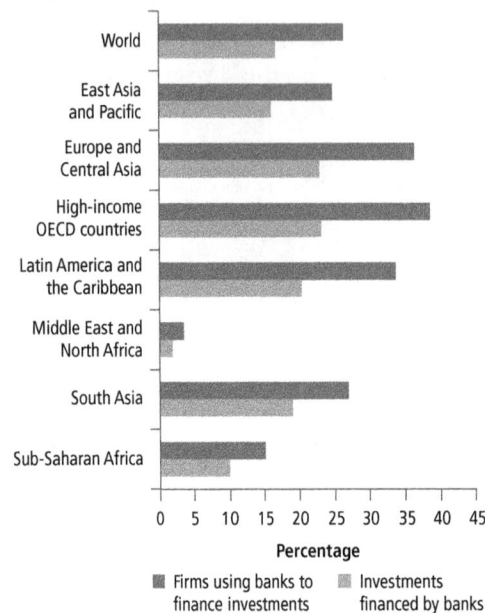

Source: Based on World Bank enterprise surveys.

Even if lending to smaller or younger firms is inherently more difficult, basic policy reforms to address credit market issues will help them. Indeed, reforms will be particularly helpful to smaller and less established firms, because they are the most disadvantaged by credit market imperfections. Critical reforms include steps to make the banking industry more competitive, the development of credit information systems, and better creditor rights.

Making the Banking Industry More Competitive

The banking sector in much of Africa is characterized by a lack of competition (it is dominated by a few large banks) and heavy government involvement (IFC 2013; Bertrand, Schoar, and Thesmar 2007). Measures that would facilitate new domestic and foreign entry into the industry could increase competition, make the lending industry more efficient, and increase the likelihood that banks will find better ways of reaching out to firms. Where government ownership of banking assets is extensive, as in Tanzania, fostering competition may require a reduction in the government's financial stake.

The banking sector should be opened up with care, however, as the system can become more vulnerable when more banks enter and begin to compete. For instance, banks may take on too much risk in more competitive environments. It is also hard to open up the financial system to competition if the supervisory structure is poor. Reforms to improve the institutions that support the financial sector, described next, are more feasible.

Strengthening Credit Information Systems

Well-developed credit information systems have improved access to finance in advanced economies. One reason why collateral requirements or interest charges are so high in some developing economies is that banks have little information on prospective clients, so they set high risk premiums. Credit information systems that permit banks to share customer repayment information can help lenders to evaluate prospective customers and bankable projects (IFC 2013). Most countries in Africa have no credit information system at all. Where credit information systems exist, they tend to be rudimentary, with low coverage of potential borrowers (figure 6.17).

Countries seeking to establish strong credit information systems require new regulations for the licensing, operation, and supervision of credit bureaus. Kenya's credit information system, for instance, significantly improved after 2008, when new regulations were approved on the licensing, operation, and supervision of credit bureaus by Kenya's central bank.[17] By

Figure 6.17 Coverage of credit bureaus is generally low in Africa

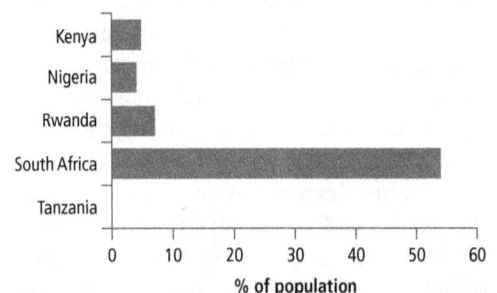

Source: World Bank Doing Business indicators.

2010 and 2011, respectively, the first two credit bureaus had started to operate. The new legislation allowed banks to share negative credit information by obligating banks to report all of the nonperforming loans on their books.

To be truly effective, credit information systems must cover not only all potential borrowers but also all prospective lenders, and they must include both positive and negative information on borrowers. The scope of credit information systems is commonly much more limited in Africa, however. In Zambia, for instance, the credit reference bureau that opened in 2007 has yet to expand its sources to retailers, trade creditors, and utility companies in order to capture a larger share of the population of potential borrowers (World Bank 2009). Similarly, in a survey following the regulatory reform in Kenya, the two most prominent concerns highlighted by the banks were the need to share positive as well as negative information and the need to incorporate the information collected by other providers, such as microfinance institutions and utility companies. The sharing of positive data enables the development of a credit-scoring system, allowing good borrowers to establish a track record and access loans at more favorable interest rates.

Strengthening Contract Enforcement and Creditor Rights Institutions

Legal rights of lenders and borrowers can facilitate the use of collateral and the ability to enforce claims in the event of default. Strong creditor rights can expand the supply of loans by providing legal protection for lenders in cases of nonpayment. The legal system should also allow borrowers to use a broader range of assets as collateral, which should allow them to obtain loans on better terms. These legal rights must also be enforced well in practice. Some of the high risk premiums that banks attach to borrowers in Africa reflect their low confidence in creditor rights and their enforcement. Contract enforcement institutions are particularly weak in most countries in the region, even upper-middle-income countries. For example, banks in Rwanda contend that insolvency and bankruptcy procedures do not function well in practice, despite the new legal framework

passed in 2009 (World Bank 2012c). Angola, Botswana, and Swaziland have among the lowest global scores on the World Bank's Doing Business indicators of contract enforcement, especially the length of time required to enforce a standard contract (World Bank 2011b).

Banks' reliance on real estate and land as prime collateral can further complicate the efforts of smaller enterprises to obtain financing. Banks typically do not use other assets, especially movable assets, as collateral for several reasons. Contract enforcement is weak, the registration of assets is poor, and the legal framework for creditor rights does not adequately support secured transactions in assets. Potential reforms include the introduction of electronic property registration and land titling systems, along with the adoption of a more modern framework of security interests over movable assets. Such a framework would allow banks to register security interests over a wide range of movable assets—including personal property, vehicles, machinery, inventory, raw materials, receivables, and intellectual property—and to enforce claims on those assets as collateral.

Reducing Constraints to the Entry and Growth of Productive Firms: Governance Is Key

A good business environment should facilitate the entry of new firms and the growth of more productive firms. Unproductive firms are pressured either to improve their productivity or to exit, and overall productivity improves.

Credit constraints, poor start-up financing, and high costs of access to public utilities are major barriers to firm entry and expansion in Africa. Another critical influence on firm entry and growth is the quality of governance. Excessive or poorly designed business regulation, corruption, and weak contract enforcement impose high entry and expansion costs, which reduce productivity through their negative effects on entry and competition (Klapper, Laeven, and Rajan 2006; Djankov 2009; see also Xu 2011).

Formal entry requirements are probably the most ubiquitous means by which governments directly regulate entry. Almost everywhere in

Figure 6.18 **Africa has the highest formal costs of setting up a business**

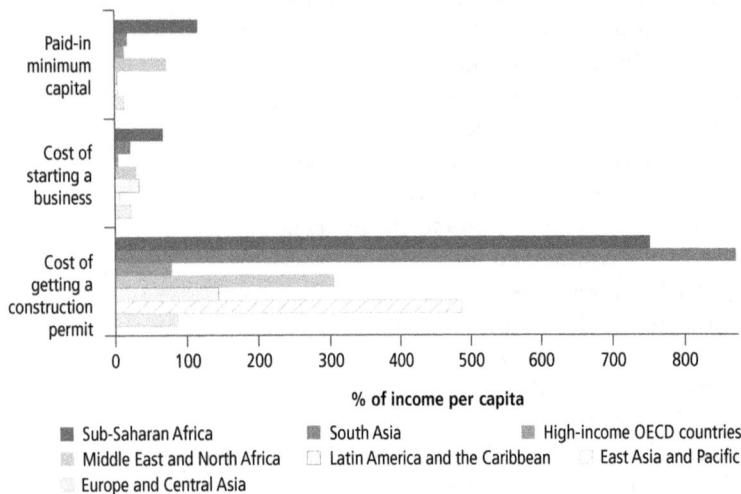

Source: World Bank Doing Business indicators, 2012.
Note: Paid-in minimum capital is the amount that the entrepreneur needs to deposit in a bank or with a notary before registration and for up to three months following incorporation.

The formal cost of setting up the standard business (as a percentage of per capita income) is 105 percent in Angola and 284 percent in the Democratic Republic of Congo, for example. These costs are high by international standards, even compared to South Africa, where the same cost is a mere 0.3 percent of per capita income.

Corruption in the granting of entry licenses and other permits also hinders the setup and expansion of firms, and it must be tackled to strengthen competitive forces in Africa. Survey evidence from Uganda on who has to pay bribes and how much they have to pay suggests that more profitable firms have to pay larger bribes when seeking access to permits, licenses, and public services. By raising costs disproportionately for more productive firms, corruption acts as a tax on efficiency. This same research suggests that if firms have better information and undertake collective action, they can improve their bargaining position when dealing with bribe takers and reduce corruption (box 6.6).

Better governance can also help by strengthening contract enforcement. Poor contract enforcement can constrain the growth of productive firms by making trust more important than efficiency in determining how production is organized. Owners and top management shy away from delegating responsibility to other employees (see, for instance, Cingano and

Africa, anyone setting up a new business needs to obtain an operating license from a local and central government authority and to acquire legal status to engage in certain transactions from the government registrar. Often, various construction permits and site use licenses are required to establish or expand a firm. Usually the time and costs associated with all of these permits and licenses are a substantial share of the overall cost of setting up a business, and they can be prohibitive (World Bank 2011b). On average, the formal costs of setting up a business are higher in African countries than elsewhere in the world (figure 6.18).

Reforms to reduce the start-up and expansion costs linked to regulation should be a priority for improving the business environment in Africa. Many resource-poor countries in Africa have steadily and significantly reduced business start-up costs over the past five years through a series of administrative and legislative reforms. For example, in countries throughout Southern Africa (including Lesotho, Madagascar, Malawi, and Mozambique), start-up costs have converged with or even fallen below those of South Africa, which have always been low by emerging-market standards. In contrast, start-up costs remain very high in some resource-rich countries (figure 6.19; World Bank 2012b).

Figure 6.19 **Business setup costs are higher in resource-rich African countries**

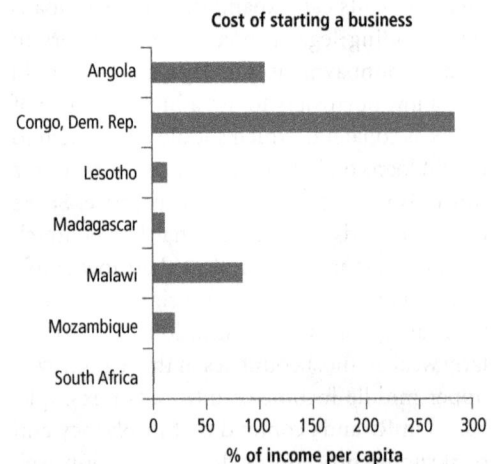

Source: World Bank Doing Business indicators, 2012.

Box 6.6

Who must pay bribes? How much? And does it matter?

Who must pay bribes and how much? A unique set of survey data on corruption, containing quantitative information on the payment of bribes by Ugandan firms, helps to answer these questions. The data have two striking features: not all firms report that they need to pay bribes, and there is considerable variation in reported graft across firms facing similar institutions and policies. These patterns can be explained by differences in control rights and bargaining strength across firms. Firms typically have to pay bribes when dealing with public officials whose actions directly affect their business operations. Such dealings cannot be easily avoided when, for example, a firm must export or import goods or make use of public infrastructure services.

How much must graft-paying firms pay? When the quantitative data on corruption are combined with detailed financial information from the surveyed firms, the size of the bribe that a firm needs to pay depends positively on current and expected future profits and negatively on expected alternative returns to capital. In other words, firms' "ability to pay" and "refusal power" can explain a large part of the variation in bribes across graft-reporting firms. These results suggest that public officials act as price (bribe) discriminators and the prices of public services are determined partly to extract bribes. Moreover, expecting high demand for bribes, a firm might find it profitable to choose a technology with higher operating costs per period and thus lower profits, but one that indirectly reduces the size of the bribe that the firm needs to pay.

Subsequently, researchers used the same data to study the relationship between bribery payments, taxes, and firm growth. Using industry-location averages to circumvent potential problems of endogeneity and measurement errors, they found that the rate of both taxation and bribery is negatively correlated with firm growth. A 1 percentage point increase in the bribery rate is associated with a 3 percentage point reduction in firm growth, an effect that is about three times greater than that of taxation. These results are consistent with the findings from the original research, which suggest that firms' investment and technology decisions are driven partly by the desire to minimize bribe payments, even though the decisions adversely affect gross profits.

The results have clear policy implications. If the size of the bribe that a firm needs to pay is an outcome of a bargaining process, collective action on the part of the business community that strengthens the bargaining position of individual firms may be a successful strategy to reduce the cost of doing business. Potentially effective measures include collecting and disseminating information about corrupt practices; informing the private sector and the public about service standards, guidelines, and norms of major service providers; increasing the ability of individual firms to commit to not paying bribes; and recognizing those who are doing a good job by resisting corruption.

Sources: Svensson 2003; Fisman and Svensson 2007.

Pinotti 2012; Bloom, Sadun, and Van Reenen 2012). Firms also have an incentive to integrate vertically or to enter into contracts only with members of their extended family and social network.

Localized Interventions to Improve the Wider Business Environment

To increase competitiveness, the ultimate policy objective is to improve the overall business environment, but in some cases localized interventions can lay the groundwork for a competitive, modern enterprise sector to emerge. Concentrating public resources in selected clusters of activity is one kind of localized intervention. Such clusters can also be used to introduce incremental reforms in the investment climate, before they are rolled out more broadly.

Firms engaging in similar or linked activities often cluster, because clustering has many potential advantages. Firms in the cluster can learn production and business management techniques from one another.[18] Transport and other types of infrastructure that serve the cluster improve as clusters grow. Together, the firms can attract more consumers, more and better input suppliers, and more skilled workers than they could attract if they were dispersed. Clusters can be especially conducive to the growth of specialized input suppliers. They also help to reduce the cost and raise the quality of specialized inputs. Investments to improve input quality or reduce input costs are less risky for a supplier when several prospective purchasers are present; when there is only one purchaser, the purchaser has the power to bargain those gains away.

In this way, clusters can exhibit "agglomeration economies"—that is, the firms in a cluster can become increasingly productive as the cluster grows and matures. Many of the potential productivity benefits from growing clusters occur through spillovers between firms—for example, firms learn from one another or downstream firms benefit from having several input suppliers located nearby. The gains from being in a cluster thus depend on how many other firms locate there, and every firm that locates in a cluster could be conferring benefits on the other firms in that cluster. A cluster that is not out of the ordinary to start with may become internationally competitive once it is big enough. But when choosing where to locate, firms fail to take this collective benefit into account. This is a form of market failure, so although clusters can emerge spontaneously, they may need some kind of public support to reach a truly competitive size.

Public support may be especially necessary to form clusters in manufacturing and tradable services, given their potential export orientation. Because they are not limited by the size of the domestic market, such clusters can truly exploit the economies of scale from clustering production. As discussed, African firms can integrate with global supply chains by specializing in specific tasks or steps in a value chain. To do so, they must be able to import inputs as easily and cheaply as their international competitors, and must have access to the same high-quality physical infrastructure and supportive regulations. Thus one option for public support is to develop clusters specializing in specific tasks within global value chains.[19]

Box 6.7 looks at the common attributes of 11 successful clusters in Africa. These clusters highlight the role of value chains (linking input suppliers with downstream firms), knowledge flows, ability to attract a skilled workforce, and coordination. All of the clusters had public support, although the form of support varied. A common pattern, however, was the spontaneous rather than publicly engineered inception of the clusters, suggesting that public support should

be concerned mainly with enabling nascent clusters to transition toward self-sustaining growth.

Special economic zones (SEZs) are an increasingly popular vehicle for supporting localized growth, especially in the form of export-oriented clusters. The idea is to support clustering by concentrating public investment (such as infrastructure) and policy reforms in specially marked zones. Some SEZs target locations that are considered to have an inherent advantage for insertion into global value chains, such as areas near ports, but the choice of a high-potential location may not be critical to success: a particular location may have no inherent advantage in a sector or task, but it may acquire comparative advantage as a cluster starts to develop and agglomeration economies arise (Collier and Venables 2007). As the experience of successful clusters in Africa suggests, SEZs should focus on supporting incipient clusters to develop beyond a critical threshold, after which they can sustain themselves. SEZs in Africa have rarely been located around preexisting clusters, which is thought to be one reason that their performance has been less satisfactory than that of SEZs in other developing regions (Farole 2011).

Creating a superior business environment within SEZs reduces the availability of public resources for improving the business climate outside of those areas. If there are significant increasing returns to clustering, then allocating public resources to SEZs is likely to be superior to spreading public resources everywhere to provide services at "a uniformly low level" (Collier and Venables 2007). SEZs do not always fulfill their potential, however, as indicated by the varied experience with SEZs worldwide. Because it is difficult to measure the extent of agglomeration economies rigorously, the causal impact of promoting clusters through SEZs is difficult to evaluate. For that reason, every potential SEZ should be considered carefully.

SEZs designed to cater to the needs of particular firms or industries to the exclusion of others are especially risky. Such SEZs concentrate resources not just spatially, but also in certain lines of activity or firms that are deemed to be "winners." This strategy assumes that the state has the ability to identify which firms stand to gain the most from agglomerat-

Box 6.7

Knowledge, technology, and the emergence of successful enterprise clusters in Africa

How have successful enterprise clusters evolved in Africa, and what lessons do they offer for encouraging new clusters to develop? A study of 11 clusters that emerged more or less spontaneously in various countries and industries provides insight into those questions.[a]

Except for the Mauritian textile cluster (originating in an export-processing zone established by the government in the 1970s), the clusters arose spontaneously because they had access to major local markets and infrastructure (all clusters); natural resources (the cut flower, fish, and wine industries); and local entrepreneurs with tacit knowledge and basic skills in trading, design, or manufacturing (the metalwork, computer, and Nnewi auto parts clusters, which started with trading or repairing and evolved into assembling or manufacturing). Strong local demand existed for their products, except for cut flowers and fish, which had strong international demand. Governments sometimes promoted clusters indirectly. For example, the handicraft cluster in Tanzania and the Suame automotive cluster in Ghana developed because the government relocated scattered, unorganized businesses to clear the city or facilitate spatial planning.

Efficiencies from a cluster-based value chain were fundamental. A value chain develops when a cluster achieves a certain scale, gains visibility, and expands further to benefit from efficiencies derived from a larger clientele, synergies among firms, the developing knowledge network, and shared facilities and services, including some provided by governments and donors (warehouses, for example).

To succeed, all clusters had to acquire, adapt, and disseminate knowledge. Horizontal and vertical links among firms—subcontracting relationships, connections with customers and suppliers, information and formal collaboration through joint ventures and franchises, membership in associations, and the movement of skilled personnel—created knowledge networks. Foreign knowledge and technology sustain several clusters. Foreign direct investment from Hong Kong SAR, China, and Taiwan, China, brought technology and know-how to the Mauritian textile industry. Nigeria's Otigba computer village imports computer hardware from China, Dubai, and Malaysia, with which it maintains technical and production channels. Kenya's Kamukunji metalworkers obtain technology from South and East Asia. Formal and informal learning and training assume numerous forms. Technology-intensive manufacturing clusters are trained by experts (locally and overseas) and offer training on the job or factory site. South African wine producers participate in viniculture forums and root stock associations. In most instances, universities and technology institutes contribute minimally to knowledge and technology flows for clusters. Even so, South African's wine industry benefits from the Elsenburg Agricultural Training Institute and the Wine Industry Network for Expertise and Technology.

All successful clusters have a labor force that is more educated than the norm for Africa, sometimes far beyond the norm (in Otigba, 55–60 percent of entrepreneurs are university graduates). In Suame—Africa's largest artisanal engineering cluster—75 percent of entrepreneurs have a primary education or less; only 2 percent have a higher education. Yet such clusters create employment for increasing numbers of university graduates, who can be an important force for continued growth and sustainability.

Government support to clusters takes several forms: defining and implementing sectoral policies, regulations, and standards; creating a special agency to promote or develop a cluster; establishing institutions to provide technical support and develop capacity; offering incentives in the form of subsidized land or infrastructure; and forging strategic alliances with industries overseas.

Industrial and professional associations facilitate collective action and cooperation. For example, Tanzanian clusters voice concerns and obtain technical advice through associations. Suame associations focus on social welfare. Associations for flower producers engage in lobbying, environmental conservation, maintaining standards, and facilitating market access, among other activities. The Wines of South Africa Association markets South African wines internationally.

Amid stiff global economic competition, the survival of these clusters depends on overcoming local challenges related to the critical mass of skills at their disposal, weak local technology institutions (disconnected from the business sector), weak government and institutional support, natural resource depletion, and the failure to meet international standards for product quality and safety. The government has a multifaceted role to play in enabling clusters to meet these enormous challenges. Aside from overall coordination, the public sector can facilitate the acquisition of knowledge and technology (through links with foreign enterprises and improved links between local institutes and businesses), establish a conducive institutional regime (clear regulations, standards, and quality assurance) in collaboration with trade and professional associations, strengthen training and skills, provide basic infrastructure, and enact policies that increase consumers' purchasing power and demand for high-quality goods.

Source: Zeng 2006.
a. The clusters were cut flowers and metalwork (Kenya), fish production and processing (Uganda), handicrafts and furniture (Tanzania), automotive parts and computer hardware (Nigeria), manufacturing and vehicle repair (Ghana), textiles (Mauritius), and wine and textiles (South Africa).

Box 6.8

Why have special economic zones failed to thrive in Africa, and what are the lessons for the future?

Government attempts to launch SEZs in Africa have met with little success. Numerous zones and industrial parks have been announced but failed to materialize; others have been "built," but never occupied. The few SEZs that have emerged are smaller than those in other regions. For example, SEZs in six African countries supported perhaps 35 firms on average, versus 350 in Honduras, nearly 300 in Bangladesh, and 3,500 in Vietnam (Farole 2011, 71). Evidence is emerging that Africa's SEZs have started to stagnate at low levels of growth (Farole 2011, 4). What could help the next generation of SEZs to do better?

In India, the Scheme for Integrated Textile Parks, inaugurated in 2005 by the Ministry of Textiles, is in its early stages but has successfully built parks and attracted firms to locate and invest in them. The parks appear to be generating the benefits associated with clustering. The scheme's most prominent innovation is to give the park users a much greater role, much earlier, in development of the park. In fact, the first order of business is not to build parks but to organize entrepreneurs.

Entrepreneurs form a group (called a special-purpose vehicle, SPV) to develop a detailed proposal for a park. To assist with this task, the SPV selects a specialized project management consultant (PMC) that is stringently vetted by the ministry. Guided by the SPV, the PMC designs, costs, and conducts a feasibility study for the project. The SPV makes the final decisions on location, project design, and costing, because the entrepreneurs constitute the "demand" for the park and have the most incentives to select the best alternative.

If the central government approves the proposal, it provides a grant for infrastructure to be shared by park users (up to 40 percent of the cost, up to a maximum of about US$8 million). The SPV finances the rest. It may solicit state grants, obtain other state and local contributions (such as subsidized land), and even obtain investment from PMCs, but the SPV must contribute at least 51 percent of the equity to ensure that members retain managerial control. No single private entity within the cluster may own more than 20 percent of the equity, and each firm occupies land in proportion to the equity it contributes. The PMC receives fees only if the project is accepted.

The combination of incentives offered under the scheme fosters interdependence among the stakeholders. Institutional mechanisms reinforce those relationships, including regular monitoring reports from the PMC to the ministry, quarterly central government reviews of the scheme, and the appointment of directors on the SPV board by the ministry, PMC, and the state.

The small size of the parks and the grants seems to reduce the incentives for interference at the state and central level. Because a central ministry rarely has local knowledge or human resources to monitor at a micro level, devolving this task to a specialized agency (the PMC) allows the ministry to focus on its strategic mission and obtain better micro data. The reporting requirements for PMCs are clear and standard. Strict rules and methods for grant disbursements help to limit the abuse of funds.

Responsibility for engagement and coordination with state agencies lies with local entrepreneurs, who are best positioned to navigate the political economy of their state. States issue the clearances that are vital for park development, especially for converting land to industrial use. Although limits on state participation in SPV funding curb the state's direct role, the ability to appoint a director to the SPV board is an incentive to participate. SPVs also have recourse to the center if issues arise with the state.

The scheme appears highly adaptable to India's diverse conditions and its textile industry. Although this model may not suit circumstances in other industries or countries, it indicates that success is more likely when incentives are carefully calibrated to the political, institutional, and entrepreneurial context.

Sources: Saleman and Jordan 2013; Zeng 2006.

ing, which is arguable. The driving principle of localizing interventions around incipient clusters should be one not of picking winners but rather of "letting the winners pick each other by locating near each other." In other words, it is important not to over-engineer who gains entry to an SEZ (see box 6.8 for an example of a more nuanced approach from India).[20]

Building Skills for the Modern Wage Sector

As discussed in chapter 3, productivity in modern wage enterprises depends on a range of skills: cognitive skills, soft skills, and managerial and business skills. Policy discussions often revolve around technical skills, but foundational skills acquired through schooling are also important. Recent research from Kenya, for instance, suggests that by raising literacy and reasoning skills, secondary school completion reduces the probability of low-skilled self-employment by 50 percent, while raising the probability of formal employment by 30 percent (Ozier 2013). These skills seem to matter because they facilitate on-the-job learning in firms. Literate workers can be trained through written instructions in job specifications and procedures, for example, and they require less hands-on technical supervision by others. Such training is rare in Africa, however, because of low literacy levels (Biggs, Shah, and Srivastava 1995).

Employer surveys from some African countries—Botswana, Lesotho, and Sierra Leone—suggest that employers are also looking for soft skills in young hires. Employers in Botswana, for instance, rate reliability and punctuality, commitment and hard work, honesty, and teamwork skills as the top skills required when hiring skilled workers (World Bank 2011a).

While there is increasing international evidence on the link between skills and productivity, firms in Africa generally do not rate skills as a top constraint. Self-reported shortages of skills tend to be higher in relatively capital-intensive industries. Skills also tend to become a constraint for high-performing firms: businesses that complain of a skills shortage consistently outperform those that do not (Barker and Mengistae 2013). This information suggests that while raising skills is not going to solve the employment problem by itself, it should be part of the policy package for improving competitiveness. Even if skills are currently not a binding constraint, they will quickly become binding as the sector takes off.

In addition to the limited availability of cognitive, soft, and technical skills among job seekers, a lack of "managerial capital" could also be constraining the competitiveness of African firms. As discussed in chapter 3, there is increasing evidence that firms in the region have visibly poor basic management practices. There may be considerable scope for improving productivity (and hence raising employment) by investing in business and management skills training, and perhaps even in individualized management consulting.

Several policy recommendations emerge from this evidence on the role of skills. They emphasize the need to focus on foundational skills and public goods such as quality assurance and information, the need for government to focus on building portable rather than job-specific skills, the need for special support to enable poor and disadvantaged groups to acquire skills, the need to develop international linkages, and the need for systems that link employers with trainers. The following discussion of these recommendations reviews interventions that have been tested in Africa and elsewhere.

Focus on Foundational Skills and on Public Goods Such as Quality Assurance and Information

The discussion on public support to build skills for youth employment often takes a short-term view of the problem and centers on technical vocational education and training (TVET), but it is equally, if not more, important to build a solid foundation for individuals to develop their skills as they progress in life. Basic schooling is a key determinant of wage workers' cognitive and soft skills. It is the foundation for the acquisition of additional skills, whether through more formal education, training, or on-the-job learning. Improving access to general schooling and the quality of that schooling—even at the basic level—is a priority for increasing the productivity of labor in the modern wage sector.

Parental investment and early childhood interventions in health and education also influence personality traits that become relevant to productivity later in life, either directly or through the fact that some personality traits will make some students more likely to succeed in school (Almlund et al. 2011). Recently, many governments have included soft skills in training programs for youth, and while there is some evidence of their impact, evidence on the significance of early childhood investments is much better established.

Governments should also reevaluate their role in providing TVET directly. As discussed in chapter 3, publicly provided TVET has a poor track record in Africa, where it is expensive but often inefficient or irrelevant to the labor market. An increasingly large share of TVET in Africa is provided by the private sector (Mingat, Ledoux, and Rakotomalala 2010; World Bank 2012d; Atchoarena and Esquieu 2002; Kitaev 2002). Although private providers may offer little training in some specific skills, this lack of interest does not necessarily mean that nascent private institutes are incapable of providing such training or that the returns to those skills are too low. Similarly, there may be an equity-based case for establishing public TVET institutes in poor or remote areas, where private entry is limited, but there may not be high enough returns to TVET training in remote areas. In many cases, low take-up of training is better addressed by improving access to credit (or grants) and providing information about training programs. In other contexts, a

better alternative for public support may be active labor market programs that have training components and target specific groups (Almeida, Behrman, and Robalino 2012).

It is also critical to make formal TVET more efficient and market relevant. Several policy recommendations are pertinent here, but they are based largely on the experience of developed countries. Box 6.9 discusses potential reforms and how they have been undertaken in Africa.

Address Information and Credit Constraints to Improve Access to TVET among Poor and Disadvantaged Groups

As discussed in chapter 3, the government could step in to provide targeted financial

Box 6.9

Reforming TVET systems in Africa

One strategy for improving the relevance and quality of skills developed through TVET programs is to grant public TVET institutions increased autonomy and accountability for results. Institutions would have the freedom to set fees, adapt training to local needs, hire appropriate staff, and choose methods of instruction. Accountability can be increased by basing financing on performance and outcomes rather than inputs, accompanied by better measurement of performance.

Governments also have a role in providing standards, accreditation, quality assurance, and information. The TVET qualifications system should be focused less on providing inputs and more on assuring that the training has provided the competencies (skills) required for the market. Lack of information about private TVET providers can constrain young people from making informed choices about training, and it can also dull providers' incentives to improve their quality. Governments can play a role in collecting and disseminating this information. Instead of measuring inputs (number of students, institutions, and teachers) as is currently the norm, the emphasis should be on tracking efficiency (dropout, repetition, and survival rates) and outcomes (share of trainees entering wage or self-employment after graduating), which are more relevant to young people's training decisions. For instance, in the Netherlands, almost all graduates of higher education institutions are surveyed a year and a half after they graduate to collect information on time taken to find a

job, type and quality of employment, and students' satisfaction with the education.

Many African countries have begun to reform their TVET systems along these lines. While this is a positive step, there is little rigorous evidence yet on whether these reforms have improved cost-effectiveness or market relevance. For instance, Ethiopia, Ghana, and Tanzania have developed national qualification frameworks to set standards. Recognizing the need for better coordination in their TVET systems, some countries have tried new governance arrangements and have introduced national coordinating bodies and national training authorities, with mixed results. Ghana, for example, established the Council for TVET (or COTVET) in 2006 as a coordinating body. A study of this reform suggests that COTVET's engagement with the private sector and collection of demand-side data could be improved and that insufficient coordination within the government has led to parallel agendas, plans, programs, and committees. Governments in Africa may need to build more capacity in the relevant agencies before they can successfully transplant complex TVET systems from developed countries.

Sources: Based on Johanson and Van Adams 2004 (mixed results of governance arrangements); Darvas and Palmer 2012 (TVET in Ghana); World Bank 2012a (TVET with a business component in Uganda); Sondergaard and Murthi 2012 (reforms in Eastern Europe and Central Asia); Krishnan and Shaorshadze 2013 (TVET in Ethiopia).

support and information that young people from poor or otherwise disadvantaged backgrounds need to access TVET markets.[21] Young women are less likely to participate in TVET than young men, and they frequently focus on narrow types of training such as tailoring or weaving, suggesting that direct financial support or information is needed to increase their take-up of training with high returns. Targeted voucher programs that have an information component, such as the Technical and Vocational Vouchers Program (TVVP) in Kenya, can improve access to training among poor and disadvantaged youth. The TVVP experience shows that flexible vouchers (not restricted to specific types of training providers) are more effective than inflexible ones. Another important lesson from TVVP is that participants are frequently mistaken about the returns to vocational education, with males strongly preferring traditionally "male-dominated" courses such as motor vehicle repair and women almost exclusively choosing traditionally "female-dominated" courses such as hairdressing. TVVP provided information on the higher economic returns in male-dominated trades, which encouraged women to take up training in those areas.

Focus Government Intervention on Building Skills That Are Portable, Not Job Specific

Government interventions should be focused on building more "portable" skills, as opposed to skills required only for a particular job or firm. More portable skills have higher social value, because they are less vulnerable to changes in the demand for skills specific to certain firms or industries. Because their current market returns could be lower than this social return, the likelihood of underinvestment is higher for more portable skills. Firms are also less likely to invest in portable skills because workers trained in such skills could be poached by other firms.

Firm-specific skills can be acquired through on-the-job training, and public support may not be necessary to supply them. Credit constraints could prevent firms from investing in firm-specific skills, but there is little evidence

that African firms are particularly constrained in providing on-the-job training. World Bank enterprise surveys indicate that on average 30 percent of formal firms in Africa provide on-the-job training, which is comparable to the standard level across low- and middle-income countries. Nor does the absence of on-the-job training in a firm necessarily signal a constraint. A recent study estimates that many firms do not provide it because the returns to such training are close to zero for them (Almeida and Carneiro 2009). Governments could consider supporting on-the-job training in specific cases where there is compelling evidence of a market failure (box 6.10), but not more generally.

Some of the constraints to firm-specific training could be addressed by broader policies to improve the business climate or productivity in firms. For example, if liquidity constraints prevent firms from investing in training, then policies that improve firms' access to finance will also have an impact on on-the-job training. To the extent that firms and workers would be more likely to reach an agreement on sharing the returns from training if contracts were enforceable, strengthening the enforceability of contracts and the rule of law could have a positive impact on on-the-job training. Sometimes, firms train workers in very specific or outdated skills because they use old technology. Policies that promote innovation and technological upgrading in firms could therefore also improve the social returns to on-the-job training.

Facilitate International Linkages in Training and Technology Upgrading in Specific Industries

Governments can facilitate technical cooperation with other countries in training and upgrading technology in specific industries, especially with other developing countries that have technical capacity in the industry. A recent example is the technical cooperation between Ethiopia's Ministry of Trade and Industry, the Ethiopian Leather and Leather Products Technology Institute, and the Footwear Design and Development Institute of India. The Footwear Design and Development Institute provided technical assistance to seven Ethiopian shoe

Box 6.10

Does government have a role in on-the-job training?

To the extent that they are substitutable, on-the-job training is by design more likely to be more market relevant than technical or vocational education in the classroom. When there is evidence that on-the-job training is being underprovided because of credit or other market failures, government subsidies could be considered. Some developing countries use subsidy schemes (in the form of levy-rebate systems) to promote on-the-job training. For example, Peru allows firms to use payroll-tax proceeds for in-service training or to purchase training at an accredited training institution. Levy-rebate systems have a mixed record of success, however. In South Africa, for example, only 35 percent of small enterprises claimed the training grant to which they were entitled—and even fewer large firms appear to be claiming them.

Some countries have also used a voucher system that subsidizes the cost of training to firms while giving them flexibility in choosing the training provider. Kenya's Jua Kali Program is a good example. An evaluation of this program, which targeted small and microenterprises, found that firms using vouchers experienced markedly greater growth in revenue and assets. While this finding is promising, it should be interpreted with caution, because the firms that participated in the program are not necessarily comparable to those

that did not. Ghana offered a similar voucher program to informal enterprises in the early 1990s, but it largely failed, apparently because of poor marketing and distribution.

Even when there is evidence that training is underprovided by some firms, governments should be cautious with on-the-job training subsidy schemes and their targeting. The returns could vary across firms. Training might be subsidized in firms in which the net returns are insufficient to justify the training, or scarce public resources might be wasted on firms that would have provided on-the-job training even without the subsidy. It is not easy to identify which firms are constrained in providing training. Many programs try to improve targeting by using proxies, such as targeting smaller firms based on the assumption that they are more likely to be credit constrained. These proxies are imperfect, and governments should also invest in better monitoring and evaluation systems for such programs. A randomized pilot, for example, could help to test whether subsidies are a substitute source of funding for on-the-job training that would have occurred in any case.

Sources: Based on Johanson and Van Adams 2004; Filmer 2012 (South Africa); World Bank 2011c (vouchers in Peru); Almeida, Behrman, and Robalino 2012 (Jua Kali).

factories in design, technical upgrading, quality assurance, productivity enhancement, and testing, which improved their productivity and the overall quality of shoes. For instance, cutting at one of the shoe factories rose from 2,000 pairs a day to 2,400, and defect rates dropped from 3 to 1 percent (Dinh et al. 2012).

If certain technical skills are in demand in several countries, but the demand is too small to justify the fixed costs of building a training center in every country, governments can cooperate to create regional hubs for technical skills training. "Importing" such skills could also make economic sense, and in response governments could ease constraints on the immigration of skilled workers. The current policy regime in most African countries is not conducive to importing technical skills. Policy makers do need to take political economy considerations into account, such as concerns about domestic jobs being taken by foreigners, but highly skilled

foreign workers may actually create additional jobs. Building a base of evidence on the net employment effects of skilled immigration can help to generate support.[22] Policies for importing skills can be designed to maximize domestic spillovers—for instance, by encouraging firms to train domestic workers in return for permits to hire technical skills from abroad.

Foster Systems That Link Employers with Trainers

Linking TVET systems to employers is necessary to ensure that the training is relevant to the market for skills. The returns to specific technical skills can vary substantially across markets and over time. For this reason, policies oriented toward improving the skills delivered through TVET should build TVET systems with employers' involvement to ensure that employers transmit information to trainers about which skills are in demand on a regular basis.

Some developing countries already produce regular reports on the supply of and demand for skills, such as the Labor Market Intelligence Reports produced by the Philippines Technical Education and Skills Development Authority (TESDA). TESDA's labor market reports are based on consultations and focus group discussions with employer associations as well as on labor market surveys (TESDA 2012a, 2012b).

Similar approaches are being rolled out in Africa. Tanzania's vocational and educational training authority has a monitoring and evaluation system based on regular data that are collected by zonal labor market analysts and mini market surveys that track current and prospective industry needs (United Republic of Tanzania and UNESCO 2012). Regular interaction between training centers and industry and commerce is promoted by attaching tutors and students to industry to gain practical exposure and by attaching industrial practitioners to training centers to teach specific topics. The success of this approach has yet to be determined.

Linkages between the training system and industry can also help youth to make the transition to work. In Africa, matching specialized skills to jobs is not a major problem, but in low-skilled wage employment, young people from disadvantaged backgrounds have trouble connecting to employers because of basic informational problems. A signal of these problems is the ubiquity of informal networks as a source of information about jobs. Young people without networks in modern firms—especially youth from poor families or rural areas, whose family members or friends are less likely to have wage jobs—will have greater difficulty finding such jobs. Recent research suggests that informal job networks also put women at a disadvantage. An experiment on hiring in Malawi found that men referred men unless specifically asked to refer women, and women referred ill-qualified women unless specifically rewarded for providing good-quality referrals (Beaman, Keleher, and Magruder 2012). Aside from disadvantaging certain groups, informal job networks reduce the productivity of job matches by causing them to be based on connections rather than qualifications and by limiting the pool of potential hires that firms can tap.

Can the transition to work be eased by inserting training graduates in firms through temporary internships and other programs? A case in point is the German-style dual system, in which theory is taught in educational institutions and practical skills are acquired through an apprenticeship (or internship) in a company. Some evidence suggests that this system reduces unemployment among graduates (Piopiunik and Ryan 2012), but it is not clear how this system can be imported at scale into Africa, where the scope for internships with firms is much more limited. If adopted, training plus insertion programs should be selectively targeted to those most in need. Latin America's Jóvenes en Acción model, described later, may be more suitable to the African context.

Governments also support insertion through employment or job search agencies. The evidence suggests that such services have limited relevance for Africa. Formal public placement agencies are underused. A survey of job seekers in 11 African cities found that only 7 percent were registered with an employment agency (De Vreyer and Roubaud 2013). Similarly, a recent study on the Middle East and North Africa found that many job seekers rely solely on personal and family connections, and most job placements occur outside of public employment services (Kuddo 2012). A review of impact studies—drawn largely from developed countries—found that these services tend to be more effective for the most educated workers, when demand for labor is high (Betcherman, Olivas, and Dar 2004).

Comprehensive training-related programs that link students to employers through internships are well-established in Latin American countries and have begun to spread to other regions, including Africa. The Jóvenes en Acción (Youth in Action) Program in Colombia, for example, provided three months of classroom-based training and three months of on-the-job training through internships in firms to unemployed young people between the ages of 18 and 25 in the two lowest socioeconomic strata of the population (Attanasio, Kugler, and Meghir 2011). Similarly, the Juventud y Empleo (Youth and Employment) Program in the Dominican Republic subsidizes training for individuals between the ages of 16 and 29 who have not completed high school, with the training followed by an internship at a private firm (Ibarraran et al. 2012). The programs involve collaboration with the private sector to provide internships and select the content of training. They usually offer a package of skills, complementing vocational training with life skills training intended to improve social interaction and work-related practices and attitudes.

Rigorous impact evaluations of several Jóvenes en Acción programs show mixed but promising results. On average, the programs increase formal wage employment at the rate of about four to six additional jobs per 100 participants. Given the low wage employment rates for African youth from poor backgrounds, this impact could be large in relative terms. The programs also lead to significantly higher earnings, but the impacts are larger for female participants, and it is unclear if there is a significant impact on males. Evaluations of Jóvenes en Acción programs and of recent training programs from India and Jordan suggest that a more comprehensive package—such as a combination of soft skills training and on-the-job training—is more effective (see Maitra and Mani 2012 for India; Groh et al. 2012 for Jordan).

These findings suggest that a targeted, comprehensive (training plus internship) program could be an effective instrument for promoting productive wage employment among disadvantaged youth. Such programs are being adopted in Africa but have not yet been evaluated, and there are serious questions about their cost-effectiveness in Africa. Jóvenes programs were estimated to be cost-effective in Latin America, in the narrow sense that their average impact on earnings exceeded the program cost per participant.[23] Because the modern wage sector is relatively small in Africa, the cost of subsidizing internships could be higher there, and impacts on earnings lower. The small size of the wage sector also makes scalability a bigger concern. Considering the mixed evidence on what type of training works best in these programs, they should be implemented on a pilot basis, and the pilots should be evaluated to find the most cost-effective model for Africa.

Improve Management Practices

Management training can have positive impacts, but more evidence is needed on how to target it. If poor management practices are as prevalent in Africa as some recent studies suggest, there may be considerable scope for improving productivity by investing in business skills training and perhaps even in individualized management consulting. Better management can make firms more productive and ultimately increase hiring. There is evidence that firms underinvest in management skills because they underestimate its value or are credit constrained.

Programs seeking to promote managerial skills in established small and medium-size firms are on the rise in developing countries, including programs that give intensive or individualized management consulting. Some have been evaluated in quasi-experimental or randomized studies, including studies by the Kaizen Institute of industrial clusters in Dar es Salaam and Addis Ababa.[24] The evaluations suggest that such programs do lead to the adoption of new management practices. The magnitude of these effects is generally small, with some exceptions. Among Ghanaian metalwork firms, for instance, the percentage of firms keeping records increased 30 percent (Mano et al. 2012).

Evidence on whether the adoption of new management practices actually improves business performance and employment is more mixed, with few studies finding statistically significant impacts on sales, profits, or survivorship. The most promising finding is from a field experiment on large Indian textile firms, in which management practices raised productivity 17 percent in the first year and led within three years to the opening of more production plants (Bloom, Sadun, and Van Reenen 2012). These results suggest that improved management practices can create more jobs.

Given the limited but promising evidence, more pilot studies in Africa would be useful, including studies that examine issues related to targeting and selectivity. For instance, is limited managerial capital a constraint only for larger firms, as the Indian study suggests? Are the returns to managerial training highest when training targets firms with the most ability or "potential" for success, and can that potential be identified? In industries where healthy competition among firms does not always occur, it is difficult to identify such potential by looking at current performance. Moreover, high-potential firms may do well even in the absence of government-supported managerial training. Small pilot programs directed at firms with alternative profiles could be useful for understanding where support is most needed.

Many Options to Promote Competitive Modern Enterprises

Modern manufacturing and services firms have been an engine of job growth in developed countries and more recently in East Asia. In the long run, the same should be true for Africa. The modern enterprise sector presently accounts for a small share of African employment, and it is growing unevenly across the region. The manufacturing sector, which has been a vibrant source of new jobs in other regions, accounts for less than 3 percent of total employment in Africa.

Because African economies are small, domestic demand alone cannot support a thriving modern enterprise sector, where so much depends on achieving scale and diversity. Trade in manufacturing (and tradable services) may be essential for modern firms in these sectors to realize their full potential for productive youth employment, but presently they export very little. Labor costs are generally not lower in African countries than in their potential competitors. If they cannot compete on the strength of low labor costs, the region's modern enterprises must compete on the strength of their productivity—but African firms are relatively unproductive.

The lack of productivity signals deeper problems that are not identical across the subcontinent. In some countries, the cost of complementary inputs to labor (electricity, overland transport, and so on) is too high. In others, bureaucratic red tape delays investors' access to land or permits or complicates efforts to move goods (inputs and output) through ports. The high costs of financial intermediation are starving investors of capital. Small domestic markets

in many countries, combined with barriers to imports and regional trade, suppress competition and reduce pressure to innovate and improve productivity, even among firms that produce for domestic markets.

Governments in Africa can do much to remedy this situation. The most important step is to improve the business climate so that entrepreneurship and productive firms can grow. Key reform objectives are to improve access to finance and infrastructure services, improve trade logistics, and ease regulatory constraints to entrepreneurship. Some efforts—such as providing physical infrastructure for public utilities and transport—require costly investment in the long run. Yet many other policy reforms are not so expensive in monetary terms and can deliver huge impacts by reducing distortions and increasing efficiency. Selective and spatially targeted support to emerging clusters can make the most of limited resources by promoting agglomeration economies. Localized interventions of this sort should assist clusters by providing good infrastructure and supportive regulation, but they should never try to force clusters into existence by trying to pick "winners."

A skills shortage does not seem to be a binding constraint on modern wage employment in Africa, but there is much evidence that a range of skills—cognitive, behavioral, and technical—matters to productivity in firms. African youths need those skills if they are to be truly productive in modern firms, particularly when this sector starts to take off. Governments should, first of all, foster a strong foundation in basic skills by improving the quality of general education. Rather than directly providing TVET, they should focus on providing "public goods" such as quality assurance and information to develop a training sector that is efficient and relevant to the market for skills. For poor and disadvantaged youths to gain access to training, governments should provide financial support in conjunction with information that enables them to obtain the right kind of training. Programs for disadvantaged youths that integrate training with internships show promise, as do programs offering managerial training—but their scalability and affordability in Africa remain unproven.

Notes

1. Africa's wage employment sector is only partially "modern," in the sense that many wage employees work without a formal contract. On average, about 57 percent of wage employees have a contract with their employer. Among young people, the share with a contract is 47 percent.

2. New thinking on international trade reflects the major impact that trade can have on productivity. An increasingly large share of the trade in goods now comes from trade in different varieties of products within the same industry; for example, the United States and European countries export cars to each other. Such trade is beneficial, because it allows different varieties to be produced at an efficient scale, which would not be possible if each variety were sold only within its country of origin. This kind of trade also allows more efficient producers to take fuller advantage of their efficiency, because a larger market—a direct consequence of lower trade barriers—has a disproportionately greater positive impact on the profitability of more efficient firms. As more productive firms gain market share at the expense of less productive ones, the industry's potential for generating employment rises (a point addressed later in the analysis of Africa's manufacturing competitiveness).

3. Less productive firms are limited to selling in the domestic market, as the price they would have to charge to recover transport and other costs of exporting would not be competitive. See, for instance, Melitz and Trefler (2012).

4. The caveat with these data is that the surveys collect information on firms that are formally registered. In most countries, all firms above a certain size are supposed to register, but in practice, the registration rates and quality of the registry information vary across countries.

5. Some evidence indicates that Sub-Saharan Africa, along with South Asia, may have the lowest labor productivity in manufacturing in the developing world. See Clarke (2011).

6. An additional reason is that African firms substitute labor for capital by using relatively labor-intensive production methods, despite the fact that many African countries have higher wages than China.

7. Moreover, foreign direct investment in Africa is dominated by investment in extractive industries (World Bank 2013a).

8. The technical term is total factor productivity (TFP).

9. As discussed later, some recent studies, notably Bloom et al. (2013), measure organizational efficiency.

10. Associations between these business environment variables and plant-level and aggregate productivity in World Bank enterprise survey data are analyzed in several papers, including Dollar, Hallward-Driemeier, and Mengistae (2005); Li, Mengistae, and Xu (2011); Harrison, Lin, and Xu (2013). See also Hall and Jones (1999); Bartelsman, Haltiwanger, and Scarpetta (2009).

11. That is, the simple average of firm productivities, not weighted by their market shares, is higher in Country A.

12. Specifically, it is possible to decompose industry productivity into the average of firm-level TFPs—which would be the industry's TFP level if all firms had equal market shares—and an "allocative efficiency" component. This is referred to as the Olley-Pakes decomposition of aggregate productivity (Olley and Pakes 1996). See also Melitz and Polanec (2012) and Foster, Haltiwanger, and Syverson (2008) for related decompositions. The Olley-Pakes decomposition can be described as follows: let a_t be the weighted average of (log) TFP of a given industry in year t and let a_{it} be the log TFP of enterprises constituting the industry with respective market shares, s_{it}, where i indexes enterprises. Then a_t can be written as

$$a_t = \bar{a}_t + \sum_{i=1}^{N_t} (s_{it} - \bar{s}_t)(a_{it} - \bar{a}_t),$$

where letters with upper bars represent unweighted industry means of variables.

13. Banerjee and Duflo (2012), for instance, show that firms are credit constrained in India. Udry and Anagol (2006) discuss evidence on exceptionally high rates of return to capital in Ghana, which suggests credit constraints.

14. In India, for example, labor laws prevent firms from adjusting employment in response to external shocks. See Adhvaryu, Chari, and Sharma (2013).

15. Among the indicators of the potential gains from reductions in trade costs are the large and persistent cross-border disparities in the price of goods, earnings, and rates of return to capital among neighboring countries across the region. These suggest substantial room for increasing employment opportunities for young people simply by making it easier for countries to trade and invest across borders, without necessarily involving large international migration of people (Habyarimana and Mengistae 2013).

16. Barker and Mengistae (2013). Beck, Dermigüç-Kunt, and Maksimovic (2005) report that firms claiming to be more constrained by access to credit are likely to grow more slowly.

17. Kenya Gazette Supplement no. 52 (Legislative Supplement no. 31) and Legal Notice no. 97, of 11 July 2008.

18. Cadot et al. (2013) found that new exporters are more likely to survive beyond the first year when other firms are exporting the same product to similar destinations. They argue that information spillovers account for the finding.

19. Collier and Venables (2007). See also Monga (2012) and Lin and Monga (2011) on the instrumentality of localization to that end in the context of industrial policy, which the framework of Collier and Venables does not necessarily assume.

20. The issue of localizing interventions in support of clusters is often intertwined with the issue of industrial policy (that is, policy targeted to specific types of industries or firms). But the two are quite distinct. Interventions to localize clusters do not rely on identifying specific firms or industries that should be clustered. For the current debate on industrial policy, as distinct from the spatial targeting of measures for improving the investment climate, some key references are Lin (2011); Lin and Monga (2011); Pack and Saggi (2006); Rodrik (2004).

21. A survey of disadvantaged youth in Malawi found that only 13 percent had ever received technical or vocational training (Hicks et al. 2011). Those who had not received any training attributed it to high costs and limited access and information.

22. That evidence base does not yet exist for Africa.

23. This assessment is based on particular assumptions about how long the earnings impact lasts. See Attanasio, Kugler, and Meghir (2011).

24. McKenzie and Woodruff (2013) review these evaluations of management and business practice training programs. Mano et al. (2012), Sonobe, Suzuki, and Otsuka (2011), and Karlan, Knight, and Udry (2012) are Africa-specific evaluations.

References

Adhvaryu, Achyuta, A. V. Chari, and Siddharth Sharma. 2013. "Firing Costs and Flexibility: Evidence from Firms' Employment Responses to Shocks in India." *Review of Economics and Statistics* 95 (3): 725–40.

Almeida, Rita, Jere Behrman, and David Robalino, eds. 2012. *The Right Skills for the Job? Rethinking Effective Training Policies for Workers*. Washington, DC: World Bank.

Almeida, Rita, and Pedro Carneiro. 2009. "The Return to the Firm Investment in Human Capital." *Labor Economics* 16 (1): 97–106.

Almlund, Mathilde, Angela Duckworth, James Heckman, and Tim Kautz. 2011. "Personality, Psychology, and Economics." In *Handbook of the Economics of Education*, edited by Eric Hanushek, Stephen Machin, and Ludger Woessmann, 1–181. Amsterdam: Elsevier.

Atchoarena, David, and Paul Esquieu, eds. 2002. *Private Technical and Vocational Education in Sub-Saharan Africa: Provision, Patterns, and Policy Issues*. IIEP/Prg.DA/01.300. Paris: International Institute for Educational Planning.

Attanasio, Orazio P., Adriana D. Kugler, and Costas Meghir. 2011. "Subsidizing Vocational Training for Disadvantaged Youth in Developing Countries: Evidence from a Randomized Trial." *American Economic Journal: Applied Economics* 3 (3): 188–220.

Banerjee, Abhijit, and Esther Duflo. 2005. "Growth Theory through the Lens of Development Economics." In *Handbook of Economic Growth*, Vol. 1A, edited by Philippe Aghion and Steven Durlauf, ch. 7, 473–552. Amsterdam: Elsevier.

———. 2012. "Do Firms Want to Borrow More? Testing Credit Constraints Using a Directed Lending Program." Massachusetts Institute of Technology, Department of Economics, Boston, MA.

Barker, M., and Taye Mengistae. 2013. "Business Environment, Market Distortions, and Employment in Africa: An Analysis of Business Survey Data on Manufacturing Industries and Services." Background paper for the Africa Region Report on Youth Employment in Africa, World Bank, Washington, DC.

Bartelsman, Eric, John Haltiwanger, and Stefano Scarpetta. 2009. "Cross-Country Differences in Productivity: The Role of Allocation and Selection." IZA Discussion Paper 4578, Institute for the Study of Labor, Bonn.

Beaman, Lori, Niall Keleher, and Jeremy Magruder. 2012. "Do Job Networks Disadvantage Women? Evidence from a Recruitment Experiment in Malawi." Working Paper, Northwestern University, Department of Economics, Chicago.

Beck, Thorsten, Asli Dermigüç-Kunt, and Vojislav Maksimovic. 2005. "Financial and Legal Constraints to Growth: Does Firm Size Matter?" *Journal of Finance* 60 (1): 37–77.

Bertrand, Marianne, Antoinette Schoar, and David Thesmar. 2007. "Banking Deregulation and Industry Structure: Evidence from the French Banking Reforms of 1985." *Journal of Finance* 62 (2): 597–628.

Betcherman, Gordon, Karina Olivas, and Amit Dar. 2004. "Active Labor Market Programs: New Evidence from Evaluations with Particular Attention to Developing and Transition Countries." Social

Protection Discussion Paper 04012, World Bank, Washington, DC.

Biggs, Tyler, Manju Shah, and Pradeep Srivastava. 1995. "Technological Capabilities and Learning in African Enterprises." Technical Paper 288, World Bank, Washington, DC.

Bloom, Nicholas, Benn Eifert, Aprajit Mahajan, David McKenzie, and John Roberts. 2013. "Does Management Matter? Evidence from India." *Quarterly Journal of Economics* 128 (1): 1–51.

Bloom, Nicholas, Raffaella Sadun, and John Van Reenen. 2012. "The Organization of Firms across Countries." *Quarterly Journal of Economics* 127 (4): 1663–705.

Briceño-Garmendia, Cecilia, and Vivien Foster, eds. 2010. *Africa's Infrastructure: A Time for Transformation.* Washington, DC: World Bank.

Cadot, Olivier, Leonardo Iacovone, Martha Denisse Pierola, and Ferdinand Rauch. 2013. "Success and Failure of African Exporters." *Journal of Development Economics* 101 (C): 284–96.

Chari, Amalavoyal V. 2011. "Identifying the Aggregate Productivity Effects of Entry and Size Restrictions: An Empirical Analysis of License Reform in India." *American Economic Journal: Economic Policy* 3 (2): 66–96.

Cingano, Federico, and Paolo Pinotti. 2012. "Trust, Firm Organization, and the Structure of Production." Working Paper 2012-133, Bocconi University, Paolo Baffi Centre on Central Banking and Financial Regulation.

Clarke, George R. G. 2011. "Manufacturing Firms in Africa." In *Performance of Manufacturing Firms in Africa: An Empirical Analysis*, edited by Hinh T. Dinh and George R. G. Clarke, 47–86. Washington, DC: World Bank.

Collier, Paul, and Anthony J. Venables. 2007. "Rethinking Trade Preferences: How Africa Can Diversify Its Exports." *World Economy* 30 (8): 1326–45.

———. 2008. "Trade and Economic Performance: Does Africa's Fragmentation Matter?" Paper presented at the Annual World Bank Conference on Development Economics, Cape Town, June 9–11.

Corrado, Carol, Charles Hulten, and Daniel Sichel. 2005. "Measuring Capital and Technology: An Expanded Framework." In *Measuring Capital in the New Economy: Studies in Income and Wealth*, Vol. 65, edited by Carol Corrado, John Haltiwanger, and Daniel Sichel, 11–45. Chicago: University of Chicago Press.

Darvas, Peter, and Robert Palmer. 2012. "Technical and Vocational Skills Development in Ghana." World Bank, Washington, DC.

De Vreyer, Philippe, and François Roubaud, eds. 2013. *Urban Labour Markets in Sub-Saharan Africa.* Paris: Agence Française de Développement; Washington, DC: World Bank.

Dinh, Hinh T., Dimitris A. Mavridis, and Hoa B. Nguyen. 2012. "The Binding Constraints on the Growth of Firms in Developing Countries." In *Performance of Manufacturing Firms in Africa: An Empirical Analysis*, edited by Hinh T. Dinh and George R. G. Clarke, 87–138. Washington, DC: World Bank.

Dinh, Hinh T., Vincent Palmade, Vandana Chandra, and Frances Cossar. 2012. *Light Manufacturing in Africa: Targeted Policies to Enhance Private Investment and Create Jobs.* Washington, DC: World Bank.

Djankov, Simeon. 2009. "The Regulation of Entry: A Survey." *World Bank Research Observer* 24 (2): 183–203.

Djankov, Simeon, Caroline Freund, and Cong S. Pham. 2010. "Trading on Time." *Review of Economics and Statistics* 92 (1): 166–73.

Dollar, David, Mary Hallward-Driemeier, and Taye Mengistae. 2005. "Investment Climate and Firm Performance in Developing Economies." *Economic Development and Cultural Change* 54 (1): 1–31.

Dutz, Mark, Sergio Kannebley, Maira Scarpelli, and Siddharth Sharma. 2012. "Measuring Intangible Capital in an Emerging Market Economy: An Application to Brazil." Policy Research Working Paper 6142, World Bank, Washington, DC.

Eifert, Benn, Alan Gelb, and Vijaya Ramachandran. 2008. "The Cost of Doing Business in Africa: Evidence from Enterprise Survey Data." *World Development* 36 (9): 1531–46.

Fafchamps, Marcel, and Simon Quinn. 2012. "Results of Sample Surveys of Firms." In *Performance of Manufacturing Firms in Africa: An Empirical Analysis*, edited by Hinh T. Dinh and George R. G. Clarke, 139–211. Washington, DC: World Bank.

Fafchamps, Marcel, and Mans Soderbom. 2006. "Wages and Labor Management in African Manufacturing." *Journal of Human Resources* 41 (2): 346–79.

Farole, Thomas. 2011. "Special Economic Zones in Africa: Comparing Performance and Learning from Global Experiences." World Bank, Washington, DC.

Filmer, Deon. 2012. "Challenges and Options for Technical and Post-Basic Education in South Africa." Policy Note, World Bank, Africa Region, Human Development Unit, Washington, DC.

Fisman, Ray, and Jakob Svensson. 2007. "Are Corruption and Taxation Really Harmful to Growth? Firm-Level Evidence." *Journal of Development Economics* 83 (1): 63–75.

Fitzmaurice, Mike, and Olivier Hartmann. 2013. "Border-Crossing Monitoring along the Northern Corridor." SSATP Working Paper 96, World Bank, Washington, DC.

Foster, Lucia, John C. Haltiwanger, and Chad Syverson. 2008. "Reallocation, Firm Turnover, and Efficiency: Selection on Productivity or Profitability?" *American Economic Review* 98 (1): 394–425.

Fujita, Masahisa, Paul Krugman, and Anthony J. Venables. 1999. *The Spatial Economy: Cities, Regions, and International Trade.* Cambridge, MA: MIT Press.

Gelb, Alan, Christian Meyer, and Vijaya Ramachandran. 2013. "Does Poor Mean Cheap? A Comparative Look at Africa's Industrial Labor Costs." CGD Working Paper 325, Center for Global Development, Washington, DC.

Groh, Matthew, Nandini Krishnan, David McKenzie, and Tara Vishwanath. 2012. "Soft Skills or Hard Cash? The Impact of Training and Wage Subsidy Program on Female Youth Employment in Jordan." Policy Research Working Paper 6141, World Bank, Washington, DC.

Habyarimana, James, and Taye Mengistae. 2013. "Labor Market Integration in Africa: Evidence from Trading Blocks." Background paper for the Africa Region Report on Youth Employment in Africa, World Bank, Washington, DC.

Hall, Robert E., and Charles I. Jones. 1999. "Why Do Some Countries Produce So Much More Output per Worker Than Others?" *Quarterly Journal of Economics* 114 (1): 83–116.

Hao, Janet, and Charles R. Hulten. 2011. "Intangible Capital and the Sources of Recent Chinese Economic Growth." Paper prepared for the Conference on Research in Income and Wealth, Productivity Program Workshop, Summer Institute 2011, National Bureau of Economic Research, Cambridge, MA, July 19.

Harrison, Ann E., Justin Yifu Lin, and L. Colin Xu. 2013. "Africa's (Dis)advantage: The Curse of Party Monopoly." NBER Working Paper 18683, National Bureau of Economic Research, Cambridge, MA.

Hicks, Joan Hamory, Michael Kremer, Isaac Mbiti, and Edward Miguel. 2011. "Vocational Education Voucher Delivery and Labor Market Returns: A Randomized Evaluation among Kenyan Youth." Report for Spanish Impact Evaluation Fund Phase II.

Hsieh, Chang-Tai, and Peter J. Klenow. 2009. "Misallocation and Manufacturing TFP in China and India." *Quarterly Journal of Economics* 124 (6): 1403–48.

Ibarraran, Pablo, Laura Ripani, Bibiana Tapoada, Juan Miguel Villa, and Brigida Garcia. 2012. "Life Skills, Employability, and Training for Disadvantaged Youth: Evidence from a Randomized Evaluation Design." IZA Discussion Paper 6617, Institute for the Study of Labor, Bonn.

IFC (International Finance Corporation). 2013. *IFC Job Study: Assessing Private Sector Contributions to Job Creation and Poverty Reduction.* Washington, DC: IFC.

Johanson, Richard K., and Arvil Van Adams. 2004. *Skills Development in Sub-Saharan Africa.* Washington, DC: World Bank.

Kalemli-Ozcan, Sebnem, Laura Alfaro, and Vadym Volosovych. 2008. "Why Doesn't Capital Flow from Rich to Poor Countries? An Empirical Investigation." *Review of Economics and Statistics* 90 (2): 347–68.

Karlan, Dean, Ryan Knight, and Christopher Udry. 2012. "Hoping to Win, Expected to Lose: Theory and Lessons on Micro Enterprise Development." Working Paper, Yale University, New Haven, CT.

Kitaev, Igor, with contributions from T. Coleman, J. Glover, and B. Kaluba. 2002. "Synthesis of Main Findings from Two Studies on Private Technical-Vocational Education and Training in Ghana and Zambia (Phase II)." Draft IIEP/Prg.DA/02.365, International Institute for Educational Planning, Paris.

Klapper, Leora, Luc Laeven, and Raghuram Rajan. 2006. "Entry Regulation as a Barrier to Entrepreneurship." *Journal of Financial Economics* 82 (3): 591–629.

Krishna, Pravin, and Devashish Mitra. 1998. "Trade Liberalization, Market Discipline, and Productivity Growth: New Evidence from India." *Journal of Development Economics* 56 (2): 447–62.

Krishnan, Pramila, and Irina Shaorshadze. 2013. "Technical and Vocational Education and Training in Ethiopia." Working Paper, International Growth Centre, London, February.

Kuddo, Arvo. 2012. "Public Employment, Services, and Activation Policies." Social Protection and Labor Discussion Paper 1215, World Bank, Washington, DC.

Li, Wei, Taye Mengistae, and Lixin Colin Xu. 2011. "Diagnosing Development Bottlenecks: China and India." *Oxford Bulletin of Economics and Statistics* 73 (6): 722–52.

Lin, Justin Yifu. 2011. "New Structural Economics: A Framework for Rethinking Development." *World Bank Research Observer* 26 (2): 193–221.

Lin, Justin Yifu, and Célestin Monga. 2011. "Growth Identification and Facilitation: The Role of the State in the Dynamics of Structural Change." *Development Policy Review* 29 (3): 259–310.

Maitra, Pushkar, and Subha Mani. 2012. "Learning and Earning: Evidence from a Randomized

Evaluation in India." Department of Economics Discussion Paper 44/12, Monash University, Melbourne.

Mano, Yukichi, Alhassan Iddrisu, Yutaka Yoshino, and Tetsushi Sonobe. 2012. "How Can Micro and Small Enterprises in Sub-Saharan Africa Become More Productive? The Impacts of Experimental Basic Managerial Training." *World Development* 40 (3): 458–68.

McKenzie, David, and Christoper M. Woodruff. 2013. "What Are We Learning from Business Training and Entrepreneurship Evaluations around the Developing World?" *World Bank Research Observer.* doi: 10.1093/wbro/lkt007.

Melitz, Marc J., and Sašo Polanec. 2012. "Dynamic Olley-Pakes Productivity Decomposition with Entry and Exit." NBER Working Paper 18182, National Bureau of Economic Research, Cambridge, MA.

Melitz, Marc J., and Daniel Trefler. 2012. "Gains from Trade When Firms Matter." *Journal of Economic Perspectives* 26 (2): 91–118.

Mingat, Alain, Blandine Ledoux, and Ramahatra Rakotomalala. 2010. "Developing Post-Primary Education in Sub-Saharan Africa: Assessing the Financial Sustainability of Alternative Pathways." World Bank, Washington, DC.

Monga, Célestin. 2012. "Winning the Jackpot-Jobs Dividend in a Multi-Polar World." Paper presented at the International Economics Association–World Bank Roundtable, "Industrial Policy in Africa," Pretoria, South Africa, July 3–4.

OECD (Organisation for Economic Co-operation and Development). 2010. *Measuring Innovation: A New Perspective.* Paris: OECD.

Olley, Steven, and Ariel Pakes. 1996. "The Dynamics of Productivity in the Telecommunications Equipment Industry." *Econometrica* 64 (6): 1263–97.

Ozier, Owen. 2013. "The Impact of Secondary Schooling in Kenya: A Regression Discontinuity Analysis." Paper presented at the Annual Meeting of the Population Association of America, New Orleans, April 11–13.

Pack, Howard, and Kamal Saggi. 2006. "The Case for Industrial Policy: A Critical Survey." *World Bank Research Observer* 21 (2): 267–97.

Piopiunik, Marc, and Paul Ryan. 2012. "Improving the Transition between Education/Training and the Labour Market: What Can We Learn from Various National Approaches?" EENEE Analytical Report 13, European Expert Network on Economics of Education, http://www.eenee.de/portal/page/portal/EENEEView/_generische_page_eenee?content=eenee-home.htm&language=us.

Rodrik, Dani. 2004. "Industrial Policy for the Twenty-First Century." CEPR Discussion Paper 4767, Centre for Economic Policy Research, London.

Rotunno, Lorenzo, Pierre-Louis Vézina, and Zheng Wang. 2012. "The Rise and Fall of (Chinese) African Apparel Exports." CSAE Working Paper 2012-12, Centre for the Study of Africa Economies, University of Oxford.

Sachs, Jeffrey D., and Andrew M. Warner. 2001. "The Curse of Natural Resources." *European Economic Review* 45 (4-6): 827–38.

Saleman, Yannick, and Luke S. Jordan. 2013. "The Implementation of Industrial Parks: Some Lessons Learned in India." World Bank, Washington, DC.

Sondergaard, Lars, and Mamta Murthi, with Dina Abu-Ghaida, Christian Bodewig, and Jan Rutkowski. 2012. "Skills, Not Just Diplomas: Managing for Results in Education Systems in Eastern Europe and Central Asia." World Bank, Washington, DC.

Sonobe, Tetsushi, Aya Suzuki, and Keijiro Otsuka. 2011. "Kaizen for Managerial Skills Improvement in Small and Medium Enterprises: An Impact Evaluation Study." World Bank, Washington, DC. http://siteresources.worldbank.org/DEC/Resources/FinalVolumeIV.pdf.

Svensson, Jakob. 2003. "Who Must Pay Bribes and How Much? Evidence from a Cross-Section of Firms." *Quarterly Journal of Economics* 118 (1): 207–30.

Syverson, Chad. 2011. "What Determines Productivity?" *Journal of Economic Literature* 49 (2): 326–65.

Tanzania, United Republic of, and UNESCO (United Nations Educational, Scientific, and Cultural Organization). 2012. "Management Issues in Higher, Technical, and Vocational Education and Training in Tanzania." In *Education Sector Analysis: Beyond Primary Education, the Quest for Balanced and Efficient Policy Choices for Human Development and Economic Growth*, ch. 8, 307–32. Dar es Salaam: Government of Tanzania and UNESCO.

TESDA (Technical Education and Skills Development Authority). 2012a. "Metals and Engineering Sector: Supply and Demand in Computer Numerical Control (CNC) Machine Operation and Other Related TVET Qualification." Labor Market Intelligence Report LMIR-ST-PO 03-05-12, TESDA, the Philippines.

———. 2012b. "Technical Education and Skills Development Monitoring and Evaluation System: Towards Increasing Efficiency, Effectiveness, and Relevance of TVET in the Philippines."

Presentation made at the Third International Congress on Technical and Vocational Education and Training, Building Skills for Work and Life, Shanghai. http://www.unesco.org/education/TVET2012/roundtable/3/M-DelaRama.pdf.

Udry, Christopher R., and Santosh Anagol. 2006. "The Return to Capital in Ghana." Discussion Paper 932. Yale University, Economic Growth Center, New Haven, CT. SSRN: http://ssrn.com/abstract=893023.

Wood, Adrian, and Kersti Berge. 1997. "Exporting Manufactures: Human Resources, Natural Resources, and Trade Policy." *Journal of Development Studies* 34 (1): 35–59.

Wood, Adrian, and Jörg Mayer. 2001. "Africa's Export Structure in a Comparative Perspective." *Cambridge Journal of Economics* 25 (3): 369–94.

World Bank. 2004. "An Assessment of the Investment Climate in Zambia." World Bank, Washington, DC.

———. 2008. *Finance for All? Policies and Pitfalls in Expanding Access.* Policy Research Report 41972, World Bank, Washington, DC.

———. 2009. "Zambia: Second Investment Climate Assessment; Business Environment Issues in Diversifying Growth." Vols. 1 and 2. World Bank, Washington, DC.

———. 2010. "The Business Environment in Southern Africa: Issues in Trade and Market Integration." Vols. s 1 and 2. World Bank, Washington, DC.

———. 2011a. "Botswana: Skills for Economic Diversification and Economic Growth." World Bank, Washington, DC.

———. 2011b. *Doing Business 2012: Doing Business in a More Transparent World.* Washington, DC: World Bank.

———. 2011c. "Strengthening Skills and Employability in Peru: Final Report." World Bank, Washington, DC.

———. 2012a. "Analysis of Uganda's System of Business, Technical-Vocational Education and Training (BTVET)." World Bank, Washington, DC.

———. 2012b. *Doing Business 2013: Smarter Regulations for Small and Medium-Size Enterprises.* Washington, DC: World Bank.

———. 2012c. "Financing Small- and Medium-Sized Enterprises in Rwanda." World Bank, Washington, DC.

———. 2012d. *World Development Report 2013: Jobs.* New York: Oxford University Press.

———. 2013a. *Africa's Pulse* 7 (April). World Bank, Washington, DC.

———. 2013b. "Tanzania Economic Update, Opening the Gates: How the Modernization of the Port of Dar es Salaam Can Transform Tanzania." Report 77729, World Bank, Washington, DC.

World Economic Forum. 2012. *The Global Competitiveness Report 2012–2013: Full Data Edition.* Geneva: World Economic Forum.

Xu, Lixin Colin. 2011. "The Effects of Business Environments on Development: A Survey of New Firm-Level Evidence." *World Bank Research Observer* 26 (2): 310–40.

Zeng, Douglas. 2006. "Knowledge, Technology, and Cluster-based Growth in Africa: Findings from Eleven Case Studies of Enterprise Clusters in Africa." Knowledge for Development (K4D) Program, World Bank Institute, Washington, DC.

Youth Unemployment in South Africa: Different Configuration, Different Approaches

South Africa's labor market—unlike most others in Sub-Saharan Africa—has a high share of wage employment off the farm, very little employment in household enterprises (HEs), and an even smaller share of employment in agriculture (4.5 percent). South Africa also stands apart from other African countries in having a high unemployment rate, estimated at 25 percent (based on a narrow definition of unemployment) in 2012.

High unemployment is nothing new in South Africa, which had an unemployment rate of 39 percent in 2005, compared to 17 percent in Africa's other upper-middle-income countries. At 51 percent, unemployment among those ages 15–24 was twice the national average in 2012. South Africa's high rate of youth unemployment reflects the high rate of unemployment throughout the country, which is worsened by circumstances specific to youth.

Especially unique is the combination of high unemployment and a very small HE sector. The ratio of HE employment to unemployment in South Africa was estimated to be 0.30–0.48 in 2012, which is much smaller than the ratio in middle-income countries of Asia and Latin America (11 and 7, respectively) or other countries in Sub-Saharan Africa (4.7). In South Africa, residual labor is not absorbed by the informal sector, as it is in other African countries or even in middle-income countries elsewhere in the world. In South Africa, larger domestic firms occupy the space that HEs occupy in many other African countries.

Conventional Perceptions of the Causes of Unemployment

High wage levels and high real unit labor costs played a part in dampening the demand for labor and encouraging industry to shift into more capital-intensive modes and sectors of production—at the expense of low-skilled workers and of industries that use low-skilled labor intensively (Mengistae 2011). While South Africa's industry has become more competitive over the last decade, it remains less competitive than that of many trading partners. Stringent labor market regulations are typically put forward as the primary cause of high unemployment. Yet close scrutiny of the evidence suggests that the story is not just about labor market rigidities. Deficiencies in economic growth, coupled with the rapidly growing working-age population, are major contributors to high unemployment in South Africa.

By many standards, South Africa has rigid labor market laws and high barriers to entry in the HE sector. The minimum wage imposed by the regulations is high, so the ratio of minimum to median wage is 1.52 for unskilled workers and can go as high as 2.66 in some sectors (Bhorat, Kanbur, and Mayet 2011). High unionization and the use of wage bargaining councils raise wages further: conservative estimates show that union jobs enjoy a wage premium of at least 17 percent. As a result, the labor market is segmented. Well-paying nonfarm wage jobs occupy the upper end of the spectrum, and a pool of the unemployed, queuing for wage jobs, occupies the lower end. High barriers to entry in the HE sector—created mainly by stringent local government by-laws, limited access to capital, and poor entrepreneurial skills—ensure that very few of those who fail to get a wage job join the nonfarm HE sector. Consequently, a high level of open unemployment coexists with a small informal sector that cannot be explained by high reservation wages among the unemployed (Kingdon and Knight 2004; Mitra 2010).

Yet the contribution of labor market rigidities to unemployment appears exaggerated.

An employment wage elasticity of –0.7 suggests that minimum wage laws and the wage premiums exacted by unions and bargaining councils do reduce employment, but the size of the elasticity also implies that wage rigidities only partially explain why unemployment is so high. It is important to note that violation of minimum wage requirements is high in South Africa, reaching 50 percent in 2007 (Bhorat, Kanbur, and Mayet 2011). Violations are highest in sectors where minimum wages are higher, suggesting that minimum wages are only moderately binding. Revised estimates of the unionization premium are also much smaller than previous estimates (Bhorat, Goga, and van der Westhuizen 2012). Indeed, recent estimates indicate that wage rigidities account for only 1 percentage point of unemployment in South Africa (Magruder 2012).

The Real Unemployment Problem: Slow Growth

To a larger extent, South Africa's unemployment problem is a growth problem, arising not only from the structure of growth but also from its slow pace in relation to demographic trends. Most of the growth in employment between 1995 and 2005 was in skilled employment, which grew 22 percent, while unskilled employment declined 13 percent (figure F4.1, panel a). Demand for unskilled labor is weak at a time when the unskilled labor force is expanding significantly. Owing to this pattern of skills-biased growth, a great scarcity of skills exists alongside high unemployment among the unskilled.

In the decade between 1995 and 2005, prior to the global financial crisis, the employment elasticity of growth (ranging from 0.6 to 0.8) and growth of gross domestic product (GDP) were comparable in South Africa and other middle-income countries, except for China and India. Population growth was not comparable, however. Rapid population growth reduced growth per capita in South Africa compared to other middle-income countries (figure F4.1, panel b). South Africa's labor force grew 46 percent between 1995 and 2005, outstripping the 29 percent growth in employment. Growth in the labor force was propelled by an increase in

Figure F4.1 Patterns in economic and employment growth in South Africa

a. Employment growth by skill category, 1995–2005

b. GDP growth in South Africa and other countries

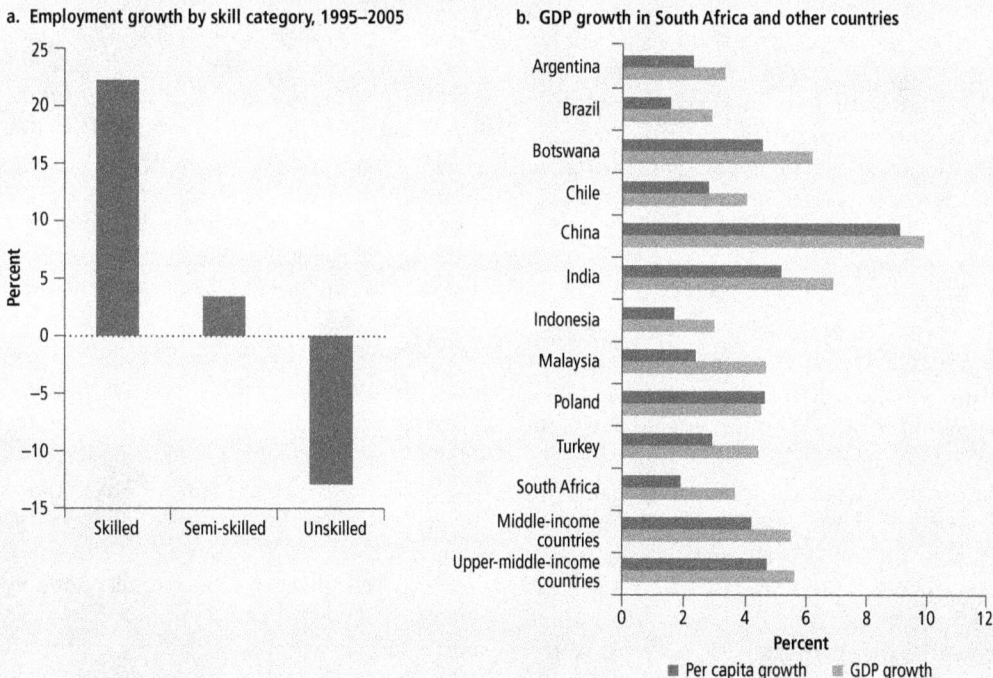

Per capita growth · GDP growth

Sources: World Bank 2011; Bhorat, Kanbur, and Mayet 2011.

labor force participation as well as population growth. Labor force participation rose 11 percentage points between 1997 and 2005, mostly because post-apartheid norms enabled greater involvement in economic activity, especially among women. At the same time, the share of the working-age population expanded by 6 percentage points between 1990 and 2010. The high unemployment that accompanied growth in the working-age population is one indication that South Africa's demographic dividend did not materialize.

Inefficient Job Search and Matching Processes

For young people in particular, the effects of South Africa's oversubscribed market for unskilled labor are amplified by frictions in job search and matching. The quality of unskilled labor is extremely varied, and unskilled workers' low level of education offers little indication of their real ability to prospective employers. Firms also face high hiring and firing costs owing to tight regulations. To minimize hiring costs, firms tend to hire unskilled labor through word of mouth and other nonpublic advertisements; to screen for productivity, they rely on referrals. For young people, with their limited experience, inability to signal their real aptitude, poor connections, and poor information on job openings, the job search can become very long and demoralizing, and the age at which they obtain their first wage job will continue to increase.

Policies to Reduce Unemployment

Various policies have been pursued and proposed to reduce unemployment in South Africa. Popular proposals on the demand side include wage subsidies, labor regulation reform, and public works; on the supply side, they include reforms in education and training systems, as well as support for entrepreneurship. What might be done to improve the potential for such strategies to work—especially for youth?

Improve the Targeting and Design of Wage Subsidies

Subsidies are expected to stimulate labor demand by mitigating the impact of high minimum wages, union premiums, or high reservation wages. Subsidies may not have much of an effect on demand for labor in South Africa, however, because it is difficult to substitute unskilled for skilled labor (Go et al. 2010). Subsidies may serve only to move those who are currently employed into other jobs, and their effects may well be temporary. High violation of the minimum wage law in sectors with the highest minimum wage ratios will further reduce the impact of wage subsidies.

Wage subsidies might be more effective if they target sectors where the response will be higher and are designed to reduce the displacement of workers from one job to another. Although preliminary evidence from an impact evaluation in South Africa showed that the wage subsidy program increased the probability of getting and keeping employment, a negligible proportion of employers claimed the subsidy. This finding suggests that the real impact of the subsidy was that it improved the efficiency of search and matching instead of reducing the real wage that the employer would have to pay. The general finding is that although youth wage subsidies may have a positive impact, their efficacy is conditioned by other labor market conditions, such as the flexibility of the labor market. A youth wage subsidy is just one instrument—of many—to tackle youth unemployment. If wage rigidities prove to be the primary cause of unemployment, eliminating labor rigidities would be a longer-term solution to the problem. If overall labor demand is low, then it will need to increase.

Provide Incentives for Labor-Intensive Growth

Public works programs have not significantly improved employment in South Africa, based on evidence from the Expanded Public Works Program (McCord 2007). A better alternative is to implement national policies that not only increase the pace of economic growth but also create incentives for labor-intensive firms to form and to locate near the pool of labor—

for example, by establishing special economic zones (as discussed in chapter 6) or offering fiscal incentives favorable to labor-intensive industries.

Reform Education and Training Systems

South Africa's long-term employment issues cannot be addressed without reforms in education and training systems. Such reforms can help to improve the productivity of the labor pool, narrow the wide gap between the skills that the labor market demands and workers can supply, and increase the signaling ability of education, which, in turn, will improve the search and matching efficiency of the labor market.

The technical and vocational education and training (TVET) system is plagued by low enrollment, low completion, and low probability of finding employment, but it could be improved by reforms that strengthen basic education (an area where South Africa performs poorly). South Africa would also benefit from restructuring the further education and training (FET) system to permit part-time learning (which would make FET more flexible and accessible) and to introduce apprenticeships and closer engagement with industry (which would make FET more relevant to the workplace). Sector education and training authorities should have a simplified bureaucracy, move to demand-driven financing, and delegate training to the most competent institutions using a performance-based financing approach (see discussion in Filmer 2012).

Revise By-Laws and Offer Focused Training to Support Entrepreneurial Activities

South Africa should make it easier for young people to become self-employed by introducing by-laws that are compatible with self-employment and by offering financial support. Although international evidence is generally mixed, the evidence on the impact of the Women Entrepreneurship Programme in South Africa suggests that well-structured entrepreneurship training would enhance success (Botha, Nieman, and van Vuuren 2006). Current proposals to strengthen business

licensing may work in the opposite direction by increasing the administrative burden for HEs (as well as small and medium enterprises).

References

Bhorat, Haroon, Sumayya Goga, and Carlene van der Westhuizen. 2012. "Institutional Wage Effects: Revisiting Union and Bargaining Council Wage Premia in South Africa." *South African Journal of Economics* 80 (3): 400–14.

Bhorat, Haroon, Ravi Kanbur, and Natasha Mayet. 2011. "The Determinants of Minimum Wage Violation in South Africa." Working Paper WP 2011-05, Cornell University, Charles H. Dyson School of Applied Economics and Management, Ithaca, NY.

Botha, M., G. H. Nieman, and J. J. van Vuuren. 2006. "Evaluating the Women Entrepreneurship Training Programme: A South African Study." *International Indigenous Journal of Entrepreneurship, Advancement, Strategy, and Education* 2 (1): n.p. http://www.indigenousjournal.com/read.html.

Filmer, Deon. 2012. "Challenges and Options for Technical and Post-Basic Education in South Africa." Policy Note, World Bank, Africa Region, Human Development Unit, Washington, DC.

Go, Delfin S., Marna Kearney, Vijdan Korman, Sherman Robinson, and Karen Thierfelder. 2010. "Wage Subsidy and Labour Market Flexibility in South Africa." *Journal of Development Studies* 46 (9): 1481–502.

Kingdon, Geeta Gandhi, and John Knight. 2004. "Unemployment in South Africa: The Nature of the Beast." *World Development* 32 (3): 391–408.

Magruder, Jeremy R. 2012. "High Unemployment yet Few Small Firms: The Role of Centralized Bargaining in South Africa." *American Economic Journal: Applied Economics* 4 (3): 138–66.

McCord, Anna. 2007. "Training within the South African National Public Works Programme." In *Human Resources Development Review 2008: Education, Employment, and Skills in South Africa*, edited by Andre Kraak and Karen Press. Cape Town: HSRC Press.

Mengistae, Taye. 2011. "Are South African Wages Too High or Growing Too Fast? A Comparison of Manufacturing Pay and Productivity in Selected Middle-Income Economies." World Bank, Washington, DC.

Mitra, Sophie. 2010. "Disability Cash Transfers in the Context of Poverty and Unemployment: The Case of South Africa." *World Development* 38 (12): 1692–709.

World Bank. 2011. World Development Indicators. Washington, DC: World Bank.

Chapter 7

Conclusion: Building an Effective Youth Employment Policy

The challenge of youth employment in Sub-Saharan Africa is not amenable to simple solutions. It reflects the intricate web of challenges and opportunities that links all countries in a globalized world. For Africa now, the key employment issue is that productivity—and therefore earnings—in many jobs is low, while aspirations, especially among young people, are high and rising. Despite progress in many countries, most of Africa's young people will not have an easy or structured transition to a sustainable livelihood, one of the core aspects of adulthood. All stakeholders have a role to play in supporting this transition.

Most African countries endorse the medium-to long-term agenda to increase employment in the nonfarm modern wage sector—in other words, to bring about a structural transformation of their economies. If Africa follows Asia's model, this effort will rely primarily on expanding export-oriented manufacturing, with its high requirements for labor. But even as governments embark on policies to foster such a transformation, they increasingly recognize that the process will take time, given Africa's small industrial base
and demographic profile. For that reason, this report has emphasized short- and medium-term strategies that will address current challenges while laying a foundation for the employment agenda to succeed in the long run.

A Programmatic Approach

Unemployment, which is typically low in low- and lower-middle-income countries, is just the tip of the iceberg. Most Africans cannot afford to be unemployed. They work, but they earn little for that work. The challenge of youth employment requires a comprehensive approach designed to relieve the constraints that prevent young people and the private sector from seizing opportunities and increasing productivity in agriculture, household enterprises, and the modern wage sector. Governments need to adopt a holistic view of how to address the situation—they need to "own" the whole problem.

There is a common tendency to believe that government-provided training in technical and vocational skills will suffice to unlock the potential of youth. However, such action, by itself, will not address the more fundamental problems that prevent young people from finding better opportunities. The gap in technical skills is only one facet of the youth employment challenge. A comprehensive approach to tackling the challenge will address constraints on both the human capital as well as the business environment sides of the problem.

As an overall principle, it is important to recognize that youths will find their opportunities in the private sector, whether in agriculture, household enterprises, or the modern wage sector. Governments should focus on providing public goods and services that support productivity in both household economic activity and enterprise economic activity. Government should be an enabler for job creation.

A key enabling action is to ensure that each cohort of youth entering the workforce has a solid foundation of skills acquired through basic education. In addition to getting children to attend school, a critical priority is to ensure that substantial learning occurs while they are in school. Given the growing evidence that social and behavioral skills are important for productivity, education systems could consider instilling such skills in combination with the other, more traditional, cognitive skills.

The defining feature of youth is that it is a time of transitions, but youth in Africa are not finding well-marked pathways to stable and productive livelihoods. While efforts should help all youth to make the transition, specific groups will face particular challenges along the way. For example, increasing young women's empowerment by increasing their agency— their control over their own destinies—has been shown to reduce negative outcomes such as early pregnancy and exposure to human immunodeficiency virus/acquired immunodeficiency syndrome (HIV/AIDS) and to have positive impacts on their earnings. And new approaches should be tried. The new communication technologies that are spreading throughout Africa (and that hold so much appeal for youth) offer innovative options for government to reach youth with messages, to help them to shape their employment aspirations, and to help youth learn about employment opportunities.

Rising to the youth employment challenge requires two kinds of action. Governments must *act now for the short term*, by addressing the immediate constraints that hold youth back from finding higher-productivity work. They also must *act now for the medium term*, by taking decisions and actions now so that the challenge of youth employment is easier to address in the future (table 7.1).

"Do Now for Now": Address the Constraints Facing Households and Firms

Priorities to Get Youth into Productive Household Economic Activities

Both farm and nonfarm household enterprises suffer from *financial exclusion*. Lifting barriers to credit, financing, and savings vehicles will support greater productivity—and growth—in the agricultural and nonagricultural sectors. Improving access to credit and financing is important for financial inclusion, but the key is to facilitate saving. Saving can be fostered through local savings groups and mobile money (especially attractive to youth), as well as the more established banking sector. Mechanisms for saving, which help to build the habit of saving, will increase the funds available for investing and enable mobilizing additional financing.

Priorities for Agriculture

Policies need to enable rural youth to *access land*. Approaches could include increasing the security of tenure, ownership, and sales to encourage fluid land markets to develop. Strategies will involve reducing the cost of land transfer, promoting rental markets, encouraging youth-sensitive land redistribution, and promoting youth-focused administration of communal or government land.

New approaches to agricultural extension promise to overcome previous shortcomings. To expand the repertoire of agricultural skills and increase access to information, these high-quality, demand-driven extension programs should target youth.

Table 7.1 Priority actions to take now to address the youth employment challenge

Area for intervention	"Do now for now": Actions to affect the current cohort of youth	"Do now for later": Actions to affect future cohorts of youth
Agriculture	1. Enable rental markets for land 2. Pilot intergenerational land transfer programs 3. Support high-quality, demand-driven extension services (covering information as well as skills) 4. Link agricultural credit to extension services	1. Establish effective land registration and transaction systems 2. Scale up intergenerational land transfer programs, based on lessons from pilot programs 3. Mainstream youth into smart interventions aimed at increasing productivity (producer organizations, livestock development, irrigation, and others) 4. Build skills through rapid improvements in education systems in rural areas
Agriculture and household enterprises	5. Promote rural village savings and loan associations and self-help groups 6. Enable financial inclusion for households 7. Use safety net programs as a platform to deliver interventions to disadvantaged youth	
Household enterprises	8. Develop a national strategy for household enterprises that reflects the voice of their ownship and youth 9. Ensure access to workspace and infrastructure for household enterprises through improved urban policy 10. Leverage nongovernmental organizations to deliver interventions that support disadvantaged youth to enter the sector by addressing multiple constraints (building a range of skills together, building skills along with providing access to finance)	5. Build foundational skills through rapid improvements in education systems 6. Address infrastructure needs of household enterprises in urban development planning
Modern wage sector	11. Reduce the cost of infrastructure services by addressing quality and efficiency 12. Address logistics bottlenecks 13. Reduce corruption and the cost of business start-up 14. Reform technical and vocational education and training and pursue public-private partnerships for delivering demand-driven training	7. Increase the quantity of infrastructure services 8. Expand regional markets for products 9. Build foundational skills through rapid improvements in education systems 10. Improve access to credit through financial sector reform
Cross-cutting areas	15. Increase awareness of opportunities and pathways to self-employment, especially for young women 16. Consider second-chance education for basic skills	11. Promote early child development and nutrition to build a stronger foundation for skills development 12. Build behavioral skills (consider reforms within the school system) 13. Reduce fertility rates to lower the size of future youth cohorts (through more girls' education, improved maternal and child health, increased access to family planning) 14. Build better employment data and a stronger evidence base to identify country constraints, priorities, and opportunities

Smart interventions to raise productivity, such as effective producer organizations, improved livestock production systems, or sustainable irrigation and water management, should mainstream youth. Projects should neither treat youth as an enclave nor ignore them.

Priorities for Household Enterprises

A first step in most countries is to develop a national strategy for household enterprises (HEs), because at present they are ignored, if not suppressed. Such a strategy will involve working with local governments as a part of urbanization and local economic development efforts. In addition to developing plans, the strategy should explicitly develop a way for the

voice of those working in the HE sector to be heard. When the needs of HE owners cannot be expressed and channeled, it is not surprising that policy makers and politicians neglect to cater to those needs.

To ensure that HEs can be established and operate legally and productively, urban policies should provide adequate locations where HEs can work and sell their products. In addition, smart urban planning should provide access to essential support services for HEs, such as lighting, water, sanitation, and effective security.

Because a very large share of Africa's new nonfarm employment opportunities will need to come from individual self-employment, projects should encourage youth to navigate a successful transition to starting up and operating an HE. Depending on the individual and sector, this assistance may include support for developing a range of skills (behavioral, life, technical, and business skills) as well as access to finance for starting a business. Integrated approaches that address multiple constraints simultaneously are promising.

Governments should leverage nongovernmental organizations (NGOs) and steer them to support young people who are well placed to enter the HE sector. Such support can involve NGOs in delivering integrated approaches to removing productivity constraints, with a focus on poorer youth. Working through NGOs is attractive, because often they can be more flexible, community driven, and responsive to clients than other service providers. Even so, government financing for NGOs to deliver integrated programs for youth should be performance based, with payment linked to the successful delivery of services that demonstrate beneficial impact.

Safety net programs (such as those that transfer cash or livestock assets) are proving to be powerful tools for poor areas and poor people to improve their standard of living and support productive investments. These programs can support youth in making the transition into productive activity (within or outside agriculture) through integrated approaches, such as programs combining public works or transfers with life skills training, especially if the overall business environment is conducive. Monitoring and *careful evaluation* are essential to identify the most cost-effective approaches.

Priorities to Create More and Better Wage and Salary Jobs in Firms

If the overall number of jobs in the modern wage sector grows, youth will benefit. Because export-oriented manufacturing has the greatest potential to generate employment in the wage and salary sector, the first priority is to remove binding constraints to export competitiveness. Governments will need to address elements of the business environment that reduce productivity at the factory level and well beyond the factory gates, such as constraints related to transportation and other infrastructure, customs, and border control.

Another priority is to develop and sustain a policy environment that enables the most productive firms to enter and grow. Here, the vital steps include improving access to finance and land, removing barriers to entry, and reducing the cost of corruption.

The poor quality and scarcity of infrastructure services clearly inhibit competitiveness, but the best immediate solution is not necessarily to provide more infrastructure. Strategies must pay attention to the cost and quality of infrastructure services. Better services—electricity, roads, or ports, for example—might be provided with existing infrastructure coupled with better policy and organization. Incentives matter for turning the available infrastructure into effective infrastructure services.

Throughout Africa, the private sector provides a wide range of vocational training opportunities. The public sector should provide post-school training programs only to carefully targeted groups. When such programs are undertaken, public-private partnerships help to ensure that training is aligned with business needs. Directly integrating firms into the training is an additional way to facilitate the transition to employment. Programs should not simply displace adult workers and substitute young workers.

"Do Now for Later": Take Action for Medium-Term Payoffs

As governments identify and implement policies to make their young and growing workforce more productive in the near term, they must also start to take action on policies that will yield payoffs in the medium term. First and foremost, many countries will need to reduce fertility rates more rapidly. Countries that have larger working-age populations in relation to their non-working-age populations will experience the most rapid gains in productivity and investment.

Countries that move urgently to improve their education systems will also gain a substantial advantage. Given the size of the cohorts coming into Africa's education systems, no country can afford to retain an education system that fails to instill the skills to pursue a stable livelihood. Underperforming education systems not only are inefficient but also condemn large parts of another generation to poverty. At the same time, children must be ready to learn when they come to school. Steps to build the foundation for effective education must be taken in early childhood—such as steps to improve the nutrition and cognitive development of children under age five. Deficiencies in skills have restricted growth in productivity in the past, and they will remain a constraint if changes are not made.

Addressing business environment constraints to the creation of more and better jobs in the modern wage sector is a long-term endeavor that will require sustained effort. Reforming land or financial markets takes time.

True regional integration that removes the limitations of Africa's relatively small domestic markets for goods and services will require a series of efforts that reinforce one another. And the payoff from some of these reforms may also take time to materialize, as investors and entrepreneurs wait to be certain that reforms have taken hold before they step in. But changes should start today.

At its core, the challenge of youth employment is closely aligned with the challenge of inclusive growth, defined not only as growth in which the poorest segments of society share, but also as growth in which young people's vitality is harnessed and rewarded. For African countries meeting this challenge, the benefits will build progressively on each other. The demographic dividend will start to yield results, and Africa's prosperity will grow and be shared.

Appendix

A Note on Data

Standardized and Harmonized Household and Labor Force Data

Many of the figures used in this report are based on data from standardized and harmonized household and labor force surveys. The data presented in these figures are derived from the authors' analysis of the World Bank Africa Region's standardized and harmonized data sets. This standardization was carried out under the Survey-Based Harmonized Indicators Program (SHIP), augmented with similarly standardized and harmonized labor force surveys (SHIP-LF). These are listed in table A.1.

The labor force participation variables were standardized and harmonized across these surveys so that the data could be aggregated in a meaningful way. When aggregated, population weights were used so the data from each survey contribute to the aggregate in proportion to the actual underlying population. The last survey from each country was used to create overall aggregates.

In addition to these standardized and harmonized data sets for the Sub-Saharan Africa region, the authors selectively analyzed data from the World Bank Research Department's International Income Distribution Database (I2D2). This is a compilation by the World Bank Research Department of household and labor force surveys from around the world.

Demographic and Health Survey Data

Certain figures are based on analysis of Demographic and Health Survey data. These data are available from www.measuredhs.com. Countries and years used in the analysis are presented in table A.2.

Table A.1 **Standardized and Harmonized Household and Labor Force Surveys used in report analysis**

Country	Type of survey	Year	Last year
Cameroon	SHIP	2001	
	SHIP	2007	x
Comoros	SHIP	2004	x
Côte d'Ivoire	SHIP	2002	
	SHIP	2008	x
Ethiopia	SHIP-LF	2005	x
Ghana	SHIP	1991	
	SHIP	1998	
	SHIP	2005	x
Kenya	SHIP	2005	x
Malawi	SHIP	2004	x
Mozambique	SHIP	2003	
	SHIP	2008	x
Niger	SHIP	2005	x
Nigeria	SHIP	2004	
	SHIP	2010	x
Rwanda	SHIP	2005	
	SHIP	2010	x
São Tomé and Príncipe	SHIP	2000	
	SHIP	2010	x
Senegal	SHIP	2001	
	SHIP	2005	x
Sierra Leone	SHIP	2003	x
Tanzania	SHIP-LF	2006	x
Uganda	SHIP	2005	
	SHIP	2010	x
Zambia	SHIP	2010	x

Table A.2 **Demographic and Health Survey Data Sets used in report analysis**

Country	Year	Transitions[a] Female	Transitions[a] Male	Education profile[b]
Benin	2006	x	x	x
Burkina Faso	2010	x	x	x
Burundi	2010	x	x	x
Central African Republic	1994	x	x	
Cameroon	2011	x	x	x
Chad	2004	x	x	x
Congo, Rep.	2005	x	x	
Côte d'Ivoire	2005	x		x
Congo, Dem. Rep.	2007	x		x
Ethiopia	2011	x	x	x
Gabon	2000	x	x	x
Ghana	2008	x	x	x
Guinea	2005	x	x	
Kenya	2008	x	x	x
Lesotho	2009	x	x	x
Liberia	2007	x	x	x
Madagascar	2008	x	x	x
Malawi	2010	x		x
Mali	2006	x	x	x
Mauritania	2000	x		x
Mozambique	2003	x	x	x
Namibia	2006	x	x	x
Niger	2006	x	x	x
Nigeria	2008	x	x	x
Rwanda	2010	x	x	x
São Tomé and Príncipe	2008	x		x
Senegal	2010	x	x	x
Sierra Leone	2008	x	x	x
South Africa	1998	x		
Swaziland	2006	x	x	x
Tanzania	2010	x	x	x
Togo	1998	x		
Uganda	2011	x	x	x
Zambia	2007	x	x	x
Zimbabwe	2010	x	x	x

a. Chapter 2.
b. Chapter 3.